SO-EJZ-380

Creating
Picturesque America

Creating
Picturesque America

Monument to
the Natural and Cultural
Landscape

Sue Rainey

Vanderbilt University Press
Nashville and London

☙ *Publication of this book was made possible partially*

through generous grants from the National Endowment

for the Humanities and the American Historical

Print Collectors Society.

This publication is made from recycled paper and meets the minimum requirements
of American National Standard for Information Sciences—Permanence of Paper for
Printed Library Materials.(∞)

Library of Congress Cataloging-in-Publication Data

Creating Picturesque America: monument to the natural and cultural landscape /
    Sue Rainey
p. cm.
Includes bibliographical references and index
Library of Congress Cataloging-in-Publication Data
Rainey, Sue.
    Creating picturesque America : monument to the natural and cultural landscape /
    Sue Rainey. — 1st ed.
        p.   cm.
    Includes bibliographical references and index.
    ISBN 0-8265-1257-7 (alk. paper)
    1. Picturesque America. 2. United States—Pictorial works. 3. Illustrated books—
    19th century. 4. Illustration trade—United States—History—19th century.
    I. Title.
E168.155 1994
741.6'4'097309034—dc20   94-33484
                                                                            CIP

Manufactured in the United States of America

For Reuben, Mark, and Sarah

Contents

Illustrations

Preface

Picturesque America was a conspicuous presence in the popular culture of the United States in the post-Civil War years. In the mid-1870s, it was the book of choice for display on the parlor table in many thousands of American homes from New York to San Francisco. Its twenty-pound bulk and one thousand pages contained, according to its subtitle, *A Delineation by Pen and Pencil of the Mountains, Rivers, Lakes, Forests, Water-falls, Shores, Cañons, Valleys, Cities, and Other Picturesque Features* of the United States. As the first publication to celebrate the entire continental nation, it enabled Americans, after the trauma of the Civil War, to construct a national self-image based on reconciliation between North and South and incorporation of the West. Its more than nine hundred pictures also provided graphic testimony of the variety, uniqueness, and potential wealth of the American landscape and the advanced civilization of its cities. This composite image both promoted and reinforced a resurgence of nationalism rooted in the homeland itself rather than in institutions of democracy, as would have been the case in the antebellum years. Contemporaries often referred to the book as a "monument," and, although unlike a statue or government building that served as the focus of public gatherings, its thousands of copies in homes throughout the land contributed with other national monuments to what Neil Harris has called the "cement of patriotism."[1]

Our heightened awareness of the power of images in contemporary culture helps us to understand *Picturesque America*'s impact. The relative scarcity of images in the 1860s and 70s—compared to the ubiquitousness of photographs, television, and computer graphics today—increased their potency. In particular, the inexpensive wood engravings in popular periodicals and such books as *Picturesque America* were arguably the most numerous and accessible images—the mass media of the day. True, the importance of photographs—especially in the form of stereographs—was growing, and such scholars as Peter B. Hales have attributed to them a major role in shaping how Americans visualized their country.[2] Yet in the decade after the Civil War printed images continued to be omnipresent and extremely potent delineators of a national collective identity.

Although *Picturesque America* has long been valued by book and print collectors, this important source for understanding late nineteenth-century attitudes about the nation's natural and cultural landscape has been neglected by historians. Cursory tributes to it as the period's most "lavish" and most popular guide to American scenery have acknowledged its cultural importance but failed to proceed to detailed analysis. Nor has there been attention to why and how it was produced: many interesting aspects of its publication have been overlooked and misconceptions abound about the role of the "editor" William Cullen Bryant and the contributions of particular artists. This study is the first attempt to analyze thoroughly the image of the United States conveyed by *Picturesque America* and to detail its publishing history.

Like many elements of popular culture, *Picturesque America* may seem at first glance entirely predictable—a rather wearisome survey of America's best-known places, its text full of the nineteenth century's commonest platitudes and formulaic descriptions. It is true that no amount of delving yields profundities in the text. Careful consideration does lead, however, to awareness of how timely the coverage of certain regions and topics was, and thus increases our understanding of the book's appeal and impact. Yet to accept its images and text as straightforward, albeit exceptionally appealing, *records* of its time is to do the book an injustice. Instead, they are cultural artifacts created by the numerous artists and writers. Guided by artistic and literary traditions, nostalgia for a less complicated past, and hope for the future, they carefully selected aspects of the contemporary scene that would coalesce to present a reassuring and appealing panorama.

Thus analysis of *Picturesque America*'s graphic and verbal images enriches our understanding of the aspirations and denials of Americans during this critical period. As a highly successful publishing venture in a volatile, competitive marketplace, the book serves as an important indicator of what the contributors and their public wanted to see—and what they preferred to avoid. Ignoring the economic recession and growing social problems of the early 1870s while stressing links with the picturesque tradition and continuity rather than change, *Picturesque America* presented a wide range of reasons for celebrating the American landscape—from finding "sermons in stones" to anticipating the extraction and use of rich natural resources. The two individuals most responsible for this celebratory view of American scenery and cities were the book's actual editor, Oliver Bell Bunce (1828-1890), and principal artist, Harry Fenn (1837-1911). Both were prominent figures in the publishing world of the 1870s whose contributions deserve greater recognition.

This study's attention to the cultural importance of illustrated books and periodicals and the artists who contributed to them also fills in some blanks in the history of publishing and popular art in this period. These artist-illustrators reached a much wider audience than did most oil painters. They popularized American art and engendered pride based on the nation's ability to produce superior illustrated magazines and books. Attention to how Harry Fenn and the other *Picturesque America* artists understood their task as well as to the models they emulated throws light on how they combined traditional and innovative approaches. My research has also led to a surprisingly large number—some 180—previously unpublished original drawings for *Picturesque America*. By comparing these with the wood and steel engravings based on them we can learn much about the artists' working methods, intentions, and values.

One of the most frequent misconceptions about *Picturesque America* is that it appeared suddenly, full-blown, bound in two hefty volumes, in 1872 or 1874. This was far from the case. Initially conceived as a series of landscape views demonstrating that the United States had scenery qualifying as "picturesque," the first images appeared in *Appletons' Journal* November 12, 1870. Part one of this study discusses the development of "Picturesque America" as a *Journal* series. The first chapter focuses on the mission of the publisher, D. Appleton and Company, to diffuse culture and on how an illustrated periodical fit into its publishing program. Chapter 2 explores why the firm chose to launch a series on American scenery and how Harry Fenn was selected as artist. The third chapter looks more closely at editor Oliver Bunce and the materials he selected for the magazine series, especially his attention to the South during the series' first year.

Part two begins with the decision to switch the series to the more ambitious and permanent format of a book in parts. This impressive product appeared twice a month over a two-year period, in forty-eight fascicles that could be bound later according to the subscriber's wishes. Chapter 4 also contains details on how Bunce introduced and orchestrated this publication. Chapter 5 explores the making of the illustrations—from artists' sketches or, in some cases, photographs, to final prints.

Finally, part three analyzes the messages of the text and pictures by subject categories. The first section of chapter 6, "A Landscape Still Picturesque," discusses how the contributors selected subjects and shaped images emphasizing, in turn, the picturesque qualities of the long-settled East—incorporating factories and railroads into appealing vistas—and a West characterized by sublime and unique scenic features virtually untouched by civilization. The second section, "A Civilization Advancing," analyzes the factors contributing to the strong message that the cities of the United States ranked as elegant and attractive, with amenities similar to those of Paris and London, and well-dressed and orderly citizens capable of enjoying them. Chapter 7 concludes with *Picturesque America*'s numerous cultural roles—from engendering respect for American artists and spawning numerous imitations, to modeling and promoting genteel touring, to fostering pride in the special qualities of the American landscape. It also interprets the book's precipitous decline in prestige by the early 1900s.

Thus, this book, like *Picturesque America* itself, deals in both fact and interpretation on many different levels, from specific detail to pervasive, though often implicit, assumptions. Through careful analysis this little-appreciated landmark of popular culture becomes a window on the post-Civil War years, opening to our view the beliefs and attitudes that determined how many Americans thought about themselves, their landscape, and the rest of the world. It not only illuminates that particular period of our nation's history, but also helps us understand the continuing force of some of those attitudes—both positive and negative.

My appreciation of wood and steel engravings sparked the curiosity that led to this study, but its gradual evolution from a brief paper dealing primarily with *Picturesque America*'s graphic images to a more comprehensive analysis of the book's history and cultural significance has been slow and not always sure. Over the years, more people than I can name have provided suggestions, information, and encouragement. I am most grateful to them all.

Marjorie Balge's class in American landscape art at the University of Virginia introduced me to *Picturesque America*, and Marjorie provided much counsel and support, especially in the initial stage of the project. Others who read early drafts and offered suggestions or assistance include Richard Guy Wilson, Bernard F. Reilly, Jr., Herman J. Viola, Ian M. G.

Quimby, Jerry N. Showalter, Joseph F. Kett, and Rona Schneider. In mid-
stream, Roger B. Stein of the University of Virginia made extremely helpful comments on two successive revisions, leading me to pay more
attention to the implied social messages in words and pictures. More
recently, David Tatham of Syracuse University and William Diebold
offered constructive suggestions, as did Richard D. Hathaway of Vermont
College of Norwich University, whose detailed criticisms were invaluable.

A number of people have generously shared information with me,
especially Joni L. Kinsey, Merl M. Moore, Jr., William Diebold, Terry
Belanger, Michael Winship, Allen Ramsier, Michael W. Schantz, John D.
Duncan, Jessie J. Poesch, Alfred C. Harrison, Jr., Mary M. Allodi, and
Rosemarie L. Tovell. Also providing valuable assistance have been
Richard C. Kugler of the Old Dartmouth Historical Society, New Bedford,
Massachusetts; Robert J. Scholnick of the College of William and Mary;
Phil Lapansky of the Library Company of Philadelphia; staff members at
the Historic New Orleans Collection and at the United States Geological
Survey Library, Denver; and members of Harry Fenn's family: William Abt,
Jean Van Antwerp, and the late Dorothy Van Antwerp Walters.

Through the years, I have been encouraged and aided by friends at
Alderman Library of the University of Virginia, especially Mildred K.
Abraham, and by many friends in the American Historical Print Collectors
Society, especially Georgia B. Barnhill, Gloria Deák, and Rona Schneider.
I am especially grateful to the American Historical Print Collectors Society
and the National Endowment for the Humanities for providing generous
subventions to ensure that the book would be fully illustrated. As is his
custom, Reuben Rainey, my husband, provided the support and encouragement to persevere, while challenging me to aim for excellence. For
that I thank him.

                                                              SUE RAINEY

PART ONE

Fighting the Illustration Wars:
The "Picturesque America" Series
in *Appletons' Journal*

CHAPTER 1

Appletons' Journal
and the Mission to Civilize

Picturesque America entered the marketplace just as publishing hit its stride as a highly profitable and influential business in the post-Civil War years. The production and sales of newspapers, magazines, and books grew at a phenomenal rate, spurred by increasing literacy, technological advances in printing that increased speed and decreased costs, more efficient and faster distribution by railroad, and, not to be overlooked, growth of advertising. In this highly competitive market, *Picturesque America* achieved unprecedented success. Published by New York's D. Appleton and Company, it came into homes in two of the most popular contemporary formats—first in the illustrated periodical, *Appletons' Journal,* beginning in November 1870, then as a book in parts from 1872 to 1874. Its visual richness—more than nine hundred wood engravings and fifty steel engravings—accounted for much of its appeal in an age hungry for images. As recently as the 1870s, many parts of the United States were known to most Americans only from verbal reports, if at all. Through inexpensive prints of scenery and cities in popular periodicals and books, many Americans were seeing for the first time what they had only abstractly imagined as their country.

The production of such a volume was an unusually expensive undertaking. Even in 1870s dollars, the sums are impressive. The illustrations alone, the majority made from on-the-spot drawings by travelling artists, cost $138,000.[1] Yet the extraordinary outlay yielded huge profits from subscription sales that may have reached one million copies. Ralph Waldo Emerson, Henry Wadsworth Longfellow, Oliver Wendell Holmes, John Greenleaf Whittier, and Harriet Beecher Stowe subscribed, as did many who sought to better their humbler positions by demonstrating good taste and interest in picturesque scenery and art. Clearly, in *Picturesque America*

D. Appleton and Company chose both subject matter and format that appealed to a wide range of Americans.

Yet even as it benefited financially from *Picturesque America*, the Appleton firm explained its motive for this project and its entire publishing program as much loftier than that of profit. Its aim was no less than to promote civilization. By disseminating information, literature, and art, it educated and thus "improved" the populace. With some conspicuous exceptions, most leading publishers shared this mission. The Harper firm, for example, subtitled its newspaper *Harper's Weekly, A Journal of Civilization.*

Buttressing publishers' confidence that such an ambitious mission could be achieved were widespread beliefs in humanity's essential goodness and in the inevitability of progress. An 1869 *Appletons' Journal* article on "Agriculture as a Force of Civilization" included the following bald statements of those beliefs: "The world is becoming morally better, while it is becoming physically more beautiful and perfect." Further, "We cannot say what engineering is not capable of doing, and to the improvement of the facilities for commerce we can assign no limits."[2] Clearly, Calvinism's emphasis on depravity and original sin had largely given way to more optimistic, comfortable concepts—articulated by Horace Bushnell, James McCosh, and others—stressing humanity's ability to intuit essential truths and to choose a moral course of action based on the intuitive "moral sense" or "conscience." Furthermore, notions derived from Romanticism and German idealism convinced many that, freed from superstition, dogma, and tradition, as well as from an overemphasis on the intellect or strict empiricism, each individual human spirit would thrive and recognize the eternal in all things. Such influential thinkers as Emerson popularized the notion that the revelation of the absolute was potentially perfect in every person. The publishers' educational role, which grew as books and periodicals became cheaper and more accessible, was to expose the populace to the best that had been thought—to truth and beauty in literature, art, and science.

Many viewed the years following the Civil War as a time of national renewal, of "the second birth of the Republic." After "the triumph of two great wars—the one with Nature, the other with man," a "new country" emerged, reunited and connected across the continent by railroad and telegraph lines.[3] This offered great opportunities to many, including publishers, who could ship books to the West Coast in just two weeks instead of the three months required to go "round the Horn."[4] But it also pre-sented unprecedented challenges to the democratic mode of government and to those who would promote the spread of civilization. The young nation already had a reputation for great technical know-how but little higher culture. For example, in 1867 Thomas Wentworth Higginson, recalling that Alexander von Humboldt had called the United States "a dead level of mediocrities," admitted that "our brains as yet lie chiefly in our machine-shops."[5] As the pool of potential voters expanded greatly beyond the relatively homogeneous descendants of Anglo-Saxon settlers, with their shared values of industry, frugality, and restraint and codes of "polite" behavior, the intellectual elite debated the compatibility of democracy and civilization. Yet when Britisher Thomas Carlyle and others questioned whether the body politic that expanded to include everyone could remain viable—Carlyle likened embracing "radical" democracy to shooting the rapids at Niagara—Americans defended the democratic ideal. Walt Whitman, for one, wrote in answer that, after all, the object of government was "not merely to rule, to repress disorder, etc., but to develop, to open up to cultivation, to encourage the possibilities . . . of that aspiration for independence, and the pride and self-respect latent in all characters."[6]

Now that the continuance of the Union under the leadership of the North was assured, many saw the creation of an educated populace—including recent immigrants and former slaves—as the primary challenge and chief hope of the nation. Popular writer and biographer James Parton stressed that the special task of "this generation and the next" was the diffusion of education and culture. In an 1869 article entitled "Popularizing Art" in *The Atlantic Monthly*, he described the challenge, with an ironic reference to "Tory friends":

Meanwhile, what our sweet and tenderly beloved Tory friends amiably style "the scum of Europe" pours upon our shores, chokes up our cities, and overspreads the Western plains. When a Tory speaks of the "scum of Europe," or of "the dregs of the people," he merely means the people whom his barbaric and all-grasping meanness has kept ignorant and poor. These people, as well as the emancipated slaves of the South, it devolves upon us of this generation and the next to convert into thinking, knowing, skilful, tasteful American citizens.[7]

In his unintended paternalism, Parton was optimistic that the leaders of his time, including publishers, could effect such a transformation.

Those "converted" would recognize there was more to life than food and material possessions. Their inborn powers of intuition combined with exposure to great literature, art, and nature would foster moral and spiritual development, not to mention good manners. This transformation was, in fact, already underway: Parton described "The Wonderful Growth of Chicago," which had two hundred churches whose purpose was "*not* the promulgation of barren and dividing opinions, but the diffusion among the whole community of the civilization hitherto enjoyed only by a few favored families."[8] The city also had many bookstores and was "becoming second only to New York" as a distribution point for publishers. As evidence, he reported that "over three thousand sets of Appleton's Encyclopedia" had been sold there, as had "several hundred sets of the Encyclopedia Britannica," at two hundred dollars a set.[9]

He also found St. Louis, with large numbers of French and German immigrants and their descendants, a pleasing surprise:

It has stolen into greatness without our knowing much about it. If Chicago may be styled the New York, St. Louis is the serene and comfortable Philadelphia, of the West. Having passed through its wooden period, to that of solid brick and stone, it has a refined and finished appearance, and there is something in the aspect of the place which indicates that the people there find time to live, as well as accumulate the means of living.[10]

He even speculated that St. Louis might become the capital of the United States someday, with "the civilization of the Continent" extending from there in every direction.[11] Similarly, newspaper editor Samuel Bowles saw signs of incipient civilization as far west as Cheyenne, in the Wyoming Territory, in 1868, when measured by the popular indicators of newpapers, churches, and permanent buildings.[12]

The spread of civilization across the continent and to all segments of the population was seen as the solution to another conspicuous problem—the growing divisions and disparities between the rich and poor. In an address to the alumni of Hamilton College in 1872, the writer Charles Dudley Warner said, "Unless the culture of the age finds means to diffuse itself, working downward and reconciling antagonisms by a commonness of thought and feeling and aim in life, society must more and more separate itself into jarring classes."[13]

Among the media for diffusing culture in this period, wood engraving was one of the most effective. Prints made from woodblocks were a popular feature of the inexpensive, large-circulation newpapers and magazines from mid-century on. Pictures could communicate more directly and effectively than verbal descriptions. They were "educators" of the multitude, including the illiterate, and their wide distribution made possible a common cultural experience that bridged class divisions. They were the period's mass media—similar in importance to television or video images today. In this period when art was thought to convey ideas of truth and beauty and thus foster moral action, inexpensive prints were seen as a solution to "the problem of civilization" as posed by Emerson in 1860, "how to give all access to the masterpieces of art and nature."[14] Frederick Hudson, a historian of American journalism, described the illustrated newspapers that started in the 1850s and increased their circulation dramatically during the Civil War as "the art gallery of the world. Single admission, ten cents."[15] A commentator in the *Hartford Times* who considered "good pictures" the most "persuasive ministers in the service of true refinement and enlightenment" recognized that not everyone could afford paintings, but stressed that "there are few who cannot manage to take some one good pictorial paper. A really *good* illustrated paper is a greater *educator* of the popular taste than any painter, however great."[16] Using the metaphor of a visitor in the home, the writer claimed that the family's "critical taste and enjoyment grow by use through the accustomed visits of the illustrated paper."

In addition to pictures, many of these "visitors" to the home brought literature and feature articles that were also important purveyors of taste and culture. Elaborating the metaphor, artist Eugene Benson compared such magazines to the presence of a "cultivated friend"

rich in souvenirs of travel, at times eloquent, and always discreet, illuminating the minds about him, and giving a zest to knowledge. . . . A home circle without an illustrated magazine is torpid and poor in its sources of pleasure. It has neither eyes for art or nature, nor a liberal interest in anything but its routine and mechanical existence. I consider the illustrated magazine one of the essentials of a beautiful home life.[17]

Yet like all mass media, this one could be abused. Whereas the magazines Benson had in mind were "educators," others offered "literary poisons" that glorified crime and seduction and could corrupt readers' minds. The culprits were the cheap story papers serializing, and sometimes illustrating, sensational fiction, such as the *New York Ledger*, Street and Smith's *New York Weekly, Saturday Night,* and *Fireside Companion,* with circulations in the hundreds of thousands.[18] The editor of the period's most popular women's magazine, *Godey's Lady's Book,* warned readers that these story papers could pollute their children's minds and admonished them to "banish" from their homes "every book and paper that fails to implant in the mind a moral gem that will bloom, and blossom, and clothe itself with beauty."[19]

Clearly, *Picturesque America*'s publisher, D. Appleton and Company, was firmly on the side of the improvers rather than the corrupters. An old and respected firm established in 1831 by Daniel Appleton (1785–1849) and continued by his five sons, it was in the postwar years New York's second largest publishing company, after Harper and Brothers. The firm had expanded rapidly since the enterprising eldest son, William Henry Appleton (1814–99), had taken the reins in 1849 after the death of his more cautious father. It established its own printing plant on Franklin Street in 1853, and in 1854 opened an elegant retail bookstore at 346–348 Broadway. Expansion in the postwar years prompted moves of the editorial and business offices to larger quarters in lower Manhattan in 1866, 1869, and 1872. And in 1868 the production plant moved from Manhattan to a one-and-a-half block area in the Williamsburg section of Brooklyn, where some six hundred people were employed in a printing plant, electrotype foundry, and bindery.[20] Although still a family-run enterprise, D. Appleton and Company had definitely entered the ranks of big business.

The firm's significant role as educator and "improver" during this time of "national rebirth" is evident from its publishing program in the post–Civil War years. Looking at this program in its highly competitive context also enables us to understand why Appleton chose to introduce an illustrated periodical in the spring of 1869—explaining it, of course, in terms of extending their educative mission to a new format. The firm's popular publications also highlight the major interests of its audiences, interests that contributed to the success of the "Picturesque America" series in *Appletons' Journal* and the book that followed.

The cornerstone of Appleton's publications for those seeking to become better educated and informed was the *New American Cyclopaedia.* This sixteen-volume work was completed in 1863, despite the Civil War, which brought much publishing activity to a standstill. Advertisements stressed its value to those who could not afford a large library:

While only men of fortune can collect a library complete in all the departments of knowledge, a Cyclopaedia, worth in itself, for purposes of reference, at least a thousand volumes, is within the reach of all—the clerk, the merchant, the professional man, the farmer, the mechanic.[21]

Another staple was the firm's all-time best seller, *Webster's Spelling Book*, which peaked at sales of 1,596,000 in 1866. Demand was especially brisk in the South, where public education was spreading and many former slaves were learning to read and write.[22] For those new to reading and to English, the firm offered such classics as *Robinson Crusoe* and *The Swiss Family Robinson* "in words of one syllable."[23] Other aids for inexperienced readers included Charles H. Moore's *What to Read and How to Read* (1871). Textbooks for all levels of learners were also an important part of the firm's publishing program.[24]

Other works gave practical advice about how to conform to prevailing tastes. John W. Masury's *How Shall We Paint Our Houses?* (1868) and Frank J. Scott's *The Art of Beautifying Suburban Home Grounds of Small Extent* (1870) provided instruction in areas in which Americans were considered deficient. Scott's volume would, advertisements claimed, enable those forced from cities by high costs to avoid afflicting "the cultivated eye with individual crudities in architecture and in decoration."[25]

Travel was an important means of furthering education and culture. From 1847, when its first *Railroad and Steamboat Companion* was published, Appleton regularly issued travel guides to the United States and Europe. After the Civil War ended, the firm wasted no time producing an 1866 edition of the *Southern Tour*. And in 1871, the *Western Tour* appeared, taking advantage of the great interest in travel on the transcontinental railroad, completed in May 1869.

Always reasonably strong in the field of history, the Appleton firm quickly offered publications to satisfy the public's intense interest in the recent events of the Civil War, including books on the military careers of Generals Philip H. Sheridan and Ulysses S. Grant in 1865 and 1868, respectively.[26] As early as 1866 it began rebuilding its Southern market with histories from the Confederate side, with the *Life of Stonewall Jackson*, followed in 1871 by the first biography of Robert E. Lee, both by Virginian John Esten Cooke.

In addition to publications aimed generally at popular education, Appleton was known for publishing the latest scientific findings and theories, thereby winning both admiration and censure at a time when science seemed to be overturning many long-held beliefs.[27] This focus on science, especially on the earth's geologic history, unquestionably contributed to the interest in *Picturesque America*. With the guidance and urging of science editor Edward Livingston Youmans (1821–87), an influential interpreter of evolution through lyceum lectures and books, Appleton became the American publisher of Charles Darwin, Thomas H. Huxley, John Tyndall, and Herbert Spencer. The firm had great success in 1860 with the first American edition of Darwin's *Origin of Species* and with later works expounding evolutionary theory. Yet Appleton published a wide range of scientific opinion. In the years the *Picturesque America* project was underway, for example, the firm published Darwin's *Descent of Man* (1871) as well as works opposing his theories and numerous books dealing with how the earth and heavens were formed.[28]

As the fields of anthropology and ethnology developed, there was also intense interest in different beliefs and customs and their changes through history. Several Appleton publications applied developmental or evolutionary theories to religion and morality.[29] Most comprehensive in this regard were Herbert Spencer's works, written to apply evolution to all aspects of the universe. At the urging of Youmans, Appleton published Spencer's *Education* in 1860 and his *First Principles*, the first volume of his *Synthetic Philosophy*, in 1864. Youmans and many other Americans saw in Spencer's ideas a new and reassuring framework for understanding the world, one that incorporated the latest scientific theories, but left room for the divine. Youmans made his position clear on this point when he announced *A New System of Philosophy*:

To Mr. Spencer the one conception which spans the universe and solves the widest range of its problems—which reaches outward through the boundless space and back through illimitable time, resolving the deepest questions of life, mind, society, history, and civilization, which predicts the glorious possibilities of the future, and reveals the august methods by which the Divine Power works evermore,—this one, all-elucidating conception, is expressed by the term EVOLUTION.[30]

The comprehensiveness of this philosophy appealed to many, as did Spencer's notion that progress, defined as "the transformation of the homogeneous into the heterogeneous," was inevitable, "not an accident, not a thing within human control, but a beneficent necessity."[31] Like the natural world, society would evolve toward higher civilization if left unimpeded.

Government interventions, in Spencer's view, would make evils worse or cause new ones rather than remedy them.[32] Thus Spencer's ideas provided a rationale for optimism despite severe social problems. They also could be used to justify the Republican party's retreat from an interventionist stance to a more limited governmental role during Reconstruction.

During this intellectual ferment, many struggled to hold to their belief that creation had been set in motion by a benevolent God while accepting scientific findings about the subsequent development of the universe and human beings. Not surprisingly, the Appleton firm, led by a family of solid Episcopalians, sponsored works that charted such a path. Spencer's thought contributed to this effort, especially his conception of the limits of scientific inquiry—that in all directions investigation led to insoluble mystery, to "the Unknowable."[33] As Youmans and others saw it, Spencer's description of the positive consciousness of a "Supreme Cause" indicated "an indestructible basis in human nature for the religious sentiment."[34]

Other works published by the firm sought more directly to reconcile belief and knowledge, such as *Primary Truths of Religion* (1869) by Thomas M. Clark, Episcopal bishop of Rhode Island, and *Religion and Science* (1873) by Joseph Le Conte, a professor of geology and natural history at the new University of California.[35] According to Le Conte, the Bible and nature were both divine books of revelation: both "have the same Author, and are, therefore, equally sacred, equally true, equally authoritative."[36] Nature could still provide a direct experiential encounter with God, even for those who had replaced literal belief in the Biblical account of creation with new conceptions of the earth's antiquity and the gradual development of the diversity of life over eons. Such convictions about nature's import were among the underlying reasons for *Picturesque America*'s popularity.

In the fields of literature and art, D. Appleton and Company had lagged somewhat behind other publishers, but in the postwar years greatly expanded its efforts. Fictional selections with wide appeal that avoided the excesses of sensationalism became best sellers, like Lewis Carroll's *Alice's Adventures in Wonderland* (1866) and German novelist Luise Mühlbach's *Joseph II and His Court* (1867). The latter heralded a growing fascination with the lives of European aristocracy and with Teutonic or Anglo-Saxon heritage.[37] Similarly, in 1870 Appleton published the American edition of Benjamin Disraeli's *Lothair*. The former British prime minister's best seller depicted life in English country houses, providing Americans a model of orderly society, at a time when numerous immigrants were changing the makeup of the nation's largest cities and anti-Catholic and anti-Irish sentiments were growing.[38] Appleton also had considerable success with novels by women writers and with inexpensive editions of Dickens, Scott, and Cooper: in 1868 the firm began issuing Dickens works "for the million," priced from fifteen to thirty-five cents.[39]

For publications in the visual arts, the arena in which *Picturesque America* would play such a significant role, D. Appleton and Company had, until 1868, depended on imports and followed the lead of other firms. With the growing popularity of illustrated periodicals and greater emphasis on the role of printed pictures in spreading culture, the firm took initiatives between 1868 and 1870 that quickly placed it in the first rank of publishers providing art for the home circle. It moved away from publishing luxury "gift books" with steel engravings recycled from European or American publications and focused on issuing less expensive volumes illustrated by wood engravings based on original designs by American artists.

For example, the three "holiday" books Appleton promoted most heavily in December 1868 and December 1869 were luxury editions with the formidable price of twenty dollars each: *The Schiller Gallery* (December 1868) and *The Goethe Gallery* (December 1869), new editions of earlier German publications with steel engravings of characters in the two writers' works, and *The Poet and the Painter* (December 1868), an anthology illustrated by reused steel engravings.[40] Steel engravings had long been the most prestigious type of illustration in wide use in books. The time-consuming intaglio process involved incising the metal plate with the lines that would hold the ink. To do this, the engraver used a combination of etching, which utilized acid to incise the lines, and engraving, which used sharp tools called burins to gouge out the lines (see fig. 4.3).

The introduction of steel to replace copper plates in the 1830s had made much larger printing runs possible and brought books illustrated with steel engravings into the price range of those of moderate means. Yet their use still involved a significant outlay in time and money when compared to printing from raised letterpress type. To print them required a special rolling press that applied great pressure to force the ink from the grooves of the plate. And good results required heavy, dampened paper. Furthermore, inking the plates and wiping the surface before each impression involved considerable labor. Thus a twenty-dollar price for the four-hundred-page *Poet and the Painter*, with its ninety-nine steel engravings, was not unreasonable, especially if one accepted Appleton's claim that it was "the most sumptuous, the most richly illustrated and altogether the most elegant gift book published in America."[41]

In the holiday season of 1868–69, however, the Appleton firm also offered a gift book illustrated by the less expensive process of wood engraving. *Wood-Side and Sea-Side, Illustrated by Pen and Pencil* was a collection of poetry that featured illustrations by the extremely popular English artist Myles Birket Foster, as well as several American artists, including Asher B. Durand and John A. Hows. Wood engravings allowed the vastly more affordable price of four dollars when bound in decorative cloth or eight dollars in Moroccan leather.

Wood engraving was a relief process that had evolved from the simple woodcuts of earlier centuries (fig. 2.9 reproduces a wood engraving). Its great advantage was that the raised printing surface could be printed on the same press at the same time as letterpress type. The innovations popularized by Thomas Bewick in England beginning in 1790—use of engraver's tools on the harder end grain of boxwood—led to more refined prints, as did improvements in printing presses and paper. By mid-century the great demand for pictures in newspapers and magazines led many artists in both Britain and the United States to turn their attention to designing for wood engraving. The humble wood engraving, long the most common means of providing pictures in books and magazines, earned new respect and attention as an art form available to the masses. By the 1860s, electrotyping was used widely to produce exact duplicates of woodcuts as well as of letterpress type. The size of press runs was no longer limited by the factor of wear and tear, yielding economies of scale.[42] Thus Appleton was able to advertise *Wood-Side and Sea-Side* as appropriate for holiday giving at four dollars.

Although D. Appleton and Company had offered its gift books with considerable pride in 1868 and 1869, the firm may well have been stung by criticisms in an important book-trade journal. *The American Literary Gazette and Publishers' Circular* of December 1, 1869, faulted American publishers with relying too heavily on electrotypes of engravings from abroad, thus "manufacturing books out of all sorts of odds and ends." It called for original American illustrations and implied that such efforts would foster the needed development of skilled engravers in this country.[43]

D. Appleton and Company's altered approach to gift books in 1870 seems a direct answer to the trade journal's challenge. For that season, the firm commissioned several American artists to illustrate William Cullen Bryant's *Song of the Sower*. The resulting designs by Winslow Homer, W. J. Hennessy, Harry Fenn, John A. Hows, Granville Perkins, C. C. Griswold, and others, engraved on wood by skilled engravers, occupied considerably more space than did the text of Bryant's poem. Bound in an elaborately decorated green cloth stamped in gold, the book was priced at five dollars. It clearly met the criteria the trade journal had outlined—an original American production with well-executed wood engravings at a moderate price.

The book was so successful that D. Appleton and Company produced a companion volume in 1871, Bryant's *The Story of the Fountain*, illustrated by several of the same artists: Fenn, Homer, Hows, and Perkins, plus Alfred Fredericks. This edition was even more successful than *The Song of the Sower*. Press comments quoted in Appleton ads called the book "a triumph of American skill and art" and praised the variety of illustrations combined with the "harmony of theme and display." The *Saturday Evening Gazette* went so far as to say,

The Messrs. Appleton deserve the thanks of all Americans who take pride in the artistic triumphs of their native land, and may lay the flattering unction to their souls that they have produced the best illustrated work that has ever been issued here.[44]

Such singular praise combined with profitable sales surely convinced the Appletons that the times demanded further projects utilizing original artwork by Americans, reproduced as wood engravings.

At the same time that the firm's leadership was forging their new approach to gift books, they laid plans for yet another initiative to bring art into the home—*Appletons' Journal*. Founded in April 1869, this magazine would be the vehicle for initiating the "Picturesque America" series about a year later. Aware of the great popularity of the illustrated weeklies, especially *Harper's Weekly* and *Frank Leslie's Illustrated Newspaper*, they also observed the way several competitors utilized their own magazines to publicize their books. Since 1850, *Harper's Monthly Magazine* had been a conspicuous example of this tactic. The Boston firm of Ticknor and Fields had published the prestigious *Atlantic Monthly* since 1857, and in 1866 launched *Every Saturday*. Two years later in Philadelphia, Lippincott and Company founded *Lippincott's Magazine*, and *Putnam's Monthly* was begun by the New York firm. D. Appleton and Company must also have been aware of the wide admiration in the United States for the French *Magasin Pittoresque* and for British illustrated magazines like *The Cornhill, Good Words,* and *Once a Week.*[45] Readers were so eager for the latest periodicals that some publishers announced the exact day, even the hour, when a new number would be ready.[46]

By the summer of 1868 the Appleton brothers felt they could wait no longer to enter this competitive and vital arena of popular education and art. What sort of magazine would best serve their purposes and be distinctive enough to succeed? The prominent science editor, Edward L. Youmans, had long hoped to edit a magazine that would educate the general public about science. But he ran up against the Appletons' wish to feature literature and art in a publication that would benefit the firm much as *Harper's Monthly* and *Every Saturday* served their publishers. Eventually Youmans and his employers arrived at the compromise of an illustrated weekly paper "devoted at once to popular science and to art and letters" with "contributions from the most eminent writers in Europe as well as America."[47] The Appletons appointed Youmans editor of the new magazine. Anticipating a spring 1869 inaugural issue, he sailed to England in September 1868 to obtain material. For Youmans, the publishing house had tendered him "an unqualified commission to use their funds to carry out the most important and considerable project they have yet undertaken."[48]

The title selected for the new weekly was *Appletons' Journal of Literature, Science, and Art.* The compromise reflected in the title produced a magazine distinctive in both content and format. Its three emphases set it apart from the popular weeklies featuring current news, *Frank Leslie's Illustrated Newspaper and Harper's Weekly.* Its numerous illustrations distinguished it from the leading literary magazines, the *Atlantic Monthly,* the *Nation,* the *North American Review,* and the *Galaxy.* Furthermore, its urban orientation made it very different from *Hearth and Home,* the new illustrated weekly aimed primarily at rural families. The 8" x 11" format was smaller than the weeklies, yet larger than the 6½" x 9½" page of *Harper's Monthly,* allowing for larger illustrations. Its page size was similar to the greatly admired *Magasin Pittoresque.* Each issue was thirty-two pages, compared to the sixteen larger pages (11" x 16") of *Harper's Weekly.* Thus, at the same price, four dollars a year, or ten cents a copy, it was a comparable value.

The Appleton firm's conception of its role as "improver" or educator was clearly evident in the *Journal's* initial number, April 3, 1869. An announcement explained that after "nearly half a century" of "promoting general education and diffusing information" through books, the publishing house would now pursue these same goals through a weekly journal—the form of literature currently so popular with the public.

The new weekly was well received. The firm's judgment about what people wanted, at least in terms of pictures and fiction, was on the mark. After the first two numbers, *Round Table* concluded that *Appletons' Journal* had "more than fulfilled the pledges of the prospectus" and that, as a "picture paper and a story paper," like *Harper's Weekly*, "it will doubtless attain and keep a large circulation."[49] One early alteration may indicate sales were not quite all the firm had hoped for; by July 1, 1869, the *Journal* was also offered in monthly parts—an alternative format allowing it to compete with the monthlies as well as the weeklies and to be sold by book dealers not handling newspapers or weekly periodicals.[50]

The announced intention of providing extensive coverage of science in the new *Journal* evidently met with little enthusiasm. Despite the intense interest in geology and evolution already clear from the firm's successful publications on these topics, for hearthside reading most families preferred lighter fare. At the end of April 1869, a disappointed Youmans wrote his frequent correspondent Herbert Spencer:

> The paper is having a curious experience. The bare announcement that it would give attention to science and valuable thought raised an almost universal condemnation of it in advance as a certain failure. And although we have had no science in it and made it as vacant of ideas as possible, it is voted heavy.[51]

Although the *Journal* in the following months did treat scientific topics rather frequently, Youmans resigned the editorship after a little more than a year. His idea for a magazine emphasizing science had simply been slightly ahead of its time, for the single-focus *Popular Science Monthly* was successfully launched by D. Appleton and Company in 1872 under his leadership.

The planned emphases on literature and art proved more popular and long lasting. The firm's success with historical novels of European aristocracy carried over into the *Journal*, where serialized novels were regular features.[52] Other offerings included short stories, poems, sketches of travel and adventure, and discussions of art, books, and related topics. The intention to offer something for everyone would be partially fulfilled, although with a heavy emphasis on New York City and local activities.

In the realm of art, the *Journal* stressed the novelty and artistic value of its illustrations, claiming that many of the original works were fine enough to be framed. In truth, many of the *Journal*'s illustrations were well-designed and skillfully engraved. The larger wood engravings in *Harper's Weekly* and *Leslie's* were more coarsely and quickly engraved, sometimes from photographs or poorly composed sketches by amateurs. Furthermore, their paper stock was so thin that the print showed through from the other side. In the smaller format monthly magazines, such as *Harper's Monthly*, most of the wood engravings were finer textured but small and rather dull. The *Journal* competed on the basis of greater variety and originality of illustrations, engraved and printed with more care. It advertised that each number would include as an "Illustrated Supplement" either a steel engraving, a large "cartoon" engraved on wood and printed on a separate sheet "suitable for framing," or an "Art Supplement" with numerous wood engravings illustrating articles on such popular topics as New York City or European gardens. The more costly steel engravings distinguished the *Journal* from most other weeklies and linked it with the gift book tradition.

During the first year of publication, *Appletons' Journal* followed these announced plans rather closely: A number of high-quality steel engravings were included, primarily of landscape paintings by well-known American artists, including John F. Kensett, J. W. Casilear, Asher B. Durand, W. S. Haseltine, and F. O. C. Darley. These images were noticeably larger than most earlier ones produced by steel plates. The other featured type of illustration, the wood engraved "cartoons" (meaning sketches for paintings), were fold-outs as wide as twenty-eight inches. Their generous width accommodated sweeping scenes of lively cities and harbors, such as "The Levee at New Orleans," drawn by Alfred R. Waud, or "The Grand Drive at Central Park," by Thomas Hogan. A number of these conveyed the quality of sketches, with lines full of movement and drama. Unfortunately they were easily damaged with repeated unfolding and refolding.

With a new format for literature, essays, and scientific information and with illustrations that could be framed as works of art, the Appletons' new periodical injected a novel competitive element into the marketplace and achieved considerable success. By September 1869, *Godey's Lady's Book* said it was "among the best of the publications which have so recently been established." The *Syracuse Journal* had even higher praise: "*Appletons' Journal* occupies a field all to itself, nearer to the popular heart, appealing not only to the judgement and intellect, but to the sense of the beautiful and the good."[53] Thus the *Journal* further enhanced D. Appleton and Company's reputation as a publishing firm that contributed to the general good through the dissemination of information and culture. But the *Journal*'s rivals did not allow it to rest on its laurels for long. Established and new competitors would challenge it to new initiatives, including the series called "Picturesque America."

CHAPTER 2

The "Picturesque" Subject and Artist Harry Fenn

"Picturesque America" began in the November 12, 1870, *Appletons' Journal.* The publisher's notices heralded "a series of papers" "consisting of splendidly-executed views of the most unfamiliar and novel features of American scenery accompanied with suitable letter-press."[1] For some months a specially dispatched artist—soon revealed to be Harry Fenn—had been working on the illustrations. Such a project was ambitious and costly. Why did the fledgling *Journal* undertake it at this particular time? And why did the editors select the picturesque features of the American landscape as their subject?

Ideally, the first question could be answered by an examination of D. Appleton and Company's records; unfortunately, few have survived the various moves, fires, and mergers in the firm's long history. Despite this documentary gap, a clear rationale for the project emerges when we examine the publishing context of late 1869 and early 1870. The heated rivalry between the *Journal* and other illustrated periodicals—especially new competitors—to attract and hold a large audience through the quality, quantity, and subject matter of their pictures prompted the Appleton firm to launch the "Picturesque America" series.

By the fall of 1869 the *Journal's* well-engraved and carefully printed art, combined with the public's enthusiasm for pictures, had stirred its major rivals to invest more heavily in illustrations. Competition between the leading pictorial weeklies, *Frank Leslie's Illustrated Newspaper* and *Harper's Weekly*, had been strong for over a decade—with the question of whose pictures were better being hotly contested. In the fall of 1869, this rivalry intensified. "To keep up with the times," Leslie's included more genre scenes, illustrations keyed to literature, and pictorial supplements.[2] The newspaper also began a sporadic series called "Across the Continent" in January 1870, appealing to public curiosity about the West.[3] Convinced that illustrations in quantity provided a competitive edge, *Leslie's* advertised a particular number as having "21 square feet of Beautiful Engravings."[4]

The Harper firm was also aware of this rivalry. Beginning in early 1870, the publisher's notices in *Harper's Weekly* newly emphasized the high quality of its illustrations, claiming the "best artists in the country." Emphasizing timeliness and accuracy, they cited a debt to "photographers in all the large cities of America, Europe, and the East for prompt and valuable contributions." In its own defense, *Appletons' Journal* claimed to have become "a household necessity" and announced that in 1870 it would feature no less than "the finest engravings" as well as "the best literature, the greatest variety, the largest quantity of any American periodical."[5]

Additional competition arose from unexpected quarters. Two other periodicals—*Every Saturday* and *The Aldine Press*—increased their emphasis on large, attractive wood engravings. With the New Year's number for 1870, the prominent Boston firm of Fields, Osgood and Company (formerly Ticknor and Fields) suddenly transformed *Every Saturday* into "An Illustrated Weekly Journal." Since 1866 it had featured selections from foreign literature, without illustrations. Now it changed to a larger format—10½" x 14½", midway in size between *Appletons' Journal* and *Harper's Weekly*—and announced it would be the "Handsomest Illustrated Journal in America," with engravings after European artists "an important and attractive new feature."[6] Not surprisingly, this announcement elicited an immediate sarcastic response from the more chauvinistic *Leslie's*: "We infer, therefore . . . that it is 'important and attractive' to disregard wholly American artists and engravers."[7]

Nevertheless, *Every Saturday* was not deterred. Many of its controversial foreign illustrations came from *The Graphic*, a new illustrated weekly launched December 4, 1869, in London. By buying electrotypes from *The Graphic*, *Every Saturday* could include high-quality wood engravings reproducing works by such English artists as Arthur Boyd Houghton and John Gilbert, and such French artists as Jean Léon Gérôme and Paul Gavarni.[8] Yet *Every Saturday* soon aborted its plan to include only foreign wood engravings, probably in response to criticism such as *Leslie's* and public eagerness for American scenes. Designs by American artists gradually began to appear.[9]

Another significant challenge to *Appletons' Journal* in the sphere of illustration came from the much-expanded *Aldine Press: A Typographic Art Journal* (renamed *The Aldine, the Art Journal of America* in January 1871), a monthly folio-size publication that had originated as a slim house organ for the New York printing firm of Sutton, Browne and Company In January 1870, *The Aldine Press* increased both its length and its coverage of American and European artists and their works. Its selling point, with considerable justification, was the superior quality of its typography and printing and "the Unequalled Excellence of the Wood-cut illustrations."[10] As a specialized art publication, *The Aldine* differed from the more general *Appletons' Journal.* But because the *Journal* had always stressed the artistic quality of its illustrations, it could not ignore *The Aldine's* offerings. The contents of these two periodicals strongly suggest that each viewed the other as a major rival and took important initiatives in reaction to the other.[11]

Despite claiming to have quickly become a household necessity, the *Journal's* financial situation was not solid enough to preclude money-saving alterations. By mid-1870, the editor had discontinued the fold-out cartoons—and the steel engravings would meet the same fate by year's end. When news of yet another competitor spread through New York publishing circles in mid-1870, the leadership of *Appletons' Journal* must have decided that a new initiative was called for. The latest challenge came from *Scribner's Monthly*, scheduled to begin publication in November 1870, featuring "the best reading matter" and "the finest illustrations procurable at home and abroad." The primary reason this new magazine posed such a threat was the popularity of its editor, Dr. Josiah Gilbert Holland (1819–81). Subscribers would be attracted to a magazine directed by the man who had written the well-loved narrative poems *Bitter-Sweet* (1858) and *Katrina* (1867) and who as "Timothy Titcomb" offered advice to young men from the country venturing upon a new life in the city. His books and lyceum lectures had spread his fame throughout the country, and some considered him "the most popular and effective preacher of social and domestic moralities in his age, the oracle of the active and ambitious young man; of the susceptible and enthusiastic young woman; the guide, the philosopher, and school-master of humanity at large, touching all questions of life and character."[12]

"Picturesque America" was announced at the end of October 1870 to begin in early November, coinciding with the first appearance of *Scribner's Monthly*. The timing of the "Picturesque America" series strongly suggests that the *Journal*'s managers hoped this new, ongoing, illustrated feature would be sufficient attraction to hold their subscribers and distract potential readers from the new competitor. The intensifying rivalry between illustrated periodicals in 1870 explains why *Appletons' Journal* would have chosen to undertake a new project at this time. But it does not in itself explain why the editors selected "Picturesque America" as their theme. The choice was a most appropriate one for interrelated reasons: Not only did it appeal to those intensely curious about unfamiliar regions of the United States; it also attracted those eager to demonstrate their appreciation of both natural landscapes and landscape art. In addition, Appleton could rise to the challenge of producing high quality original illustrations designed by American artists, as well as expand its "improving" role. By providing examples of "touring in search of the picturesque" the series could educate new audiences in this approach to appreciating scenery, while entertaining those already indoctrinated.

In this period of peace and renewed optimism following the wrenching turmoil of the Civil War, images of the "most unfamiliar and novel features of American scenery" held great appeal. With the threat of a permanently divided nation laid to rest and a railroad route to the Pacific shore just completed, the reality of a continental nation could be grasped more readily than ever before.[13] Most were eager to put the painful years of War and Reconstruction behind them and anticipated the return of a recovering South to national life. Thus they wanted information about a region that had been largely off limits for more than a decade, but which held special attractions due to its mild climate and lush vegetation.

Furthermore, as more and more people moved West, building "mushroom" cities and cultivating land, Americans wanted to know where crops would flourish, valuable minerals could be found, and fortunes made. They also wanted pictures and descriptions of the mountains, waterfalls, rock formations, and great trees of the West, whose scale was so much larger than anything more commonly seen in the East. Visual documentation of such features could complete the expanding nation's self-image, and provide new bases for national pride. Some in large Eastern cities had been able to see images of such spectacular scenery in Albert Bierstadt's massive paintings of Yosemite and the Rocky Mountains or in Carleton Watkins's photographs of Yosemite. More had viewed scenic regions in stereographs, a popular addition to many parlors and lending libraries in this period. Yet stereographs, priced at $1.50 to $6 a dozen and requiring the separate purchase of the stereoscopic viewer, were neither as accessible nor as ubiquitous as the wood engravings entering the home in popular periodicals.

Neither stereographs nor exhibitions of paintings and photographs had adequately satisfied the curiosity of large numbers of Americans; nor had popular lithographs, published by Currier and Ives and other firms, which frequently presented either bird's eye views of cities or idealized views of general types of scenery rather than specific places. The hunger for more images can be seen in the illustrated features in the *Journal*'s competitors in 1870, like *Leslie's* "Across the Continent" and *Every Saturday*'s "Graphic America." In offering its readers pictures of the "novel and unfamiliar" scenery of their country, *Appletons' Journal* responded to insistent demands.

Increased opportunities for travel naturally heightened this interest. The rail system had doubled in mileage since the close of the Civil War, making travel more convenient and less expensive.[14] The growing number of people with the means and leisure to travel weighed the pros and cons of different vacation destinations. The new middle-income travellers— merchants, clerks, and "mechanics" (referring to those engaged in small manufacturing of all sorts)—were not drawn to such expensive resorts as Saratoga and Newport, favored by the old moneyed elite. As alternatives some took seriously the suggestions in newspapers and magazines to explore new areas in the Catskills and the Finger Lakes of New York State, newer seacoast resorts like Naragansett, Rhode Island, or regions farther afield like the Maine coast or the mountains of North Carolina. Others followed the advice of the Brooklyn clergyman Henry Ward Beecher (1813–87) to find refreshment from the stresses of city life by spending a month in the country with a wholesome farm family. Still others were enticed by tales of more active vacations involving fishing, hunting, hiking, and camping. Whereas travel in many parts of the West was still risky, a number of areas accessible to the population centers of the East coast offered wilderness adventure without real danger. The Appletons could provide an interested public with information about such areas, stimulating the market for their travel guides at the same time.

Yet the project they planned was something quite different from a travel guide or a travel account. This venture to disseminate original landscape art sought to profit from and feed national pride in both the American landscape and American art. The recent clamor for greater

2.1 Thomas Nast, "The Artist in the Mountains," *Harper's Weekly,* July 21, 1866. Wood engraving, 2⅛" x 2⅜₆". Courtesy the American Antiquarian Society.

excellence in American-produced illustrations coincided with the culmi-nation of a period of great creativity and achievement among American landscape painters. Following the lead of Thomas Cole (1801–48) in the 1820s, more and more artists had chosen landscape over portraits and his-torical scenes as their preferred subject matter. By mid-century, the sight of artists with sketch pads working under their umbrellas had become so common it inspired cartoons (see figs. 2.1, 2.2). Yet these travelling artists also inspired admiration and respect, for it was widely believed during this period that special talent for seeing beauty and grandeur enabled artists to guide others to encounters with the divine in nature.[15]

2.2 F. S. Church, "Return of Our Artist with his Summer Sketches," *Harper's Weekly*, September 13, 1873. Wood engraving, 10⅞" x 9⅛"; page, 16" x 11".

Generations raised on Wordsworth saw nature as the great teacher of moral and religious truths, and subscribed to such familiar sentiments as,

> One impulse from a vernal wood
> May teach you more of man,
> Of moral evil and of good,
> Than all the sages can.[16]

By attending to and savoring their emotional responses to nature and shaping them into art that revealed God's handiwork, landscape artists participated in a highly significant mission. From mid-century to at least the early 1870s, American artists and art critics showed a strong consciousness of this religious aspect of the artist's role. The works of the English critic John Ruskin (1819–1900), widely read beginning in the 1850s, reinforced convictions about the beneficial effects of art that was "true to nature." As one American art critic explained, landscape held first place in the art world because the purpose of art was the expression of our highest emotion, and "Where can we find a nobler or purer emotion than in the contemplation of what we call 'Nature,' God's creation?" Thus, he said, "the love of God impels the modern landscape painter to portray . . . God's handiwork as seen in his groves, his mountains, his seas, his clouds, and all the other expressions of his goodness, majesty and power."[17] By sponsoring the creation of landscape art produced by travelling artists in search of divine handiworks the *Journal* embarked on an endeavor of the highest import.

The Appletons' choice of the word *picturesque* emphatically linked this new venture with a long and still-admired tradition of touring "in search of the picturesque" and with the prestigious British and Continental view-books published earlier in the century, replete with engravings after artists' renderings of picturesque scenery.[18] The notion that it was a pleasurable and worthwhile activity for everyone, not just artists, to travel through the countryside in search of memorable views—those that would make appealing pictures—had spread gradually in the United States after being imported from Britain early in the nineteenth century. Ironically, the enthusiasm for picturesque touring predated the spread of Wordsworthian love of nature in Britain and was, in fact, criticized by Wordsworth as an overly rational, intellectual approach to the natural world. But American nineteenth-century popular thought merged the two impulses into a pervasive enthusiasm for seeking out memorable landscapes and responding to them, as Wordsworth said, "with a heart / That watches and receives."[19]

But—just as Charles Dickens noted at Niagara Falls that the sight that brought him close to God was, to his wife's maid, "nothing but water" and "too much of that!"—many had yet to develop this sensibility.[20] Unlike English travellers who did not expect their servants to share their response to scenery, Americans tended to believe that this appreciation could be taught and would benefit all, both culturally and spiritually. In his 1835 "Essay on American Scenery," Thomas Cole lamented that most Americans were so preoccupied with making money that they were indifferent to the beauties of nature, and urged cultivating a taste for scenery.[21] In 1844, the Boston clergyman Warren Burton, in a series of lectures later published as *The Scenery-Shower*, entreated parents and teachers to train the young to appreciate scenery, for the "faculty" for the beautiful, the picturesque, and the sublime developed with practice.[22] As late as 1870, the Appletons evidently judged rightly that there were still many eager to refine their skills in this approach to touring and thus to identify themselves with and join the ranks of those schooled in appreciation of art and nature.

"Touring in search of the picturesque" did require some instruction. It involved the moderate intellectual challenge of classifying scenes according to three aesthetic categories established since the latter half of the eighteenth century as descriptive of particular qualities in a landscape—*beautiful, sublime,* or *picturesque.* By the mid-nineteenth century the definitions and distinctions of these terms were taken for granted.

The *beautiful* was characterized by the smooth curving lines, harmony of color, and limited size of pastoral landscapes and calm lakes. Idealized Italian landscapes in paintings by Claude Lorrain (1600–82) had long provided models of the beautiful—balanced compositions of gentle curves and suffused golden light, they evoked feelings of peace and contentment, of humanity in harmony with a benevolent natural order.

The *sublime*, in contrast, was characterized by vast height or depth, darkness, powerful motion, or loud noise. Such scenes aroused feelings of awe or wonder, filling the mind and blotting out other thoughts. They could take one's breath away and cause the heart to skip beats. Fear was also a frequent response to the sublime. Viewed from a safe distance, towering peaks, deep canyons, roaring waterfalls, or dramatic storms could produce just enough terror to provide a thrill or a shudder or frisson, as it

was often called.[23]   Many works of the Italian painter Salvator Rosa
(1615–73) depicting wild and threatening storms, mountains, and declivi-
ties were considered ideal representations of the sublime.

The *picturesque* was less extensive in scale than the sublime and much
easier to discover in the landscapes of Britain and the eastern United
States. It was characterized by irregularity of form, rough texture, pleasing variety, and contrasts of light and dark. Its effect was to arouse curiosity and interest, and therefore provide delight.

From the mid-eighteenth century, these aesthetic categories had been
argued and refined in Britain in the writings of Edmund Burke (1729–97),
Uvedale Price (1747–1829), Richard Payne Knight (1750–1824), and others who sought to understand their emotional responses to different types
of natural landscapes and landscape paintings.[24] The great popularizer of
touring in search of "scenes" that resembled paintings—or, indeed, theater sets—was the Hampshire clergyman and amateur artist William
Gilpin (1724–1804). His enthusiastic accounts of touring the rugged
waterfalls and cliffs of the English Lake District and the mountains of
Scotland and Wales encouraged many Britons to follow suit.[25] For many,
this interest had overtones of nationalism, as they nurtured preferences
for typical British landscapes over the "classic" Italian scenes in Claude
Lorrain's paintings. In addition, anti-aristocratic sentiments valued infor-
mal "nature" over the symmetric "art" of formal gardens. Furthermore, it
was a means of enjoying the landscape available to those without enough
land to create a landscape garden.

In the view of Gilpin and others, associations with history or literature
greatly heightened a scene's picturesque interest. Architectural antiquities and ruins, objects that evoked reflection on the passage of time and
on man's inevitable end, became favorite subjects of artists, writers, and
tourists. The Romantic movement's concern with ancient origins and
medieval legends fed such interests. Landscapes associated with literature
also held special appeal, such as the places described in Byron's *Childe
Harold's Pilgrimage*, Samuel Rogers's *Italy*, and later, Scott's novels.[26]

This popular activity which imbued sightseeing with cultural and literary significance was carried across the Atlantic by books and periodicals, as well as by emigrating British landscape artists, and by travelers in
both directions.[27] Educated Americans with the money and leisure to
travel eagerly adopted the new approach to touring. With the "Picturesque America" series, *Appletons' Journal* participated in the accelerating

democratization of picturesque touring from an upper-class pastime rooted in art and literature to a way for middle-class tourists to take possession of the landscape.

In naming their new series "Picturesque America," the Appletons also linked it to a specific tradition in the graphic arts, the "picturesque views" that had naturally flowed from the popularity of picturesque touring. Many of these views utilized the compositional elements long admired in Claude Lorrain's landscape paintings: a dark foreground with trees or other elements framing the main subject, a light middle ground, and a zigzag of light and dark planes or a curving road or river leading the eye into the distance. They differed from Claude's ideal landscapes and the depictions of "generalized" nature preferred by such academic artists as Sir Joshua Reynolds in that they represented "particular" nature or actual places, and for this reason are frequently called "topographical views."

Prior to about 1830, British and Continental publishers offered numerous rather costly series of views in the form of copper engravings, etchings, or aquatints, often gathered together and accompanied by text in viewbooks.[28] When the development of steel plate engraving facilitated longer runs, the number of viewbooks increased greatly and their prices decreased.[29] By making such views accessible to a mass audience as inexpensive wood engravings in a popular periodical and, later, a serialized book, *Picturesque America* represented a further democratization of such prints.

With the great proliferation of picturesque views, a number of formulaic approaches to picture composition emerged. Many of these conventions were still in vogue by the time of *Picturesque America*. These included a rich variety of texture and detail in the foreground, whether of plants, animals, rocks, architectural elements, or people; framing elements, such as trees, cliffs, or parts of buildings, on one or both sides; dramatic effects in the sky, including storms, rainbows, sunrise or sunset, or moonlight; and recurring compositional points of view, ranging from panoramic views from a height, akin to the conventional bird's-eye view, to slightly elevated viewpoints, to the occasional more intimate closeup from ground level in a forest or a city street. The overall aim was to achieve pleasing variety and contrast within a balanced composition.[30]

The artists also came to follow certain patterns in their choices of subjects, influenced by notions of what constituted sublime, beautiful, and picturesque landscapes. Favorite subjects were water in motion in stormy

seas or cascading waterfalls; geological oddities, such as unusual rock formations and caves; steep, snowy mountain peaks; gnarled and twisted trees
that exuded antiquity; and Britain's alternative to Roman ruins, Gothic
architecture, particularly when already crumbling or partially destroyed.[31]
Almost without exception, the views included at least one small human figure, providing scale and serving as a stand-in for the viewer. Some scenes
resemble seventeenth-century Dutch and Flemish paintings in their celebration of country life and rural roads and carriages. In towns or cities,
favorite subjects included harbors crowded with boats and fisherfolk, busy
markets, cathedrals, and castles. Furthermore, by the 1840s artists gave
considerable attention to trains and railroad bridges and even managed to
make mining sites attractive.

Not only were British viewbooks exported to the United States, but
British artists and engravers also crossed the Atlantic to try to duplicate
their successes at home. Early and relatively costly aquatint series like
Picturesque Views of American Scenery (1819–21) and *The Hudson River
Portfolio* (1821–25) found limited audiences in the young republic.[32] A
projected series of small steel engravings called *The American Landscape*—
engraved by Asher B. Durand after paintings by Thomas Cole, Durand,
and others—did not find enough subscribers in 1830 to go beyond the
first of the ten numbers proposed.[33] More successful was the English
import *American Scenery*, published in thirty parts by the London firm of
George Virtue from 1837 to 1839, with steel engravings after designs by
the British artist William H. Bartlett (1809–54), who toured the United
States in 1836–37. With text by the popular American writer Nathaniel
Parker Willis (1806–67), the book enjoyed wide sales through Virtue's
New York office at seventy-five cents a part, or a total of $22.50.[34]

At mid-century a number of American publications with steel engravings of American scenery achieved respectable sales, such as *The Home
Book of the Picturesque* (Putnam, 1852), which reproduced the works of several leading landscape painters, T. Addison Richards's *Landscape Annual*
(Leavitt and Allen, 1854), and *The Scenery of the United States* (D. Appleton
and Company, 1855), which reused plates from *Meyer's Universum*.[35] The
canon of the most notable American scenery established in these and
other similar publications became the starting point for later projects,
including *Picturesque America*. Understandably, the earlier books, like
Willis's *American Scenery*, concentrated on the most accessible and most
noted scenic features, those of the Northeast. Treatment of the South and

West was very cursory—showing primarily Natural Bridge in Virginia, Tallulah Gorge in Georgia, and a few towns along the Mississippi.[36] Just as Willis and Bartlett had sought out the spots already famous in travel literature, prints, and paintings, those who came after them used *American Scenery* as a guide. In consequence certain scenic features became obligatory stops for travellers, leading to the establishment of more and more tourist facilities.[37] In the 1850s images of many of the same areas reached an even wider audience in the form of small wood engravings in such popular periodicals as *Harper's Monthly*.[38] The "Picturesque America" series would use the same medium to further publicize well-known tourist attractions and expand the canon by establishing new ones.

The public's avid curiosity about the American landscape, combined with the popularity of touring in search of the picturesque, goes far to explain why a series called "Picturesque America" would have appealed to the Appletons. But what sparked the idea? The answer lies in a particular incident recorded frequently enough to lend it credulity: At a social gathering including some of the Appletons, artist Harry Fenn overheard "an Englishman sneeringly say that the scenery of America had nothing picturesque about it. Mr. Fenn remarked in the hearing of the heads of the house, 'If they will make it worth my while, we will show the young man if there is any thing picturesque in America.'" A transplanted Englishman himself, Fenn was now clearly taking the part of his adopted homeland. A few months later, he received a letter from the Appletons "asking him to come over and talk to them about that suggestion he had made."[39]

Although the record fails to include who in the firm overheard Fenn's remark and who later met with him to discuss it, we can surmise that one of the participants was George S. Appleton (1821–78). The third eldest of the Appleton brothers, he was called "the active mind" of the firm and was often credited with "fine artistic taste." After studying at the University of Leipzig, he established his own bookselling and publishing business in Philadelphia. In 1865 he joined the family firm in New York and became known for his "fertility in resources and in projecting new enterprises."[40] The history of publishing uniformly gives George S. Appleton credit for conceiving *Picturesque America* and numerous other Appleton art publications.[41]

Fenn probably met with George S. Appleton and one of the *Journal*'s editors, Oliver Bell Bunce, who would eventually oversee the production of the new series and the book that followed. The meeting must have taken place before the fall of 1870 because the *Journal* of October 29 announced that the project had been underway for some months. Although no records of the understanding reached between Fenn and the company have been found, subsequent events suggest that Appleton commissioned him to make an extensive sketching tour in the South and agreed to publish a series of his views in the *Journal*. Fenn was already a familiar figure at the firm, having contributed numerous works to the *Journal* in its first year of publication. Yet he was not on the Appleton staff, and it was not a foregone conclusion that he would be commissioned for this project despite his having suggested it. Whoever selected him, and it was probably Bunce in consultation with George S. Appleton, made an inspired choice. Fenn's experience and talent perfectly suited the challenges and aims of this new project.

Born in Richmond, Surrey, probably in 1837, Harry Fenn had an early interest in drawing and painting. By the age of twelve he was attempting careful renderings from nature.[42] He was also attracted to dramatic landscapes; in 1856, at about the age of nineteen, he came to the United States, primarily to see Niagara Falls[43] (see fig. 2.3). Like so many others, he evidently sought an encounter with the divine in that most famous of sublime features. He stayed on, working at first as a wood engraver, for which he had been trained in the workshop of the Dalziel brothers, the leading wood engraving establishment in London. In learning this skill, Fenn selected a career path common to many aspiring artists in this period in the United States as well as Britain.[44] He produced wood engravings for *Frank Leslie's Illustrated Newspaper* in 1857 and 1858 and probably worked for other publishers as well.[45]

After six years in the United States, during which time he married Marian Thompson of Brooklyn, Fenn went to Italy to study painting, probably in 1862 or 1863. He is said to have given away his gravers before sailing, telling his fellow engravers that he "intended thereafter to use only brush and pencil." They, in turn, "scoffed at his ambition."[46]

Upon his return a year or so later, Fenn did abandon engraving for painting and drawing. Yet in the 1860s in New York it was becoming difficult to earn a living from painting alone. Even such celebrated painters as Frederic Church and Albert Bierstadt found their sales dwindling. With more American artists training in Europe, especially Paris, and more European paintings being imported, critics and patrons were developing new tastes—for the more intimate, atmospheric Barbizon landscapes or

2.3 Harry Fenn, about 1875. Courtesy of William Abt.

the grandiose figure paintings of Gérôme, Meissonier, and others.[47] A less risky way for an artist to make a living was to produce illustrations for books and the burgeoning periodical market. The advantages of earning steady income and reaching a mass audience outweighed the disadvantages of being limited to black and white and depending on engravers to translate one's work. This was the path Fenn chose.

One of his earliest book commissions was sixteen illustrations for a large project memorializing the Union effort in the Civil War, *The Tribute Book* (Derby and Miller, 1865) by Frank B. Goodrich. In this book, Fenn occupied a prominent place as a specialist in landscape views alongside well-known illustrators who most often depicted figures, such as Augustus Hoppin, John McLenan, and Hammatt Billings. Fenn's views of the falls of Minnehaha (p. 284) and the English ship *George Griswold* (p. 383), both engraved by N. Orr, were among the largest and most attractive in the book, exhibiting the attention to texture and light effects that became hallmarks of Fenn's style. In both of these illustrations, Fenn used the format of a circle broken at the bottom—a popular convention used frequently in *Picturesque America* by Fenn and the other artists—that had the effect of increasing three-dimensionality and drawing the viewer into the scene.

At least two other early jobs gave Fenn the opportunity to depict scenic spots in the United States: *Trenton Falls: Picturesque and Descriptive* (N. Orr and Company, 1865), edited by N. P. Willis, and Albert D. Richardson's popular *Beyond the Mississippi* (American Publishing Company, 1867), a celebration of the building of the transcontinental railroad. Fenn's eight Trenton Falls views used perspective more skillfully than did the rather flat images carried over from earlier editions. Fenn probably had his own on-site sketches to work from because Trenton Falls was a regular stopover on the route to Niagara in this period. For *Beyond the Mississippi*, however, he probably worked from photographs or other prints or paintings to make his six designs, including depictions of far-flung places like the Taos Pueblo and Mount Shasta. Even so, he created memorable images that undoubtedly furthered his reputation—particularly an illustration of the massive redwood "Grizzly Giant."

During the same period, from 1865 to 1869, Fenn created illustrations based on meticulous nature studies for the respected Boston publisher Ticknor and Fields. This placed him in association with the highly skilled wood engraver, A. V. S. Anthony (1835–1906), who oversaw the firm's gift book production. As early as 1865, Fenn contributed designs to Ticknor and Field's edition of John Greenleaf Whittier's *National Lyrics.* In 1867 he drew the iris and attendant dragonfly for the frontispiece to Henry Wadsworth Longfellow's *Flower-de-Luce,* as well as the title page for Harriet Beecher Stowe's poem "A Day in the Pamfili Doria" in her *Religious Poems.* For Professor and Mrs. Louis Agassiz' *A Journey in Brazil* (1868), he demonstrated his skill at drawing tropical vegetation—so in vogue at the time—in such a way as to facilitate effective wood engraving, even when working from photographs (see fig. 2.4). In this period Fenn also contributed a number of illustrations to Ticknor and Field's magazine for children, *Our Young Folks.* The detailed nature study accompanying Lucretia Hale's "The Four Seasons" (June 1866) (fig. 2.5) is especially effective and representative of the type of close observation of nature recommended by John Ruskin.[48]

While establishing himself as a book illustrator in black and white, Fenn became active as a watercolorist as well. He was among the early members of the American Watercolor Society, elected at the second meeting of the society January 2, 1867. He contributed four works to the society's First Annual Exhibition, held in conjunction with the 1867/68 winter exhibition of the National Academy of Design, and was represented by three to five paintings in succeeding years.[49] As might be expected, the subjects of most of Fenn's works exhibited in the first three annual exhibitions came from his stay in Italy in the early 1860s. From 1870/71 to 1873, his subjects derived mainly from his travels for "Picturesque America."

In practicing and exhibiting in the watercolor medium during this period, Fenn was participating in one of the most dynamic, innovative movements in American art. Watercolor had been little appreciated or practiced in the United States before the British Loan Exhibition of 1857/58, in which half of the paintings were watercolors, including many by J. M. W. Turner (1775–1851).[50] Because Fenn came from England, however, he surely would have been familiar with works of such British landscape watercolorists as John Robert Cozens, Thomas Girtin, and Richard P. Bonington, as well as Turner. Technical innovations introduced by these artists had resulted in works rivaling oil paintings in their density of color—and deemed appropriate as major exhibition pieces.[51] More and more artists who abandoned the studio to draw and paint directly from nature recognized watercolor's practical advantages—it was fast, easily transportable, and capable of capturing light effects. These same qualities

2.4 Harry Fenn, "Cocoeiro Palm," frontispiece, in Louis Agassiz, *A Journey in Brazil* (1868). Wood engraving, 5⅞" x 3¹¹⁄₁₆".

2.5 Harry Fenn, nature study, accompanying
Lucretia Hale, "The Four Seasons and a Little about
their Flora, May and June.—Spring and Summer,"
Our Young Folks, June 1866, 363. Wood engraving by
W. H. Morse, 2⅜" x 2¾".

made the medium a favorite of artists involved in landscape illustration,
like Fenn, although they often worked in pencil as well. The popularity of
the medium with artists naturally led to more watercolor exhibitions, usually sponsored by associations formed primarily for that purpose, as was
the American Watercolor Society. And, as the public gradually accepted
the idea that works on paper could be taken seriously as durable, highly
finished pictures, they began to sell.

   Fenn's prominence as well as his earnings, however, would always
derive more from his illustrations in widely circulated magazines and
books than from his watercolor paintings. He first achieved fame when
Ticknor and Fields hired him to prepare all the illustrations for a gift edition of John Greenleaf Whittier's *Snow-Bound* (1868), brought out for
Christmas 1867. *Snow-Bound* was Whittier's greatest popular success. First
published in 1866, it recalled a familiar, simpler past, when most
Americans lived in extended families on self-sufficient farms. Its depiction
of a storm-enforced period of leisure and play also held great appeal.[52] In
a prefatory note, Whittier commended Fenn's illustrations for their "faith-

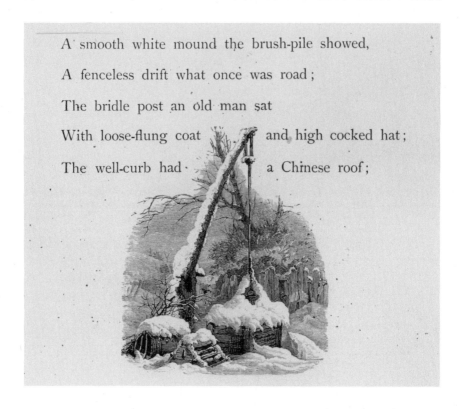

A smooth white mound the brush-pile showed,

A fenceless drift what once was road;

The bridle post an old man sat

With loose-flung coat and high cocked hat;

The well-curb had a Chinese roof;

2.6 Harry Fenn, ["The well-curb had a Chinese roof"], in John Greenleaf Whittier, *Snow-Bound. A Winter Idyl* (1868), 13. Wood engraving by A. V. S. Anthony, 2⅜" x 2¼".

fulness" to "the spirit and the details of the passages and places" in his ballad[53] (see fig. 2.6).

This edition was hugely successful, so much so that it is frequently credited as the first illustrated gift book published in this country. Although this is incorrect, considering the many illustrated annuals produced from the 1820s, the claim suggests its great impact.[54] Engraved by A. V. S. Anthony, the small images successfully combine variety with harmony. The formats vary widely, from sharp rectangles to rather amorphous vignettes, but Fenn's intricate lines and care in rendering light effects, as well as the consistently high quality of the engraving, create a pleasing whole.

In 1869, Fields, Osgood and Company (the successors to Ticknor and Fields) followed up with an elaborate gift edition of Whittier's *Ballads of New England* (1870), featuring Fenn's landscape settings as headpieces and tailpieces for each ballad.[55]   Additional illustrations were contributed by other artists whose subsequent reputations have surpassed Fenn's, including Winslow Homer, F. O. C. Darley, Sol Eytinge, Jr., Samuel Colman, and W. J. Hennessy. Yet in 1869 Fenn's reputation was soaring, and at least one critic found his work the most appealing:

The most charming illustrations in this beautiful book are the pictures of Mr. Fenn, who in studies of the very scenes described by the poet has reproduced all the moods and sentiments of the New England landscape: the pathos of the rainy and cloudy coasts, the tender serenity of the river-bordered fields, the life and brightness of the villages, the sadness of the lonely farm, the solemnity of the hill-side graveyard.[56]

Harry Fenn's popularity derived from his skill at depicting scenes in such a way that they evoked feeling but were also perceived as accurate. By the late 1860s many publishers sought his landscape and nature illustrations as well as his illustrations to poetry. *Harper's Monthly Magazine* commissioned him to illustrate the lead story for March 1868, "The Minnesota Pineries," using photographs as the bases for his drawings. Several of the twelve designs, including the opening one, are larger, more striking, and better engraved than the magazine's usual fare. In intricacy of detail, they are akin to the best work by Charles Parsons (1821–1910), art director for Harper's from 1863 to 1893. The similarities in composition, light effects, and flexible formats, as well as complexity of detail, between Parsons's work and Fenn's suggest that Parsons served as one of Fenn's mentors and models for fine small-scale work. Comparing Fenn's illustration for J. D. Sherwood's poem "The Silent City at Greenwood" in *Harper's Monthly* (January 1869) with Parsons's for another Sherwood poem in the preceding number reveals obvious similarities in style and technique (see figs. 2.7, 2.8). Furthermore, the two men, Englishmen by birth and early members of the American Watercolor Society as well as illustrators, were friends and both residents of Montclair, New Jersey.[57]

Yet Fenn's association with *Harper's Monthly* was relatively brief at this time. He contributed as a freelancer to the new periodical *Hearth and Home: An Illustrated Rural, Literary and Family Weekly* in March 1869. Also in the spring of 1869, Fields, Osgood and Company hired Fenn to do a rush job, illustrating stories of camping in the Adirondacks by the Reverend William H. H. Murray (1840–1904), minister of Boston's Park Street Congregational Church. *Adventures in the Wilderness* was a great success,

HARPER'S
NEW MONTHLY MAGAZINE.

No. CCXXIV.—JANUARY, 1869.—Vol. XXXVIII.

THE SILENT CITY AT GREENWOOD.

SHIPS SAIL PAST THIS SILENT CITY, BUT THEIR OWNERS QUIET LIE.

I.

THERE'S a city vast yet voiceless, growing ever street on street,
Whither friends with friends e'er meeting, ever meeting never greet;
And where rivals fierce and vengeful calm and silent mutely meet:
　　　　　　　　　　Never greeting ever meet.

II.

There are traders without traffic, merchants without books or gains;
Tender brides in new-made chambers, where the trickling water stains;
Where the guests forget to come, and strange, listening silence reigns:
　　　　　　　　　　Listening silence ever reigns.

III.

Ships sail past this silent city, but their owners quiet lie,
And no signals fly from top-tree 'gainst the glowing, crimson sky,
Telling the neglectful owner that his well-built Argosy
　　　　　　　　　　For the Fleece is sailing by.

2.7 Harry Fenn, "Ships sail past this silent city, but their owners quiet lie," accompanying John D. Sherwood, "The Silent City at Greenwood," *Harper's Monthly Magazine*, January 1869, 1. Wood engraving, 3⅜" x 4⅜"; page, 9½" x 6½".

2.8 Charles Parsons, illustration accompanying John D. Sherwood, "A Pilgrimage upon the Rhine," *Harper's Monthly Magazine*, December 1868, 1. Wood engraving, 5⅞" x 4⅜"; page, 9½" x 6½".

leading to an unprecedented number of visitors to the region that summer.[58] Although Fenn probably created these illustrations from his imagination, aided by his familiarity with typical forest and lake scenery of the
Northeast, his participation in this popular publication is significant. It
identified him with the important cultural movement that was legitimizing
play and leisure activities, including adventurous outdoor recreation. It
may also have reinforced his enthusiasm for fishing and hunting, activities
he would depict frequently in *Picturesque America*.

Liberal Christian clergymen had already struck blows against the
Protestant work ethic. For example, in *Work and Play* (1864), Horace
Bushnell had insisted that play as well as work was essential, saying "nothing fires or exalts us, but to feel the divine energy and the inspiring liberty
of play."[59] Now Reverend Murray endorsed the therapeutic value of adventure in the wilderness.[60] Whereas several decades earlier hunting and fishing were looked down upon as diversions for the rich or the unemployed
poor, now a minister recommended such activities as refreshing to all, but
especially city dwellers. A wilderness experience was made relatively pain-
less, as Murray described it, by the assistance of a hired guide who carried
and rowed the boat, set up camp, and cooked the meals. Recounting his
own adventure as "the first gentleman" to run rapids, he insisted that
"heroic sports" make "heroic men" (p. 84). To the "ladies," he offered the
enticement of a restful campsite and boating on calm lakes. Yet women as
well as men would benefit from direct contact with sublime scenes that
reminded them of divine creation: "I know of nothing which carries the
mind so far back toward the creative period as to stand on the shore of
such a sheet of water, knowing that as you behold it, so it has been for
ages" (p. 65). Ministers, in particular, needed this experience, for "the
preacher sees God in the original there, and often translates him better
from his unwritten works than from his written word" (p. 24).

During 1869, Fenn had ties to another influential clergyman and lec-
turer who stressed the role of feelings and imagination as a route to
faith—Henry Ward Beecher of Brooklyn's Plymouth Church. A primary
message of his widely read novel *Norwood* (1867) was that intuitive powers
enabling all to experience God in the realm of nature were superior to
the faculties of intellect.[61] Beecher was also known to admire artists and
their works, so it must have boosted Fenn's career when he was selected to
supply illustrations for Beecher's *Life of Jesus, the Christ*. The publisher J. B.
Ford issued the first chapter as a holiday book in 1869, with two landscape

illustrations by Fenn.[62] Ford also published a weekly edited by Beecher called the *Christian Union*, for which Fenn produced a special "cartoon" for the 1869 Christmas number. These assignments linked Fenn with another leading clergyman who taught that nature was revelatory of the divine and attempted in his preaching and writing to reconcile the findings of science and Biblical scholarship with religious faith.[63]

When D. Appleton and Company began publishing *Appletons' Journal* in April of 1869, they wasted no time in hiring Fenn to provide artwork. He contributed two small views to the "New York Illustrated" art supplement in the April 24 issue, and more as the series continued in subsequent numbers. Fenn's illustrations for "New York Illustrated," which was issued in late 1869 as a book, were more dynamic in both style and format than most by other artists. His foldout "View of Castle Garden and New York Bay" was the featured cartoon in the *Journal*'s seventh number, May 15, 1869; a steel engraving of "West Point and the Highlands" (after his oil painting) appeared September 11, 1869; and another foldout—of Fairmount Park in Philadelphia—appeared September 25, 1869. Two wood engravings of noticeably superior quality, "The Cape Ann Cedar Tree" and "Star Island, Isles of Shoals," appeared October 9, 1869[64] (see fig. 2.9). Comparing "The Cape Ann Cedar Tree" with the illustrations from *Harper's Monthly* (figs. 2.7, 2.8) also gives some indication of why contemporary audiences would have found Fenn's work in *Appletons' Journal* bold and out of the ordinary. The work is essentially a portrait of a tree, the larger size giving Fenn space to feature details of the plants crowding the foreground frame. Whereas the highly irregular branches and twisted trunk of the tree would have immediately identified the subject as picturesque, the monumentalizing approach makes the conventional prospect view framed by trees that Fenn prepared for *Harper's* seem almost a miniature by comparison. Thus, while proficient in utilizing the picturesque conventions, Fenn did not limit himself to that vocabulary.

By late 1869 Fenn had proven himself an innovative illustrator of significant features of both American scenery and cities, an artist whose works evoked sentiment but were perceived as faithful to the actual scenes. He was identified with popular books stressing the growing nostalgia for rural life and the psychological and religious benefits of experiences in a safe and convenient "wilderness." When George S. Appleton and Oliver Bunce needed to choose an artist for their new "Picturesque America" series, Fenn was the outstanding candidate.

2.9 Harry Fenn, "New England Coast Scene.—The Cape Ann Cedar Tree," *Appletons' Journal*, October 9, 1869, 240. Wood engraving by James Langridge, 9¼" x 6½".

From Fenn's point of view, the commission offered an excellent opportunity. He could build a following for his interpretations of the American landscape while improving the *Journal*'s competitive stance among its rivals. By setting out in search of the picturesque to create a series of landscape views, he could associate himself with such admired artists as J. M. W. Turner, Samuel Prout, David Roberts, William Henry Bartlett, Myles Birket Foster, Thomas Cole, and Frederic Church. It was also Fenn's golden chance to communicate his enthusiasm for dramatic scenery and historic cities and, most important, "his own reverential sense of beauty." According to a friend, "the pursuit and the understanding of Nature and the unveiling of her beauties that others might feel and see them as he did were to Harry Fenn far more than an emotional or artistic delight; they were his religion."[65]

CHAPTER 3

Oliver Bell Bunce and the Rediscovery of the South

Oliver Bell Bunce oversaw the entire *Picturesque America* project, from its first incarnation in *Appletons' Journal* to part 48 of the serialized book. Along with Fenn, he decisively shaped the outcome. William Cullen Bryant had no involvement with the *Journal* series, and, despite being named editor of the book, his participation was late in coming and limited to writing a preface, editing copy, and reading proof. Bunce was the actual editor of both text and illustrations. As author of twelve sections, he was also the primary writer. His beliefs, interests, and preferences were crucial determinants of the contents.

Like Fenn, Bunce's career had developed along several specialized lines. He had joined the Appleton firm in 1867 as a thirty-nine-year-old with considerable writing, editing, and publishing experience. When *Appletons' Journal* was launched in 1869, he was appointed assistant editor, serving first under Youmans, then under Robert Carter (1819–79), a long-time newspaper editor who had worked on the first edition of Appletons' *American Cyclopaedia.* Accounts differ on the date Bunce became chief editor of the *Journal,* but it was apparently after the "Picturesque America" series was well underway, and perhaps not until 1873.[1] Bunce's heavy involvement with the successful series may well have influenced the firm to promote him.[2]

Before settling in at D. Appleton and Company, Bunce had tried his hand at writing drama and fiction, as well as at publishing. By the age of twenty-five he had written three plays, the most successful being a comedy called *Love in '76* (1857). Of his three novels, *Bensley* (James C. Gregory,

1863) was the most popular. His first publishing enterprise, Bunce and Brother, produced two works by the popular American novelist Ann Sophia Stephens, who frequently satirized the nouveau riches: *Fashion and Famine* (1854) and *The Old Homestead* (1855).[3] In the early 1860s, he managed the New York publishing house of the late James C. Gregory. In that role he gained valuable experience in producing heavily illustrated books like the 1863 gift book of nature poetry, *In the Woods with Bryant, Longfellow and Halleck,* with wood engravings after John A. Hows. *Publishers' Weekly* eulogized him as "the pioneer" in publishing superbly illustrated books of poetry for the Christmas trade.[4]

After the Gregory firm dissolved, Bunce apparently entered into another publishing partnership in New York, Bunce and Huntington, with F. J. Huntington. In 1866 that firm produced at least two books noteworthy for their illustrations. *Festival of Song: A Series of Evenings With the Poets,* with seventy-three wood engravings based on designs by members of the National Academy of Design—including Winslow Homer, Frederic Church, John F. Kensett, Albert Bierstadt, Jasper Cropsey, and Worthington Whittredge—was designed as a conspicuously elegant volume that would attest to the owner's interest in poetry and art.[5] Dramatically successful in terms of sales was a Civil War novel sympathetic to the South, *Surry of Eagle's Nest* by John Esten Cooke, who would later write for *Picturesque America.* For illustrations, Bunce and Huntington commissioned four striking designs from Winslow Homer, who had served as a special artist-reporter for *Harper's Weekly* during the war.[6]

Thus, by the time Bunce joined the Appleton firm in 1867, he was experienced in selecting both literature and graphic images that appealed to the public and had already produced gift books with original illustrations similar to those that the *American Literary Gazette and Publishers' Circular* would call for in 1869. The illustrators he chose were among the best working in the media of steel and wood engraving. These credentials made him an attractive candidate for a post at Appleton, where he was an editor from 1867 until his death in 1890.[7]

During those years, Bunce came to play a prominent role in New York publishing circles. His opinions on the state of the trade were quoted frequently in the *American Literary Gazette and Publishers' Circular* (which became the *Publishers' and Stationers' Weekly Trade Circular* in 1872). Furthermore, his home on 21st Street became a gathering place for aspiring as well as established authors and artists. Those who attended Bunce's "salon" on Sunday evenings included writers Richard Henry Stoddard, E. C. Stedman, William Henry Bishop, and artists Winslow Homer, Frederic Church, R. Swain Gifford, Thomas Moran, E. A. Abbey, and Arthur Quartley.[8]

The few descriptions of Bunce convey the impression of a rather crusty, outspoken man whose irritability increased with advancing tuberculosis the last twenty years of his life. William H. Rideing, a contributor to *Picturesque America*, reminisced about the usual course of a hopeful writer's first encounter with him:

A lean, stooping, gray-visaged man, intellectual looking, spruce in attire, quick in movement, imperious in manner, he disconcerted you by the flash of his eyes, and then dashed your manuscript on the desk before him, flattening it with resounding blows of both hands, hunching his shoulders, and working his mouth as a dog does while he stiffens himself for an attack. But there was no bite to Bunce. All those menacing demonstrations were but a necessary defence against the impulses which, unguarded, would have embarrassed him through too many indiscretions of sympathy and generosity. He had the tenderest of hearts under that alarming demeanour, as you were likely to discover before even your first meeting with him ended.

Rideing goes on to say Bunce "liked to argue on art and literature, starting invariably with an emphatic 'I affirm,' and what he affirmed was so different from the opinions of others that conversation with him never missed being breezy; sometimes it whirled in the vortex of a tempest."[9]

Throughout his years as a publisher and editor, Bunce continued to write, much as Fenn continued to paint for exhibition while working as an illustrator. In 1881 he achieved wide sales with a reworking of pieces from his columns in *Appletons' Journal* titled *Bachelor Bluff: His Opinions, Sentiments, and Disputations*. Even more successful was a short guidebook Bunce wrote for those new to urban social circles called *Don't: A Manual Of Mistakes And Improprieties More Or Less Prevalent In Conduct And Speech* (1883). And in 1884 Charles Scribner's Sons published Bunce's prescription for an unpretentious yet charming family haven, "wherein the best that is within us may blossom," *My House: An Ideal*. With such books of moral and practical advice, Bunce assumed a role analogous to that of *Scribner's Monthly* editor J. G. Holland, although his influence was less far-reaching, without the celebrity attendant upon the lyceum circuit and national bestsellers.

Bunce's books and articles in *Appletons' Journal* reveal a political and social moderate whose opinions coincided with the Appleton firm's mission to "improve" and educate, and with the *Journal*'s appeal to the family circle. Sharing the confidence typical of his class, he saw civilization advancing and a bright future for the nation. Despite the quantity of trash being published, he was convinced literary taste was improving, citing as evidence the demand for books of scientific investigation; for example, Darwin's works "were more read and talked about than the most popular novel."[10] In the face of larger, more heterogeneous cities, he stressed the importance of social order and the crucial role of the family in promoting it. These concerns sometimes led to unconventional opinions, as Rideing suggested. In the August 16, 1873, *Journal* he called for suffrage for all heads of households—whether male or female—since they would have the greatest direct interest in the conservation of social order (p. 217). He must have applauded such *Journal* series as "The 'Dangerous Classes' of New York, and Efforts to Improve Them" (1870) by Charles Loring Brace.[11]

Bunce's convictions about progress read like popular applications of Herbert Spencer's theory that evolution leads inevitably to the development of civilization. In *Appletons' Journal* for July 19, 1873, he defended the current "Period of Greed," lamented by so many, in his "Editor's Table" column. He maintained that increased desire for possessions and pleasures resulted naturally from the diffusion of ideas through public education, books, and newspapers:

Culture and education have created a desire for the prizes of life, and at the same time given the means whereby they may be obtained. The Period of Greed is nothing more than the entirely natural outcome of advanced general civilization. Our public schools have opened the floodgates—can we expect anything more than that the flood should rush in to occupy its new possessions? (90)

The "prizes of life" that Bunce listed reveal much about his own values and his understanding of his evidently largely female audience:

An active, socially-disposed, cultivated person wants a tasteful home, good dresses, choice dinners, books, pictures, music, horses, summer vacations, foreign travel, social intercourse. . . . Never before, perhaps, in the world has the passion of greed been so little like a miser's desire to accumulate, and more nearly a generous, no doubt undisciplined, but still a hearty eagerness to enjoy. (90)

Thus he embraced the notion that enjoyment, or play, was a legitimate goal, as had Bushnell, Beecher, Murray, and others. Bunce also reiterated the reassuring national ideology of social and economic fluidity, affirming

that such delights and "prizes" were accessible to all who "earnestly struggle for them," "with a strong will and a firm hand." Far from being an evil,
greed was a "powerful motor in civilization" that had led to "the discovery
of continents," settlement of the wilderness, and the new inventions that
"have made civilization what it is" (90). These attitudes were entirely consistent with D. Appleton's publishing program in general and with the fun-
damental optimism of both the "Picturesque America" series and the book
that followed.

Moreover, the pages of the *Journal* reveal that Bunce was avidly interested in "the picturesque," and often used the term in his "Table-Talk" column and in stories relating his own travels. His accounts of railroad trips
with his wife show the couple in lively debate about the qualities of
scenery: She thinks a "tumble-down mill" mars a landscape, while he, like
most artists, finds dilapidated buildings picturesque.[12] Another story
shows their interest in the picturesque could outweigh convenience: On
the way back to New York City from Washington, D.C., they make a detour
to upstate New York to see the stratified rocks of Watkins Glen and find
this route "the nearest way home" because it provides a new experience of
scenery.[13]

To Bunce it was obvious that "cultivated persons" desired summer vacations, books, and pictures. His own talent for producing illustrated publications combined with his keen interest in picturesque scenery and new
travel destinations predisposed him to favor the idea of "Picturesque
America" and to see in that idea a compelling attraction for many readers.
In addition, his previous experience with illustrations made him aware
that Harry Fenn's comparatively bold style, full of energy and movement,
was currently popular with the public and particularly appropriate for representing picturesque scenery.

By the summer of 1870 George S. Appleton, with the support of
Bunce, convinced the current editor—either Youmans or Carter—to initiate the "Picturesque America" series. Their decision to send Fenn on a
tour of the South and to feature Southern scenery first was highly significant at that particular time. To suggest that regions of the former
Confederate states, which were still often viewed as backward and morally
corrupt and where many cities had been badly damaged and rail lines
destroyed, were now appropriate destinations for travellers and artists "in
search of the picturesque" signaled a return to normalcy. It also promoted cultural reunification based on appreciation of art and nature.

The decision to present the South in an attractive light was in keeping with Bunce's 1866 publication of *Surry of Eagle's Nest*. The firm's leaders also probably shared the growing sentiment in the North that Southern whites had been punished enough, a feeling often accompanied by waning enthusiasm to push for governmental intervention to assure the rights of freedmen. The commercial motive of attracting Southern subscribers surely played a part as well.

The role of the "Picturesque America" series in fostering reconciliation has been overshadowed by that of such later series as "The Great South," which began in *Scribner's Monthly* in 1873.[14] Furthermore, Bunce rearranged the material in the book that followed, and the initial focus on the South was lost. A detailed look at the early history of the series resurrects this emphasis, and also allows us to explore other ways the *Journal* and its competitors sought to appeal to the public. It was this competition that eventually prompted the Appleton firm to switch from a magazine series to a subscription book on the American landscape.

The first mention of a series of views with accompanying text to be called "Picturesque America" appeared on the back page of the October 29, 1870, *Appletons' Journal*:

The Publishers give notice that they have, for some months been gathering from various sections, by an artist specially dispatched for the purpose, material for a series of papers to be called PICTURESQUE AMERICA consisting of splendidly-executed views of the most unfamiliar and novel features of American scenery accompanied with suitable letter-press. The first of these *papers* (A Journey up the St. John's and Ocklawaha [Oklawaha] Rivers, Florida) *will shortly appear.* (536)

The next issue, November 5, included a longer announcement and named the "specially dispatched" artist, "Mr. HARRY FENN, one of our most accomplished draughtsmen." (By this time Fenn was considered an American artist.) After ascending the St. John's and Oklawaha rivers in Florida, Fenn had "traversed Georgia, the Carolinas, Eastern Tennessee, and Virginia, and returned with his portfolio filled with a series of very striking and beautiful sketches" that were then in the hands of the best engravers. Since returning from his Southern tour he had also made sketches in a number of Northern localities.

With the November 12 issue, the much-heralded series began with "A Journey up the St. John's and Ocklawaha Rivers"—a truly novel and dramatic opening that presented the attractions of a swamp, a setting long viewed as evil and forbidding. Further it applied the picturesque conventions to a landscape radically different from the picturesque regions of the Northeast—which, in turn, most resembled Britain. According to David C. Miller, this positive portrayal "marked the induction of the swamp into the canon of the predominant American landscape tradition."[15] On the other hand, Bunce's choice was not surprising, for Florida was just coming to national attention as a desirable destination for both adventure and recuperation. Jacksonville, Green Cove Springs, and several other towns were already winter havens for invalids, and regular boat trips had recently been instituted on the St. John's River. An 1869 guidebook by Ledyard Bill, *A Winter in Florida* (Wood and Holbrook), prompted the *New York Times* to observe that "the thousands who would know all about Florida before going there, will find this book just the thing."[16] At least two of the *Journal*'s competitors, *Harper's Monthly* and *Every Saturday*, ran illustrated stories on Florida in October 1870.[17] The eight-page section in *Appletons'* consisted of two large and ten small illustrations and several columns of text printed on smoother paper than the rest of the *Journal*.

The writer that Bunce selected to accompany Fenn and prepare the text was Thomas Bangs Thorpe (1815–78), a seasoned journalist who had specialized in tales of adventure and descriptions of picturesque scenery. Familiar with the swamps of the Lower Mississippi from his days as a newspaper editor in New Orleans, he was well known for his humorous tales of alligator shooting, bear hunting, and fishing with bow and arrow in *The Hive of the Bee-Hunter*, published by D. Appleton and Company in 1854. He had written on natural history for *Harper's Monthly* in the 1850s and promoted travel to the Juniata River via the Pennsylvania Central Railroad in 1860 as editor of the *New York Spirit of the Times*.[18] He had also contributed several articles to *Appletons' Journal*.

Thorpe was a highly competent, predictable practitioner of the art of landscape description in the picturesque mode. By selecting him to initiate the series, Bunce could be confident of the outcome. Although Thorpe finds the Florida landscape "strange" and "wild," his choice of words, formulaic descriptions, and reactions would have been familiar to nineteenth-century readers. Compared with the temperate regions to the north, Thorpe finds the barren sands instances of "suffering Nature," whereas the luxuriant vegetation of the "hidden recesses" of the swamps are full of the "wildest effects." In describing their river journey, he rather playfully introduces a frisson of danger by suggesting they feared their small "ill-shaped omnibus" of a steamboat might wreck against a cypress knee and subject them to "a miserable death, through the agency of mosquitoes, buzzards, and huge alligators" (578–79).

Winding through the dense vegetation with "the avowed purpose of hunting the picturesque" in this land "which the pencil of the artist has heretofore scarcely touched," the travellers were rewarded "at every turn" by "a picture of novel interest." This was just the quality of river journeys that the Reverend William Gilpin had praised—the variety and surprises that kept the traveller in "agreeable suspense." But instead of finding rock outcroppings, castle ruins, and distant vistas of irregularly shaped hills, they find a dead cypress covered with turkey buzzards "waiting patiently for the decomposition of an alligator," tangled masses of blossoms and vines, a large white crane stalking water snakes, a huge water oak blocking the channel, or the marvelously transparent waters of Silver Spring. Fenn captures the profusion of unusual flora and fauna and the closeness and eerie darkness of the swamp in his almost full-page illustrations full of sinuous lines and bold contrasts (see fig. 3.1).

In keeping with the picturesque preference for night scenes, the dramatic climax of Thorpe's piece is his overwrought description of the "theatrical display of the swamp by torchlight":

From the most intense blackness we have a fierce, lurid glare, presenting the most extravagantly-picturesque groups of overhanging palmettos, draped with parasites and vines of all descriptions . . . we enter what appears to be an endless colonnade of beautifully-proportioned shafts, running upward of a hundred feet, roofed by pendent ornaments, suggesting the highest possible effect of Gothic architecture. The delusion was increased by the waving streamers of Spanish moss . . . [which] hung down like tattered but gigantic banners, worm-eaten and mouldy, sad evidences of the hopes and passions of the distant past. ("Journey Up the St. John's," 582)[19]

Here the decay of the natural world rather predictably reminds them of the past, as had architectural ruins in more usual picturesque settings. In resorting to metaphors comparing natural features to works of civilization, in this case to Gothic arches hung with banners, Thorpe used a device common in descriptions of American wilderness that lacked literary and historical associations. As a way of rendering the strange more understandable, this approach would be used by many *Picturesque America* writers.[20]

3.1 Harry Fenn, "Florida Swamp," *Appletons' Journal*, November 12, 1870,
580. Wood engraving by F. W. Quartley, 9¼" x 5¹³⁄₁₆".

The travellers also amused themselves by shooting alligators—an activity that would soon attract many "sportsmen" to Florida's swamps and lead to the animal's decimation. Fenn depicted himself holding a gun, watching an alligator with two offspring. They also relished a chance encounter with two "Florida crackers" who had set up a camp to make cypress shingles. Struck by how uncomfortable and monotonous such an existence must be, Thorpe rather patronizingly commented that the men were, nevertheless, "civil, full of character, and in their way not wanting in intelligence." He and Fenn also found their hut, which Fenn illustrated, "the very model of the picturesque," with a charm and "contrast of colors" "impossible to be conceived of in the mere speculations of studio-life."[21]

The publishers, apparently satisfied with this vivid beginning, used the series to entice new subscribers. On November 19, 1870, they advertised that anyone subscribing to *Appletons' Journal* for 1871 before December 20 would receive the last eight numbers of 1870 free, beginning with "the number containing the first of our illustrated papers on Picturesque America," which "promises to be one of the most valuable pictorial series ever issued on American localities."[22]

Western North Carolina was featured next. Like Florida, this area was receiving increased attention in the press as a new field for painters and vacationers in search of the picturesque. The *Journal* had already promoted the region in its first foray into Southern scenery, a three-part series in October 1869 called "Novelties of Southern Scenery" by travel writer and landscape artist Charles Lanman (1819–95). The opening image of a very pointed peak supported Lanman's claim that in "treasures" of mountain scenery the Southern states were "not one whit behind the Northern States," for they could boast of fourteen peaks higher than Mount Washington, "the king of the North."[23] And in the summer of 1870, the *Journal* urged artists to paint the mountains of Virginia and North Carolina and spare the art galleries "further illustrations of scenery in the Catskills, on Lake George, or among the New-England hills."[24]

The November 26 and December 17 numbers featured the region near the French Broad River in North Carolina. Each number contained a pair of facing full-page views printed on heavy calendered paper, with the other side left blank. This special treatment as art supplements, or "extra sheets," was a new approach that made the prints more obviously "suitable for framing" than the usual wood engravings with type on the back. Fenn's images made a strong case for the area's appeal as a tourist destination, including "gorges of fearful height," huge cliffs, and weird and fantastic masses of rock. The first pair, "The Lover's Leap—At Early Sunrise" and "The Lover's Leap—Approach by Night," depicted a well-known rock formation near the Warm Springs Hotel thirty miles from Asheville in different light and from different viewpoints. The morning view (fig. 3.2) emphasized its stratification and fissures, features that were of great interest in this period as evidence of geologic time, of the eons taken to form and erode such rocks. Fenn included a glimpse of an artist's umbrella and easel, a favorite device for stressing accuracy as well as the importance of artists as guides to appreciating the natural world.

The unsigned description of the Warm Springs resort, set amid "lofty mountains, majestic and fatherly, standing with a saintly presence like a benediction over the gentle valley," further enticed visitors (Nov. 26, 644).[25] Lofty mountains also appeared in Fenn's views in the December 17 *Journal*, but in the case of "A Farm on the French Broad River, North Carolina," he emphasized how precarious farming was on such a steep slope. The facing view, "Chimney Rock, Hickory-Nut Gap," presented "one of Nature's most wonderful freaks" (737).

With the December 31 number of *Appletons' Journal*, the series' coverage of Florida resumed with a pair of virtuoso wood engravings depicting exotic plants found in a backyard in St. Augustine (see fig. 5.23) and in a garden in "Pilatka" (Palatka). In each, Fenn captures a striking variety of textures and forms in the tropical foliage, creating images far different from conventional picturesque views, but clearly in that category in terms of irregularity, variety, roughness, and contrast. The fact that these views appeared at the end of December probably heightened their appeal to readers in colder regions.

With the inaugural "Picturesque America" feature on the St. John's and Oklawaha rivers and the full-page views of North Carolina and Florida, *Appletons' Journal* had indeed produced some "splendidly-executed views of the most unfamiliar and novel scenery," as promised.[26] Critical response to the magazine was generally favorable: One writer, praising it for resisting the temptation to profit from sensationalism, termed it "an instrument of civilization," accessible to both "the poor man's market" and "the rich man's parlor."[27] Yet the *Journal*'s position was far from secure. The new *Scribner's Monthly*, whose three-dollar subscription price undercut the *Journal*'s by a dollar, claimed to have sold fifty-thousand copies of its inaugural November 1870 number before the end

3.2 Harry Fenn, "The Lovers' Leap—At Early Sunrise," *Appletons' Journal*, November 26, 1870. Wood engraving by Harley, 8⅞" x 6⅛".

of October. It heralded a special holiday number containing "one of the finest series of Landscape Illustrations ever prepared in this country."[28] *The Aldine* and *Every Saturday* and their illustrations were also promoted vigorously, especially their holiday numbers.[29]

In response, the *Journal* advertised its own holiday supplement, illustrated by Fenn, Sheppard, and others, and offered yet another premium: "ten splendid steel engravings," selected from the sixteen that had already appeared in the magazine.[30] In addition, most likely to reduce expenses, Appleton abandoned the short-lived experiment of using "extra sheets" for the "Picturesque America" series. The January 7 number contained two facing full-page wood engravings of the French Broad River printed on the same paper as the rest of the magazine, with text on the back—the approach that would henceforth be used throughout the series. Furthermore, perhaps to heighten interest, "Picturesque America" subjects expanded to include more than "the most novel and unfamiliar scenery." In the first few months of 1871, the series addressed industrial towns and historic cities—subjects that had figured prominently in earlier picturesque views of Britain and Europe as well as the United States.

With the January 28 number, the "Picturesque America" feature moved to the front page, with the focus on Southern scenery interrupted by a story on one of the nation's oldest industrial sites—Mauch Chunk (now Jim Thorpe), Pennsylvania. In this long-time tourist attraction, the dramatic natural setting combined with technology to produce a strong candidate for "the most picturesque town in the Union." The unsigned article was the first Bunce wrote for the series. He communicated his enthusiasm for the "Swiss-like village" nestled in hills near the Lehigh River, which served as the transportation center for the surrounding coal-mining region and was accessible by both the Erie Railroad and the Central Railroad of New Jersey. Fenn's illustrations supported Bunce's excitement about seeing in one view "the river, a canal, two railways, a road, and a street, packed in a space scarcely more than a stone's-throw wide," and the ceaseless string of "long, black coal-trains" of "marvelous length . . . like so many huge anacondas" (see fig. 3.3). Bunce was perhaps even more impressed by the statistic that the trains and barges transported some 54,000 tons of coal weekly.

The highlight of their visit was their ride up the Mount Pisgah Inclined Plane and on the Gravity Railroad, which had been thrilling tourists since 1826. Fenn's view stressed the steepness of the tracks, nicely complementing

3.3 Harry Fenn, "Mauch Chunk and Mount Pisgah," *Appletons' Journal*, January 28, 1871, 94. Wood engraving by Harley, 8⅞" x 6⅜".

Bunce's speculations about what would happen if the car broke loose (see fig. 4.9). His musings present a classic example of the "technological sublime," in which new machines and industries become transcendent symbols of powerful forces for good or utilitarian ends but also induce fear and awe.[31] He observes, "One discovers that his imagination takes a strange pleasure in depicting the terrible whirl through space and the horrible splintering upon the rocks." This is the first of several examples in *Picturesque America* of the thrill passengers on trains and boats derive from unaccustomed speed and the possibility of danger. Later conspicuous examples include E. L. Burlingame's comparison of experiencing the downgrade after the highest point on the Union Pacific Railroad with falling from a fourth-story window (II, 177–78), L. J. G. Runkle's description of the "mad excitement" of riding on the cow-catcher in the canyon of the Columbia River (I, 43–44), and W. H. Rideing's account and James D. Smillie's illustration of descending the Long-Sault Rapids of the St. Lawrence at full steam (II, 373, 375).

This article is also the first instance of *Picturesque America*'s aesthetic approach to industrial sites, concentrating almost exclusively on the attractive or stimulating visual aspects of the scene while failing to deal with such disturbing issues as the way resource extraction mars the landscape and creates dangerous and unhealthy working conditions. The focus on the picturesque aspects of the scene was a familiar and reassuring response to the changing industrial landscape.

Coverage of the South resumed in the February 4 number with Fenn's view of an old mill at Reem's Creek, North Carolina, the first of many depictions of mills, a favorite picturesque element in the landscape. Indeed, years earlier Thomas Cole had called mills "the Castles of the United States."[32] The next two numbers, February 11 and 18, featured illustrations by Fenn of the Natural Bridge in Virginia, with text by John Esten Cooke.[33] Bunce made clear that in addition to introducing much "unfamiliar" scenery, the "Picturesque America" series would not neglect those special precincts that had long been attracting reverent pilgrims. Yet Fenn's first image of this landmark was striking in its originality, offering even jaded armchair travellers a fresh viewpoint (fig. 4.5).

In early 1871, after initiating the series so prominently with views published from November 1870 to February 1871, Fenn made a surprising move. He took another assignment in direct competition with *Appletons' Journal*: a commission from *Every Saturday* to travel to Pittsburgh and the

Pennsylvania oil fields. Of course, Fenn had a long-standing relationship with that magazine's publishers, who had used many of his designs in *Our Young Folks* and Whittier's *Snow-Bound* (1868) and *Ballads of New England* (1870). At the beginning of 1871, when James R. Osgood began publishing under his own name after James T. Fields's retirement, he decided to alter *Every Saturday*'s emphasis on European illustrations and reprints from foreign periodicals. Henceforth the magazine would feature events at home as well as abroad; furthermore, it had made arrangements on an "extensive scale" with American artists to treat "whatever there is of interest in the busy life about us."[34]

Osgood and the magazine's editor, Thomas Bailey Aldrich (1836–1907), probably had seen Fenn's "Picturesque America" illustrations and concluded that a competing series on American localities would serve their weekly well. They commissioned Fenn to travel by train to Pittsburgh and Oil City, Pennsylvania, with Ralph Keeler (1840–73), a popular writer who was also art editor of *Every Saturday*.[35] On February 11 they announced

a series of papers illustrating points of scenic and industrial interest in the United States, on a grander scale than has ever been undertaken by any pictorial newspaper. The first of the series will be entitled "The Taking of Pittsburg," by Mr. Ralph Keeler, with original designs by Mr. Harry Fenn. . . . These gentlemen have been on an extended tour of the country which they are to depict.

Fenn's self-portrait looking out the back of the train launched the series March 4, calling attention to it and to him as the artist (fig. 3.4).

At this time Pittsburgh's importance as an industrial metropolis was growing. It was a leading supplier of iron and steel for the railroads, as well as a major glass manufacturing center. Although smoke and soot rendered it dark and sunless, many viewed the city's setting as picturesque and its industrial activity as exciting. It was a popular subject, having been featured as the "Iron City" in the February 18, 1871, *Harper's Weekly*, with illustrations by C. S. Reinhart. *Every Saturday* tried to get the upper hand by coverage in greater depth, over a five-week period, by a popular writer and artist.

Expressing excitement about the "inconceivable wealth" of the region, Keeler described the "busy life" in the factories and foundries of Pittsburgh, and in the newly developed oil fields. Fenn's views, compared with those for "Picturesque America," contain more human interest, more

3.4 Harry Fenn, self-portrait, "On the Way to Pittsburgh—Great Bend on the Alleghenies," *Every Saturday*, March 4, 1871, 200. Wood engraving by J. L. L., 8¾" x 11¾".

depiction of workers and machinery. Two of the more interesting ones use dramatic light effects: In depicting workers in the glow of molten metal, "Casting Steel Ingots" recalls John Ferguson Weir's oil painting, *The Gun Foundry* (1866), which had been exhibited at the Paris Exposition of 1867 (see fig. 3.5). And side-by-side views of the top and bottom of a blast furnace present striking industrial images unlike anything in *Picturesque America* (see fig. 3.6). The views of the oil fields include dark closeups called "Boring for Oil" and "Burning Gas," as well as a hillside covered with derricks and dramatically burning wellheads (April 1, 1871).

Unfortunately—or perhaps fortunately for Appleton—several of *Every Saturday*'s wood engravings based on Fenn's designs were murky and unattractive. Having depended to a large extent on electrotypes from the London *Graphic* or genre scenes that could be engraved in a leisurely fashion, the magazine was relatively inexperienced at producing good quality wood engravings quickly. "Among the Glass Workers," engraved by J. P. Davis, is a muddy gray, with ill-proportioned men who resemble grotesque gnomes—perhaps due in part to Fenn's comparative lack of practice in drawing people. Furthermore, the dark prospect views of Pittsburgh are among the least attractive of the wood engravings reproducing Fenn's drawings and may have disappointed him.

After his excursion to Pennsylvania for *Every Saturday*, the *Journal* managed to lure Fenn back to the "Picturesque America" series. The publishers surely realized the rather dull images they had used in his absence— Paul Dixon's "A Nook on the Hudson" (February 25) and A. C. Warren's "New Hampshire Scenery" (March 11)—fell far short of the drama of Fenn's best work. They announced Fenn's return with considerable fanfare on the back page of the March 25, 1871, number:

The publishers of APPLETONS' JOURNAL have the pleasure of announcing the completion of arrangements by which Mr. HARRY FENN will for a time give his professional services exclusively to the prosecution of the series of views entitled "*Picturesque America*," which for a few months past has been a conspicuous and attractive feature in the JOURNAL. Mr. Fenn will this spring visit South Carolina, Georgia, Tennessee and Virginia, after which he will proceed to sections North and West; and when the summer heats are over, he will visit other Southern localities. It is the design to illustrate every portion of the Union, in a manner far superior to anything of the kind hitherto attempted. . . . (360)

This announcement, used again April 1 and 8, becomes significant in light of Fenn's work for *Every Saturday*, which appeared March 4, 11, 18, and 25, and April 1.

Fenn may have strayed because his initial commission with *Appletons' Journal* was limited to the early illustrations or because he was dissatisfied with his pay. Given that Fenn and Bunce traveled together soon after the new agreement was forged, the promise of more such journeys may have influenced Fenn to return. He no doubt had noted that more unified and interesting articles resulted when writer and artist traveled together—as on the St. John's River and at Mauch Chunk.

The number announcing Fenn's return to the "Picturesque America" series included two full-page illustrations by him of historic East Hampton, Long Island (see fig. 6.30), probably derived from drawings made the previous summer or fall. Sometime in March, Fenn and Bunce traveled from New York to Charleston by steamer, and in April they visited Lookout Mountain and Chattanooga. While they were travelling, the *Journal* pub-

3.5 Harry Fenn, "Casting Steel Ingots," *Every Saturday*, March 11, 1871, 237. Wood engraving, 5¾" x 4¾". Courtesy the American Antiquarian Society.

3.6 Harry Fenn, "Top of a Blast Furnace," *Every Saturday*, March 18, 1871, 260. Wood engraving, 5¹⁵⁄₁₆" x 6⁷⁄₁₆". Courtesy the American Antiquarian Society.

lished other views of the South by Fenn: four of Savannah (April 8), two of Florida—the lighthouse at St. John's Bar and the Pine Barrens (April 22)—and yet another French Broad scene (May 20). The brief text accompanying this final North Carolina view encouraged immigration— and reconciliation—by praising the healthy climate, good soil, and cheap land of the region near Asheville (587).

In the time it took to prepare the text and pictures from Bunce and Fenn's travels in South Carolina and Tennessee, the *Journal* also published some Western landscapes. Eager to provide curious Americans with views of this region, Bunce departed from the practice of using artist's depictions made on-the-spot. Fenn's two May 13 views of the Yosemite Valley were drawn from photographs "by Anthony"; and apparently one of them was not very clear, for Fenn's rendering of Half-Dome is muddled.[36] For depictions of areas that were just being explored, like the Humboldt Range in Nevada and the Shoshone Falls of the Snake River in Idaho Territory, the *Journal* used drawings by the prolific Alfred R. Waud, probably based on photographs or sketches by others (May 27, June 3).[37] The unsigned texts emphasized that future travellers and artists would make "the public as familiar" with the wonders of these regions "as they now are with the famous Yosemite" (654). After this brief attention to the West, however, the series returned to the South, with a July 1 article on the picturesque old town of St. Augustine, with unsigned text by Robert Carter introducing a note of conventional Gothic gloom in describing the "bloody" history and dungeons of Fort San Marco (now called Castillo de San Marcos). Fenn's unusually attractive views probably derived from his 1870 trip to Florida. (see fig. 5.48)

The first article coming from the new arrangement between Fenn and the Appletons, "Charleston and Its Suburbs," appeared July 15, 1871.[38] The integration of text and pictures makes this and the other articles from their Southern tour among the best in the series. The feature on Charleston was the first to deal with a Southern city, and Bunce's awareness of being a sojourner in a different and recently hostile land makes it of more than usual interest. The front-page illustration of "A Road-Side Scene near Charleston" depicted a black woman sitting under a rough arbor, surrounded by four children, preparing sweet potatoes to sell to "wayfarers of African hue" (see fig. 3.7). This image is unusual in the series for its primary attention to people. It is also notable for representing blacks quietly intent upon their work, unlike the demeaning

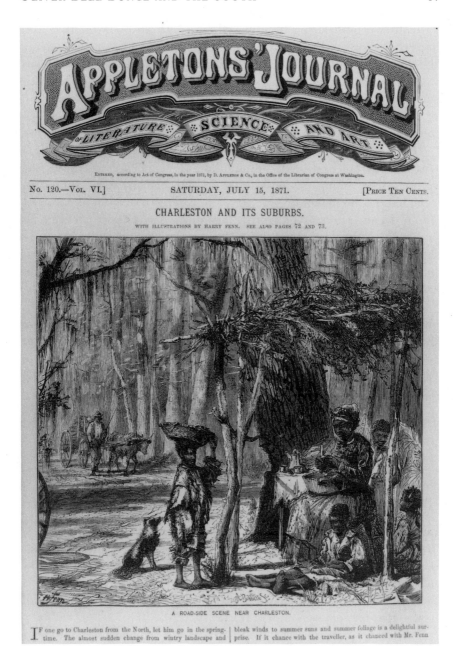

3.7 Harry Fenn, "A Roadside Scene near Charleston," *Appletons' Journal*, July 15, 1871, 1. Wood engraving by A. Bobbet, 5¹⁵⁄₁₆" x 6⁷⁄₁₆"; page, 11" x 8".

caricatures emphasizing frivolous or superstitious behavior that were appearing more and more frequently in periodicals. Conspicuous among these were some of the "Southern Sketches" by William Ludwell Sheppard in the July and August 1870 *Appletons' Journal*. The "Picturesque America" series and the book that followed can also be faulted for some caricatures of blacks, but this early image is noteworthy for its serious and dignified interpretation.

The positive impressions of the South build upon one another in the Charleston feature, exuding admiration and conciliatory feelings. The contrast of the sunny weather with the stormy northern March Bunce and Fenn left behind makes it seem they have entered a "terrestrial paradise." The text and pictures highlight the age of the city with its old churches and "noble private mansions standing in a sort of dingy stateliness amid their embowering magnolias." Rejecting comparisons with Venice, Bunce finds the walled gardens English in fashion. The war damage he mentions does not appear in Fenn's images.

While visiting Fort Sumter, where the Civil War began, Bunce experiences "something of a sensation" climbing over the ruins and picnicking with those who had defended as well as those who had assailed the walls (59). Similarly, when he and Fenn are invited by Charleston friends on an expedition to the Ashley River, he finds the day especially memorable because of the harmonious meeting of former antagonists:

There were in our small company a Northerner, who had fought under the Union flag, a descendant of one of the proudest names of Revolutionary fame; a Virginian, also of a family of renown, whose love of daring and danger had led him into many a strange adventure under Mosby; an Englishman, whose enthusiasm for the Confederate cause had brought him all the way from London to do battle under Lee; another Englishman [Fenn?], whose sympathies for the Federal cause had been marked all during the war.

The kinship of family and educational background was reasserting itself, despite political differences. Bunce also expresses sorrow over all the former mansions burned by Sherman's soldiers, together with the hope that the plantations will "attain a prosperity under the new dispensation as brilliant as that they enjoyed under the old" (61).

After the interruption of two more Western views in the number for August 12—of the Columbia River by R. Swain Gifford—attention to Southern history and scenery continued August 26 with the report of

Bunce and Fenn's visit to Lookout Mountain, Tennessee. The wood engraving on the front page illustrated the unusual formations of "Rock City," while two full-page images showed different views of the Tennessee Valley from the top of Lookout Mountain (see fig. 5.16). The fierce struggle over control of its rocky heights in the Civil War's "Battle above the Clouds" had imbued this spot with great interest. However, the chief drama in Bunce's text arises not from the battle, but from his skepticism about whether the mountain will reward their search for the picturesque. From "the mountain-loving Mr. Fenn," Bunce learns that "a half glance" through the trees during the ascent is often more picturesque than an open view from the summit—long a chief principle of picturesque viewing. He also learns that one must spend time getting to know a mountain to appreciate its variety and "changing aspects." Those who "make a hurried jaunt to its Palisades, glance at the prospect . . . and then hurry back again" miss a great deal.

The trip to Lookout Mountain took Bunce and Fenn first to the busy rail center of Chattanooga, but no depictions of the city appeared in the series. Having been burned and "denuded" of all its trees during the war, and flooded since, it was "dreary enough in the brightest sun" and "forlorn beyond description" in the rainstorm they experienced (239). There was nothing picturesque about this "rude place" that seemed more like an "extemporized mining-town of the far West than an old settlement of the East." The only positive note was that the buildings going up everywhere signaled returning prosperity (239).

More appealing was Augusta, Georgia, featured in the September 23 number, whose "handsome streets" and "embowered villas" had not been damaged during the War. The writer described the city hall and its grounds as a scene with "more of the rich, quiet charm that pertains to an English university-town than is usually found in our rude, new-made American cities" (353–54). Revealing the cultural dominance of the Northeast as the norm or standard, the suburb of Summerville, with its "villages and cottages, embowered in trees," was judged "more Northern" than Southern, "with houses like our own" (354).[39]

Although a city full of rude architecture lacked appeal, a crude cabin in a lonely mountain setting could be picturesque, as could mountain people. The October 14, 1871, number opened with Bunce's article "On the Tennessee" and Fenn's depiction of the riverside log cabin where they obtained a meal from a "pleasant-faced" and "intelligent" woman who kept the windowless cabin as "neat as a pin." This experience led Bunce to reflect on "the native superiority of American character" and how different were the "simple, rude people of the Tennessee hills" from the peasants of Europe (423). His admiration probably derived in part from a sense of kinship, for they, like most New Englanders and, indeed, like Bunce and Fenn, were mainly descendants of settlers from England and Scotland. In this period, "American" was still commonly identified with the strain of Anglo-Saxon Protestants who were the first immigrants, as distinguished from more recent arrivals, such as Irish Catholics.

Following the three articles based on Fenn's and Bunce's Southern tour, the series came to a virtual halt.[40] By at least April of 1872, the Appleton editors had decided to end the series in the magazine and produce a serialized book.[41] The new publication would use some of the material from the series, but go far beyond it. What prompted the Appleton firm to make this drastic change in format? The account in Bunce's obituary in *Publishers' Weekly* says only that Fenn's early "Picturesque America" illustrations were considered "so striking as to suggest further work in the same line but in a different format."[42] More compelling was the need to respond to attempts by competing periodicals to match or surpass the series—in a way that would make good business sense.

Appletons' Journal could no longer make facile claims to supremacy in the graphic arts; its rivals also constantly emphasized the quantity and quality of their pictures—frequently with justification. In the fall of 1871, *Frank Leslie's Illustrated Newspaper*, never reluctant to make sweeping boasts, said it held first place in reporting news events—by "say 100 to 0"—and that it illustrated "every week about ten times as many items of news as any American journal."[43] Known for its reporting of disasters and scandals, *Leslie's* featured "Life Sketches in the Metropolis" with striking illustrations of glamorous New York society, followed by the shocking contrast of "Our Homeless Poor," in the first half of 1872.[44] *Harper's Weekly*, in turn, stressed the excellence and popularity of Thomas Nast's cartoons—most notably his satires of the Tweed Ring—and claimed to have "one-third more reading matter" and more illustrations, as well as "more than *double*" the circulation of any similar publication.[45]

Every Saturday bragged that "everybody" considered its illustrations "greatly superior" to those in any other illustrated paper (June 24, 1871). Further, it claimed that its representations of "American Scenery, Life, and

Character" surpassed all others, suggesting that the firm was aware of its rivalry with the "Picturesque America" series and hoped to profit from its greater emphasis on depicting people. In reality, in mid-1871 *Every Saturday* did offer *Appletons' Journal* vigorous competition through its striking images of people—especially Winslow Homer's depictions of outdoor activities in New England.[46]

The main illustrated monthlies, the long-popular *Harper's Monthly* and the new *Scribner's Monthly*, also sought to attract readers with articles about scenic regions of the United States, frequently the same areas selected by *Appletons' Journal*.[47] The striking images of "The Wonders of the Yellowstone" in *Scribner's Monthly* in May and June 1871, prepared by Thomas Moran, attracted much attention because they were the first views of the region to appear in a popular magazine. *Scribner's* illustrations were also widely praised in the press for their "careful presswork" and "delicacy and finish."[48]

Already faced with formidable competition, the publishers of *Appletons' Journal* were confronted at the end of 1871 with an all-out effort by *The Aldine* to surpass them in their own field: artists' interpretations of American scenery. *The Aldine*'s prospectus for 1872 announced:

America.
"I love thy rocks and rills,
Thy woods and templed hills."

The glories of the unrivaled scenery of our country afford an exhaustless field for the exercise of the painter's art. Many attempts have been made to gratify the popular longing for scenes of "home, sweet home," but it will be universally acknowledged that, so far as our illustrated periodicals are concerned, such attempts have hitherto proved miserable failures—mere caricatures or topographical diagrams rather than pictures. It remains for the publishers of THE ALDINE to inaugurate an artistic movement that shall be worthy of the subject—that shall give American scenery its rightful preeminence in the pictorial world.

In this age and country of universal travel it is astonishing how comparatively few are acquainted with scenes not to be viewed from the windows of a railway car. To ordinary American "tourists" the mission of THE ALDINE will be to reveal the undiscovered beauties to them "so near, and yet so far."

William Cullen Bryant's endorsement led the list of "Commendations from Individuals and the Press" following the above announcement. He said that although England generally produced the best engravings, he had "never seen anything comparable to the work of *The Aldine*" in terms of careful inking and delicate lines. The Appletons would have been stung by this singular praise, especially since they had just published a complete edition of Bryant's poetry and featured him in a front-page *Journal* story with portrait.[49] Furthermore, *The Aldine*'s characterization of the scenic views in other periodicals as "miserable failures" must have struck a blow, as did the charge that previous series had shown scenery only along the rail routes.[50]

The Aldine had in essence challenged *Appletons' Journal* to a risky duel. Part of *The Aldine*'s ammunition was the announcement that it would be publishing works by a number of prominent American artists in 1872, including several who had provided designs for the *Journal*. The list included, among others, W. T. Richards, Wm. Hart, George and James Smiley [sic], Granville Perkins, F. O. C. Darley, Paul Dixon, and J. How[s]. As promised, beginning in January 1872, *The Aldine* began to publish large, well-engraved views of the American landscape that were comparable to the best of the *Journal*'s, and superior to some. *The Aldine* was by this time already widely recognized as the leader in terms of wood-engraved illustration. Newspapers from all parts of the country praised the magazine as "unrivalled" and "a model of perfection" performing a "priceless service in domiciling Art in America."[51]

Thus by early 1872, Bunce and the Appletons realized they needed to take decisive action in order to head off *The Aldine*'s formidable challenge and avoid losing the advantage of the current popularity of their "Picturesque America" series. Their ingenious solution avoided taking up the white glove by exiting the field and finding a new one. They decided to expand the series in more permanent and elegant form, as a serialized book that would induce subscribers to agree to a two-year commitment. Thus, although the *Journal* would no longer benefit directly from the "Picturesque America" series, the publishers could hope to reap large profits. Subscription sales in those years often proved more lucrative than bookstore sales, for canvassing agents could cover towns that did not have bookstores or libraries.[52] The advantage of being able to pay in small increments rather than a lump sum was also attractive to many subscribers. Furthermore, with the commitment of substantial funds from subscribers, the firm's investment in the illustrations assured a high quality product and a way to meet the competition offered by *The Aldine*.

The "Picturesque America" series to this point had barely scratched the surface of the riches of the American landscape. The series had featured several unfamiliar regions, and at least one of the stars of American scenery—Natural Bridge—but there were countless more in both categories. By highlighting Charleston, St. Augustine, and East Hampton, the *Journal* had begun to put to rest the notion that the United States lacked historic buildings. The enlarged publication could feature other cities of the North and Middle West and include many recent amenities that would demonstrate cultural sophistication as well. It could also build on the positive image of American technology started with the coverage of Mauch Chunk. The expanded publication could enhance the favorable image of Southern scenery and cities and greatly increase the coverage of other regions, from New England to the Far West, with its picturesque rock formations, forests, waterfalls, sublime mountains, and canyons. The new work, in a more concentrated format, could become a cyclopedia for fostering pride in the natural and cultural landscape of the United States. Their ingenious solution would pay off handsomely.

PART TWO

"The Most Magnificent
Illustrated Work Ever Produced
in America"

CHAPTER 4

"A Monument of Native Art"

D. Appleton and Company began publishing *Picturesque America*, "the most magnificent illustrated work ever produced in America," in June of 1872.[1] Canvassing agents with sample pages spread out from the firm's offices in major cities to sign up subscribers for the entire work.[2] Because the series was to run to forty-eight parts and the arrangement was strictly payment on delivery, both agents and subscribers committed themselves to an ongoing relationship over the next two years. Every two weeks, the agent would deliver a part and collect fifty cents. Subscribers included the literary and intellectual elite, including James Russell Lowell and Oliver Wendell Holmes; such prominent clergymen as Henry Ward Beecher; editors such as J. G. Holland and George W. Curtis; statesmen Hamilton Fish and Schuyler Colfax; wealthy businessmen, including August Belmont, Cyrus W. Field, and Jay Cooke; as well as clerks and laborers.[3]

Judging from the sample book and subscription list of an agent in Philadelphia, most subscribers were men, and most ordered *Picturesque America* from their places of business.[4] A significant number were members of the rising middle class—such as merchants, craftsmen, skilled workers, and bookkeepers and clerks. For them, subscribing to *Picturesque America* provided a means of signaling their interest in culture and art, as well as in their country's scenic beauty. During a period when men made most major decisions about family expenditures, but most books, especially light fare like novels, were bought by women, the predominance of men's names suggests that subscribing to *Picturesque America* was viewed as more than a matter of simple entertainment.[5]

Each twenty-four-page part was enclosed in a light blue paper wrapper decorated with an artist's brushes and palette (with Fenn's monogram),

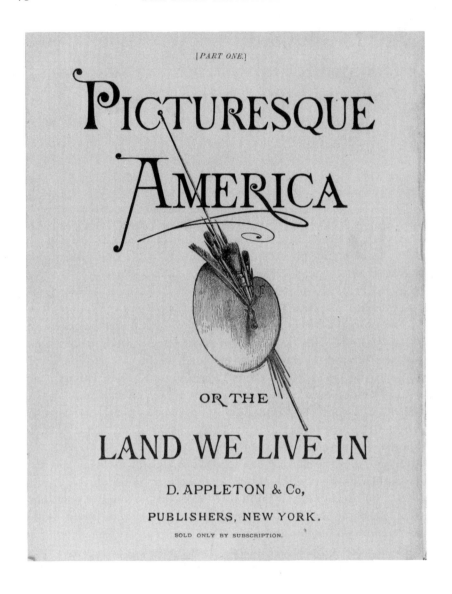

4.1 Front wrapper, part 1 of *Picturesque America*. 13⅜" x 10⅛".

PUBLISHED IN PARTS. PRICE, FIFTY CENTS EACH PART.

The most Magnificent Illustrated Work ever produced in America.

PICTURESQUE AMERICA;

OR,

THE LAND WE LIVE IN.

A PICTORIAL DELINEATION OF

The Mountains, Rivers, Lakes, Forests, Water-falls, Shores, Canyons, Valleys, Cities, and other Picturesque Features of our Country.

THIS truly superb work, which has now been for several years in active preparation, will consist of a complete description and elaborate pictorial illustration of the greater part of the North American Continent. It will portray the great mountain-ranges, the superb lakes, the beautiful valleys, the grand primitive forests, the cascades, the magnificent rivers, the towns and cities, in brief, all the picturesque aspects of our land, from Canada to the Gulf, from the Atlantic to the Pacific.

For several years artists have been specially employed in visiting different parts of the Union for the purpose of procuring designs for this work. The views, hence, will not only be original and trustworthy, but possess the vividness of personal observation, and include the movement and life characteristic of each locality. The volume will be something more than a gallery of landscapes; it will exhibit our people in their methods of living and travelling, and delineate the picturesque phases of commerce, as well as the sublime forms of our hills; it will show the often beautiful setting of our cities, and portray the active and brilliant panorama of our bays and rivers. All the marvellously varied phases of our country will be set forth with the utmost fulness, so that the work will, in its completeness, form a splendid pictorial cyclopædia of American life, scenery, and places. The very best artistic talent of the country has been employed upon the designs, and the engraving has been executed without limitation of expense, by the best skill obtainable. The articles have been written either by writers who accompanied the artists, or by those specially acquainted with the field described. They are accurate and graphic pen-pictures, supplementing the artists' delineations with suitable fulness and effect.

The publishers claim that no publication of the kind has ever been attempted in the country on a scale so large, with design so liberal, and with results so really magnificent. They offer it to the American public as not only the greatest and fullest exposition of our country that has yet been made, but as a monument of native art worthy the genius and reputation of our people. The enterprise is a large one—*the illustrations alone will cost fully one hundred thousand dollars*—but the publishers have determined to spare no expense in carrying out the project, assured of the hearty response of the American people.

The engravings will consist of steel and wood. The steel plates will be printed on heavy, toned, plate-paper; the wood illustrations will be of the finest character, and abundantly interspersed through the text, which will be printed on heavy, extra-calendered, toned paper. In all particulars of manufacture, care will be taken to secure a thoroughly elegant and sumptuous work.

CONDITIONS OF PUBLICATION.

This work will be published in semi-monthly parts, at Fifty cents each, payable on delivery; the carrier not being allowed to receive money in advance, or give credit.

Each part will contain one highly-finished engraving on steel, and a large number of finely-executed woodcuts.

The work will be completed in Forty-eight parts; the size imperial quarto. It will be printed on heavy, toned, highly-calendered paper, made expressly for this work, in the best manner known to the art.

Subscriptions received only for the entire work. Subscribers removing, and not being regularly supplied, will please address the Publishers, by mail, or otherwise.

D. APPLETON & CO., Publishers, 549 & 551 Broadway, New York.

Entered, according to Act of Congress, in the year 1872, by D. APPLETON & CO., in the Office of the Librarian of Congress, at Washington.

4.2 Back wrapper, part 1 of *Picturesque America.* 13⅜" x 10⅛".

emphasizing that this was primarily an art publication (fig. 4.1). On the back was printed the prospectus that D. Appleton and Company used to promote it (fig. 4.2). This lengthy description stressed its uniqueness: "The publishers claim that no publication of the kind has ever been attempted in the country on a scale so large, with design so liberal, and with results so really magnificent." The publishers kept silent about its link with the series in *Appletons' Journal,* probably thinking it counterproductive to mention that any material was being reused. They emphasized its comprehensiveness—"a splendid cyclopaedia of American life, scenery, and places"—rather than the original, more limited emphasis of the *Journal* series on "the most unfamiliar and novel features of American scenery."

This more comprehensive emphasis may have been intended in part to offer something different from *The Aldine*'s focus on scenery. Yet it was also in keeping with the period's fascination with all-inclusive schemes. Furthermore, it was consonant with Bunce's confidence that civilization was inexorably advancing and that the United States now had many features worthy of the attention of artists, including sites of manufacturing, centers of transportation, and elegant cities and suburbs. Without naming Harry Fenn or anyone else, the prospectus stated that for several years artists had been travelling to different parts of the country to "procure designs" for the work. These drawings would yield printed images with the sought-after qualities of originality, accuracy, and animation or expressiveness. As the prospectus put it, "The views, hence, will not only be original and trustworthy, but possess the vividness of personal observation."

The promotional copy also stressed the expense the Appleton firm had incurred in producing the artworks. Part of the motivation for this was doubtless to get the competitive upper-hand by outspending rivals such as *The Aldine;* yet the firm also intended to foster pride in American art, and claimed that it would "spare no expense" to produce "a monument of native art worthy the genius and reputation of our people." The cost estimate increased from $80,000 to $100,000, and the following year it was $130,000. The selling points of one steel engraving per part and the special heavy paper enabled the canvassing agent to justify the twenty-four dollar total price. Indeed the price was reasonable compared to other publications featuring steel engravings.[6]

The addition of the subtitle, *The Land We Live In,* suggests that the Appletons may have looked to a popular English work as a precedent. *The*

Land We Live In: A Pictorial and Literary Sketchbook of the British Empire, first issued in London by Charles Knight in 1847, contained both steel and wood engravings and covered cities, manufacturing, mining, and transportation, as well as natural beauty, picturesque towns, and antiquities. Many of its wood engravings were produced by the Dalziel firm, where Harry Fenn apprenticed a few years later. Thus Fenn might have suggested this work and its title as a model for the expanded *Picturesque America.*[7]

In response to the launching of subscription sales of *Picturesque America* in June of 1872, Harper and Brothers took some countermeasures of its own. The *Harper's Monthly* for July 1872 opened with a story entitled "In Search of the Picturesque" by Constance F. Woolson, who was later to write for *Picturesque America.* This humorous story pokes fun at the notion of picturesque travel, as the narrator and her sister are led by their grandfather in search of a picturesque countryside that no longer can be found near the smoky factory city of "Marathon."[8] Although such attitudes were becoming more prevalent, they were not yet common enough to prevent *Picturesque America* from attracting a wide audience. The *Harper's Monthly* for August, furthermore, opened with a feature on the same region covered in the opening article of *Picturesque America,* Mount Desert Island in Maine, with illustrations by Fenn's friend Charles Parsons.

The first two parts of the new subscription book emphatically demonstrated that it would cover the entire nation. Part 1 opened with Bunce's article on the coast of Maine, then reprinted the first eight pages of Thorpe's article on the St. John's and Oklawaha rivers in Florida that had initiated the *Journal* series. Part 2 completed the St. John's article and continued with "Up and Down the Columbia," written by Lucia J. G. Runkle, illustrated by R. Swain Gifford. Thus, in the earliest parts, Bunce chose to range from the far North to the far South on the East Coast, then to jump to the West Coast. He judged rightly that this emphasis on the entire continental nation would appeal to readers in 1872, just as the focus on the South had appealed in 1870. With the trauma and disruptions of the Civil War receding, the opportunities for travel and enterprise in the more remote and less populated areas of the nation were of interest to many, and publications like *Picturesque America* only enhanced their appeal.

Part 1, which agents probably used to persuade subscribers to sign up for the entire book, included strikingly varied elements, and thus in itself

4.3 Harry Fenn, "Cascade in Virginia," with self-portrait, *Picturesque America*, I, title page. Steel engraving by Robert Hinshelwood, 9" x 7"; page, 12⅝" x 9½".

exhibited an important hallmark of the picturesque. First came a steel engraving, after Fenn, of the coast of Florida, showing a mass of palms and cacti. Next came the decorative steel-engraved title page, depicting scenery more typical of traditional picturesque tours—a cascading waterfall with rainbows in the spray, protruding cliffs, and overarching trees (see fig. 4.3). To make it clear that the images were based on personal observation, Fenn included in the scene an artist with easel, palette, and umbrella (the artist's wide moustache suggests a self-portrait) at work painting the waterfall. The words *Picturesque America* formed by letters of gnarled wood were superimposed on the scene. The complete title page followed, with copyright on the verso, then the preface.

The name of William Cullen Bryant has long been associated with *Picturesque America*. He is credited as editor, and some have assumed he took an active role in selecting the material. Yet Bryant's participation in the project dates from late June of 1872, after it was well underway. The first title page printed for volume I does not carry his name, nor is the first preface signed by him. These original versions, now quite rare, were probably distributed with part 1 to the earliest subscribers. About this time it evidently occurred to Bunce or George S. Appleton that the name of William Cullen Bryant as editor would enhance the appeal of the new book—just as the publishers of *The Aldine* recognized the value of including his praise in their advertising. The seventy-eight-year-old Bryant had become an instition whose opinions and endorsements were influential, particularly in projects connected with natural scenery and art. In a letter to the Appleton firm dated June 24, 1872, Bryant agreed to edit the work, with the stipulation that it not "proceed beyond fifty numbers."[9] He later recounted that his task was to read the proofs, "correct the language, omit superfluous passages and see that no nonsense crept into the text." In the end, he found this very tiresome, as he wrote, rather ungraciously, to his friend the Reverend Orville Dewey on August 20, 1874:

Every part of it, except a few of the first sheets, passed through my hands; and I do not remember that I was ever more weary of any literary task, for the mere description of places is the most tedious of all reading. . . . I wish you had done it in my stead.[10]

Bryant was also asked to provide a preface for the work, and this was likely one of the first tasks he turned to. He relied heavily on the original version, probably written by Bunce, but more than doubled it in length.

He included at the end an emphatic acknowledgment that Bunce was responsible for selecting the book's text and illustrations. Both versions (see appendix B) repeat the major points in the promotional prospectus and highlight some of the most important themes that recur in the body of the text. The two prefaces stress the comprehensive nature of the project and the "almost boundless" opportunities this country offers to "the artist's pencil." They claim America has "a variety of scenery which no other single country can boast of," and Bryant relates this variety to the three categories of scenery—"whether beautiful or grand, or formed of those sharper but no less striking combinations of outline which belong to neither of these classes," that is, the picturesque. Furthermore, both versions indulge in the landscape chauvinism so prevalent at the time. As Bryant rephrased the earlier text:

In other parts of the globe are a few mountains which attain a greater altitude than any within our limits, but the mere difference in height adds nothing to the impression made on the spectator. Among our White Mountains, our Catskills, our Alleghanies, our Rocky Mountains, and our Sierra Nevada, we have some of the wildest and most beautiful scenery in the world. On our majestic rivers—among the largest on either continent—and on our lakes—the largest and noblest in the world—the country often wears an aspect in which beauty is blended with majesty.

Departing from the previous version, Bryant adds the observation that the recently completed transcontinental railroad provides "easy access to scenery of a most remarkable character," making a European tour unnecessary—indeed, almost unpatriotic:

For those who would see Nature in her grandest forms of snow-clad mountain, deep valley, rocky pinnacle, precipice, and chasm, there is no longer any occasion to cross the ocean. A rapid journey by railway over the plains that stretch westward from the Mississippi, brings the tourist into a region of the Rocky Mountains rivalling Switzerland in its scenery of rock piled on rock, up to the region of the clouds.

Bryant declares that in the magnificent forests of the West the United States surpasses Switzerland and even the cedars of Lebanon. In so doing he strikes a theme that had appeared in many of his poems, the great antiquity of the natural world: These groves contain "trees of such prodigious height and enormous dimensions" that "we might imagine them to have sprouted from seed at the time of the Trojan War." This natural antiquity is also evident in the "remarkable" chasms of the West, which, he says, have "enriched our language with a new word": cañon or canyon.

Such chasms report "of some mighty convulsion of Nature in ages that have left no record save in these displacements of the crust of our globe." The varied scenery of the West also includes the desert, which, "in all its dreariness," still offers "subjects for the pencil."

The theme of the revelation of God in nature that recurs in Bryant's poems occurs here only indirectly. He says the prairies are so vast the spectator is "overpowered with a sense of sublimity." In his 1833 poem "The Prairies," he described his own response to the prairies of Illinois: "I behold them for the first, / And my heart swells, while the dilated sight / Takes in the encircling vastness." As was expected with sublime scenery, his thoughts turned to the divine:

> Man hath no part in all this glorious work:
> The hand that built the firmament hath heaved
> And smoothed these verdant swells, and sown their slopes
> With herbage, planted them with island-groves,
> And hedged them round with forests. Fitting floor
> For this magnificent temple of the sky—

Bryant reiterates that the purpose of *Picturesque America* is "to illustrate with greater fulness, and with superior excellence" both those well-known places "which attract curiosity by their interesting associations" and those unfamiliar yet "glorious" spots "in the by-ways of travel." Indeed, in dealing with the celebrated stars of American scenery that Bryant says are already familiar to all through paintings, engravings, and photographs— "the banks of the Hudson," "Niagara," and "the wonderful valley of the Yosemite"—*Picturesque America* provides depth of coverage through multiple images that could give the armchair traveller a sense of seeing the region from many different viewpoints. (This was one of the advantages of relying primarily on less expensive wood engravings.) Many less-visited areas, on the other hand, "will become familiar to the general public for the first time through these pages." This claim is certainly justified in relation to unheralded spots in the byways of travel, and to a somewhat lesser degree with regard to regions that had only recently begun to attract tourists, like Maine, Florida, Western North Carolina, some parts of the Great Lakes, the "Dalles" (Dells) of Wisconsin, the transcontinental railroad corridor, the Rocky Mountains, the northern coast of California, and the Columbia River in Oregon.

Immediately following the preface is the opening of the first article, "On the Coast of Maine," with "Picturesque America" repeated once again

PICTURESQUE AMERICA.

Castle Head, Mount Desert.

ON THE COAST OF MAINE.

WITH ILLUSTRATIONS BY HARRY FENN.

THE island of Mount Desert, on the coast of Maine, unites a striking group of picturesque features. It is surrounded by seas, crowned with mountains, and embosomed
with lakes. Its shores are bold and rocky cliffs, upon which the breakers for countless centuries have wrought their ceaseless attrition. It affords the only instance along our Atlantic
coast where mountains stand in close neighborhood to the sea; here in one picture are

4.4 Harry Fenn, "Castle Head, Mount Desert," *Picturesque America*, I, 1. Wood
engraving by F. W. Quartley, 5⅜" x 6¼"; page, 12⅜" x 9½".

above Fenn's depiction of the towering cliffs of "Castle Head, Mount Desert" (see fig. 4.4). Bunce's choice of Mount Desert Island for part 1 of the serialized book is significant. It was becoming popular as a tourist destination, especially for residents of New York and Boston, who could catch the regular steamers from Portland, and many of whom were potential subscribers to *Picturesque America*.[11] Furthermore, its scenery could decisively counteract the frequent charge that the coastlines of the United States were dull. Two of the most stinging criticisms had been penned some twenty years earlier by George William Curtis and James Fenimore Cooper. Curtis, who in 1872 was the well-known political editor of *Harper's Weekly*, had said in 1852, after several years' travel in Europe, that the United States had "no coast scenery"; similarly, in *The Home Book of the Picturesque* in the same year, Cooper had called his homeland's coasts "low, monotonous and tame," lacking "bold promontories."[12] *Picturesque America* aimed to show that these two had obviously not included Maine in their reckoning.

In his text, Bunce acknowledges that Maine is the only place on the Atlantic where mountains are neighbors to the sea. There the tourist in search of the picturesque could find the variety and contrast epitomizing that category of scenery: "In one picture" are "beetling cliffs" and "restless breakers," "green islands" and "placid mountain-lakes," and "rugged gorges" and "sheltered coves." According to Bunce, "It is a union of all these supreme fascinations of scenery, such as Nature, munificent as she is, rarely affords" (I, 2). Thus, the coast of Maine was a splendid, comparatively accessible choice for the opening of this new publication intended to illustrate the "glorious" places in the United States.

The varied and relatively unfamiliar scenery of the region also provided the raw material for a short course in picturesque touring. Just as the Appleton firm sought to educate and "improve" in many of its other publications, *Picturesque America* had a didactic purpose. It offered instruction in the correct way to tour, to turn sightseeing into a cultural and educational activity and to learn from what nature had to teach. The pupils who needed educating were two new types of tourists: the recently wealthy entrepreneurs who had not yet absorbed the ways of polite culture and those recently enabled to travel by decreasing railroad and steamboat fares. With limited interest or limited leisure and means, these excursionists typically spent only one day at a famous spot like Niagara Falls or Lookout Mountain. Bunce had been aware of these hurried visitors in his *Journal* story on Lookout Mountain, and he warned that those who took only a quick look would miss much. A poet in the August 9, 1873, *Harper's Weekly* similarly complained that at Niagara, "the tourists, ruthless wanderers, brush from every rose its dew, / Seeking only more excitement— something wondrous, something new."[13] To those accustomed to the slower pace of picturesque touring, the new tourists often seemed more interested in stimulating activity than in quiet contemplation and were too content to follow the dictates of the guidebooks about where to go and what to see.[14]

By writing the keynote article himself, Bunce was able to set forth his own explorations with Fenn as an instructive model of how to appreciate fully a region's scenic attractions and realize the cultural and spiritual benefits of encounters with nature. The leisurely, contemplative mode of touring depicted in "The Coast of Maine" and much of *Picturesque America* requires taking time to observe the changing effects of weather and to explore beyond the beaten path or the scenic overlook—always with the enticing possibility of encountering a storm or sunset that made one forgetful of all else, or discovering a scenic feature that made one feel connected with primal creation, or at least the distant past. As the elegantly dressed excursionists in Fenn's illustrations suggest, such unhurried touring was an option primarily for those with considerable means. Yet the model that *Picturesque America* provided could serve as a goal for those aspiring to higher incomes and more leisure; indeed, by subscribing to the book and displaying it in their homes, they associated themselves, if only vicariously, with the cultural tradition of picturesque travel and appreciation of art and nature.

Bunce's description of how he and Fenn explored Mount Desert Island is entirely in keeping with the approach and the mind-set of the late nineteenth-century picturesque tourist and landscape artist, a mind-set absorbed from the surrounding culture and its literature, art, and travel writing. Adopting an artist's view of the world, the tourist could seek aesthetic and sensual pleasure from the discovery and close observation of "pictures"—groupings of varied attractive elements of natural scenery, such as mountains, lakes, sea coasts, cliffs, rock formations, and trees. Such pictures could include both expansive prospect views from lookout points and more intimate close-up views. In each case, certain effects of light or weather could enhance the picture for the careful observer.

The diary of *Picturesque America* artist R. Swain Gifford reveals the typical preoccupation with such effects. During an 1869 trip by steamer from

New Bedford, Massachusetts, to New York, Gifford recorded that he spent the day watching "strange tricks of fog" and the "beautiful atmospheric changes near sunset" and that he rose early the next morning to see the sunrise. When he went to Central Park with two friends after arriving in New York and a sudden thunderstorm forced them to seek shelter in a cave, Gifford wrote: "We stood motionless and scarcely a word passed between us during the storm so deeply were we impressed by its awful and majestic power. When the sun again lighted up the landscape we instinctively turned toward each other and walked quietly out of our retreat."[15]

The tourist who went the extra mile in search of "pictures," to "discover" something not described in the guidebook, or to find an observation point that lent new drama to a scenic feature would be amply rewarded. And finally, by a direct, unmediated encounter with this natural element, the tourist could experience feelings ranging from sensual delight in the beauty of nature, to worshipful appreciation of the Creator and the created order, to forgetfulness of self and mystical union with the natural feature.

The painterly language of Bunce's account of their approach to Mount Desert Island by steamer demonstrates how well he had absorbed the artist's view of the world. Bunce and Fenn were pleased that delays in their voyage caused them to approach Mount Desert as the sun was sinking behind the mountains rather than at midday, "when the landscape, under the direct rays of the sun, possesses the least charm" (I, 2). In the setting sun, the mountains, which Fenn depicted in a steel engraving,

lift in gloomy grandeur against the light of the western sky, and, with the movement of the steamer, break every moment into new combinations of rare beauty. Now they lie massed, one against the other, in long, undulating lines, now open into distinct groups; now Green Mountain fronts the sea with all its stern majesty, now Newport rises apparently from the very water's edge in one abrupt cliff a thousand feet in height. It is a dissolving view that for an hour or more presents a superb succession of scenic effects, which the spectator watches with entrancing interest. (I, 2)

After finding accommodations in the treeless village of East Eden (now Bar Harbor), which was so lacking in beauty that Bunce "wonders whether the notion of naming places by their contraries is a legitmate Down-East institution," he says visitors will have two priorities before turning to the pleasures of fishing and boating. They are to seek close-up encounters with picturesque landmarks as well as expansive views from high vantage points: "to explore the long series of rocks and cliffs on the shore" and "to ascend Green Mountain (now Cadillac Mountain), and enjoy the superb view." Bunce affirms the necessity of a leisurely pace for these explorations in comments scattered throughout the text. He mentions that many people stay overnight at the cottage on the top of Green Mountain to see the view from the summit at sunrise. The frequent fogs, however, can shroud the view, disappointing those in a hurry. The better approach is to learn to delight in the foggy effects, the succession of "dissolving views: "It is a rare pleasure to sit on the rocky headlands, on the seaward side of the island, on a day when the fog and sun contend for supremacy, and watch the pictures that the fog makes and unmakes" (I, 10).

Storms, even more exhilarating, allow the momentary thrill of threatening danger. Bunce stresses the "extreme grandeur," or sublimity, of the cliffs at "Spouting Horn" during a violent storm: "The scene is inspiriting and terrible. Visitors to Mount Desert but half understand or appreciate the wonders if they do not visit the cliffs in a storm" (I, 8). Needless to say, only those staying for an extended period could be reasonably assured of experiencing such a spectacle and the accompanying thrill.

The careful observation of scenic features that Bunce and Fenn undertake is also not for the hurried. Central to *Picturesque America* is the idea that the search for the picturesque involves choosing an appropriate vantage point and then investing time and emotional energy in understanding what nature has to teach. Bunce provides a classic account of this endeavor as he prescribes how to appreciate the cliffs of Mount Desert:

People in search of the picturesque should understand the importance of selecting suitable points of view. . . . It is often a matter of search to discover the point from which an object has its best expression; and probably only those of intuitive artistic tastes are enabled to see all the beauties of a landscape. . . . To the cold and indifferent, Nature has no charms; she reveals herself only to those who surrender their hearts to her influence, and who patiently study her aspects. . . . No indifferent half glance will suffice. Go to the edge of the cliffs and look down; go below, where they lift in tall escarpments above you; sit in the shadows of their massive presence; study the infinite variety of form, texture, and color, and learn to read all the different phases of sentiment their scarred fronts have to express. When all this is done, be assured you will discover that "sermons in stones" was not a mere fancy of the poet. (I, 8–10)

Thus, according to Bunce, the goal of the tourist is to experience to the fullest extent "all the beauties of a landscape," but is not limited to sensual enjoyment. Nor does the experience lead to the pantheistic identification of the universe with God. The ultimate motivation is to discover evidence of God, or divine creation, and the feeling of reverence this can evoke. Bunce's directions for achieving this twofold experience make use of verbs that imply the passage of time: go and search, sit, surrender your "heart," study patiently, and learn. Thus, he provides a kind of epistemological map for experiencing nature—in its "infinite variety of form, texture, and color"—as revelatory of the divine.[16]

In resorting to a quotation and in failing to specify the doctrinal content of the "sermons in stones," Bunce was typical of most *Picturesque America* contributors. Their admiration of the power, beauty, and variety of nature led to fervent but vague theistic affirmations that to them seemed clearly linked to liberal Protestant Christianity but avoided divisive sectarian dogmas. For example, Felix de Fontaine says that the scenic marvels of the French Broad river are "manifestations of power and beneficence" that "link the creature with his Maker." He goes on to describe how "the denizen of the city . . . worships" in such natural temples "from the regions of icebergs to the jungles of the equator." In such places, both tourists and artists (Frederic Church comes quickly to mind) find "the holiest of aspirations" (I, 132–34).[17]

For several of the writers, encounters with nature result in affirmations exemplifying the familiar "argument from design" espoused by the eighteenth-century Deists. For example, Thorpe observes that "in the great order of Nature," Spanish moss "has its purposes" to consume "the hard and iron-like woods" and make way for new growth (I, 270).[18] As James Turner has pointed out, this "quasi-scientific, empirical demonstration of God's existence" based on the intricate and complex design of the universe was one of two main arguments for belief in God in this period. The other, more in keeping with Bunce's approach, "looked beyond the sensible world, into man's heart, and found there primal religious impulses or immediate intuitions of the divine, deeper than reason, that testified to the reality of God."[19]

The intense immersion in a work of nature that Bunce recommends, involving the "surrender of the heart," could lead to such an "immediate intuition of the divine." This is quite different from the primarily intellectual exercise that Gilpin and others had prescribed for picturesque tourists almost a century earlier. That approach had stressed the pleasures of analyzing a scene and comparing and contrasting it to an ideal land-scape, as Claude might compose, for example. Bunce—like others in this period, including Henry Ward Beecher, W. H. H. Murray, and, John Ruskin, all imbued with the sentiments of the Romantic poets—stressed a more emotional response to an actual scene. In such interactions, scenic features typically categorized as "picturesque" could have an impact simi-lar to that usually associated with the sublime. We can see similarities between Bunce's directions and those of R. Swain Gifford regarding Niagara Falls. Gifford, who thought he derived more benefit from read-ing Emerson than from hearing a sermon, wrote that the "best way for one to enjoy them [the falls] fully would be to get away entirely alone and lie down and allow it all to take entire possession of your mind. The impres-sion of Infinite power made upon my mind will, I am sure always remain."[20]

Gifford's recommendations and reponses, like Bunce's, resemble those of earlier writers. In particular, Bunce's series of verbs and "surrender of the heart" bring to mind British novelist Anthony Trollope's recommenda-tions in 1862 for a memorable encounter with Niagara Falls. After a quick look at the falls from the many observation points, Trollope wrote, the visi-tor should proceed to Goat Island, which divides the river above the falls, and walk out on the wooden bridge leading from it to the observation tower: "*Go down* to the end of that wooden bridge, *seat yourself* on the rail and there *sit* till all the outer world is lost to you" [italics added]. He went on to suggest that "in these moments, the less of speaking" the better:

To realize Niagara you must sit there till you see nothing else than that which you have come to see. You will hear nothing else, and think of nothing else. At length you will be at one with the tumbling river before you. . . . The cool liquid green will run through your veins, and the voice of the cataract will be the expression of your own heart. You will fall as the bright waters fall, rushing down into your new world with no hesitation and with no dismay; and you will rise again as the spray rises, bright, beautiful, and pure.[21]

Bunce's directions for discovering "sermons in stone" on Mount Desert Island are a somewhat diluted version of Trollope's suggestions for maxi-mizing one's mystical experience of the sublime at Niagara. Yet by instructing tourists in how to extract important lessons and derive spiritual benefit from previously unknown, even unnamed, natural features,

Picturesque America greatly enriched the possibilities for picturesque touring and appreciation of nature in the United States.

Bunce follows his own prescriptions, and he and Fenn leave their "vehicle" and set out in search of Thunder Cave (now Thunder Hole). A "superb forest-walk" leads them first past fine birches "that would have filled any artist with delight," mentioning specifically the American painter Worthington Whittredge (1820–1910), "whose birch-forests are so famous" (I, 12). Bunce describes a particularly striking "forest-picture" in the painterly language typical of the landscape descriptions of the time:

The trees were mostly evergreen, and the surface of the ground covered with outcropping rocks and tangled roots, all richly covered with mosses. The broken light through the dark branches, the tint of the fallen pine-leaves, the many-colored mosses which painted every rock in infinite variety of hue, the low, green, branches of the fir and the spruce; all made up a picture of ripe and singular beauty. (I, 12)

Thereafter they reach Thunder Cave, where Fenn's careful observation while sketching enables him to "detect" that the action of waves on the many large stones in the cavity produced the thunderlike sound. Then, by departing from the usual paths and first forcing their way through undergrowth and then clambering down a rugged rock pile, they are rewarded for their efforts by "discovering" a natural obelisk and a sheer cliff that reminds them of the battlements of an "old Norman castle . . . standing in grim and gloomy grandeur." These somber thoughts greatly enhance the interest of the discovery for them: "There was an air of neglect and desolation, as if it were an old ruin, and we found it impossible to dissociate the grim and frowning walls from the historic piles that look darkly down upon so many European landscapes" (I, 13) (see fig. 4.4).

Bunce's delight in the cliff, which they name "Castle Head," and his decision to place Fenn's illustration of it at the beginning of the book demonstrate that he and Fenn were keenly aware of the lack of historic architecture in this country and were quick to seek substitutes in "natural antiquities." Bunce is also rather smug about their having found it. He said the "Castle" escapes the notice of "the customary visitor" who keeps to the path along the top of the cliff; only "those who boldly clamber down" to the shore are able to see it (I, 13). In his *Journal* story about his trip to Colorado in 1873, Bunce also indicates his preference for going beyond the well-known scenic landmarks:

One's sensations, to be truly enjoyable, must be spontaneous. The attitude of admiration is detestable. The beauty that I discover fills me with delight; the beauty that I am directed to admire may win a few conventional phrases of appreciation, but never really enters my heart.[22]

Thus it is the "picture" he finds and studies, even names, that evokes the most intense feelings. Ironically, by describing and depicting such previously overlooked places in *Picturesque America*, Bunce and Fenn denied others the privilege of discovery and lengthened the list of must-see sights. For many less independent souls than Bunce, the validating printed description or image would lend importance to their travel experiences— as photographs, postcards, films, or video images do for many today.

This delight in finding natural features that resemble works of civilization and using metaphors to describe them, such as the obelisk and "Castle Head," recurs frequently in *Picturesque America*. Thorpe likened the trees of the Florida swamp to a Gothic colonnade. Elsewhere in volume I the cliffs along the Columbia River are described as "columns, and obelisks, and shafts" (42); natural rock formations are compared to Gothic architecture in Weyer's Cave (213), the Grand Canyon of the Yellowstone (298), and Tower Falls (300); and trees in Savannah's Bonaventure Cemetery (127) and northern California (418) are likened to columns. These metaphors rendered familiar the strange and unusual; moreover, they also enhanced the significance of a natural feature by an illusory identification with cultural history.[23]

That it was Bunce's intention to provide instruction in picturesque touring in the initial article of *Picturesque America* is supported by the fact that the article he commissioned to open the second volume reiterated many of the same themes. In the "Highlands and Palisades of the Hudson," E. L. Burlingame (1848–1922), a young writer working on the revision of Appletons' *American Cyclopaedia*, provides a second introduction of sorts, replete with guidance for the tourist. He stresses that *Picturesque America* differs from ordinary guidebooks in that it informs readers about the best way to achieve the proper "frame of mind" in approaching places. To explore the Hudson Highlands, he recommends sailing downriver from Poughkeepsie as the "true way . . . to learn the noblest beauties of the Hudson's grandest region."

Watching the growing picturesqueness of the stream, and noting the gradual rise of the hills, the increasing grandeur of their outline, and the deepening majesty of their presence, until, with his heart full of this slowly-gaining beauty, one finds himself among the perfect pictures which lie in the very midst of the mountain-group. (II, 2)

Passing slowly along the shores and studying them well puts "one in the truest mood for the first sight" of the more spectacular scenery to come (II, 6).

Like Bunce, Burlingame recommends investing time in studying the ever-changing effects of light and the seasons on views such as that of Storm King and "Cro'-Nest" (now Crow's Nest) mountains. The view from West Point is a scene "no other river can show":

Sit and watch it lying under the sky of a cloudless autumn morning, when its out-lines all seem mellowed with a touch of golden haze, and it is framed by the many-colored splendors of the foliage of late October; or see it when the perfect beauty of the new green of spring is over its hills . . . or, best, perhaps, and cer-tainly grandest of all, when the overhanging thunder-cloud of a summer afternoon comes slowly nearer . . . until . . . you find yourself overtaken by the tempest; see this picture of the Hudson in one of these aspects or in all, and you will grant that no Old World vaunted Rhine can show you more and truer beauty than is thus given in our own home. (II, 9)

Thus, Burlingame reiterates that knowing the most effective way to approach a scene and choose a viewpoint, as well as carefully observing it under different conditions, can enhance one's enjoyment and reveal the greatest beauty. And, in this case, the added benefit would not be "ser-mons in stones" but the conviction that the Hudson equals or surpasses the "Old World vaunted Rhine"—the inevitable comparison.

After setting forth an ideal model of the leisurely picturesque tour, Bunce provided descriptions and images that would educate subscribers about the "marvelously varied phases" of the United States. He relied heav-ily in the first few parts on material that had already appeared in *Appletons' Journal.* Yet in every case the material was rearranged, and the larger page, larger type size, and more generous leading (space between lines) resulted in a substantially different look. Comparing the opening of the section on Natural Bridge as it appeared in the *Journal* with the page from *Picturesque America* reveals that the lowest portion of the wood engraving, including tiny figures that made the arch seem incredibly high, was removed to make

4.5 Harry Fenn, "Natural Bridge," *Appletons' Journal*, February 11, 1871, 168. Wood engraving by Harley, 9⅞" x 6½"; page, 10¹⁵⁄₁₆" x 7¾".

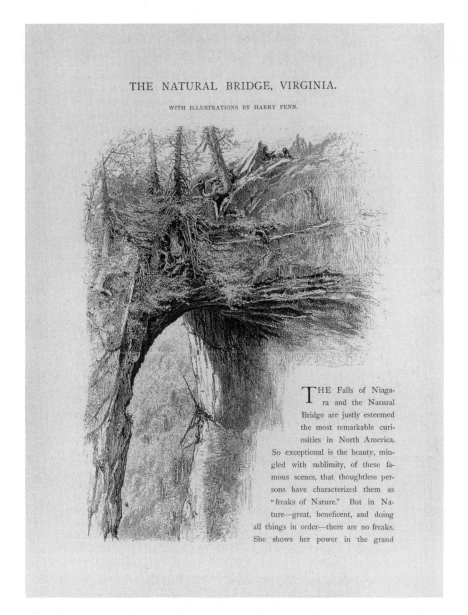

THE NATURAL BRIDGE, VIRGINIA.

WITH ILLUSTRATIONS BY HARRY FENN.

THE Falls of Niagara and the Natural Bridge are justly esteemed the most remarkable curiosities in North America. So exceptional is the beauty, mingled with sublimity, of these famous scenes, that thoughtless persons have characterized them as "freaks of Nature." But in Nature—great, beneficent, and doing all things in order—there are no freaks. She shows her power in the grand

4.6 Harry Fenn, "Natural Bridge," *Picturesque America*, I, 82. Wood engraving by Harley, 8¼" x 6¼"; page, 12⅝" x 9½".

4.7 Harry Fenn, "St. James's Church, Goose Creek," *Appletons' Journal,*
July 15, 1871, 61. Wood engraving by Cullen, 2⅚₆" x 3⅝".

at the top. In addition, most of the wood-engraved title was obliterated.
The revisions produced a less crowded, better balanced page (see figs. 4.5,
4.6). Bunce also made numerous additions and changes, including commissioning text and more illustrations of the Columbia River in the
Northwest and new text by Felix G. de Fontaine on the French Broad
region of North Carolina. Fenn's illustrations predominated in the first half
of what would become volume I. Thereafter, Bunce published primarily
new material that had not appeared in the *Journal*, and the works of other
artists appeared more and more frequently. Volume I contained articles on
thirty-four regions, fourteen of which had been illustrated and described in
the *Journal*. Thirteen articles in the first volume concerned regions in the
South, including West Virginia.

Bunce was selective in deciding what to include in *Picturesque America*.
He rejected a number of wood engravings that had appeared in the
Journal series.[24] Most were rather dull compositions utilizing picturesque
conventions, but even some of Fenn's illustrations were rejected. The
views of the Yosemite Valley Fenn made from photographs were passed by
in favor of designs from on-the-spot drawings by James D. Smillie. Fenn
reworked some designs, probably at Bunce's request, to enhance their dramatic qualities and increase their size: He transformed the small, rather

4.8   Harry Fenn, "St. James's Church, Goose Creek," *Picturesque America*, I, 209.
Wood engraving by W. J. Linton, 6¼" x 6⅜".

straightforward view of "St. James's Church, Goose Creek" from the July
15, 1871, *Journal* article on Charleston into the larger nighttime image in
Picturesque America, replete with such Gothic details as leaning tombstones,
arching trees, and hanging moss (see figs. 4.7, 4.8).[25] Using a lower viewpoint, he also exaggerated the height of the church. He similarly transformed the *Journal* image of the inclined plane railroad at Mauch Chunk
into an impressively steep, yet delicate, depiction that merges gracefully
with the opening text (see figs. 4.9, 4.10).

Other less theatrical changes show that Bunce wanted the graphic
images to be pleasing, with contrasts of light and dark rather than a dull

4.9 Harry Fenn, "Mount-Pisgah Inclined Plane," *Appletons' Journal*, January 28, 1871, 94. Wood engraving by Cullen, 5⅞" x 3¼".

MAUCH CHUNK.

MAUCH CHUNK, doubtless the most truly picturesque town in the Union, is situated in the very heart of the Pennsylvania coal-region. Its name, in the original Indian language from which it is derived, means "Bear Mountain." It lies in a narrow gorge between and among high hills, its foot, as it were, resting on the picturesque little Lehigh River, and its body stretching up the clefts of the mountains. It is so compacted among the hills that its houses impinge upon its one narrow street, and stand backed up against the rising ground, with no space for gardens except what the owners can manage to snatch from the hill-side above their heads. As proof of what can be done in a narrow space, this

4.10 Harry Fenn, "Mt. Pisgah," *Picturesque America*, I, 109. Wood engraving, 9" x 6¼"; page, 12⅜" x 9½".

4.11 Frederick L. Vance, "An Old Mill in the Housatonic Valley," *Appletons' Journal*, October 5, 1872, 380. Wood engraving by John Filmer, 8⅛" x 5⅛".

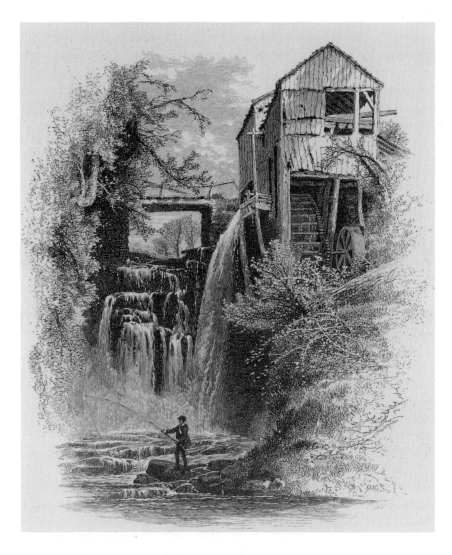

4.12 J. D. Woodward, "Old Mill, Sage's Ravine," *Picturesque America*, II, 296. Wood engraving, 7" x 6".

gray. For example, one of G. H. Smillie's *Journal* illustrations was reworked to replace the nearly uniform gray in much of the image with a greater range of tones, from white snow to black conifers.[26] Comparison of two views of the same mill or two very similar mills in the Housatonic Valley in Connecticut sheds light on the type of image Bunce wanted the *Picturesque America* artists to create. Frederick L. Vance's image in the *Journal* was pleasant, but the rectilinear format, straight lines, flatness, and emphasis on repeated patterns created a serene, somewhat static composition (see fig. 4.11). J. D. Woodward's "Old Mill, Sage's Ravine" in *Picturesque America* was strikingly different (see fig. 4.12). The low viewpoint making the mill seem higher, the light and shadows creating the illusion of depth, the different position of the figure, and the more precarious condition of the building and the bridge all enhanced the drama and the picturesque quality of this image. Also, the popular vignette format allowed the artist and engraver to emphasize the rough texture and irregular lines considered hallmarks of the picturesque.

To obtain the additional illustrations for *Picturesque America*, Bunce eventually commissioned a number of artists in addition to Fenn to provide drawings. Some he sent off on journeys, but he was also quick to save money by obtaining drawings from artists who had already made pilgrimages to scenic areas. This was the case with four artists mentioned frequently in the New York and Boston newspapers in the late 1860s: R. Swain Gifford, William Hart, James D. Smillie, and Casimir Clayton Griswold. They may have arranged with Bunce in advance to provide *Appletons' Journal* with illustrations, or Bunce may have contacted them after learning of their travels from reports in the press or from works they exhibited. Gifford, who set out for California and Oregon in July 1869, only two months after the completion of the transcontinental railroad, provided several views of the Far West that appeared in the *Journal* in August 1871. Later he provided additional illustrations of the region for *Picturesque America.*

William Hart (1823–94), an associate of the National Academy and one of the organizers of the American Watercolor Society (where he would have encountered Fenn), travelled to Lake Superior in the summer of 1870, as was duly reported in the papers.[27] Bunce turned to him to provide illustrations for *Picturesque America*'s section on that region, which appeared with parts 17 and 18 in the spring of 1873. James D. Smillie (1833–1901), who would also have known Fenn in the American

Watercolor Society, travelled to California by train in 1871 and spent considerable time drawing and painting in Yosemite Valley.[28] He may well have planned to provide the *Journal* with some views, perhaps for the "Picturesque America" series. He eventually supplied the text and illustrations for "The Yosemite," but considering the timing, it is almost certain Smillie did not have a specific commission for the book when he set off. In addition, Casimir Clayton Griswold (1834–1918), some of whose views of the seacoast near Newport appeared in *Appletons' Journal* as early as January 22, 1870, and later in *Picturesque America*, had chosen to paint the area prior to any Appleton commissions.[29]

Artists aside from Fenn that Bunce commissioned to travel to prepare illustrations for *Picturesque America* include A. R. Waud, Granville Perkins, John Douglas Woodward, William Hamilton Gibson, and Thomas Moran. Jules Tavernier, William Ludwell Sheppard, and A. C. Warren may also have travelled for the book, although it is difficult to be sure without more evidence. Several of the artists Bunce engaged, including Waud, Warren, Perkins, Smillie, Sheppard, and Gibson, had already done work for the *Journal* or other Appleton publications and most had provided illustrations for rival periodicals. Bunce turned to them as specialists in landscapes and city views in a time when more and more illustrators tended to specialize, or were cast in such roles by art directors.[30] It is not surprising that no women artists participated in the project, for during this period the working conditions of a landscape artist or illustrator—painting or drawing outdoors, sometimes living in a tent—were considered "obviously impossible for a woman," especially an unmarried woman.[31]

Although several of these artists, specifically Waud and Sheppard, were also considered skilled at depicting people, such depictions would never play a major role in *Picturesque America*. Figures are almost always present in the illustrations—providing scale, enhancing the picturesque quality of the scene, or serving as a stand-in for the viewer—but they are subordinate to the main subject, whether landscape or city scene. The difference in approach is clear when one compares illustrations by Fenn and Waud for *Every Saturday* with their views for *Picturesque America*. Figures, either individual portraits or groups, are the subject of several of Fenn's *Every Saturday* illustrations.[32] Furthermore, Waud, who was commissioned by *Every Saturday* as "special artist" after Fenn returned to the Appleton firm in March 1871, had earned his reputation depicting Civil War soldiers and battles for *Harper's Weekly*. His *Every Saturday* illustrations of Mammoth Cave, New

Orleans, the Mississippi, and St. Louis consist of almost as many character sketches as landscapes.[33] Yet his *Picturesque America* views, like Fenn's, include people only as additions to the landscape or cityscape. The pattern is so clear it must have been the result of a directive from Bunce.

Fenn illustrated twenty-four of the sixty-five sections of *Picturesque America*. The next most prolific contributor was John Douglas Woodward (1846–1924), who did ten himself, as well as one with Fenn. Woodward, who was twenty-six in 1872, was gaining recognition through his landscape illustrations in *Hearth and Home* and a commission to provide views of his home state, Virginia, for *The Aldine* in 1873. Bunce commissioned him to cover Mackinac Island and the south shore of Lake Erie for volume I. Obviously pleased with the results, Bunce later hired him to illustrate eight articles in volume II, more than any other contributor.

Granville Perkins (1830–95) was the third most prolific of the *Picturesque America* artists, illustrating eight articles about Eastern rivers and cities. Perkins, a Baltimore native, was a frequent contributor of marine and landscape views to *Frank Leslie's Illustrated Newspaper* and *Harper's Weekly*, as well as *Appletons' Journal*. During Cuba's struggle for independence beginning in 1868, his views based on his travels there in the early 1850s gained him recognition and the approbation of Admiral David G. Farragut. Bunce might well have been impressed by the February 1872 *Aldine* feature on Perkins, which said his paintings were much admired for "the natural life-like beauty of their sky and water effects."[34] Bunce attempted to capitalize on Perkins's apparent strengths by commissioning him to illustrate the Delaware Water Gap, the Neversink Highlands, Harper's Ferry, Brandywine Creek, the Juniata and Susquehanna rivers, and two cities he knew well, Philadelphia and Baltimore.

Alfred R. Waud (1828–1912), commissioned by Bunce after *Every Saturday* eliminated illustrations at the end of 1871, was the artist for five sections covering the Mississippi and the Midwest. He appears to have made journeys specifically related to his *Picturesque America* commissions, although he sometimes reused drawings he had made on earlier assignments.[35] A respected illustrator, Waud had done a great deal of work for *Appletons' Journal*, including early foldout cartoons, and it is not surprising that Bunce turned to him to illustrate regions with which he was already familiar.

The other artists did three or fewer sections. R. Swain Gifford did three sections in volume I, based on his sketches from his 1869 trip west. Thomas Moran (1837–1926), to whom Bunce turned for Western views after Congress's celebrated purchase in June 1872 of his *Grand Canyon of the Yellowstone* to hang in the Senate Chamber, did three in volume II. William L. Sheppard (1833–1912), a Richmond native, did "Scenes in Virginia" and "West Virginia" in volume I and "Washington" to close volume II.[36] James D. Smillie and William Hamilton Gibson each did two sections. In addition to providing the images and text for the Yosemite Valley feature, Smillie illustrated the one section covering part of Canada, following the popular tourist route on the "St. Lawrence and the Saguenay" to Montreal and Quebec. Gibson (1850–96) was a young artist who had contributed botanical sketches to Appletons' *American Cyclopaedia*. Bunce sent him first to Rhode Island, then to the Connecticut coast.

William Hart, C. C. Griswold, and Jules Tavernier did one each. Originally from France, Tavernier (1844–89) came to New York in 1872 and quickly found work with *Harper's Weekly* and *The Aldine*, which published his striking view of Niagara Falls in November 1872. He covered northern New Jersey. A. C. Warren (1819–1904) did nine city views for steel engravings, although he was not the primary artist for any of the sections. (Appendix A contains brief biographies of the *Picturesque America* artists, including details about their work for the publication.[37])

Most of these artists were involved in a full range of professional activities, and travelling for *Picturesque America* offered the opportunity to find subjects for exhibition pieces as well as for the book. From 1871 through 1876, several artists exhibited works from their sketching tours for *Picturesque America* in the annual exhibitions of the American Watercolor Society. For example, at the Fourth Annual Exhibition during the winter of 1870/71, Fenn showed four works from his travels for the "Picturesque America" series: *The Convent Gate, St. Augustine, Florida; Home of Howard Payne, Author of Home Sweet Home, East Hampton, Long Island; Sketches on the Ocklawaha River, Fla.*; and *Coquina Quarry, Anastasia Island, St. Augustine Fla.* Similarly, in the Fifth Annual Exhibition, during the winter of 1871/72, Fenn's works included *The Mouth of the St. John's River, Fla.* and *Study from the Sister Islands, Niagara.* The Sixth Annual Exhibition, in 1873, included Fenn's *Entrance to Watkins Glen; Cavern Cascade, Watkins Glen*; and *Goat Island, Niagara.* James D. Smillie and A. R. Waud also exhibited watercolors of areas they illustrated for *Picturesque America*: Smillie, in 1871/72 and 1873, contributed works depicting Yosemite, and A. R. Waud showed a painting of a boat, *Hotel Dieu, near South West Pass (La.)*, in the Eighth Annual Exhibition (1875).[38]

Although it can be shown that artist and writer sometimes toured together for *Picturesque America,* in more instances this pattern was not followed. A careful examination of the articles for evidence of whether artist and writer travelled together suggests that in eighteen cases the writer did accompany the artist; nine of these are quite clear from the text (plus the unique case of James D. Smillie, who was both author and artist for "The Yosemite"); and in nine other cases the close congruency between text and illustrations makes joint travel seem likely. At least some of these tours were carefully planned in advance, as is indicated by Thorpe's comment that "by the aid of influential letters and previously-made arrangements" they "secured the good-will of the captain of the steamer" they boarded to explore the St. John's River (I, 19). In six cases it is clear that artist and writer did not travel together.[39] In the remaining instances, which constitute the majority of articles, it is likely that the artist travelled independently and that Bunce commissioned a writer familiar with the region. The prospectus on the back wrapper of each part states that the articles were written by individuals who either accompanied the artists or were "specially acquainted with the field" described. Some had even published travel accounts. Before Lucia J. G. Runkle wrote "Up and Down the Columbia" for Bunce, her "Letters from Next Door," recounting her summer 1869 trip to California and Oregon Territory, appeared in the *New-York Tribune.*[40] Bunce was quick to cut costs and save time by relying on such writers when the opportunity presented itself.

In addition to Bunce, who made the largest contribution with twelve articles, twenty-seven others wrote for *Picturesque America.* Most were professional writers, journalists, or editors—the new authorities in the dawning age of mass communications. Only two represented the more traditional authority of the clergy. William Carey Richards (1818–92), a Baptist minister and brother of the artist T. Addison Richards, covered Connecticut. His previous writings included *Georgia Illustrated* and numerous contributions to periodicals. Thomas M. Clark (1812–1903), the Episcopal Bishop of Rhode Island and author of the Appleton publication *Primary Truths of Religion* (1869), wrote the sections on Providence and Newport.[41]

Other established writers or editors enjoying considerable reputations in the 1870s but no longer widely known today include a number of Virginians and West Virginians: David Hunter Strother (1816–88), writer and illustrator of many articles about the South published in *Harper's*

Monthly Magazine in the 1850s under the pen name of "Porte Crayon"[42]; Richmond native John Reuben Thompson (1823–73), editor of the *Southern Literary Messenger* from 1847 to 1860 and literary editor of the *New York Evening Post* the last years of his life; George W. Bagby (1823–83), who succeeded Thompson as editor of the *Southern Literary Messenger* from 1860 to 1864 and was famous for his humorous writings under the pen name of "Mozis Addums"; John Esten Cooke (1830–86), a prolific writer who was well known for his romantic novels, *Leather Stocking and Silk* (1854) and *The Virginia Comedians* (1854), and had more recently published several Civil War novels, his own war reminiscences called *Wearing of the Gray* (1867), and the first biography of Robert E. Lee, published by D. Appleton and Company in 1871.[43]

A number of writers contributed to *Picturesque America* early in their careers and later acquired considerable reputations, including regional novelist Constance Fenimore Woolson (1848–94), a niece of James Fenimore Cooper, who contributed four articles; Rossiter Johnson (1840–1931), writer of history and editor of the *Annual Cyclopaedia* and the "Little Classics" and other series; Edward Livermore Burlingame (1848–1922), who worked on the revision of the *American Cyclopaedia* between 1872 and 1876 and later edited *Scribner's Magazine* from its beginning in 1887 until 1914; G. M. Towle (1841–93), a Boston newspaper editor and writer of history books; and William Henry Rideing (1853–1918), who came to America from England at the age of seventeen and, after leaving the staff of the *New York Tribune,* wrote seven articles for *Picturesque America*. The most frequent contributor after Bunce was the reporter Rodolphe E. Garczynski, who wrote eight articles (and about whom nothing else is known).[44]

During this period, when increasing numbers of women turned to writing as an occupation, especially the writing of fiction, three women in addition to Woolson contributed to *Picturesque America*: Lucia Gilbert Runkle (1837–1923) was the first woman in the United States to write editorials for a daily newspaper, the *New York Tribune*;[45] Susan Nichols Carter, wife of Robert Carter, the second editor of *Appletons' Journal*, wrote books about drawing and painting and was principal of the Women's Art Schools at Cooper Union and an editor for G. P. Putnam; and "Sallie" A. Brock (ca. 1840–after 1900) of Richmond, later Mrs. Sarah A. Putnam, who had published her memoirs of *Richmond during the War* and edited a compilation of Southern war poetry, *The Southern Amaranth*.[46]

The fact that Bunce commissioned a number of Southern writers in addition to Brock to describe various parts of the South, including some who had been soldiers or journalists for the Confederate cause, further supports the view that *Picturesque America* promoted national reconciliation—as did the "Picturesque America" series in the *Journal* that initially focused so positively on the South. With no interest in waving the "bloody shirt," Bunce enlisted the participation of former Confederate supporters, such as John Esten Cooke, John Reuben Thompson, William Tappan Thompson, and Felix G. de Fontaine, several of whom had conveniently relocated to New York. Thompson (1812–82) was founder and editor of the *Savannah Morning News* and creator of the "Major Jones" books popular in the 1840s.[47] De Fontaine (1834–96), a Bostonian sympathetic to the Southern cause, wrote the *History of American Abolitionism* (D. Appleton, 1861) and was one of the South's leading war correspondents, writing for the *Charleston (S.C.) Courier* and publishing the *Daily South Carolinian* (Columbia, 1864–65). From 1868 to 1871, he was managing editor of the *New York Telegram*.

The only evidence I have found related to payment of the writers comes from James D. Smillie's diary for April 2, 1873, where he records receiving eighty dollars for approximately twenty-one pages of text. More prominent writers may have been paid more, plus expenses and a weekly stipend when travel was required. An 1875 agreement between Bayard Taylor and D. Appleton and Company indicates that the prominent poet and travel writer would receive ten dollars for each full page of type for any article he wrote for *Picturesque Europe* (1875–79), a publication that followed upon the success of *Picturesque America*.[48] If Smillie's experience was anything like the other writers, it was money well earned, for Bunce was a demanding editor.[49]

With so many writers involved it is difficult to generalize, but usually the articles that recount an actual journey by railroad, steamer, carriage, horseback, or on foot, with interesting details of people and places, prove the more lively and readable today. These accounts enabled the reader to experience the journey vicariously in a way not possible with a dry recounting of history and facts. A superior example is Henry A. Brown's[50] account of his journey to the Catskills with Fenn, which begins:

It was mid-August when we started for the Catskills. Though it was early when we left New-York City, no air was stirring, and the hot morning gave promise of a hotter day. The train steamed out of the huge depot into the glare of the early sunlight, and the dust began to whirl up beneath the wheels in a white, dry cloud. We have rushed with lightning-speed along the eastern bank of the Hudson—now plunging into a dark, damp tunnel cut through the overhanging rock; now whirling around some promontory, jutting out into the placid river. (II, 117–18)

Another of the more interesting pieces, Constance Fenimore Woolson's account of Mackinac Island, benefitted from her long familiarity with the region, although she probably did not travel with Woodward as he sketched. Her lively account is peppered with comments of local people and interesting historical perspectives. In contrast, the general overviews of a city or region make dull reading, as William Cullen Bryant noted. *Picturesque America*'s gradual distribution in small increments allowed subscribers to savor each new section, lingering over the images and perhaps reading part or all of the newly arrived text, whereas reading the entire book from start to finish would have been a dull and daunting task.

Whether commonplace or stimulating, the articles that Bunce commissioned and gradually disseminated to the public were viewed as informative, educational accompaniments to the "splendid" artworks that were the main attraction to subscribers. Most important, the text and pictures together enhanced Appleton's reputation for publishing high quality works that "improved" the family circle. Complaints increased during this period about book agents using high-pressure techniques to sell cheaply produced subscription books that were worthless, even "absolutely wicked and demoralizing," such as *The Mysteries of Life in the City of Satan*. *Picturesque America*, in contrast, was singled out as an admirable exception—along with histories and dictionaries of the Bible.[51] Naturally, such attitudes contributed to its success.

The project was also admired for its scale. The Appletons claimed, with considerable justification, that no publication of the kind had "ever been attempted in the country on a scale so large." For the world of publishing, it was comparable to the huge new corporate ventures in other realms that were becoming emblematic of the age—ventures requiring a unifying vision and coordination of many disparate elements. Examples include organizing and equipping an army, building a transcontinental railroad or a water supply or septic system for a large city, organizing a large mining operation, and refining and transporting oil. Mass producing and distributing, over a two-year period, an eleven-hundred-page book in forty-eight parts, with almost a thousand illustrations in two different media was a highly complex project. It required the coordination of a large number of artists, writers, and engravers, as well as hundreds of type-setters, printers, electrotypers, binders, and subscription agents. Bunce and the Appleton firm, with its (for the time) mammoth manufacturing plant and large sales force, met the challenge. *Picturesque America*, in turn, benefitted from the growing appreciation of large, costly, and complex ventures. Many subscribers who proudly displayed it in their homes were impressed by the enterprise and expense required to produce it as well as by the magnificence of the result.

 CHAPTER 5

Reconciling Truth and
Poetry in Illustrations

Selecting and Interpreting Scenery and Cities

W hen the *Picturesque America* artists set out on their journeys, how did they decide where to set up easel and
umbrella and begin to draw? Further, once they
selected a subject, how did they employ the picturesque conventions as
well as innovative approaches to create images combining fidelity to the
actual scene with "poetry"—the type of image that most appealed to critics
and the public alike?

Picturesque America's opening section on Mount Desert Island reveals
that Fenn and Bunce shared a cluster of ideas about their task—ideas
derived from the literature and art of the picturesque tour and from the
widely held belief that the artist's mission was to reveal divine creation.
Although not always so clearly stated, internalized criteria about what constituted picturesque, beautiful, and sublime scenery shaped the searches
of the other artists as well. The situation was similar to that in nineteenth-
century Britain, where, as Christopher Mulvey describes it, this "development in bourgeois taste" had

redrawn the visual map so that only those features which could be described as
picturesque could be seen by the traveller. At the beginning of the eighteenth
century, Defoe would have passed by everything that was attracting the attention of
the English tourist 150 years later.[1]

The artists immediately recognized certain landscape combinations—
such as scenes filled with the irregular lines of jagged rocks, twisted trees,
and intricate foliage—as appropriate for inclusion in the book. Several
artists depicted themselves at work before such stereotypically picturesque

5.1 Jules Tavernier, "Eagle Rock, Orange," *Picturesque America*, II, 48. Wood engraving by A. Measom, 8⅞" x 6⅛".

scenery, two conspicuous examples being Fenn's title page vignette (see
fig. 4.3) and Jules Tavernier's view of Eagle Rock on Orange Mountain
(New Jersey), complete with female companion admiring the impressive
outcropping and stump as well as the artist's work (see fig. 5.1; also II, 306).

Sometimes a scene clearly met the criteria, but finding a spot from
which to draw it was difficult. In order to capture a particularly grand
view—encompassing rocks, trees, river, and mountains—D. H. Strother
recounted that his determined artist companion, whom he called "our
perplexed Salvator," "dismounted, and scaling a rude cliff, nestled amid
the gnarled branches of a dead cedar, hanging a hundred feet above the
road" (I, 382).[2] Similarly, to reach a desired viewpoint in Yosemite Valley,
James D. Smillie climbed "a slit in the rock and got a great slit in [his]
breeches and wondered how [he] was ever going to get down."[3]

In other settings, finding both subject and point of view could take
time. For example, in Charleston, Bunce related that at first

The search for the picturesque that would meet the necessities of our purpose was
not expeditious. It is only after walking around a place, and surveying it from different situations, that an artist can settle upon his point of view. We were three
days in Charleston ere Mr. Fenn discovered the prospect from St. Michael's belfry.
(I, 200)

That prospect included the rich juxtaposition of varied elements and
reminders of history that were thought to make a city view picturesque: a
busy street leading to the Old Custom House, a jumble of roof lines and
"quaint" chimneys, numerous boats and ships, and several islands in the
bay, including that occupied by Fort Sumter (see fig. 5.2). Using a popular device, Fenn framed all these elements with the arches and balustrades
of St. Michael's belfry. He included a young black man pausing in his
work to admire the view—a sympathetic figure despite his exaggerated
features, for he seems to share the artist's appreciation of the prospect.

In an area sparse in dramatic natural and cultural features, however,
finding suitable subjects could be a challenge. This is clear from a letter of
William Hamilton Gibson, whom Bunce sent to the coast of Rhode Island
in September 1872. Gibson wrote his mother afterwards,

All through the day would I pass by little bits of landscape that I thought would
compose rather prettily, but nevertheless I made up my mind . . . to sketch only
such bits as I knew would be particularly attractive, and of course it would take
nearly the whole day before I could find and sketch more than two.[4]

5.2 Harry Fenn, "A Glimpse of Charleston and Bay, from the Tower of St. Michael's Church," *Picturesque America*, I, 201. Wood engraving by Harley, 9" x 6½".

Most conspicuous on the visual map that guided the artists and writers were the landscapes and historic cities that conformed to the picturesque aesthetic. But by the 1870s enthusiasm for technological innovation, scientific knowledge, and civic amenities had altered that map considerably. The artists and writers were often struck by natural or manmade features that forced them to weigh competing values. For example, excitement about a new railroad bridge came very close to eclipsing the interest of the writer W. S. Ward and the artist John Douglas Woodward in the picturesque waterfall of the Genesee River at Portage, New York. With its strong geometric forms, the bridge was clearly the "least picturesque" feature of the scene. Yet this "triumph of the bridge-builder's skill . . . said to be the largest wooden structure of its kind in the world" was captivating. Woodward drew it and the falls below from a distant, low viewpoint that emphasized the height of the bridge (fig. 5.3). Bunce, in turn, chose to open the section on "The Valley of the Genesee" with this view. Ward related the artist's explanation of why only this distant view of the bridge was included:

"This is a tour in search of the picturesque," he says; "and the straight lines, sharp angles, and cut-stone buttresses of a railway-bridge do not belong to that order of beauty." Assenting to this just estimate of the artist's mission, we turn away from this hasty survey of the bridge to the contemplation of the rough-hewn, rugged walls of the chasm it spans. (II, 354)

Thus, although artist, writer, and editor all found the bridge fascinating, their dedication to the picturesque dictated that they gave considerably more attention to the waterfalls and rugged chasm. Five views of these features followed the one of the bridge.

In the article "In West Virginia," the artist-writer team similarly distinguished between a rock formation primarily of scientific interest and one of picturesque interest, preferring the latter because of its emotional impact. They first came upon "a singularly perfect and beautiful exhibition of arched strata"—a half-circle that appeared "drawn by an engineer" and hewn by a "master-mason" (I, 377, 382). Yet they concluded that this formation, with its "artificial regularity," which "excites no other emotion than that of pleasing curiosity," would "more appropriately adorn a geological museum than a landscape-gallery" (382). Still, Bunce found it sufficiently interesting to open the section with Sheppard's image of it.

The formation the travellers then suddenly came upon, however, "Chimney Rocks," was "of quite another character," according to Strother, and aroused greater enthusiasm:

THE VALLEY OF THE GENESEE.

WITH ILLUSTRATIONS BY J. DOUGLAS WOODWARD.

Railroad-Bridge, Portage.

THERE is said to be a mountain-peak in Potter County, Pennsylvania, standing upon which the observer may mark the fountain-head of two rivers. Though flowing through adjacent gorges, their courses are soon divided, the one tending southward, while the other marks out a winding way to the harbor at Charlotte, there losing itself in the waters of Lake Ontario. To follow down the pathway of the southward-flowing stream would lead the traveller through every variation of climate and verdure that our land affords—now shadowed by the rugged peaks of the Alleghanies, then over rough rapids and dangerous shallows, till the smoky precincts of Pittsburg are reached, with the blending waters of the Monongahela. Still farther, and bearing west by south, its course leads through fruitful valleys, and along the busy wharves of Cincinnati, Louisville, and Cairo. Here the clear, fresh waters of the mountain-rivulet are finally merged and lost in the expanse of the Mississippi; and, afloat on the bosom of the Father of Rivers, we are borne on its sluggish current to the delta, and the borders of the Southern gulf.

This tour of fancy ended, the river-voyager retraces his path till he stands again upon the Northern summit, and girds himself for the second and northward journey.

116

5.3 J. D. Woodward, "Railroad-Bridge, Portage," *Picturesque America*, II, 353. Wood engraving, 7½" x 4¼".

At the butt of a sharp spur rises a towering architectural mass, which any one familiar with the Old World would pronounce a well-preserved feudal ruin, and a purely American imagination would conceive to be the chimneys of a burnt factory. As the probabilities of finding a feudal castle and a modern factory in this region are about equal, we must deviate a little from the highway to obtain a better view of the startling object. (I, 382–83)

Like "Castle Head" on Mount Desert Island, this formation excited, indeed "startled," the travellers because of its resemblance to an ancient castle, with the attendant associations of chivalric deeds and battles. Of course the artist chose to draw it, emphasizing such typically picturesque features as broken, irregular lines of the "towers" of rock, delicate foliage, and strong lights and shadows (I, 383). The travellers' excitement, replaced by "vague regrets" when closer inspection dispelled the illusion, once again demonstrates their interest in finding features comparable to Old World antiquities in their "traditionless" country.

American cities also presented dilemmas to the artists, who wanted to demonstrate age and quaintness, as well as modern amenities and imposing new buildings. For example, artist and writer both admired the harmony and regularity of the handsome new buildings in Chicago's business district rebuilt after the fire of 1871 (II, 516), even though they could not be considered picturesque.

Thus the artists for *Picturesque America*, like the writers, used a set of internalized criteria—albeit tempered by current interests and enthusiasms—to guide them in sorting out and categorizing what they encountered in the natural and cultural landscape. But this was just the first step. They then had to choose how to represent their subjects in memorable and appealing ways.

The easiest choice involved materials. Judging from the extant original drawings, pencil was the artists' favorite medium for preparing sketches for wood engravings. They frequently added touches of Chinese white or gouache for lighter areas, such as clouds, water, or white or light-colored objects. Woodward regularly used an off-white paper, whereas Waud most often used tinted papers of tan, pale gray, mint green, gray-blue, pink, or reddish brown.[5] Tinted paper could serve the artist well by establishing the middle tone in the scene, allowing the artist to use different weights of pencil lines or shading to depict the subject, and use white for the highlights. When preparing a design for a steel engraving, on the other hand, the evidence suggests the artists frequently worked in watercolor.

A greater challenge was to create depictions that were accurate and "poetic" at the same time. All of the artists embraced this goal, and, indeed, *Picturesque America*'s prospectus had promised views that were not only "original and trustworthy," but also possessed "the vividness of personal observation."

For at least a quarter century American landscape painters had turned increasingly from creating idealized compositions in the studio to drawing and painting particular landscapes outdoors. This was in keeping with the desire to represent the special qualities of the American landscape as well as to be scientifically accurate. Such prominent older artists as Asher B. Durand, in his 1855 "Letters on Landscape Painting" in *The Crayon*, and the popular critic John Ruskin emphasized the value of sketching from nature. Ruskin, whose ideas first became known to Americans in 1847 with the first American edition of *Modern Painters* (vols. I and II), is the art expert most frequently mentioned in *Picturesque America*. His advice to young artists to "go to Nature," "rejecting nothing, selecting nothing, and scorning nothing," and such claims as "if you can draw the stone *rightly*, everything within the reach of art is also within yours" reinforced the growing interest of artists in Great Britain and the United States in observing and recording nature's particularity and appreciating the minute as well as the grand.[6] This approach had already been used by the Pre-Raphaelites, whose intricate representations of both nature and medieval scenes created a stir when included in an exhibition of British art shown in New York, Philadelphia, and Boston in 1857/58.[7] American artists including John Henry Hill, William Trost Richards, Henry Roderick Newman, Fidelia Bridges, and Charles Herbert Moore emulated the Pre-Raphaelites and briefly aroused public interest. Yet most critics and painters felt this approach sacrificed both unity of composition by overemphasis on details and creativity or imagination by strictly literal renderings.

Several *Picturesque America* artists took great care in observing and sketching nature, to the extent that they became accomplished amateur botanists or geologists. Although few of their drawings for *Picturesque America* are primarily close-up nature studies, many of them represent trees, plants, and rocks carefully enough that species can be identified. This was quite different from the depictions of general rather than specific types of rocks, trees, and clouds in most earlier picturesque views. Some of the artists may have followed Ruskin's recommendation to use J. D. Harding's *Lessons on Trees* (London: Day and Son, 1850) to learn how

5.4 J. D. Woodward, nature studies. Sept. 16, 17, 18, 19, 1870, Staunton, Va.
Pencil on paper, 11" x 8½". Courtesy the Diocese of Virginia.

5.5 A. R. Waud, *Racine from the Lake.* ca. 1872. Pencil on green-beige paper, 7⅜" x 9⅞". Courtesy The Historic New Orleans Collection, accession no. 1977.137.14. II i, ii.

to represent different kinds.[8] They also clearly spent considerable time outdoors drawing specimen plants, trees, and rocks. The exquisitely detailed nature studies by John Douglas Woodward (fig. 5.4), made shortly before he worked on *Picturesque America,* demonstrate the powers of observation admired by W. H. Rideing when he and Woodward visited the High Falls of the Delaware: "That keen eye of his discovered effects in the smallest nooks, underneath the fronds of the tiniest fern, among the grains of sand that lodged in the crevices, and in the swaying shadows of the forms around" (II, 473).

Fenn was also a student of botany and geology, as had been demonstrated in many of his illustrations for *Our Young Folks.* His close-up view of the top of Natural Bridge portrayed the countless tiny breaks in the rock's surface, as well as the jumble of tree roots and branches growing on the top (fig. 4.6). Although this work has some similarities to earlier rock studies in oils by Ruskin, Durand, and David Johnson, the medium of

5.6 A. R. Waud, "Racine," *Picturesque America*, II, 525. Wood engraving, 4" x 9¼".

black-and-white wood engraving necessarily dictated great differences. Fenn's work depends mainly on line and secondarily on tone to convey all the details of texture and "color." By exploiting the medium's capacity to represent texture, Fenn and the masterful wood engraver Harley conveyed appreciation of nature's intricacy and created an image that was profoundly "picturesque," although vastly different from the more usual views of Natural Bridge depicting the arch from below.

In addition to striving to represent details of the natural world with fidelity, the artists for *Picturesque America* also took pains to represent accurately the man-made environment. This can be seen in the crisp detail of Alfred R. Waud's drawing of Racine, Wisconsin, from the lake, featuring its "good harbor" and "immense piers" (fig. 5.5). Waud diligently recorded the buildings along the shoreline and scattered careful renderings of the lighthouse pier and several boats across the paper. Unlike most *Picturesque America* artists, Waud did not redraw his designs on the woodblock himself, so, in this case, he apparently left the placement of the boats, as well as the elaboration of the lake's surface and the sky to the imagination of whoever put the scene on the block (fig. 5.6)

In another instance, Waud provided notes to insure that the wood engraving of the imposing new courthouse in St. Louis would be accurate with respect to architectural details and lighting. On the back of his drawing, he pointed out that the building's pilasters were Ionic on the "1st

5.7 J. D. Woodward, *Green River, Gt Barrington, Berkshire Co., Mass.*, October 9, 1872. Pencil and white on paper, 7" x 10". Courtesy the Diocese of Virginia.

story," Corinthian on the second and third. He also drew a plan showing the siting of the building with respect to the points of the compass, and wrote:

The Sun shines on the front of the building only for an hour or two after sunrise. I leave the shadows to the artist who puts it on the wood— I have left out many trees to show the park[?] Plan will show how light falls. Front of light buff stone— prison and wall brick ornate & strong relief in architecture.[9]

Accuracy was essential, but there was widespread agreement that a strictly literal approach was not enough; it did not result in "art." The landscape artist should also be a "poet," interpreting the scene and conveying something of his or her emotional response to it. The spirit and animation imbued by the artist would result in works of greater artistic value than those of "mere topographical accuracy" or the "painted photographs" critics derided.[10] They would be preferable to actual photographs; for although the public appreciated photography's faithfulness to a particular

5.8 J. D. Woodward, "Green River, at Great Barrington," *Picturesque America*, II, 301. Wood engraving by F. W. Quartley, 5⅛" x 6¼".

subject, most still thought of photography as a craft derived from technology that lacked the emotional intensity of true art.[11] Photography's potential in this regard was not yet recognized. In his Preface, Bryant, following the lead of the earlier preface, pointed out this difference by saying, "Photographs, however accurate, lack the spirit and personal quality which the accomplished painter or draughtsman infuses into his work."

Bryant viewed landscape artists, on the other hand, as those whose imagination, like that of British artist J. M. W. Turner, "transfigures and glorifies whatever they look at." Bryant's reference was anything but off-hand. Ruskin's intense admiration for Turner had led many to consider his paintings and prints supreme examples of the successful combination of truth to nature and poetic interpretation—which Ruskin described as a

5.9 J. D. Woodward, *Lower Falls of the Genesee, Rochester*, July 14, 1873. Pencil and white on paper, 9⅞" x 7". Courtesy the Diocese of Virginia.

THE VALLEY OF THE GENESEE. 367

Lower Falls.

farther, following the line of the river along its eastern shores, we enter Monroe County, and approach the city of Rochester.

This city stands in the same relation to the valley as does a storage and distributing reservoir to the streams from which the supply is received. In its early days, the life of the city was dependent upon the harvest of the valley; when these were abundant, then all went well. Having already referred to the wheat-product of the valley, we can readily understand the need and consequent prosperity of the city, which has long been known as the "Flour City of the West." Although now ranking as the fifth city in the State, there are yet living many persons whose childhood dates back of that of the city in which they dwell. From a brief historical sketch on the subject, we learn that, in expressing aston-

5.10 J. D. Woodward, "Lower Falls," *Picturesque America,* II, 367. Wood engraving, 8" x 6³⁄₁₆".

5.11 J. D. Woodward, *Cushing's Island from Peak's, Portland Bay,* August 20, 1873.
Pencil and white on paper, 7" x 10". Courtesy the Diocese of Virginia.

higher order of aesthetics. Still a towering figure in landscape art twenty
years after his death, Turner is mentioned several times in *Picturesque
America,* his name sometimes linked with Ruskin's.[12] Fenn and Moran, in
particular, admired and emulated his works.[13] His numerous contributions to viewbooks, despite their small scale and lack of color, offered
exemplary models of sublime effects: their dramatic skies suggested infinity; their wild seas implied danger; and their towering mountains invoked
awe.[14] Furthermore, admiration for Turner spilled over to those American
landscape artists seen as uniting fidelity to a particular scene with poetic
interpretation. For example, art critic Henry Tuckerman said that John F.
Kensett "does not merely imitate or emphasize or reflect nature—he interprets her—which we take to be the legitimate and holy task of the scenic
limner."[15]

To balance the demand for accuracy with the demand for "poetry," the
Picturesque America artists used a range of approaches, from simply tacking
on conventional picturesque details to adopting bold new viewpoints and
formats designed to involve the viewer in the artist's emotional response

5.12 J. D. Woodward, "Cushing's Island," *Picturesque America*, II, 412. Wood engraving by [James H.] Richardson, 3⅞" x 9⅛".

to the subject. They frequently transcended the engraved photograph to convey a sense of delight or excitement about the beauty or the interest of a scene. Occasionally, they achieved the sought-after goal of revealing the power and benevolence of the Creator.

The most obvious and often the least convincing approach to animating a scene was to embellish a straightforward composition with conventional picturesque details such as figures, animals, birds, vehicles, boats, twisted trees, smoke, clouds, and rainbows. The goal of fidelity to the natural and cultural environment obviously did not extend to such transient features as the changing effects of weather and time of day or people and animals enlivening a scene.

A favorite device was the addition of interest in the sky, either by turning day to night or sunlight to storm or by adding a rainbow or other dramatic light effects, such as a rising or setting sun. Ruskin had stressed that the sky was constantly "talking" to us, producing "picture after picture, glory after glory" for "our perpetual pleasure."[16] Among the examples of this type of manipulation is Woodward's view along the Green River, at Great Barrington, Massachusetts. His drawing features a magnificent old tree with twisted branches, as well as a picturesque wooden bridge (fig. 5.7). But on the woodblock Woodward enhanced the romance of this charming bit of nature by adding a rainbow—the conventional sign of divine benevolence—against a dark sky and two lovers gazing at it (fig. 5.8).

5.13 J. D. Woodward, *Fairy Arch of Giants' Stairway, Mackinaw* [sic] *Island*, July 8, 1872. Pencil and white on paper, 10½" x 8½". Courtesy the Diocese of Virginia.

5.14 J. D. Woodward, "Fairy Arch," *Picturesque America*, I, 285. Wood engraving by Harley, 8⅛" x 5¹⁵⁄₁₆".

5.15 Harry Fenn, *Lookout Mt. Tenn.*, [1871]. Pencil and wash on blue paper, ca. 18" x 12¼". Private collection of Mrs. Donald Fenn van Antwerp.

5.16 Harry Fenn, "Lookout Mountain.—View from the Point," *Picturesque America,* I, 54. Wood engraving by James Langridge, 8¹⁵⁄₁₆" x 6¼".

A similar comparison of original drawing with wood engraving shows that the rainbow as well as the boatloads of tourists and the birds were added to Waud's image of "The Jaws," in the Wisconsin Dells (II, 536).[17] Also obvious is Waud's "Sunset, Lake Michigan" (II, 519), in which the disparate shafts of sunlight loom like divine fingers over the windswept waves and ships. Surely these illustrations and others with bolts of lightning and writhing trees must have seemed trite to many viewers even in the 1870s.

Yet the inclusion of some human interest was considered essential, not banal, as most artists and critics continued to find scenes devoid of any connection with human history sterile and lifeless. Comparing numerous extant drawings for *Picturesque America* with the wood engravings shows that the artists added such details as figures, animals, paths, boats, and wagons even more frequently than they dramatized atmospheric effects. This was the rule rather than the exception. Often the additions were legitimate and either were or could have been part of the scene when the artist drew it. Sometimes the artists sketched such details in the margins, suggesting their presence. This is true of a number of drawings by Waud and Woodward, who subsequently incorporated the details in the image. For example, Woodward's pencil and gouache drawing of the Lower Falls of the Genesee at Rochester, New York, included the stick figure of a fisherman in the upper margin (fig. 5.9). On the woodblock, he inserted the fisherman below the falls (fig. 5.10). He also adopted a slightly lower viewpoint that made the falls seem higher, and increased the volume of water and spray. He further enlivened the scene by conventional, but in this case reasonably subtle, details of a crescent moon and clouds tinged by moonlight, as well as that icon of progress, smoke from a factory chimney.

Such additions could transform rather stark, even dull, scenes into more interesting ones. In his image of Cushing's Island in Portland Bay, Maine, for example, Woodward filled in the foreground with rocks, surf, and children clamming and enlivened the distance with numerous sailboats (figs. 5.11, 5.12). Sometimes the changes gave scale to a prominent landscape feature, as in Woodward's image of "Fairy Arch" on Mackinac Island in Lake Huron (fig. 5.13). On the woodblock, he added tourists—one scrambling up to the opening in the rock—and boats to the already vivid rendering of the arch adorned with twisting branches (fig. 5.14). The one extant drawing for a wood engraving by Fenn that has come to light so far shows that he made similar changes and additions on the woodblock. To his drawing from the top of Lookout Mountain, he added numerous hikers enjoying the view, as well as a self-portrait, and enhanced the drama of the composition by stretching the tree trunk to fill the space (figs. 5.15, 5.16).

The fact that the artist could and did add such details was one of the reasons many preferred an artist's rendering of a scene to a photograph—or to an engraving based on a photograph. In addition, with the freedom to manipulate viewpoint, composition, and lighting, artists could transform ordinary scenes into vivid, or at least interesting ones. Thus, although the subjects appearing in *Picturesque America* were sometimes already familiar through periodical illustrations based on photographs, many preferred the artist's interpretations in the book. Comparing two wood engravings from *Frank Leslie's Illustrated Newspaper* with two of Waud's Cincinnati views illuminates several possible reasons.

In *Leslie's* illustration of the new public hospital (May 11, 1872), the building occupies three-quarters of the picture, with the foreground taken up by a low bridge over the Miami Canal, called "the Rhine" in this predominantly German quarter (fig. 5.17). The picture doubtless presents an accurate view of the large building, but is dull and heavy in its strong horizontality. Waud chose a completely different, low viewpoint, near the canal, and included only the front portion of the building (fig. 5.18). From this angle, with considerable foreshortening, the bridge looks curved, older, and appropriately picturesque, and the building's height and mansard roof and towers—so fashionable at the time—are emphasized. With changes on the woodblock, the illustration printed in *Picturesque America*, significantly titled "The Rhine" rather than "the Cincinnati Hospital," includes more details—boats, carriages, people, and clouds (fig. 5.19). The result is a pleasingly varied depiction of the lively quarter—with the different elements more balanced than in the *Leslie's* view.

Comparing *Leslie's* engraved photograph of Cincinnati's Tyler-Davidson Fountain, which had been erected at great expense by one of the city's millionaires and was considered "one of the most beautiful fountains in the world" (II, 165), with Waud's illustration reveals further advantages of the artist's freedom of choice. Whereas the camera's foreshortening resulted in a jumbled composition (fig. 5.20), Waud highlighted the main subject by depicting it at night and by making the nearby buildings fade into the background (fig. 5.21). Thus, he created a clearer, more focused compo-

5.17 "Ohio. The Cincinnati Public Hospital. From a Photograph by Winder," *Frank Leslie's Illustrated Newspaper*, May 11, 1872, 133. Wood engraving, 4½" x 9". Courtesy the Library Company of Philadelphia.

5.18 A. R. Waud, *On the Rhine, Cincinnati,* [1872]. Pencil on paper, 8½" x 10¾". Courtesy The Historic New Orleans Collection, accession no. 1977.137.34.18.

5.19 A. R. Waud, "The Rhine," *Picturesque America*, II, 161. Wood engraving, 4¾" x 6¼".

sition that at the same time probably provided more accurate information about the fountain's design and waterplay.

Many, and possibly a majority, of the views in *Picturesque America* depend on such subtle approaches as Waud's to achieve the "spirit, animation, and beauty" the publishers promised. Yet some, particularly works by Fenn, Moran, and Smillie, achieve a heightened drama conveying the artist's emotional response to the scene, and occasionally elicit feelings of excitement, fear, awe, or tranquility. In these works, the artists frequently departed from the conventional approach typical of the picturesque tradition—the frontal, prospect view from a slightly-elevated viewpoint, utilizing Claude Lorrain's formula of a dark foreground with trees framing the main subject in the middle ground. Instead, their scope is less extensive, concentrating on the foreground or middleground, similar to the approach of the painters of the Barbizon school in France (fl. 1830–1870). In addition they show a great range of viewpoints, some dramatically high or low, resulting in extreme verticals or diagonals. Some compositions are characterized by great three-dimensionality and motion. Some depart

5.20 "Ohio. The Fountain Presented to the City of Cincinnati by Messrs. Davidson & Probasco.—From a Photograph by Winder," *Frank Leslie's Illustrated Newspaper*, May 11, 1872, 133. Wood engraving, 8¾" x 6¾". Courtesy the Library Company of Philadelphia.

5.21 A. R. Waud, "The Tyler-Davidson Fountain," *Picturesque America*, II, 163.
Wood engraving by John Filmer, 6⅛" x 5⁷⁄₁₆".

from a dark foreground, while others dispense with framing elements altogether.

In this shift toward a more dramatic and expressive style, the *Picturesque America* artists could draw upon many models and precedents, including recent wood engravings, especially British and European, and photographs and paintings. In the 1850s and 1860s, rekindled interest in the medium of wood engraving in Britain led artists and engravers to try new approaches. Their experiments were facilitated by the technical advance of electrotyping, which allowed minute lines to stand up to long press runs. Skilled engravers translated the works of popular artists like George John Pinwell, Frederick Walker, Arthur Boyd Houghton, John Gilbert, Gustav Doré, and Myles Birket Foster into wood engravings that in fineness of detail were comparable to those on steel.[18] Yet they were often very different from steel engravings in the greater use of white space and bold contrasts and in the use of line—either sparsely to define form or intricately to represent a rich diversity of texture. French wood engravings in such publications as *Magasin Pittoresque* and *La Vie à la Campagne* were also noted for their emphasis on texture. Such differences allowed for more self-expression and thus appealed to both artists and the public. Some of these artists and their works were well known in the United States and served as models for the *Picturesque America* artists.

This was especially true of the works of Birket Foster, perhaps the most admired landscape illustrator of the time. Fenn had become familiar with Foster's works as well as the developments in wood engraving during his apprenticeship in the Dalziel brothers' wood engraving firm. Foster was a "constant visitor" at their London offices, where most of his works reproduced on wood were engraved. Fenn almost certainly schooled himself in landscape drawing by copying Foster's illustrations, for the Dalziels urged their apprentices who aspired to draw on wood to copy the landscapes of Foster and the figures of John Gilbert "as the best models for style and manner."[19] Even after resettling in the United States in the late 1850s, Fenn probably kept up with his "teacher's" current work. He was not alone in looking to Foster: Edward Austin Abbey said that when he began his career in New York in the early 1870s, an illustrator's reference library included "as many as he could afford of the gift books illustrated by Birket Foster."[20] The Appleton firm was well aware of Foster's appeal and, in 1869, widely advertised that illustrations by him appeared in their gift book of poetry, *Wood-Side and Sea-Side.*[21]

It was, however, a spectacularly successful earlier work, *Birket Foster's Pictures of English Landscapes*, that Fenn looked to for models in several instances as he created images for *Picturesque America*. Published for Christmas giving in 1862 by Routledge, Warne, and Routledge, the book contained richly detailed and varied images that celebrated the labor of field and cottage and made common, everyday scenes along path and brook appealing.[22] Thus in subject matter, as well as in the close-up, intimate point of view, the book differed from traditional picturesque views of scenic and historic landmarks. Perhaps its success, like that of Fenn's *Snow-Bound* illustrations, was largely due to nostalgia, for the English countryside had been drastically altered by the enclosure of formerly open lands, and more than half the population was long since employed in industry.[23]

Comparison of these works with some of Fenn's views for *Picturesque America* strongly suggests that Fenn was so familiar with Foster's compositions that they influenced the scenes he selected and the details he included. Two images in particular seem to have served Fenn as examples of wood engraving's capacity to capture textures, as well as of the appeal of humble backyard scenes and natural "bits" of landscape glimpsed en route. Although the particulars are entirely different, Foster's "At the Cottage Door" probably suggested to Fenn the rich possibilities of line and texture in the St. Augustine backyard he depicted in "Scene in St. Augustine.—The Date Palm" (figs. 5.22, 5.23). Similarly, in creating a composition dominated by an arching tree along the French Broad, Fenn clearly had in mind Foster's "At the Brookside" (figs. 5.24, 5.25). Although the North Carolina scene includes a more impressive rocky river, the use of trees and vines as well as foreground rabbits and birds clearly indicates borrowing. Even more striking is the foxglove plant in the foreground, reproduced by Fenn in an almost exact mirror image of Foster's, even though the plant was not native to the United States. One important difference, however, is that Fenn has given more emphasis to diagonal elements, an approach he often used to animate his compositions.

Similarly, Fenn adapted Foster's grouping of two horses drinking from a brook, led by the rider of the white horse, for the foreground of "The White Mountains, from the Conway Meadows"[24] (figs. 5.26, 5.27). Taking care to make the man's clothes conform to those worn by American farmers at the time, Fenn must have assumed that such a group could be found as readily in New England as in the English countryside.

5.22 Birket Foster, "At the Cottage Door," *Birket Foster's Pictures of English Landscape* (1863), no. 19. Wood engraving by the Brothers Dalziel, 7" x 5⅜".

5.23 Harry Fenn, "Scene in St. Augustine.—The Date Palm," *Picturesque America*, I, 189. Wood engraving by Harley, 8¹⁵⁄₁₆" x 6⁵⁄₁₆".

5.24 Birket Foster, "At the Brookside," *Birket Foster's Pictures of English Landscape* (1863), no. 20. Wood engraving by the Brothers Dalziel, 7" x 5⅜".

5.25 Harry Fenn, "The French Broad," *Picturesque America*, I, 133. Wood engraving by F. W. Quartley, 8¹³⁄₁₆" x 6⅜".

5.26 Birket Foster, "The Watering Place," *Birket Foster's Pictures of English Landscape* (1863), no. 13. Wood engraving by the Brothers Dalziel, 7" x 5⅜".

5.27 Harry Fenn, "The White Mountains, from the Conway Meadows," *Picturesque America*, I, 150. Wood engraving by Harley, 6⅜" x 6⅝₁₆".

The dramatic models provided by photography in this period included the radically new type of image seen through the stereoscope. The illusion of depth achieved by this popular device impressed the general public and inspired some artists to try for greater three-dimensionality.[25] Photographers, landscape painters, and illustrators all used similar compositional devices, such as placing a fallen log diagonally in the foreground to increase the illusion of depth.[26] Fenn's use of such devices, as well as his penchant for steep verticals and narrow passages, may have been influenced by photography.[27]

The *Picturesque America* artists were probably also influenced by celebrated contemporary paintings from striking viewpoints, such as Church's *Niagara*. For example, Smillie's Yosemite Valley view from the "Foot of Sentinel Falls" (I, 479) recalls the unusual viewpoint of Bierstadt's monumental work of a few years earlier, *The Domes of Yosemite* (1867). Some views also show similarities to paintings of expansive coastal scenes by John F. Kensett and Martin Johnson Heade that lack compositional elements framing the view on either side (see, for example, several of Fenn's "Lake George and Lake Champlain" views).

Fenn was especially apt to try fresh, dramatic approaches when charged with depicting famous places that had already been painted and engraved ad infinitum, as in his close-up rendering of the top of Natural Bridge. His only hope for arousing viewers' interest in other such familiar spots as the Catskills, the Palisades, Niagara Falls, and the White Mountains was to show them in ways that enabled viewers to "see" with fresh eyes. Comparing several of Fenn's views of famous tourist attractions with earlier images will demonstrate how he could move beyond the tradition in which he worked to bold and innovative approaches. The medium, the relief wood engraving that could be combined with type on the page, facilitated experimentation by freeing the artists from the confining rectangle of the easel or full-page format.

In depicting the Catskill region—one of the earliest, most accessible goals of New Yorkers in search of the picturesque—Fenn followed the lead of William Henry Bartlett in *American Scenery* and many other painters in picturing the famous "Mountain House" hotel, which had provided comfortable accommodations since the 1820s. Both artists drew the hotel from afar, yet Fenn's view is not nearly so distant as Bartlett's. In Bartlett's prospect view, which is framed on both sides by trees, the hotel is so effectively distanced by the intervening foreground, complete with prop-like figures and deer, that it seems lost in a vast wilderness, an incongruous element in the wild scene (fig. 5.28). The same vantage point was used by other artists, such as Thomas Cole in the 1840s and Jasper Cropsey in 1855.[28] In contrast, Fenn's rendering from a closer rock outcropping gives more emphasis to the building and its dramatic setting, suggesting that the hotel is a vacation spot offering comfort as well as adventure (fig. 5.29). The repeating steep diagonals stress the mountains' abrupt rise from the valley like a bastion or wall, as is described in the first paragraph. The stepped format makes for a completely different look from the more usual rectangle, with the indistinct edge of the vignette enabling the viewer to "enter" the scene.

Several of Fenn's images of the familiar Palisades of the Hudson also show his attempt to open viewers' eyes. The usual frontal view showed the cliffs rising from the river, such as that included in *The Hudson River Portfolio* (1825), whereas the drama of Fenn's viewpoints is obvious.[29] "The Palisades" looks down at the river from the top of the almost perpendicular rock formation (fig. 5.30). The dizzying view of tiny boats almost directly below animates the composition, as do the silhouetted trees and the horizontal rocks jutting across the verticals. Fenn has further heightened interest by reversing the conventional formula for the use of light: the foreground is the lightest part of the engraving, set off against the dark trees and rock formations. The irregular format of the lower right draws the viewer into the landscape, for the white of the page leads without impediment to the inviting platform of the flat rock. Another dramatic view of the Palisades by Fenn, this time from below, stresses the picturesque activity of fishermen, as well as the cliff looming above them (II, 22).

Like the views of the Natural Bridge, the Catskills, and the Palisades, many of Fenn's images of Niagara Falls, Trenton Falls, and the White Mountains offered the public a new look at familiar sights. The Appleton firm stressed Fenn's "faculty of seizing upon unconventional points of view" and imbuing his drawings with spirit in promoting his next project, *Picturesque Europe*.[30]

Occasionally the *Picturesque America* artists were able to fashion images that moved beyond "animation" to impart feelings of awe or serenity in the face of nature's power or beauty. To reveal "creation" in their works required manipulation of light effects in a much more subtle way than simply inserting a rainbow. Compared with painters working in oil on

5.28 W. H. Bartlett, "The Two Lakes and the Mountain House on the Catskills," in
N. P. Willis, *American Scenery* (1840), vol. 1, opposite 105. Steel engraving by J. C.
Bentley, 4¾" x 7¼".

large canvases, they were at a considerable disadvantage when they
attempted to represent the drama of the sky without color on relatively
small pages.

The very nature of the different media also made it more difficult for
the *Picturesque America* artists to achieve images that could evoke wonder,
much less awe. Compared to oils for exhibition—one-of-a-kind objects
that required a special trip to view, most likely with some reverence—the
Picturesque America prints were ubiquitous and familiar, comfortable additions to the family circle that could be handled and looked at time after
time. This made them accessible and pleasing to many, and well suited to
represent the more intimate picturesque, but it also meant they were less
likely to evoke the feelings associated with the sublime.

Despite these disadvantages, some of the *Picturesque America* artists
managed to create sublime images. Perhaps the best example is Smillie's
"Under Trinity Rock, Saguenay," which the artist visited on a tour up the
St. Lawrence River to the Saguenay (fig. 5.31). The storm clouds hovering

THE CATSKILLS.

WITH ILLUSTRATIONS BY HARRY FENN.

The Mountain House.

ABOUT one hundred and forty miles from the sea, on the western bank of the Hudson, the chain of mountains which, under various names, stretches from the banks of the St. Lawrence to Georgia and Tennessee, throws out a broken link toward the east. Clustering closely together, these isolated mountains, to which the early Dutch settlers gave the name of "Catskills," approach within eight miles of the river, and, like an advanced bastion of the great rocky wall, command the valley for a considerable distance, and form one of the most striking features in the landscape. On the western side, they

5.29 Harry Fenn, "The Mountain House," *Picturesque America*, II, 116. Wood engraving by F. W. Quartley, 7½" x 6⅛"; page, 12⅝" x 9½".

The Palisades.

lower shore, and its terraced road on the steep hill - side behind. From this road we again look out on the long reaches of broad and open river; and the wilder and grander aspects to which we have grown accustomed disappear. Yet the quieter scene is very beautiful; and, looking southward from the high terrace, a pleasant country meets the view, where along the river-banks are the little country-places that make homes for crowded-out New-Yorkers.

5.30 Harry Fenn, "The Palisades," *Picturesque America*, II, 20. Wood engraving by F. W. Quartley, 8⅞" x 6¼".

5.31 James D. Smillie, "Under Trinity Rock, Saguenay," *Picturesque America*, II, 387.
Wood engraving, 7¹⁵⁄₁₆" x 6⅛".

around the top of the "face of fractured granite" increased the majesty of the huge rock rising some eighteen hundred feet above the ship, which was dwarfed at the base. Smillie skillfully manipulated highlights and shadows to create an image of the insignificance of human activity in the face of nature's power.[31]

Two examples of images by Fenn that achieve a sense of the infinity of creation utilized fog to enhance distance: his steel engraving of "The Catskills, Sunrise from South Mountain" (fig. 5.32) and the wood engraving "Glimpse of Lake Champlain, from Summit" (II, 281). In several other wood engravings, he attempted, with less success, to use dramatic storms to evoke awe or fear—for example, "Looking toward Smuggler's Notch from the Nose" (II, 286), "Gate of Crawford Notch" (I, 156), and "Sinking Run above Tyrone" (II, 144).

Smillie's "Entrance to Thousand Islands," depicting a sunrise reflected in calm water, evokes feelings of harmony and contentment—the sense of serenity that Ruskin called "the still small voice."[32] This serene type of sublime view across still water has certain similarites to the "Luminist" works of Fitz Hugh Lane, John F. Kensett, and others.[33] Comparing this wood engraving with a large oil by Asher B. Durand of a similar subject highlights the differences between the two media and the skills involved in producing effective wood engravings. Durand's *Early Morning at Cold Spring* (1850) shows a solitary figure standing near a group of tall, enfolding trees (fig. 5.33). He looks across a still body of water toward a village dominated by a church steeple. A golden glow permeates the entire painting, as the morning light is reflected in the water and from the ground where the man stands. The use of color harmonizes all aspects of the scene and conveys a sense of peace and benevolence.[34]

Smillie's "Entrance to Thousand Islands" achieves a similar mood, although no color is used (fig. 5.34). The solitary figure this time is an artist with sketch pad who gazes across the water at the sun rising over distant islands, one of them crowned by a lighthouse. The sun glows white against the gray tone of the sky and casts a beam of light across the water, depicted by breaks in the parallel lines. The reflected light on the arching trees, branches, rocks, and boat of the foreground helps unify the composition. The higher viewpoint in the engraving heightens the effect of the shaft of sunlight across the water and allows more details to be shown in the somewhat foreshortened foreground.[35] Durand's low viewpoint, on the other hand, contributes to the stability and peacefulness of the scene.

5.32 Harry Fenn, "The Catskills, Sunrise from South Mountain," *Picturesque America*, II, opposite 127. Steel engraving by S. V. Hunt, 8⅜" x 5¾".

5.33 Asher B. Durand, *Early Morning at Cold Spring*, 1850. Oil on canvas, 60" x 48".
Lang Acquisition Fund, The Montclair Art Museum Permanent Collection, Montclair, N.J.

5.34 James D. Smillie, "Entrance to the Thousand Islands," *Picturesque America*, II, 370. Wood engraving by Harley, 7¾" x 6⅛".

The two works are comparable in the care with which foreground rocks and foliage are rendered, although Smillie has included more silhouetted branches in the immediate foreground, adding picturesque detail to the smaller scale work. There is also a striking difference in the abruptness of the foreground in Smillie's view: without an intervening slip of land, the shaft of light on the water seems to reach the viewer. The indistinct lower edge, lacking the ruled line defining the other edges, enhances this effect. Thus the wood engraving has a more accessible quality than Durand's painting by virtue of its composition, as well as by the great differences in scale and modes of viewing. Smillie's achievement, in face of the severe limitations of the medium, is impressive.

The medium of wood engraving also offered the artist some distinct advantages, specifically the possibilities for innovative formats. The fact that the raised metal type could be distributed around the relief woodblock however the artist chose allowed the artist to select viewpoints that resulted in irregular shapes. Just as Fenn took advantage of this to create fresh images of familiar landmarks, he and other *Picturesque America* artists arranged juxtapositions that increased the illusion of three-dimensionality in their works. For example, when Waud drew "Fourth Street, Cincinnati," he included the outline of a building on the right, which provided a space for a narrow column of type (fig. 5.35). On the page in the book, this odd white building filled with type moves toward the viewer, whereas the street, lively with progressively smaller carriages and pedestrians, recedes dramatically (fig. 5.36). In other instances, the artists chose highly irregular shapes for extreme vertical or diagonal features (for example, II, 558; II, 419, 431). On the other hand, they frequently used the more conventional circle broken at the bottom, a format popular in gift books and magazines. This shape could heighten the feeling of serenity, as in Fenn's pastoral scene in the Conway Meadows (fig. 5.27). But when Woodward broke the circle with a pier jutting directly toward the viewer in "Owl's Head Landing" at Lake Memphremagog, Vermont (fig. 5.37), he created a strikingly three-dimensional effect and gave this familiar shape a whole new look. The considerable departure from his earlier drawing indicates his clear intention to heighten the drama of the image on the page (fig. 5.38).[36]

Occasionally the artists experimented with other devices to add variety, such as etching-like decorative borders—sometimes in the form of foliage bursting out of the composition (for example, II, 437, and fig. 6.4). This approach would appear more frequently in page designs in the next decade. Another variation was to fill the page with a number of small images. Such composites were an appropriate way to express the variety that was a hallmark of the picturesque and appeared frequently in illustrated newspapers and on decorative bindings. They are especially numerous in volume II of *Picturesque America.* Only one sketch showing a composite layout has been found—a group of St. Louis scenes by Waud—and it is not clear to what extent the artists were responsible for choosing this format.[37] Smillie's diary indicates that Bunce specifically requested a "full page combination of views about Montreal."[38] In several instances, the composites have a trompe d'oeil effect, depicting a group of sketches tacked on a board. This emphasized that the drawings were two-dimensional objects—art on paper—but at the same time created a three-dimensonal effect, for the drawings look as if they could be taken off the page (I, 251, and II, 410, 443).

Using Photographs to Depict the West

Despite *Picturesque America*'s emphasis on the superiority of artists' interpretations to photographs, Bunce did make use of photographs in a number of instances. His heaviest use of photography was to provide Western subject matter for his artists. For the more established tourist attractions of the Yosemite Valley, the Columbia River, and the coast of California, he had been able to obtain material from James D. Smillie and R. Swain Gifford, artists who visited the regions prior to the *Picturesque America* project. To justify its claim of comprehensiveness, however, *Picturesque America* needed to include the much-talked-about regions that were just being systematically explored and surveyed—the Yellowstone Valley, the Rocky Mountains, and the Grand Canyon. But in the early 1870s, these regions were still relatively inaccessible, being far from the one transcontinental railroad route and lacking tourist facilities. Furthermore, their exploration could involve real danger. For example, one member of the 1870 Yellowstone expedition became lost, and a promising young writer, Frederick Wadsworth Loring, hired by *Appletons' Journal* to accompany Lt. George M. Wheeler's 1871 expedition in what is now Arizona, was killed by Apaches—a shock that surely must have impressed Bunce with the need for caution.[39]

5.35 A. R. Waud, *Fourth St. Looking East from the Carlisle Building* [Cincinnati], [1872]. Pencil on paper, 14¼" x 11¹⁄₁₆". Courtesy The Historic New Orleans Collection, accession no. 1977.137.34.11.

Fourth Street, Cincinnati.

the bloodiest Indian battle of the river-valley, when, in 1774, one thousand Americans were attacked by the flower of the Western tribes under the chieftain Cornstalk. The battle raged all day, but the Indians were finally overpowered, and retreated to their towns on the Chillicothe plains.

Kentucky, which comes up to the Ohio at the mouth of the big Sandy River, is one of the most beautiful States in the country. It is wild without being rugged, luxuriant but not closely cultivated; once seen, its rolling meadows are never forgotten. It is like some beautiful wild creature which you cannot entirely tame, in spite of its gentleness.

Stretching back from the river are vast parks; there is no underbrush, few fences,

5.36 A. R. Waud, "Fourth Street, Cincinnati," *Picturesque America*, II, 160. Wood engraving by [Philip] Meeder and [F. Y.] Chubb, 7½" x 6⅜"; page, 12⅜" x 9½".

LAKE MEMPHREMAGOG

WITH ILLUSTRATIONS BY J. DOUGLAS WOODWARD.

Owl's Head Landing.

THE journey northward may be made in thirty-six hours, or it may be extended
through several weeks. The route from the metropolis divides the Connecticut
Valley, that fair reach of glistening stream and forest dell leading beyond into mountain
mysteries. Nature wears her bridal robes, softly colored, fragrant, and bright—

5.37 J. D. Woodward, "Owl's Head Landing," *Picturesque America*, II, 451. Wood
engraving by F. W. Quartley, 7" x 6½"; page, 12⅜" x 9½".

5.38 J. D. Woodward, *Owl's Head Landing, Lake Memphremagog*, Sept. 18, 1872. Pencil and white on paper, 7" x 10". Courtesy the Diocese of Virginia.

Thus, for the Yellowstone region and the Colorado Rockies, rather than following his usual practice of commissioning an artist to make on-the-spot drawings, Bunce obtained photographs for the artist's use from the latest government-sponsored surveys. This avoided possible danger and also saved time and expense. As a result, *Picturesque America*'s timely depictions of these areas were among the earliest distributed to a mass audience, and thus helped to incorporate these regions into the national self-image.

By 1872, just as the *Picturesque America* project got underway, the Yellowstone region was well on its way to becoming a primary symbol of the nation's scenic richness and uniqueness. The *Journal*'s rival, *Scribner's Monthly*, had been closely associated with publicizing it, in cooperation with the U. S. Geologist in charge of explorations, Ferdinand V. Hayden (1829-87), Montana boosters, and the financial agents for the Northern Pacific Railroad, Jay Cooke and Company.[40] The latter fervently hoped the persistent tales of Yellowstone's wonders would prove true and that it would become a tourist attraction equal to Niagara, once their railroad reached its northern edge (the current terminus was Bismarck in Dakota Territory). This hope led Cooke and his colleagues to promote both exploration of the region and publicity about what was found. As a result, between 1870 and 1872 the Yellowstone Valley—that mystifying region rumored to be full of strange phenomena—was sufficiently documented and promoted to become the first national park, established by Congress in late February 1872 "for the benefit and enjoyment of the people."

Visual materials, including the earliest wood engravings, photographs, and paintings, were crucial in informing the public and government officials about this special region. The first widely circulated images appeared in *Scribner's Monthly* in May and June 1871. They accompanied "The Wonders of the Yellowstone" by Nathaniel Pitt Langford, a leading citizen of Montana Territory with ties to the Northern Pacific, who participated in the Doane-Washburn expedition, the first organized reconnaissance of the region in the summer of 1870. The wood engravings were prepared by *Scribner's* chief landscape illustrator, Thomas Moran, from rough sketches by two members of the party.[41] Although exaggerated and inaccurate in a number of instances, Moran's images stirred the interest of the public as well as Congress. The assignment also marked a turning point in Moran's career, convincing him that the region offered subjects of unprecedented interest for his art. He went there himself the summer of 1871, as a guest of the Hayden survey, with loans from *Scribner's Monthly* and the Northern Pacific sponsors. The photographs from the 1871 expedition by the survey photographer, William H. Jackson (1843-1942), as well as Moran's watercolors and second set of wood engravings—this time based on personal observation and appearing with Hayden's article in the February 1872 *Scribner's Monthly*—were instrumental in persuading members of Congress to establish the park.

Bunce must have been keenly aware of these developments, including the excitement generated by the *Scribner's* articles. Naturally he wanted to feature the Yellowstone region in *Appletons' Journal* as well, not only to appeal to public interest and meet *Scribner's* competition, but also to promote Western tourism. At about the same time the park bill was being considered, Bunce obtained some of Jackson's photographs for Harry Fenn to use in making illustrations. The May 11, 1872, *Appletons' Journal* included two full-page wood engravings after Fenn, "The Giant Geyser" and "Yellowstone Falls," and a brief text called "Scenes in the Yellowstone

Valley." Since Bunce's attempt to obtain an article from Hayden had been unsuccessful, he based this text primarily on the report of Lt. John W. Barlow, the leader of a rival military reconnaissance team that had also explored the Yellowstone region in the summer of 1871.[42]

Yet even before this article appeared, Bunce was planning fuller Yellowstone coverage in his new project, *Picturesque America.* Responding to Hayden, who was miffed that the *Journal* article overlooked his survey's role in the establishment of the new national park, Bunce wrote on May 2 that complete coverage, with ample credit to Hayden's work, would appear in *Picturesque America.* He also urged Hayden to use the *Journal* as "the medium" for gaining public recognition.[43] Having ruffled Hayden once, Bunce agreed, albeit reluctantly, to provide electrotypes of Fenn's illustrations for use in Hayden's report—in return for the use of the photographs.[44] This cooperative exchange set the pattern for several more in the following year, as Bunce sought to provide *Picturesque America*'s subscribers with accurate and timely images of Western scenery.

For *Picturesque America,* Bunce repeatedly urged Hayden to prepare an article on the Yellowstone region. In the end, however, Bunce composed the article himself, relying heavily on quotations from Hayden's report of the 1871 explorations. He was careful to point out at the beginning the nation's debt to Hayden "for an accurate detailed knowledge of the strange features of this remarkable land" and for "the idea of converting the valley into a national park" (I, 294-95). "Our Great National Park" contained the only map in the book, as well as sixteen wood engravings drawn by Fenn using Jackson's photographs, including the two that had appeared in the *Journal.* (A steel engraving of "The Upper Yellowstone Falls" after a watercolor by Moran was prepared later and distributed with part 36.[45]) The section appeared in parts 13 and 14, which, calculating that *Picturesque America*'s twice-monthly publication began in June 1872, would have first appeared in December. This timing may have been planned to spur gift sales for the holiday season, as well as to predate *The Aldine*'s March 1873 coverage of the region, with illustrations by Thomas Moran.[46]

To create an effective wood engraving from a photograph, the artist, in this case Fenn, needed to enhance the image in several ways due to film's shortcomings. In 1872 film was not orthochromatic; that is, it was unable to capture the variety of nature's tonal effects. Greens printed black, and blues were lost entirely. Furthermore, filters that would later enable film

found, from
simple milky turbid-
ness to a stiff mortar.
On the east side of
the Yellowstone, close to
the margin of the river
are a few turbid and mud springs,

5.39 Harry Fenn, "Hot Springs," *Picturesque America*, I, 310. Wood engraving by [Philip] Meeder and [F. Y.] Chubb, 5" x 6¼".

to record clouds had not yet been produced, so skies were a monotonous gray. Backgrounds were often lost in overexposure.[47] Comparing one of Fenn's Yellowstone views of Mammoth Hot Springs (fig. 5.39) with Jackson's photograph (fig. 5.40) shows some of the ways Fenn altered the original to achieve the dramatic type of image he favored.

In his rendering Fenn sharply increased the steepness of the terraces and made other changes to enhance the illusion of depth. Whereas in the photograph it is difficult to gauge how far back the terraces extend and how far away the background mountain is, Fenn added six receding figures to help measure the hot springs formation. He also introduced more steam or haze, which helps define the space. By making the mountain in the background lighter and the forest separating it from the terraces more prominent, he has accentuated the distance between them. Not having been there himself, working only from the photograph, Fenn overcompensated

5.40 W. H. Jackson, *Gardiners River Hot Springs*, ca. 1872, photograph. National Museum of American Art, Smithsonian Institution, Transfer from S.I., NMAA/NPG Library.

for the flatness of the photograph and created a somewhat exaggerated, inaccurate view.[48]

Despite Thomas Moran's conspicuous association with the Yellowstone region, it is not surprising that Bunce relied on Fenn in the spring of 1872. At this point, before the purchase of his oil painting *The Grand Canon of the Yellowstone* by Congress, Moran was still known primarily as *Scribner's* landscape illustrator, just as Fenn was known as the illustrator of the "Picturesque America" series in *Appletons' Journal*. Their status was more or less equal. Because photographs were available and Fenn was adept at reworking them, Bunce chose to stay with his most successful landscape interpreter.

A few months later the situation had changed. Moran quickly gained national prominence in June when Congress paid $10,000 for his painting, which was to hang in the Senate lobby. Bunce soon commissioned

him to illustrate "The Plains and the Sierras," dealing with the scenery
along the transcontinental railroad—the fast, new tourist route west.
Thomas and Mary Nimmo Moran set off in August 1872 on a rather hurried journey to San Francisco. The next year Bunce commissioned illustrations from Moran of the Colorado Rockies and the canyons of the
Colorado River. Thus Moran illustrated all three sections dealing with the
West in volume II of *Picturesque America.*[49] He was the rising star of Western
landscape art, and Bunce doubtless thought his participation would
enhance the sales and prestige of the publication.

For each of the sections he illustrated, Moran relied on photographs,
but to varying degrees. Photographs of the Rocky Mountains substituted
for visits to the sites; for the scenery along the railroad and that of the
canyons of the Colorado, they supplemented his own observations and
sketches. We will look at these sections in the order of Moran's travels or,
in the the case of the Rocky Mountains, in the light of the photographs he
obtained.

Although Moran apparently made some sketches on the 1872 railroad
journey, in preparing the wood engravings he relied heavily on photographs by A. J. Russell, many of which had been included in Hayden's
1870 publication *Sun Pictures of Rocky Mountain Scenery.*[50] He may have
seen Jackson's photographs of the railroad route as well. Thus Moran's
subjects were largely determined by the photographers who preceded
him, who in turn frequently chose rock formations and canyons that were
already landmarks on the Western journey.

In the transition from photograph to design for wood engraving,
Moran used approaches similar to Fenn's, although the fact that he had
seen the actual sites probably resulted in somewhat more accurate representations. Moran introduced picturesque details of rocks and trees in
the foreground and more often than Fenn dramatized the skies with
storms or moonlight. For example, his depiction of "Monument Rock,
Echo Cañon" (fig. 5.41) considerably doctors Russell's starkly impressive
photograph (fig. 5.42). He highlights the rock formation against a night
sky with a full moon and adds tiny figures on horseback for scale and
human interest. The rather incomprehensible light on the face of the
rock defines its shape, and foreground details add interest.[51]

Moran worked up his drawings for "The Plains and the Sierras" in early
1873, and the exceptionally long section was included in parts 31, 32, and
33, originally issued in September and October 1873. As early as January

of 1873, the highly organized Bunce had asked Hayden for some of Jackson's photographs from the survey of the Colorado mountains planned for that summer. And he had enlisted Moran's services to prepare the illustrations for "The Rocky Mountains."[52]

Before the Rocky Mountain photographs were available, however, Bunce engaged Moran to prepare illustrations of the canyons of the Colorado River—just as Maj. John Wesley Powell's explorations were heightening interest in a region long designated on maps as "unexplored." Powell's expeditions had begun under private sponsorship in 1867, but by the summers of 1871 and 1872 were government supported. Powell's first published report appeared in 1872. Aware of the attention and support Moran's artworks had generated for the surveys of the Yellowstone by Hayden, necessarily a rival for government funds, Powell had hoped to include Moran in his party in 1872. Moran declined, however, because of heavy commitments, including the Appleton commission. But in the summer of 1873 Moran had an "intense desire to see the Grand Cañon," both because he had been offered several commissions to illustrate it—for *The Aldine* and *Scribner's Monthly* as well as *Picturesque America*—and because it promised to be a spectacular subject for large oil paintings. When Powell, who could provide safe passage if anyone could, offered to escort him to the canyon region in the summer of 1873, Moran agreed with enthusiasm.[53] His travelling companion was J. E. Colburn, a young *New York Times* reporter who also had several commissions for articles about the region. He wrote "The Cañons of the Colorado" for *Picturesque America*, as well as articles for his own newspaper and *The Colorado Tourist*, a periodical sponsored by a coalition of railroad companies.[54]

Although Moran made a number of sketches on this trip, in completing his six illustrations for *Picturesque America* the following winter he relied heavily on photographs from Powell's earlier expeditions—most of which were made by John K. "Jack" Hillers (1843-1925), who accompanied Moran and Colburn on much of their trip.[55] Moran's rendering of "Marble Cañon" (II, 507) was probably based on a photograph by Hillers,[56] and Colburn stated that the view of "Kanab Cañon" (II, 511) was also.

In September of 1873, Bunce took further steps to obtain some of Jackson's recent photographs of Colorado from Hayden's summer survey. Although Denver and the new city of Colorado Springs had been accessible by railroad from Cheyenne since 1870 and were quickly developing as

5.41 Thomas Moran, "Monument Rock, Echo Cañon," *Picturesque America*, II, 181. Wood engraving by F. W. Quartley, 8⅞" x 6³⁄₁₆".

5.42 A. J. Russell, *Monument Rock, Mouth of Echo Cañon* (Utah), 1867/68, photograph. Russell, A. J., 10, U.S. Geological Survey Photographic Library, Denver, Colo.

tourist centers—Bunce himself had visited Colorado that summer—much of the vast mountainous area rising abruptly from the plains west of these cities was still difficult to traverse and lacked facilities for travellers.[57] Rather than sending an artist to obtain views of the high mountain regions, Bunce took the more expedient and economical course of relying on the survey's photographs. His September 23 letter to Hayden—which rather puzzlingly does not refer to their correspondence about photographs of Colorado earlier in the year—requested the use of fifteen or sixteen of Jackson's photographs for *Picturesque America*.[58] Notice of agreement came quickly from Jackson, but several months passed before the photographs were actually in hand. With regard to the text, in March 1874 a clearly exasperated Bunce asked Hayden whether or not he would comply with his earlier agreement to write it.[59] Bunce eventually turned to a member of Hayden's Colorado survey party, W. H. Rideing, a young reporter for the *New York Times*.

Among the Jackson prints Bunce was able to supply Moran in early 1874 was one of the Mountain of the Holy Cross. This most celebrated photograph from the expedition confirmed the truth of persistent tales that the Rockies hid a peak etched with a cross of snow—a fact that many took as evidence of God's particular blessing on the nation and its Manifest Destiny to spread Christianity and civilization westward. Moran would undertake his own journey to see this remote mountain the following summer and thereafter complete his famous oil painting that received a medal and much attention at the Centennial Exposition in Philadelphia in 1876, *The Mountain of the Holy Cross* (1875). In early 1874, however, he prepared an illustration for *Picturesque America* (fig. 5.43) based solely on Jackson's photographs—one of the mountain itself, in which all the terrain is well above timberline, and another of a picturesque waterfall, cascading through conifers, photographed by Jackson on the difficult climb up to the point where the cross of snow could be seen.[60] The composition of this wood engraving foreshadowed that of Moran's 1875 painting, although the mountain is considerably more distant in the later work. In both, Moran departs from the actual topography to create a composite view different from what can actually be seen from any one spot. As Moran scholars have pointed out, manipulation of this sort was consistent with his concept of artistic truth, which involved representing the scene in such a way that it conveyed the artist's emotional response. Although similar to the goal of the other *Picturesque America* artists to combine fidelity with poetry, Moran's

5.43 Thomas Moran, "Mountain of the Holy Cross," *Picturesque America*, II, 501. Wood engraving by J. Augustus Bogert, 8¹⁵⁄₁₆" x 6¼".

concept seems to move a step further from literal accuracy. His "Mountain of the Holy Cross" emphasized the height and otherworldly nature of the peak. With its chaotic jumble of trees and rocks in the foreground, separated by turbulent clouds from the distant peak, the image is a prime example of a romantic landscape, fraught with meaning and conveying a sense of awe in the face of divine power and benevolence.[61] First distributed with part 45 of *Picturesque America*, in April 1874, it was one of the earliest depictions to reach a wide audience and contributed to shaping the public's image of this newly discovered scenic treasure. Moran's wood engraving was much more dramatic than the image included in Hayden's report—a dark-toned engraving after William Henry Holmes.

Comparing several of Moran's other images of the Rocky Mountains with the Jackson photographs he most likely used shows that the artist frequently added picturesque foreground details and created compositions from two photographs.[62] Similar to the arrangement with the Yellowstone illustrations, in exchange for the use of Jackson's photographs, Bunce allowed Hayden to reproduce some of Moran's Colorado wood engravings in his official report.[63] In this way, these works reached more viewers, shaping many Americans' images of the Rocky Mountains.

One additional use of photography for Western images should also be mentioned, producing a steel engraving. Fenn's image of Mirror Lake in Yosemite Valley clearly seems derived from an 1872 photograph by Eadweard J. Muybridge (1830–1904), except for Fenn's addition of a derby-hatted hunter in a canoe firing at a deer, reflecting the current rage for hunting and fishing. The tonal technique of the steel engraving reproduced the photograph's effects remarkably well.[64]

Bunce may have occasionally sanctioned or agreed to the use of photographs as the basis for drawings of Eastern localities as well. This seems to have been the case with three of Fenn's works for the section "On the Savannah," which are strikingly similar to photographs by George N. Barnard (1819–1902), General Sherman's photographer.[65] Perhaps Fenn had not actually visited Savannah or had had too little time there to make on-the-spot drawings. Nevertheless, Bunce wanted to publish images of this historic Southern city in the "Picturesque America" series in *Appletons' Journal* and, so, apparently allowed Fenn to resort to photographs.

These various uses of photographs were the exception rather than the rule, however, in producing the illustrations for *Picturesque America*. In most cases the travelling artist recorded the scene on the spot and redrew it on the woodblock, attempting to achieve both fidelity to nature and poetic interpretation. The works were then prepared for mass distribution.

Producing the Prints—From Drawing to Wood or Steel Engraving

The return of an artist with a full portfolio—the raw material for an armchair tour of a region—generated great excitement at the Appleton firm. If Gibson's experience may be taken as typical, Bunce eagerly looked through the drawings, "gave vent to his admiration with loud praise," and called "old and young" Appleton and other staff members to see them. Bunce would then use his highly selective critical eye to choose the scenes to include in the book. Although Gibson met with greater success, Bunce, by his own reckoning, often rejected two thirds of the drawings brought to him "on account of the subjects not being interesting, the artists sketching whatever they come across that looks 'pretty' and not hunting for the most interesting alone."[66]

After the winnowing process, the artist, with the clear exception of Waud, redrew the image in reverse on the whitened woodblock. He used India ink, sepia, or pencil, sometimes with wash, making whatever additions or changes he deemed desirable—probably with suggestions from Bunce and sometimes Fenn as well.[67] When finished, each artist typically signed the block with his last name, initials, or a distinctive monogram (see appendix A.) Although photography came to be used widely in the mid-1870s as a quick means of transferring drawings to the block, this technique was definitely not used in the production of *Picturesque America*. This is clear from the numerous changes in proportion and detail between the extant original drawings and the wood engravings, as well as from the documentary evidence of Smillie's diaries and Gibson's letters.[68]

Creating the image on the block was slow, painstaking work. Smillie's diaries show that reworking his designs and preparing the blocks for the "St. Lawrence and the Saguenay" article consumed most of his studio time from August to December 1873. It required good light, but was still hard on the eyes, especially if the artist attempted to lay down intricate lines to guide the wood engraver in creating tonal effects.[69] Because there is little written documentation and the drawings on the blocks were necessarily destroyed in the engraving process, it is difficult to know exactly what techniques the artists used. The well-known wood engraver William J.

5.44 R. Swain Gifford, *The Three Sisters* [1869]. Pencil and wash on paper, 6¼" x 9¼". Private collection.

Linton (1812–97), who emigrated from England in 1866 and engraved numerous blocks for *Picturesque America*, recalled that, although their approaches varied widely according to subject and format, the artists often left the details of shading up to the engraver:

> In landscape subjects the drawings are usually worked in with Indian ink or sepia, and the engraver has to find the lines most appropriate to the same. There are exceptions to this manner of drawings,—as, for instance the *Pine Forest* by Langridge (Vol. II. p. 213), a great part of which might have been drawn in pencil lines and engraved fac-simile; and the same peculiarity occurs in the light edges of vignettes, and in the lighter portions of other cuts,—light trees and grasses especially.[70]

Linton's memory may have been skewed by his passion to defend the engraver's art. In his opinion, the more the artist left to the engraver, the better. Looking at the engravings, however, it seems clear that those artists with training as wood engravers or experience designing for that medium, like Fenn and Moran, were generally more successful than were novices in drawing on the wood in a way that aided the engraver to make an attractive engraving. They were aware of how best to exploit the qualities of the

5.45   R. Swain Gifford, "The Three Sisters," *Picturesque America*, I, 425. Wood
engraving by W. J. Linton, 6⅛" x 9⅟₁₆".

medium. They knew how to represent form through line and shading
and probably took the trouble to lay down fine lines in various configura-
tions to guide the engraver in appropriately representing surfaces and
shadows. Smillie found the task challenging, despite his skill as a steel
engraver, and sought "technical suggestions" from the wood engraver
Harley.[71] Painters in oil or watercolor had even more difficulty. According
to the prominent engraver A. V. S. Anthony, most had trouble producing
effective illustrations for wood engravings, for without color their works
"lose form and light and shade" and are "stale, flat, and muddled."[72]

Such difficulties are apparent in several contributions by R. Swain
Gifford, whose experience was primarily with oil and watercolor painting.
Apparently anticipating preparing black-and-white wood engravings, he
made several grisaille watercolor sketches of scenery in California and
Oregon that probably served as the basis for his renderings on the woodblock for some of his *Picturesque America* illustrations. The simple tonal
effects in shades of black, white, and gray in Gifford's watercolor of the
Oregon mountains called "The Three Sisters" (fig. 5.44) provided the
engraver, W. J. Linton, with little guidance. The resulting indistinct

expanses of gray and white give scant information about the actual terrain (fig. 5.45). Another grisaille watercolor by Gifford, this one of "Castellated Rock" in northern California, similarly lacks detail in the rendering of the rock surface (fig. 5.46). The engraver, J. Filmer, perhaps based on Gifford's drawing on the block, added lines in an effort to define the intricate surface (fig. 5.47). Yet the result is still awkwardly one-dimensional. Thus, depending on their background and experience with wood engraving, the artists varied greatly in the specialized skill of drawing on wood.

The artists were normally paid for each completed drawing on the block. Smillie received $35 for full-page blocks, $32.50 for three-quarters of a page, $25 for a half-page, and $10-20 for smaller images. For a composite of Montreal views, he received $45.[73] The artists also received reimbursement for travel expenses and a travel stipend. This may have varied with the artist's prestige, as Smillie received $250 for a trip of fifteen working days up the St. Lawrence and Saguenay, while Gibson expected $40 a week on his second commissioned trip.[74] Even this was quite respectable pay considering that weekly salaries for newspaper editors at the time ranged from $25 to $60 and reporters generally earned only $20–30 a week.[75] No records have been found of how much other artists or the engravers were paid.[76]

Some have written that the works of the different *Picturesque America* artists are indistinguishable—reinterpreted as they are by engravers and reproduced in black and white—and, too frequently, primarily a monotonous gray.[77] There are, however, some characteristic differences and distinguishing qualities. Fenn's works most often exhibit use of a loose, bold line, strong movement through diagonals, and skill in manipulating tones from black to white. In contrast, Woodward's works display a tighter line, with careful, short pencil strokes. Woodward uses many of the same compositional devices as Fenn but makes a specialty of rendering trees well and using them to determine the shape of his compositions. Perkins's works improve through the course of the publication, but generally use a horizontal arrangement, with a calm, rather static effect. He uses tone more than line, and his figures are poorly drawn (at least as the engravers interpreted them). Waud's works are always competent, but matter-of-fact and less dramatic than Fenn's, using gentler diagonals and more precise lines. The drama of Moran's works is often heightened by turbulent skies similar to Turner's.

The Wood Engravings

After receiving the woodblock complete with design, the wood engraver used specialized tools—burins, tint tools, scoopers, and chisels—to cut away the white areas, leaving the lines to print in relief and interpreting the tonal areas with some combination of lines and stipple. To make the minute parallel lines that represented smooth surfaces, still water, or blue skies, the engraver typically used a mechanical device called a ruling machine.[78] The meticulous work, which required the use of a magnifying glass, took time—at least several days to complete one full-page design for *Picturesque America*. To produce a woodblock surface large enough for such images, it was frequently necessary to join blocks of boxwood together, since the diameter of a single trunk was seldom more than five or six inches. Careful examination of the prints sometimes reveals a break at about the midpoint, which the engraver has not quite concealed (see figs. 4.6 and 6.30, for example).[79] When finished with a block, the engraver, like the artist, usually signed it with last name or initials, sometimes followed by "Sc.," (for *sculpsit*, "he or she engraved"). Most often the convention of artist's name on the left, engraver's on the right was followed, although not as consistently as with steel engravings.

The growing demand for wood engravings in periodicals and books encouraged more and more individuals to learn this exacting skill. The number of wood engravers in the United States grew from around twenty in 1840 to some four hundred in 1870.[80] Their ranks included many natives of England and Scotland who had received excellent training in British firms and sought opportunities in the less crowded American field. A number of German and French engravers also emigrated to the United States. The field increasingly provided employment for women, especially after New York's Cooper Union began to offer classes for women in 1859. Most wood engravers practiced their craft in New York City, the leading publishing center, either as free-lancers or as employees of engraving or publishing firms.[81] The engraving firms clustered in lower Manhattan near City Hall and Printing House Square, as did the publishing firms. From their offices in the light-filled upper lofts along the east side of Broadway between Spruce Street and John Street, the engravers did not have far to go to D. Appleton and Company, at 549–551 Broadway.[82] The engravers formed a close-knit community who knew one another and could recognize each other's work by characteristic uses of the graver—distinctions that were often lost on the untrained observer.[83]

5.46 R. Swain Gifford, *Castellated Rock, California* [1869]. Pencil and wash on paper, 9" x 6¼". Private Collection.

5.47 R. Swain Gifford, "Castellated Rock," *Picturesque America*, I, 416. Wood engraving by John Filmer, 8⅞" x 6⅛".

Firms and individuals tended to specialize in either "fine" work—for small format book and magazine illustrations and the more mechanical representations required for machinery and furniture catalogs—or "coarse" work for the illustrated newspapers. The type of work required for *Picturesque America*, like that for *Appletons' Journal* and competing periodicals of similar size or slightly larger, fell midway between the "fine" and "coarse" work.[84] This was seen as an important advantage by William J. Linton. In his *History of Wood-Engraving in America*, published in 1882, he had high praise for the work in *Picturesque America*, to which he contributed: "The imperial quarto size of the page gave scope to the engraver; and there was no more need either for the weakening refinement of small book-work or for the haste of newspaper requiring. The best landscapes engraved in this country (and nothing of later years in England will equal them) are to be found here."[85]

To make the wood engravings for *Picturesque America*, the Appleton firm hired many of the same craftsmen who had previously worked for *Appletons' Journal.* Some thirty-two different names can be counted on the prints, not all of which are signed. (I have not been able to identify any women among them.) Those that appear most frequently, sometimes last name only, are [Joseph S.?] Harley, F. W. Quartley (English-born, 1808–74), John Filmer (English-born), John Karst (German-born, 1836–1922), Alf. Harral, [James H.?] Richardson, Henry Linton (English-born), and his brother, W. J. Linton. Other well-known engravers, such as J. Augustus Bogert and [?] Annin, contributed a small number of blocks to *Picturesque America.* Sometimes one engraver was responsible for the majority of the illustrations of a particular region; in other cases the works were distributed to several different engravers, with no ascertainable pattern. When a block was produced at an engraving firm, more than one person may have worked on it—with the tasks divided according to the specialites of landscape, figures, and architecture. Others, usually apprentices, were employed to cut away the excess wood. The engravers may have been paid by the hour, as Elbridge Kingsley reported was the common practice.[86]

Many of the wood engravings do achieve the highest standard, equal to that in *The Aldine* or the finest gift books published in the United States or Europe. Yet the skills of the engravers varied, as did those of the artists. The great range of styles and techniques results from the different engravers' preferences as well from the artists' decisions about whether to represent a scene primarily in line or in tone. A drawing characterized by line was appropriately reproduced as a "black line," "reproductive," or "facsimile" engraving, in which the engraver closely followed the lines put down by the artist. This required cutting away the wood on both sides of the lines with two strokes of the burin, leaving raised lines to receive the ink, and gouging out other areas of void or white space. An outstanding example of a primarily black-line engraving is Quartley's rendering of "The Convent-Gate" in St. Augustine, based on a Fenn drawing (fig. 5.48). It demonstrates how closely a well-executed wood engraving can resemble an etching or drawing.

A primarily tonal work, on the other hand, was interpreted by the engraver in the "white-line" technique. In this approach the engraver incised a multitude of fine cuts into the woodblock to represent shading and texture. Since these lines were recessed below the woodblock's surface they did not receive the ink and appeared white on the printed page. Linton, a staunch defender of the art of wood engraving who considered black-line work mere copying, preferred white-line because he thought it allowed and demanded more creativity on the part of the engraver. Artists, concerned that their drawings be accurately reproduced, might well have preferred the black-line style and those engravers most skilled in its execution.

Among the many excellent examples of primarily white-line engraving are James Langridge's "General View of Trenton Falls" based on a Fenn drawing (fig. 5.49) and W. J. Linton's engraving of Marble Cañon after Moran (II, 507). Both of these effectively represent forms by a wide range of tone, and surfaces by a variety of textures. They meet Linton's criteria for good engraving: careful gradation and wide range of black-to-white shading, firm cuts, and "meaningful lines." Too often, however, the primarily white-line engravings are mostly a dull gray, with gradations handled so poorly that the differences in distance are not clear. (For some exceptionally bad examples, see I, 40, 46, and 48; and II, 416.)

The majority of *Picturesque America*'s wood engravings combined these two means of image reproduction, with some exhibiting more of the black-line and others more of the white-line technique. Many of the most attractive ones avoid large areas of gray and utilize the white of the paper to represent light areas in the scene or reflected light. In terms of book design, such engravings are more compatible than darker toned ones with *Picturesque America*'s amply spaced, large type. The lighter touch and more extensive white areas more closely match the weight of the lines of type.

5.48 Harry Fenn, "The Convent-Gate," *Picturesque America*, I, 186. Wood engraving by F. W. Quartley, 4⅜" x 3⅛".

5.49 Harry Fenn, "General View of Trenton Falls, from East Bank," with self-portrait lower right, *Picturesque America*, I, 454. Wood engraving by James Langridge,
9⅛" x 6¼".

(For some especially attractive pages, with engravings that combine the two styles, see I, 185; II, 12, and 423.)

As these comments indicate, the wood engravings are uneven. Some, especially those by Harley, Quartley, and W. J. Linton, are usually of high quality—manifesting clarity of form, the illusion of three-dimensionality, and good light-dark contrast—whereas the work of others, such as Filmer and Richardson, is frequently characterized by areas of dull grey and indistinct forms. Some sections of *Picturesque America* exhibit uniformly good engraving—often primarily the work of one engraver—while others are consistently poor. For example, the engravings of St. Augustine, primarily by Harley (I, 183–97), are for the most part excellent; several of the Lake Superior region (I, 393–411) by Richardson and others are of inferior quality. The extent to which these differences result from the skill of the artist rather than the engraver is difficult to determine. In the case of William Hart's illustrations of Lake Superior, his lack of familiarity with the medium of wood engraving was likely a major factor in their shortcomings.[87]

To print the wood engravings for such a large-scale project, it seems likely that numerous power presses, probably the stop-cylinder type—would have been used. Improvements in this type of press in the 1850s and 1860s resulted in finer textured, clearer impressions of wood engravings than had been attainable with the Adams bed and platen steam press. Certainly, electrotype plates were used for printing the wood engravings as well as the text. Skilled pressmen enhanced the quality of the image by making ready the press and applying overlays to certain areas of the impression surface. In addition, the use of dry rather than wet calendered paper that had been smoothed by "cold-rolling" between cylinders of iron and hardened paper pulp contributed to sharp impressions. These techniques resulted in a highly uniform, well-printed product.[88]

The Steel Engravings

The second type of illustration in *Picturesque America* was the steel engraving, which retained the prestige acquired from 1830 to 1860. The "List of Engravings on Steel" at the beginning of each volume attested to this by crediting the artist and engraver of each print. This medium was usually more successful than wood engraving in reproducing a picture

distinguished by tone, such as a watercolor or oil painting. In fact, when
the artist anticipated that a scene would be reproduced as a steel engraving, he often used watercolor to record it, if Fenn's painting of Richmond
from the James may be taken as typical (figs. 5.50, 5.51).

Each volume of *Picturesque America* contains twenty-four steel engravings in addition to the vignettes on the engraved title pages. One steel
engraving was distributed with each part, but seldom did its subject correspond to the regions covered in the text pages and wood engravings. Nor
was every article illustrated by a steel engraving, as there are thirty-four
articles in volume I and thirty-one in volume II. The sequence of distribution was determined by expediency, depending on what prints were ready.
(See appendix C for the order in which they originally appeared.) Inter-
leaving tissues protected adjoining sheets from offsetting of the ink.

The principal artists of the wood engravings did the artwork for many
of the steel engravings as well. Fenn did nine, plus the two title-page
vignettes; Perkins did six; Woodward three; Sheppard two; and Waud one.
A. C. Warren, who frequently drew city views for *Appletons' Journal* and
Harper's Weekly, did nine views of cities. Smillie's diaries provide the only
record of payment for such artwork: he received forty-five dollars for
"Mount Shasta" and fifty dollars for "The Golden Gate."[89]

A number of steel engravings included in *Picturesque America* had
already appeared in *Appletons' Journal* during the first year of publication
as "embellishments" or "art supplements." Fenn's view of "West Point and
the Highlands" (September 11, 1869) was reused in this way, as were
plates after paintings by such well-known artists as F. O. C. Darley, J. W.
Casilear, J. F. Kensett, Wm. S. Haseltine, and A. F. Bellows.[90] Although
these artists are often listed as having participated in *Picturesque America*,
they did not actually travel and sketch for the project. The Appletons simply reused plates already on hand when an appropriate opportunity arose.
In at least two instances, however, the plates were either altered or
replaced before inclusion in *Picturesque America*, demonstrating that the
firm did indeed take pains with this publication.[91]

Bunce apparently obtained several other steel engravings for
Picturesque America by commissioning reproductions of completed oil
paintings by leading landscape artists, including William and J. M. Hart
and Homer Martin. The engraving of Worthington Whittredge's "The
Rocky Mountains" in volume II is a copy of one of his paintings deriving
from his western trip in 1866.[92]

5.50 Harry Fenn, *Richmond From the James*, [ca. 1870]. Watercolor and pencil on buff paper, 10⅝" x 18½". M. and M. Karolik Collection. Courtesy the Museum of Fine Arts, Boston.

The engravers hired to execute the steel plates for *Picturesque America* were among the most prominent landscape engravers of the time, many of whom had previously done plates for *Appletons' Journal*. They included Robert Hinshelwood, Samuel Valentine Hunt, William Wellstood, E. P. Brandard, and G. R. Hall.[93] All of them came originally from England or Scotland, where the demand for books of steel engravings had been steadily diminishing with the increasing popularity of the less expensive wood engravings.

The steel engraver employed a combination of etching, in which acid corrodes the metal where lines have been drawn through a coating of resin by an etching needle, and true engraving, in which a sharp-pointed burin cuts into the metal. Like the wood engravers, steel engravers used a ruling machine to make minute parallel lines to represent skies and placid lakes.[94] The whole process was much slower and more painstaking than wood engraving. Yet the extremely fine lines of a steel engraving, often visible only with a magnifying glass, could render tone and light effectively. As Estelle Jussim has pointed out, the varying density of ink absorbed by the paper from the intaglio plate gives "a dimension of added

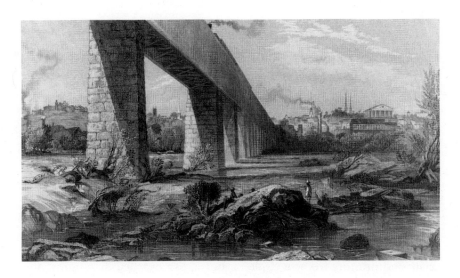

5.51 Harry Fenn, "Richmond from the James," *Picturesque America*, I, opposite 73. Steel engraving by Robert Hinshelwood, 5⅞" x 9".

light and shade which no relief process can match."[95] The light effects in several of the *Picturesque America* plates are striking, in particular the luminosity in "Indian Rock" after William S. Haseltine (I, opp. 509), and "Baptism Bay, Lake Superior" after William Hart (I, opp. 393). Jussim analyzes the differences in technique between the intaglio steel engraving and the relief wood engraving, and the resulting differences in detail and texture:

The one-stroke positive black-line manipulation of the steel engraving far exceeded the two-stroke-for-each-side-of-a-black-line manipulation of black-line wood engraving for high density detail, and, just as importantly, for variety of texture.[96]

Because the minute lines constituting the "high density detail" of steel engravings are usually imperceptible at normal viewing distance, the medium could represent a variety of textures without apparent lines—quite a different effect from that of wood engraving's more obvious use of line. Yet skillful wood engraving could also represent certain textures very effectively.

As color photographs do today, steel engravings lent glamour to a book. Bunce and the Appletons included them to make the new publication more attractive to the public, but producing the plates was slow, labor intensive, and expensive. Printing from them required special hand-operated presses that applied more pressure than those used for raised type or relief wood engravings (or electrotypes made from them).[97] The paper had to be dampened, and, for each impression, the surface of the plate had to be wiped clear after inking before printing. With such costs in mind, Bunce and the Appleton firm understandably chose to limit the number of steel engravings in the book to one per part.

Actually, the steel-engraved illustrations of *Picturesque America*, printed on hand-operated plate presses, were among the last of their kind. By 1876 a steam press for steel plates had been developed and was in use in the Appletons' manufacturing plant in Brooklyn. The steam press greatly facilitated printing from steel plates, but it also excelled in printing photogravures, which, along with the halftone process, would supercede steel engravings by the late 1880's or early 1890s.[98]

Despite steel engraving's continuing prestige, tastes were changing in the United States as they had in England, as is shown by the popularity of books illustrated by wood engravings. There was a growing appreciation of reproductions that revealed the hand of the artist. Photoengraving would eventually allow the exact reproduction of the artist's lines, but, in the meantime, some preferred the bold look of wood engravings to "prim" steel engravings. A short story by Constance Fenimore Woolson in the November 1870 *Harper's Monthly* illustrates the changing taste. Woolson uses details related to book illustration to help define her main character, a twenty-eight-year-old "woman of the world." After flinging her gentle friend's illustrated edition of Wordsworth into the river, she says, "I will replace it with a Robert Browning full of strong wood-cuts, liebchen, and you will forget those prim steel engravings of nondescript scenery."[99]

The Appletons wisely appealed to both tastes—and to people of different ages, education, and status—by including both types of illustration in *Picturesque America*. The volumes interspersed the more conventional medium for picturesque views, steel engraving, and the increasingly popular wood engraving that could be somewhat more expressive of the artist's style. Bunce was also careful to maintain a balance throughout the entire work between the comfortable predictability of traditional approaches and the drama and surprise of fresh ones.

The Appleton firm took great care in producing the illustrations, eventually spending as much as $138,000, over half of the estimated quarter-million-dollar total cost of the publication.[100] The unifying vision of the Appletons, Bunce, and Fenn and the other artists resulted in what was advertised on the back wrapper as "the greatest and fullest exposition of our country" that had yet been made. Although not all of the illustrations lived up to the publisher's claims of being "original and trustworthy" and possessing "the vividness of personal observation"—or "poetry," for that matter—great numbers of them did. Many surpassed literalness as well as sentimentality to achieve a memorable, appealing view of a particular time and place. Furthermore, the artists' manipulations of subject matter and presentation—from enhanced drama to nostalgic or optimistic fictions—reveal much about the ideals and values shared by many in their time. The text would reinforce these implicit and explicit messages.

PART THREE

Reassuring Messages
in Words and Pictures

 CHAPTER 6

"Delineation by Pen and Pencil"

Picturesque America's editor, Oliver Bell Bunce, shaped the uneven, diverse contributions of thirteen artists and twenty-eight writers into a reasonably harmonious whole. He was guided by his artistic and scenic preferences and his conviction that Americans wanted to know about dramatic scenery and new vacation destinations as well as technological and cultural progress. He also believed that civilization was inevitably advancing toward a better future through the dissemination of knowledge and art and the inculcation of traditional virtues like thrift and industry. Consequently, he selected images and commissioned essays presenting a highly positive view of the country's past, present, and future.

Like the Appletons, Bunce believed it was time to lay to rest sectional animosities and foster a strong national identity based on pride in the country's outstanding topographical features and advances in technology and culture. By making attractive images of such features accessible to the family circle in an affordable publication, Bunce and the Appleton firm offered a way for many to align themselves, symbolically at least, with those who appreciated both art and nature and had time and money enough to travel in search of the picturesque. At the same time, the high quality of the publication justified further pride in the nation's artistic accomplishments.

For the frontispieces and engraved title pages that set the tone for each volume, Bunce chose contrasting yet complementary subjects illustrating both the comprehensive nature of the project and the parallel emphases on the natural and cultural landscapes.[1] For the steel-engraved frontispieces, he commissioned images of the nation's most famous scenic attraction and its largest and most celebrated city. Volume I opens with Fenn's expansive aerial view of Niagara Falls, full of mist, relentless

6.1 Harry Fenn, "Niagara," *Picturesque America*, I, frontispiece. Steel engraving by
S. V. Hunt, 5¼" x 9¼".

movement of water, rainbows, billowing clouds, and shafts of light (fig.
6.1). It conveys a sense of nature's power undiminished by the numerous
bridges, walkways, and towers that made possible a safe encounter with the
natural wonder.

The frontispiece of volume II, New York from Brooklyn Heights, shows
a harbor crowded with sailing ships and a few steamboats and an impressive jumble of buildings, among which the steeple of Trinity Church and
the west pier of Brooklyn Bridge are prominent (fig. 6.2). When A. C.
Warren prepared this image in 1872, Brooklyn Bridge was in the early
stage of construction. His imaginative rendering of the pier includes turrets that were never built. Yet the bridge, which would be completed in
1883, was already a powerful symbol of American civilization's advance
and New York's importance as an international commerical center, and it
was important to include it.[2]

The images Bunce selected for the steel-engraved title pages of each
volume highlighted other important aspects of the book's coverage: in
volume I, a quintessentially picturesque waterfall, with rainbows in the
spray and overarching trees, is identified in the "List of Engravings on

6.2 A. C. Warren, "City of New York from Brooklyn Heights," *Picturesque America*, II, frontispiece. Steel engraving by G. R. Hall, 5⅝" x 9½".

6.3 Harry Fenn, "Dome of the Capitol," *Picturesque America*, II, title page. Steel engraving by E. P. Brandard, 9" x 7¼"; page, 12⅝" x 9½".

Steel" only as a "Cascade in Virginia" (see fig. 4.3). Thus it represents one of many unheralded spots worthy of attention from the artist or tourist in search of the picturesque—indeed, Fenn has included himself painting it—and contrasts neatly with the focus on the sublime and celebrated Niagara Falls on the facing page.

For volume II, Bunce commissioned Fenn to create a title-page image that captured the essence of urban sophistication. In contrast to the distant view of New York City on the opposite page, this close-up shows elegantly dressed men and women enjoying the park at the base of the Capitol in Washington, D.C., and strolling up its majestic steps (fig. 6.3). The recently completed dome appears disproportionately tall and floats ethereally above the letters of the book's title, dominating the image. The trees are literally bent in the service of art, as they provide a medium-toned background for the title and, with the letters, form an arch framing the lower part of the composition. The image clearly conveyed that the United States was graced by elegant public spaces comparable to the parks of London and Paris and civic architecture equivalent to St. Paul's Cathedral and St. Peter's Basilica. Whereas the capital city had long been denigrated by both foreign and American visitors as being so devoid of amenities that it was a national embarrassment, *Picturesque America* displayed conspicuous evidence to the contrary.[3]

Finally, Bunce suggested the book's comprehensiveness by choosing an image of manufacturing to open the first section of volume II, "The Highlands and Palisades of the Hudson." The subject of Fenn's dramatic "Poughkeepsie, and its Founderies [*sic*] at Night" (fig. 6.4) differs sharply from "Castle Head," the rock formation on the coast of Maine opening volume I. Yet one would be hard pressed to decide which image is more picturesque. Fenn's interpretation supports E. L. Burlingame's comment in the text that although by day one might "quarrel a little with the smoke" of Poughkeepsie's busy foundries, by night they "become the most strangely beautiful and striking feature in many miles of the Hudson's scenery" (II, 3). Although Burlingame goes on to say "they light the river like weird beacons," and their sound crosses the water "like the panting of giants," Fenn's image plays down the scene's eeriness. His small circular composition contains the energy of the operation. His high vantage point reduces the fiery furnace to two dramatic shafts of light, with the source silhouetting the two tiny workers. The marginal decorations, suggesting etchings, further soften the composition and distance it from a realism

6.4 Harry Fenn, "Poughkeepsie and its Founderies at Night," *Picturesque America*,
II, 1. Wood engraving by W. H. M. [W. H. Morse?], 6⅛" x 6⅛"; page 12⅜" x 9½".

that might have been disturbingly forceful. Thus for *Picturesque America*, probably with Bunce's encouragement, Fenn created a manufacturing image very different from the views of steel plants in Pittsburgh he prepared for *Every Saturday* (see figs. 3.5, 3.6). *Picturesque America* would incorporate images of the exterior of foundries, factories, and mills into picturesque settings without depicting the machinery and workers at close range—conveying the message that technological advances were compatible with appreciation and preservation of natural scenery.

Of course, the text and pictures gave greatest attention to scenic features, with approximately two-thirds of the images primarily of natural scenery. Of those, more than four hundred depicted places east of the Mississippi and north of the Mason-Dixon line; approximately sixty were of the South; and approximately a hundred and twenty of places west of the Mississippi. The views of towns, cities, and industry in the same three broad divisions number approximately two hundred of the Northeast and Middle West, fifty-five of the South, and only two of the West. Despite the claims to comprehensiveness, several areas of the nation were in fact neglected, such as Alabama, Mississippi, Arkansas, most of Kentucky, the whole of Texas and the Southwest, except for the Grand Canyon and some of the canyons of Utah, the Northwest above the Columbia River, and much of the Great Plains. Some of these areas had not yet recovered from the War's devastation or lacked access by railroads or navigable rivers; others may have been thought to have few picturesque features.[4]

To present a positive image of the United States, one that would foster collective pride and unity and present reassuring evidence that the nation's landscape still qualified as picturesque despite unprecedented changes on many fronts, Bunce had to be highly selective. To demonstrate the United States' emergence as a world leader required that a host of negative images and attitudes be dispelled and that many contemporary problems be minimized or avoided altogether.

The most stinging criticisms—frequently voiced by visitors from Great Britain and Europe as well as Americans like James Fenimore Cooper and George William Curtis—included charges that the United States lacked the ancient monuments of a long-established civilization, that its coasts were low and dull, that it had no majestic mountains like the Swiss Alps, and that its countryside was unkempt rather than "groomed" like England's. Furthermore, critics declared that its cities were inelegant and its people rude, devoid of taste, and mainly interested in money. Bunce and his contributors would have been aware of these negative attitudes in much travel literature. The burden of countering them created an underlying tension that determined many of Bunce's choices—and those of the artists and writers.

Many other observers of the American scene were highly disturbed by contemporary trends that included increasing materialism, commercialism, and the widening gap between the rich and poor. Bunce was surely aware of strikes by laborers, accidents in mines, turbulence in Southern legislatures and the rise of the Ku Klux Klan, bloody skirmishes between settlers and American Indians in the West, homeless children, unhealthy living conditions among immigrants in crowded cities, and unprecedented corruption in government and business. Indeed, in 1873, Bunce suggested that the current era might be characterized as the "Period of Labor Organization," or the "Period of Social Convulsion."[5] That September brought the "Panic of 1873," when banks were forced to close and the New York Stock Exchange suspended trading for ten days.[6] Yet Bunce also knew that airing such problems would detract from the positive image he wanted to create in *Picturesque America*. The need to deny or at least softpedal such problems constituted another underlying tension that shaped many of Bunce's choices.

The strategies for creating a positive "delineation by pen and pencil" took several forms, some obvious and some subtle. The most obvious way was to assert directly the superiority of some element in the natural or cultural landscape. Such claims, sometimes shrilly stated, appear in the text often enough to constitute a litany and show that one important motivation of the project was to compensate for feelings of national inferiority. One writer claims, "There is no season so glorious in any country as an American autumn" (I, 317), while another says the scenery of the Adirondack lakes "is not surpassed on earth" (II, 420). Burlingame says, "It would be impossible to find a more glorious drive" than that from Truckee, California, to Lake Tahoe, Nevada, and ranks it with "the great passes of the world" (II, 196). He also finds the Sierras repeat every phase of Alpine scenery, "often with greater beauty" than in Switzerland (II, 20). Other superlatives include that Richmond's gigantic flour mills are "the largest of the kind in the world" (I, 73), "No city has an avenue of such length" as New York's Fifth Avenue, and Central Park is "unapproached in this country and unexcelled abroad" in its "union of art with Nature" (II, 555, 557).

The more subtle and, ultimately, more significant strategy the artists and writers used to create reassuringly positive images was to conform in approach and subject matter to the tradition of picturesque viewbooks. By giving attention to effects of light and weather and to foreground details like trees, rocks, carts, animals, and people, by frequently using trees or architecture to frame compositions, and by stressing the historic aspects of a region, they linked the United States of the 1870s with the historic and much-admired landscape of the Old World, which Americans hoped to equal or surpass. In addition, by featuring such standard subject matter as waterfalls, rivers, rock formations, and mountains, and by utilizing the familiar conventions when depicting picturesque spots "unknown to art" as well as landscapes unlike the traditional picturesque, the writers and artists rendered these areas appealing or at least less strange. The traditional aesthetic and literary formulas also provided them a framework for incorporating recent technological advances into familiar, nonthreatening scenes. And by depicting a largely homogeneous society in attractive cities and small towns unchanged from an earlier time they created visions of order and stability that could build confidence about the future.

A Landscape Still Picturesque

Picturesque America conformed to, and indeed expanded, the tradition of picturesque touring by emphasizing the types of natural features of most interest to tourists in search of the picturesque (in its widest meaning, encompassing also the beautiful and the sublime). These included water in motion in waterfalls, waves, and rivers, and such geological features as rock formations, canyons, caves, and mountains. These aspects of the natural landscape had long attracted naturalists, artists, writers, and tourists, and recent controversies and advances in science had heightened their interest for many. *Picturesque America*'s artists and writers sought out such features—both famous and little known—in all parts of the country. There is a striking difference, however, in the way they were depicted in the East and West.

The artists show most of the scenic attractions in the East as comfortably accessible, with paths, benches, bridges, boats, stagecoaches, and hotels. In many images, women in elegant garb gaze at the view, picnic, or take boat rides alongside their male companions—except when a strenuous hike is required, as on Mount Mansfield or in the Adirondacks. Men fish in the streams and hunt in the forests. Nature in the East is shown as a realm for enjoying one's leisure time—for restorative "play" as well as quiet contemplation.

In the West, however, the artists emphasize wilderness and sublime scenery as yet untouched by civilization. They include fewer figures, except in Yosemite Valley, the only area where women tourists are shown. With the exception of Cliff House, the popular excursion destination near San Francisco, they depict no tourist facilities. In reality, comfortable accommodations for travellers *were* still scarce in most regions, but even where they existed, the artists chose not to include them in their pictures. Although Smillie mentions that there are three hotels in Yosemite Valley, he depicts none (I, 488).

Although some scenic spots in the West had come to be associated with engineering feats, these recent changes do not appear in the images. Moran's view of Donner Pass, for example, left out the snowsheds protecting the Central Pacific tracks even though they were renowned for their length (thirty-seven miles) and cost ($2 million).[7] Photographers had recorded the progress of the snowsheds, and Bierstadt's 1871 *View of Donner Lake* depicted them. For *Picturesque America*, however, Moran did not include them, although his view of Donner Lake appears to be from a vantage point similar to Bierstadt's.

In choosing to represent this area with no sign of the railroad or the snowsheds (although he used the railroad to reach it), Moran emphasized the sublimity and wildness of the scenery and ignored the changes brought by technological development. This approach is typical of the depiction of the West in *Picturesque America*.[8] Disregarding settlements, farms, herds of cattle, mines, and mills, the artists focused almost entirely upon natural scenery, emphasizing the unchanging monuments of natural antiquity. Occasionally a tiny train appears almost lost in the distance (II, 191), but trains are never the primary subject. A few hardy travellers on horseback or on foot are shown, as are a few covered wagons in Northern California. More frequently the landscapes are either devoid of life or peopled by American Indians, suggesting circumstances before the coming of European Americans.

Two steel engravings after F. O. C. Darley, the popular illustrator of the works of Cooper and Irving, were included in "The Plains and the Sierras" section, although their subjects, "Emigrants Crossing the Plains"

(II, opp. 176) and "Californians Lassoing a Bear" (II, opp. 201), are more suggestive of 1853 than 1873. No town or city in the vast region between St. Louis and Oakland is depicted. Moran includes a memorable image of "The Oaks of Oakland" from the end of his transcontinental railroad journey. Yet even the sophisticated, thriving city of San Francisco, with hotels and theaters rivaling New York, receives scant attention. The only view of the city is Smillie's steel engraving entitled "Golden Gate: from Telegraph Hill" (I, opp. 560), which gives major attention to the huge bay illuminated by a sunset, and tucks the city's buildings under the hill.

This pictorial celebration of largely untouched nature in the West proclaimed that wilderness was still a special quality of the landscape of the United States. True, the choice to avoid depicting recent changes in certain areas suggested regret about the loss of wilderness. Yet the stronger message was that progress could be accommodated within the vast Western lands, and that nature's sublimity and development could coexist without conflict. The text, in contrast, far from avoiding change, conveyed unqualified enthusiasm for advancing development. The writers were always relieved to come upon settled areas—farms, ranches, towns, and mills—and they greatly appreciated the conveniences of hotels when they existed. They found uninhabited areas desolate and looked forward to the spread of "civilization" to these regions, facilitated by the railroads. Such strong preferences naturally supported the development of Western tourism and precluded concerns about any detrimental effects—even though many recognized that some places of natural beauty in the East were already conspicuously degraded.

The writers and artists also reacted negatively to the featureless plains and the deserts. A treeless expanse did not fit the picturesque aesthetic, as the English traveller Isabella Bird wrote of the plains east of the Rocky Mountains:

The lack of foreground is a great artistic fault, and the absence of greenery is melancholy. . . . Only once, the second time we forded the river, the cottonwoods formed a foreground, and then the loveliness was heavenly.[9]

Picturesque America artist A. R. Waud similarly hoped that "patches of woodland" would soon be added to the buffalo grass plains of Dakota Territory, "to increase the interest and beauty of the scenery" and "break the monotony."[10]

To create attractive images of the plains, Moran always managed to include some foreground details—clumps of brush and small streams or a

man on horseback—and interesting backgrounds—whether rock formations, buttes, or mountain ranges. No images of actual desert are
included, despite Bryant's statement in the preface that regions where
"rains never fall" offered "subjects for the pencil."

The great attention to waterfalls in *Picturesque America* continued a
popular convention of picturesque touring and at the same time demonstrated the country's ample riches. Not only did the United States have
the famous Niagara, but also Yosemite Falls—higher than Switzerland's
Staubbach—Multnomah Falls in Oregon Territory (I, 34), the falls of the
Yellowstone region, and numerous falls in the East, such as those at
Cayuga Lake in New York, as well as innumerable little-known cascades
awaiting the attention of tourists. Approximately ninety-five images of
waterfalls appear in *Picturesque America.*

Water in motion had long held great fascination—whether falling
from a great height or roaring down a boulder-strewn cascade—as evidence of nature's power and energy, and of the union of apparent oppo-
sites. In his "Essay on American Scenery," Thomas Cole said that
waterfalls present to the mind

the beautiful but apparently incongruous idea of fixedness and motion—a single
existence in which we perceive unceasing change and everlasting duration. The
waterfall may be called the voice of the landscape, for, unlike the rocks and woods
which utter sounds as the passive instruments played on by the elements, the
waterfall strikes its own chords, and rocks and mountains re-echo in rich unison.[11]

For many the chords struck brought the individual into communion
with the divine. This had long been especially true of Niagara Falls, whose
scale and volume so far surpassed any waterfall in Europe. It became the
mecca for those seeking an encounter with the sublime—like Harry Fenn.
As Mulvey writes, "Niagara was the ultimate in Romantic landscape; it all but
guaranteed an encounter with the Wordsworthian divine; those who could
not get in touch with this emotional reality elsewhere could by way of travelling to Niagara give themselves the awful moment." Travel writers from the
first half of the nineteenth century often saved Niagara for the climax of
their books, and then were at a loss for words, finding it "indescribable."[12]

Long before *Picturesque America*, however, the anticipated encounter had
become problematic, and although Fenn's frontispiece recognized Niagara's continuing special place as the country's premier scenic attraction,

Bunce chose to place the article about it near the end of volume I. Tourists had already heard and read and seen too much for their experience to be spontaneous. Furthermore, the approach to Niagara had been so marred by ugly buildings that the writer Rodolphe Garczynski compared it to "a diamond set in lead" (I, 435). In addition, the commercial exploitation of the falls had become an example of what to avoid—and was used as such in the push to establish Yellowstone National Park. As Garczynski described it:

In no quarter of the world is the traveller fleeced as at these falls. He cannot take a single glance at any object of interest without having to pay dearly for it. Still there are few people who can afford to visit the place who do not go there; for man's impertinence and rapacity, though they poison the pleasure, cannot rob the scene of its awful sublimity. (I, 438)[13]

Although the falls still impressed by their sublimity—even stunned like great grief—the encounter had been diluted by familiarity and the degradation of the surroundings. Whereas Trollope managed to shut out everything else, Garczynski says, "Sit as long as you will on the scanty remnant of Table Rock, or as long as the photographers, the Indian-curiosity people, or the owners of side-shows in the neighborhood will permit you, and, after all, you have not seized the idea of Niagara, and you will not be able for some time" (I, 439).

Instead, he recommends first seeing the falls from the many different viewpoints entrepreneurs had provided (I, 439). His description of making the rounds of these spots brings to mind the series of artificial thrills at contemporary theme parks: "The great feat, of course, is to descend the stairs underneath the Table Rock from Barnett's, and to penetrate under Horseshoe Falls as far as one's courage will permit" (I, 439). Two of Fenn's illustrations depict the memorable ordeal of walking at the base of the falls, being buffeted by wind and spray, especially "The Cave of the Winds" (fig. 6.5; see also I, 437).

Thus, although Niagara remained impressive, it had become practically impossible to experience any sort of unmediated encounter with divine power there. Instead of finding the falls indescribable, Garczynski responds with a torrent of words. Yet he often seems without conviction, paying lip service to the conventions of sublimity, as when he writes that the visitor's first gaze is "too productive of the stupefaction of extreme awe" to take in all the details (I, 438).

6.5   Harry Fenn, "The Cave of the Winds," *Picturesque America*, I, 445.   Wood engraving, 9¼" x 6¼".

In contrast, it becomes clear later in volume I that the places now more likely to be found "indescribable" are the new goals of the most adventurous: Yellowstone and the Grand Canyon of the Colorado. These are sites with no European counterpart; in fact, they are unique in all the world. In Yosemite Valley, Smillie is similarly awed by the evidence of cliffs crumbled by water's destructive power: "No words can convey . . . the effects of mountains of granite, sharp and fresh in outline, piled one upon the other" (I, 482). He chooses to depict several impressive rock piles, including one at the base of Yosemite Falls, where it is just one element in a highly charged depiction of nature's power. Comparing Smillie's preliminary drawing with the wood engraving shows that he heightened the "freshly created" quality of the scene with both wind and light (figs. 6.6, 6.7). The spray travels even farther from the vertical, and stronger light allows the lower falls to glow. The easily overlooked tiny figures, who have scrambled up on one of the rocks to contemplate the sublime sight, do not detract from the impression that this is nature's realm.

In the descriptions and images of several other waterfalls the emphasis shifts subtly to stress the aesthetic experience as much as or more than the spiritual. Exulting in the ever-changing lines and colors of the falls, the writers describe an intense perception of the beautiful that fills them with love and admiration for its creator. This aesthetic approach is in keeping with Ruskin's admiration for the exquisite lines of falling water:

In water which has gained its impetus, we have the most exquisite arrangements of curved lines, perpetually changing from convex to concave, and vice versa . . . presenting perhaps the most beautiful series of inorganic forms which nature can possibly produce. . . . [E]very motion of the torrent is united, and all its curves are modifications of beautiful line. . . . [T]hey are an instant expression of the utmost power and velocity.[14]

In the images of waterfalls, the *Picturesque America* artists, especially Fenn and Woodward, attempt to represent such powerful motion through line—an artistic task long recognized as extremely difficult.[15] In depicting Catskill Falls, of which "there is nothing more beautiful in American scenery" (II, 120), Fenn uses myriad curved lines to emphasize the dynamic motion of the falling water. His full-page illustration differs from most earlier views primarily in the greater turbulence in the lower part of the falls and the complete lack of an interceding foreground (fig. 6.8).[16] The small figures facing the upper falls in this image convey great admiration, as does Fenn's

6.6 James D. Smillie, *View of Yosemite Falls*, [1872]. Charcoal on paper, 18⅝" x 12½". HEH 92.22. Courtesy the Henry E. Huntington Library and Art Gallery, San Marino, California.

6.7 James D. Smillie, "Yosemite Falls," *Picturesque America*, I, 485. Wood engraving
by A. Harral, 8⅞" x 6⅜".

6.8 Harry Fenn, "Catskill Falls," *Picturesque America*, II, 121. Wood engraving by W. J. Linton, 9¾₆" x 6¾₆".

6.9 Harry Fenn, "Under the Catskill Falls," *Picturesque America*, II, 123. Wood engraving by W. J. Linton, 9⅛" x 6⅟₁₆".

portrait of himself gazing raptly at "the great white veil of falling water" in a second full-page view, "Under the Catskill Falls" (fig. 6.9).

This view is strikingly different from a nearly contemporaneous one by Winslow Homer that appeared September 14, 1872, in *Harper's Weekly*.[17] Homer's faintly humorous "Under the Falls" focuses on two stylishly dressed young women leaning on walking sticks on the ledge behind the falls and gazing at the column of water without even a hint of awe—an image suggesting a mocking attitude toward picturesque touring similar to that in Woolson's short story and Mark Twain's *Innocents Abroad* (1869). In contrast, Fenn's depiction of himself admiring the same column lacks irony, and illustrates the kind of close observation from different angles and unusual viewpoints that Bunce prescribes in his keynote article—that leads to the "surrender of the heart" and learning nature's lessons.

The sort of rapt admiration depicted in Fenn's illustrations is expressed at length by Garczynski in his account of visiting Trenton Falls. "Creeping" close to the bank, he responds with "alternate ecstasy and awe" to the color, line, and roaring of the falls:

The color is an extraordinary topaz hue, like nothing ever seen in any other land, or in any other part of America. It resembles a cascade of melted topaz, or of liquid, translucent porphyry. . . . Gazing steadily upon it, and letting its beauties infiltrate slowly into the mind, we realize how bold is the leap, how vigorous is the curve. . . . And then come the sunlight and its golden arrows to glorify the whole, and raise the pulse of ecstasy to maddening height. . . . And the diapason of its [the chasm's] roaring becomes, to the ear of the man penetrated with the beautiful, a loud hymn of triumph and praise to the great Maker of all. (I, 457–58)

Garczynski seems able to lose himself more readily in aesthetic and spiritual ecstasy at Trenton Falls than at Niagara, perhaps because Trenton Falls, although long a tourist attraction, did not have quite the carnival atmosphere of Niagara.

Waves, another manifestation of water in motion, evoke interest and admiration in *Picturesque America*, and for some lead to an ecstatic experience. Writers and painters had traditionally found stormy seas sublime— in fact some British visitors had compared Niagara to storms at sea. The continuing popular appeal of a windswept coastline is clear from Woodward's image of "Pulpit Rock, Nahant," which opened the section on "The Eastern Shore, From Boston to Portland" (fig. 6.11). Whereas the original drawing was obviously made in good weather, when sailboats ventured forth (fig. 6.10), Woodward sought to enliven the image with waves, spray, and a dark sky. Even more dramatic is Fenn's view of the Maine coast, "The 'Spouting Horn' in a Storm," with the mast of a wrecked ship, an example of the sublime associated with danger and man's weakness in face of nature's power (fig. 6.12). The metaphor of battle to describe the confrontation of sea and rocky coast had become a literary convention used by several *Picturesque America* writers.

The higher waves and rocky coast of northern California provided new evidence to combat the old charge that the coasts of the United States were low and dull. The attention given them offers another example of how the West became the primary locus of sublime natural scenery in this period. In "On the Coast of California," Garczynski observes, "Nothing can be more tumultuous or less pacific than the waters of the Pacific Ocean along the Mendocino coast" (I, 555). The waves are higher although less frequent than in the Atlantic, and "The curves described by the falling crests of such waves are infinitely finer than any thing which the Atlantic presents; and the boiling fury with which they crash upon the beach and churn the sands is, at first sight, appalling" (I, 555). To experience the ocean aesthetically, however, as well as to understand what is special about the West, he recommends lying on the beach:

Get, if you can, upon a level with the water, and catch the color of the tips of the waves when they are raised up heavenward; . . . then you will forget the ideas of battle . . . and you will live only in color. For the moment, whether you have ever handled a brush or not, you will be a painter, and you will know all the glories of color, and you will find the tears welling from your eyes, and will comprehend the inspired madness of Turner and the heroics of Ruskin. It is not that these things cannot be seen everywhere, for they can, but here the type is on so large a scale that he must be trebly blind who cannot read the book of Nature. . . . This is why the West is breeding our poets. (I, 562)

This "living only in color" is a different experience from observing the natural order and thereby being convinced of God's existence—the "argument from Design" alluded to by several of the older writers, including Thorpe, Richards, and Cooke. Garczynski, one of the youngest writers, expresses the most intense response to color and light; his passion for such perceptions brings to mind the Impressionists. It is not possible to conceive of the clergyman W. C. Richards lying on the sand or writing a description of waves anything like this one.

Rivers, perhaps the most common manifestation of water in motion, play a crucial role in *Picturesque America*. The book's emphasis on river

6.10 J. D. Woodward, *Pulpit Rock, Nahant, Mass.*, October 1, 1872. Pencil and white
on paper, 10¾" x 7¾". Courtesy the Diocese of Virginia.

THE EASTERN SHORE, FROM BOSTON TO PORTLAND.

WITH ILLUSTRATIONS BY J. DOUGLAS WOODWARD.

Pulpit Rock, Nahant.

THE coast of New England between Boston and Portland is for the most part
irregular and rocky, and in many spots picturesque. Nature seems to have supplied it with
every variety of sea-coast aspect and beauty, from
the jagged mass of frowning and rough-worn
rock overhanging the waters to the long, smooth
reach of broad, curving beaches, and the duller landscape of green morass extending unbroken to the water's edge. There is no coast on the Atlantic seaboard which presents a
wider choice for the lover of marine pleasures; for the rich city-man and his family who
seek in proximity to the ocean their summer recreation from the cares and excitements of
the year; for the artist searching to reproduce on canvas the visible romance of Nature;

6.11 J. D. Woodward, "Pulpit Rock, Nahant," *Picturesque America*, II, 395. Wood
engraving by W. J. Linton, 6¹⁵⁄₁₆" x 6¾₆".

6.12 Harry Fenn, "The 'Spouting Horn' in a Storm," *Picturesque America*, I, 9.
Wood engraving by W. J. Linton, 8⅞" x 6⅜".

travel reinforced the link with the European tradition of picturesque touring. Recommended by the Reverend William Gilpin as allowing the traveller to enjoy a constantly changing series of scenes, almost like theater, this mode of touring had been represented in Turner's *Rivers of France* and numerous volumes illustrating the Thames and the Rhine. River travel had obviously been the most expeditious in many regions of the United States prior to the railroad, and in less developed areas still was.

At least twenty articles in *Picturesque America* are organized around a river corridor. The contributors show detailed knowledge of the location and length of major rivers and their tributaries, and this awareness is clearly still the key element in their visualization of the country's geography east of the Mississippi. True, there is great enthusiasm for the railroads and new bridges over rivers, so vastly more efficient than ferries. And the new transcontinental railroad clearly provided a way of expanding one's mental image of the country. Eventually the network of tracks across the land would replace rivers as a means of conceptualizing distances and locations of cities and geographical features—just as that function even later passed to the highway system. Yet it is clear that in the early 1870s, at least for the New Yorkers leading the *Picturesque America* project, rivers were still the most important factor. Whereas there are some forty images of railroads, it would be difficult to count the number of boats depicted within the book's covers. In the mind-set of the contributors boats still dominated travel and commerce.

The major rivers of the Northeast had long been important routes and naturally could not be neglected in any comprehensive look at the United States. From 1825, when the Erie Canal opened, the Hudson, the Erie Canal beside the Mohawk, the St. Lawrence, the Connecticut, and the Housatonic were all routes on the conventional northern tour followed by visitors from Britain and Europe as well as by American tourists. Travellers tended to admire these regions for the pleasing combination of forested mountains, winding rivers, and cultivated fields. Because these valleys, especially the Connecticut and the Hudson, were among the earliest regions to be settled and cultivated by Europeans, they had long had the "groomed" look that resembled agricultural landscapes and river valleys of the Old World. They were also rich in historical and literary associations as the locus of important events of the French and Indian War, the Revolutionary War, and the War of 1812, and the setting of legends and novels of Irving and Cooper.

6.13 J. D. Woodward, "Connecticut Valley from Mount Tom," *Picturesque America*, II, opposite 80. Steel engraving by S. V. Hunt, 5⅜" x 8⅞".

Yet by 1870 these long-settled areas also contained numerous manufacturing centers, and train tracks often skirted the river banks, offering a faster, if noisier, means of travel (which the *Picturesque America* artists and writers sometimes took advantage of). Instead of focusing on the changes brought by factories and railroads, the text and images of *Picturesque America* largely sidestepped them and stressed the long histories, attractive old towns, and picturesque and beautiful scenery of these regions.

To retain the impression of pastoral landscapes and quiet villages appropriate for "summer repose" when exploring the upper Housatonic, the "true tourist," writes Baptist clergyman W. C. Richards, departs from the railroad. That route would have led the tourist past "a tract of new activities and industries, of glass-furnaces and sand-quarries, of lumber-mills and cotton-looms, of woollen-mills and populous hamlets" and finally reached the "rich manufacturing village" of North Adams, Massachusetts, where "Chinese cheap labor" had long been prominent in the shoe factories (II, 314–15). Instead, by following "rural windings" and taking time to "bide through changing skies, and hours, and moods of

Nature," the "lover of the beautiful" will "find innumerable views to gaze upon" in "village-nooks" and "near crests and remote hill-tops" (II, 300)— views compatible with an earlier, remembered time.

Artist J. D. Woodward followed this advice, choosing to draw magnificent old trees shading village streets, small bridges over streams, and cascading waterfalls. In addition, a number of illustrations in the section on the Connecticut Valley follow the popular convention of depicting prospect views from "crests" or "hill-tops," in this case from Mount Holyoke and Mount Tom, long favorite excursion destinations for travellers between Boston and New York. The panoramic scale of these views rendered them sublime, impressing tourists with nature's immensity and variety and with the relative insignificance of human efforts.[18] Woodward's steel engraving of the view from Mount Tom (fig. 6.13) recalls Thomas Cole's *View from Mount Holyoke* (1836) but reverses the composition. It also is a more uniformly "civilized," sunlit scene wherein the jumble of rocks and trees merely provides picturesque foreground rather than juxtaposing a storm-tossed wilderness.

Also in keeping with the conventions of picturesque touring, Woodward chooses to depict old mills and an old furnace, representing the long-established industries rather than more recent and more disruptive large-scale factories (II, 89, 291, 296). Yet the writer Richards does not avoid technological feats altogether. He celebrates the "engineering skill" demonstrated in the nearly completed Hoosac Tunnel through the Berkshires, connecting Boston with the Hudson River and "second in length only to the famous Mount-Cenis tunnel under the Alps" (II, 317). Woodward, in turn, drew the tunnel works, but from such a distance they are almost lost in the trees in the background of a picturesque scene (fig. 6.14).

Similar approaches mark the sections dealing with other rivers in the East, both major and minor. Both writers and artists sought to demonstrate that the regions still qualified as picturesque despite recent changes, and that they were worthy goals of tourists. This was relatively easy amidst the steep banks of the Hudson Highlands, the Delaware Water Gap, and the Juniata. But along the Susquehanna, the writer Rodolphe Garczynski and the artist Granville Perkins encountered several areas greatly altered by resource extraction. To make them in any way appealing required some ingenuity. The heavily timbered riverbanks near Williamsport, Pennsylvania, were so ugly Garczynski compared them to a "slaughter-house." For his illustrations, however, Perkins selected spots that still had

Hoosac Mountain and Tunnel Works.

ing village, where "Chinese
eap labor" has been a spe-
lty and a success for years in the
)e-shops. It is the upper "metropo-
" of Berkshire, and is more thickly
idded about with wild and romantic
)ts than its southern sister. Gray-

6.14 J. D. Woodward, "Hoosac Mountain and Tunnel Works," *Picturesque America,*
II, 316. Wood engraving by Harley, 6" x 6⅛".

many trees (II, 213, 215). The rock quarries and coal mines along the West Branch of the Susquehanna, with their accompanying iron furnaces and rolling mills, seemed at first like "blots upon the landscape," but had some virtue in diversifying "the monotonous beauty of the scene" (II, 222). Perkins represented these operations in an appealing composite of the coal mine at Hunlocks (fig. 6.15) in a circular format, surrounded by smaller, irregularly shaped images of other operations. The spaces beside the central circle contain delicate branches, but also seem to provide room to receive the logs rolling down from the scenes in the upper corners and the smoke from the furnaces at the bottom. By managing to make even such operations as logging and mining appealing, and by depicting many more traditionally picturesque scenes along the Susquehanna, Perkins supported Garczynski's message in the text that the area was a worthy tourist destination, with special attractions for fishermen.

In other sections of the country where rivers flowed through landscapes different from pastoral New England or mountainous New York or Pennsylvania the writers and artists necessarily directed attention to other features—whether unusual flora and fauna or fast-growing cities. Nevertheless, the traditional approach of following a river's course in search of appealing views provided a means of "reading" these regions. A prime example is the article on Florida's St. John's and Oklawaha rivers that opened the series in *Appletons' Journal* and focused on the exotic plant and animal life. In her article on the Columbia River—so different from both the Hudson and the Rhine—Runkle similarly emphasized the huge forests as "the crowning glory of the place" and, utilizing the conventional theater metaphor, compared the sudden changes from verdant to arid stretches to the effects of "supernatural scene-shifters" (I, 45–46). Also different were the rolling hills of the Ohio River valley, the nation's first "West." In her journey from Pittsburgh to Louisville, although Woolson stressed the region's rich history and found many views along the riverbank to admire, her focus was definitely on the towns and cities. Many had experienced dramatic growth since early in the century, and two were of particular interest: Pittsburgh, a center of steel and glass making and the nearby burgeoning oil industry, and Cincinnati, another contender for the title of "Queen City of the West."

In describing and depicting the Mississippi River, the writers and artist would have been aware of a long history of negative responses to this river

6.15 Granville Perkins, "Scenes on the North Branch of the Susquehanna," *Picturesque America*, II, 217. Wood engraving by [James H.] Richardson, 9¼" x 6¼".

so unlike any in Europe. Earlier travellers found the muddy Lower Mississippi monotonous and gloomy and the treacherous navigation between New Orleans and St. Louis sometimes terrifying. Charles Dickens called it "an enormous ditch" running liquid mud and hoped never to see it again.[19] Another English traveller, Thomas Hamilton, wrote, "I have never felt how awful a thing is nature, till I was borne on its waters, through regions desolate and uninhabitable."[20]

Thomas Bangs Thorpe did manage to make the Lower Mississippi somewhat appealing by recounting the region's exploration and settlement, as well as its natural history. He admitted the scenic monotony, but as a counterweight he echoed the observation of earlier travellers that in the way land is constantly being formed in the Delta one can actually see creation, "from water to ooze, to mud, to soil; from grass to shrubs, to ferns to forest-trees" (I, 266, 267). He gave considerable attention to the forests, with their cypresses, magnolias, and live oaks—"the most picturesque tree of our continent"—and found something of the sublime and "mysterious" in this scenery: "Destitute though it be of the charms of mountains and water-falls, with no distant views . . . it nevertheless inspires a sort of awe which it is difficult to define or account for" (I, 269). The artist Alfred R. Waud chose to depict a number of such forests, as well as Southwest Pass, made lively with several boats, a channel marker, and porpoises (I, 264). He made no attempt, however, to represent the vast expanse of the Mississippi, the sublimity of which would probably have been impossible to convey in a small wood engraving.

Both Thorpe and Waud also found much of interest in the busy New Orleans waterfront, with its relatively long history. After paying tribute to keelboats of the past, and the "remarkable race of men" who had taken them upriver, Thorpe described the "broad-horns" still used to carry the agricultural products of the West to New Orleans, for distribution to the world. Demonstrating the mind-set of continued reliance on boats, he said these "huge edifices," comparable to "a whole block of country-stores afloat . . . will be seen probably for all time in the harbor of New Orleans" (I, 273). Waud's wood engraving of the harbor showed two broad-horns, with their immense "sweeps to keep them off the snags," alongside a large steamboat of the type that would soon make them obsolete, if the railroad did not (I, 274).[21]

The response to the Upper Mississippi, however, was altogether different from that to the lower. Above its confluence with the muddy Missouri just north of St. Louis the river was clear and blue, and the farther north

6.16 A. R. Waud, "A Cross-Street in Dubuque," *Picturesque America*, II, 332. Wood engraving, 6⅛" x 4⅜".

one travelled the more picturesque the scenery became. *Picturesque America* devotes twice as much space to this region as to the Lower Mississippi.

The coverage jumps from New Orleans to St. Louis, which opens Garczynski's long section on "The Upper Mississippi," also illustrated by Waud. Despite its lack of picturesque setting, St. Louis receives considerable attention. With a population of approximately 220,000, it was not only one of the oldest, but also one of the most important cities in the "West," disputing "with Chicago the title of Metropolis of the West," according to Garczynski. He commented that the recently completed Eads Bridge, "one of the largest and handsomest in the world, over which all the trains from the East directly enter the city, will have a great effect upon its fortunes" (II, 324).

Beginning the journey upriver, Garczynski soon noted how much more blue the river was, and above Keokuk the unfolding "panorama" began to look more and more European to him, with bluffs like "Cyclopean walls" (II, 330). He found Dubuque's steep terraces and stairways as "quaint as any of the scenes in the old cities of Lombardy" (II, 332), and Waud's wood engraving supported this notion (fig. 6.16). The bluffs near Eagle Point were covered with a "rich mantle of green" like English downs (II, 334). Above the mouth of the Wisconsin river, the water was "as clear and limpid as that of Lake Leman" in Switzerland (II, 338).

Garczynski discovered a scenic climax near Trempealeau Island, where the river "lies like a lake" surrounded by hills and bluffs of "every possible combination of picturesque lines." He proclaimed that every painter and poet in America should visit the spot, and it should become the "summer headquarters" of all who love the scenery of this country. Echoing a literary convention, he described the multi-faceted appeal of the spot: "Trempealeau is a study for the painter, a theme for the poet, a problem for the geologist, a clew for the historian. Whoever will study it with his soul rather than his wit shall not fail of exceeding great reward" (II, 343).22 With fervid nationalism, he continued:

It is a grief that Americans should wander off to the Rhine and the Danube when, in the Mississippi, they have countless Rhines and many Danubes. . . . Is Drachenfels one whit more castellated than any of the nameless bluffs about and around Trempealeau? . . . And, if any one, after seeing these things, shall pine for the castled crags of the Rhine, let him come and survey Chimney Rock, near Fountain City. (II, 343–46) (fig. 6.17)

6.17 A. R. Waud, "Chimney Rock, near Fountain City," *Picturesque America*, II, 342.
Wood engraving, 6⅞" x 6⅛".

Garczynski's extreme enthusiasm for the Upper Mississippi is easier to understand if we keep in mind the strongly adverse reactions the Mississippi had often evoked and the general feeling that the landscape of the United States was inferior because of the lack of ruins and ancient monuments.

Picturesque America adheres to the tradition of the coastal tour as well. Despite such variations as touring primarily on foot, as in "On the Coast of Maine," or skirting the edge of one of the United States' vast inland lakes, as in "Lake Superior," still the device of presenting a series of coastal views was reassuringly familiar. In books like William Daniell's *Voyage around Great Britain* (1814), Turner's *Picturesque Views on the Southern Coast of England* (1826), and Clarkson Stanfield's *Coast Scenery* (1836), the majority of the views were of the towns and harbors dotting the coast, whereas in *Picturesque America* the artists most frequently depicted dramatic cliffs or magnificent trees. Where monuments of architecture were lacking, they turned to natural monuments. Woodward's drawing of Lake Erie, which focuses on a large evergreen clinging to a boulder, is a striking example (fig. 6.18). On the block, he added figures and boats and enhanced the drama of the sky (fig. 6.19).

Picturesque America also illustrated interesting geological features. Fascination with unusual rock formations and caves had intensified along with debate over the earth's origins and the development of geology as a science. By the early 1870s many had come to accept Charles Lyell's theory of uniformitarianism, which held that slow, ongoing uniform processes such as weathering and erosion had sculpted the earth's surface over eons. Others clung to the Biblical account of creation and found French geologist George Cuvier's theory of catastrophism more acceptable. This held that a series of sudden catastrophes, such as uplifts and volcanoes, had dramatically shaped the earth's surface.[23]

The writers of *Picturesque America*, however, clearly accept the notions that earth's geological timetable is inconceivably long, and that volcanic activity and uplift, as well as gradual erosion have all molded the earth's surface. As Bunce's use of "sermons in stones" suggests, they also seem confident—like Joseph Le Conte, Louis Agassiz, and Edward Hitchcock (author of *The Religion of Geology*, 1852)—that further understanding of geology will confirm divine creation and providence.

The writers speculate about how various formations developed, mention geologic ages and specific types of rocks, and take for granted that

6.18 J. D. Woodward, *Lake Erie from Mouth of Rocky River*, June 17, 1872. Pencil and white on beige paper, 10½" x 8⅜". Courtesy the Diocese of Virginia.

6.19 J. D. Woodward, "Lake Erie, from Bluff, Mouth of Rocky River," *Picturesque America*, I, 528. Wood engraving by Harley, 8⅞" x 6⅛".

their readers have heard of such leading geologists as Agassiz, Lyell, Benjamin Silliman, and H. D. Rogers.[24] For example, T. M. Clark wrote of the fissure in the cliffs near Newport known as "The Purgatory":

It was formerly the prevailing theory that this fissure was occasioned by a sudden upheaving of the rock; but, after careful examination, Professor Silliman came to the opinion that it was probably formed by the gradual eating away of the softer portions of the stone at a very early period. (I, 368)[25]

The writers also describe the contemporary interest among lay persons as well as geologists—and the new specialists, paleontologists—in finding and collecting fossils and observing rock strata, the main clues in the mystery of geological time.[26] For example, Garczynski recounts that "enthusiastic geologists" in his party at Trenton Falls, where large trilobites had been found and the proprietors had a museum of specimens, used a rest period to search for fossils (I,459).[27]

In keeping with such intense interest, the artists are careful to depict individual rocks and larger geological formations with great specificity. Many of them probably followed Ruskin's advice to study geology themselves.[28] As a consequence, the rocks, cliffs, and canyons are much more accurately rendered than in many earlier picturesque views. The interest in stratification leads artists, as well as Bunce, to select as subjects regions where rock strata are exposed. In the East, the locations included Watkins Glen, Ausable Chasm, and Trenton Falls, among others, while Moran's illustrations for "The Cañons of the Colorado" introduced to a wide audience the countless layers of sediments in the deep canyons of the West just being explored and mapped. The reliance on line in wood engraving rendered the medium particularly appropriate for this endeavor—when well-drawn and engraved, wood engravings were better able to represent rock layers than steel engraving had been.

Unusual rock formations, shaped by wind and water over eons, continued to attract artists and travellers, serving as natural substitutes for architectural antiquities. A rock formation is the main subject in at least one hundred images in *Picturesque America*, and several regions where rock formations cluster, like Rock City on Lookout Mountain, the Pictured Rocks of Lake Superior, and the Dells ["Dalles"] in Wisconsin, are featured. Recurring designations include: chimney rocks in North Carolina, Mackinac Island, West Virginia, and the Upper Mississippi; cathedral rocks and cathedral spires; natural bridges, arches, and tunnels; palisades on

Lake Superior, the Hudson, and in Utah; and gardens of the gods and devil's gates, slides, and doorways.

Caves, which at midcentury had attracted intense interest as displays of the creative energies of nature, were still of some interest—Weyer's Cave in Virginia and Mammoth Cave in Kentucky are described and illustrated.[29] But excitement about caves seems to have lessened or gone out of style, whereas excitement about the canyons of the West, which expose eons of geologic history to the light of day, has increased.

Mountains were both the foundation and the apex of geological formations. *Picturesque America* adhered to the tradition of picturesque tours and numerous British and Continental viewbooks that had featured the mountains of Wales, Scotland, and Switzerland. Artists' interest in depicting mountains had increased in the 1850s and 1860s, reinforced by Ruskin's emphasis on mountains as "the bones of the earth" and "the beginning and the end of all natural scenery."[30] Ruskin considered them uniquely important subjects because of the way they stimulated the imagination and afforded the opportunity to reveal divine power and force.[31] In addition, scientists and lay persons alike were keenly interested in the phenomena that formed and shaped mountains, especially volcanoes and glaciers, which, in turn, became favorite subjects of artists.[32]

Picturesque America's publication, beginning with the *Journal* series in 1870, coincided with a period of even more intense interest in mountains and mountaineering. In these years American periodicals featured the expeditions of Britons John Tyndall and Edward Whymper in the Swiss Alps and the explorations and surveys of the Sierra Nevadas and the Rocky Mountains sponsored by California and the federal government. Stories and poems set in the mountains of the West gained popularity.[33] Clarence King of the California Geological Survey became a national celebrity with the publication of his exciting account of the ascent of Mount Tyndall in "Mountaineering in the Sierra Nevada" in the *Atlantic Monthly* beginning in May 1871. Its appearance in book form in 1872 prompted the publishers' trade journal to comment: "The mountain fever is the most glorious disease a-going, and it is 'catching' from this book."[34] King's elegant writing style caused some to call him the American Ruskin. His description of "the strange renewal of life" imparted by climbing above timberline, although not religious in any doctrinal sense, was entirely in keeping with the widespread desire to expand one's consciousness by a "spiritual" encounter with nature:

6.20   Harry Fenn, "The Mount Washington Road," *Picturesque America*, I, opposite
151. Steel engraving by S. V. Hunt, 7⅜" x 5⁵⁄₁₆".

The lifeless region, with its savage elements of sky, ice, and rock, grasps one's nature, and whether he will or no, compels it into a stern, strong accord. Then, as you come again into softer air, and enter the comforting presence of trees, and feel the grass under your feet, one fetter after another seems to unbind from your soul, leaving it free, joyous, grateful![35]

Picturesque America shares the contemporary enthusiasm for scaling peaks and confirming the beauty and sublimity of this country's mountains as compared with ranges elsewhere in the world, especially the Swiss Alps. The artists and writers give much attention to the well-known mountains of the East, which were often accessible by roads or even railroads, as was Mount Holyoke. They depict climbing them as strenuous and safe, though still somewhat adventurous group endeavors—for example, the riders on Mount Washington (I, 158) and the climbers on the Nose of Mount Mansfield (II, 283). In order to render such mountains sublime, in several instances Fenn distorts their height and dramatizes the scene by using such conventions as fog, twisted trees, and awestruck figures (see fig. 6.20 and II, 276, 281, 286). On the other hand, an older writer like Richards finds all the beauty one could want in the familiar forested Berkshires and states that tourists "familiar with Swiss scenery" claim they resemble "Alpine pictures" more than any other American mountains (II, 314).

Picturesque America stresses, however, the abundance of mountain riches yet to be discovered by the artist and tourist. For example, D. H. Strother finds the mountains of his home state West Virginia "savage" (I, 377) and ends his article with these words:

Will not some of our famous masters of landscape-art who have buried the Hudson and White Hills under mountains of canvas, and venturously plucked the mighty hearts out of the distant Andes and Rocky Mountains, condescend to accept this challenge from the virgin wilderness of West Virginia? (I, 392)

Strother's "challenge" recalls the highly effective charge two decades earlier by Alexander von Humboldt in *Cosmos*, urging landscape painters to "pass the narrow limits of the Mediterranean" and venture to other continents, especially to the "humid mountain valleys of the tropical world."[36] *Picturesque America* now challenged artists and travellers to explore the byways and newly accessible areas of the United States, not only the mountains of West Virginia and the South, but also the vast mountainous regions of the West.

The renowned snowy volcanoes of the Cascade range of Oregon and northern California, which Bierstadt had painted by 1865, received attention in volume I: "Up and Down the Columbia" depicted Mount Rainer and Mount Hood, the latter in both wood and steel engravings after Gifford (I, 31, 32). The "Northern California" section included Gifford's view of the volcanic peaks called "The Three Sisters," the Lassen Buttes, and a steel engraving after Smillie of Mount Shasta (I, opp. 424). Mount Shasta was of particular interest since Clarence King had revealed it to be the site of active glaciers—hitherto unknown in the United States—in the March 1871 *Atlantic Monthly*.[37] Garczynski's rush of words describing Mount Shasta combines an ecstatic response to the colors emanating from the glacial ice with the thrill of possible danger from the ancient volcano. He finds the colors so beautiful and varied—from "intense blue" and "lurid purple" to "emerald green" and "tender pink"—that he wants to watch them "for days." Yet sometimes, he says,

one cannot but feel a sudden contraction of the heart as the thought flashes upon the mind that Shasta is still active, and that that light, transparent cloudlet is smoke issuing from its inmost secrets. The imagination and the memory combine to tell how this might be, how volcanoes in Europe, notably Vesuvius, slept calmly, as if extinct and dead, for more than a thousand years, and then woke up to hurl death and destruction for leagues around. (I, 423)

Volume II of *Picturesque America* gives attention to the Sierras and the Colorado Rockies, with both sections stressing that the articles only skim the surface of the vast alpine regions. Burlingame forecasts explorations of the Sierras by climbers and tourists "far from the railway route," where "there is Alpine scenery, not only as grand as the great, world-known views in the heart of Switzerland, but even of almost the same character." These will be "the scene of triumphs" like the ascent of the Matterhorn, "perhaps—though Heaven forbid!—the witness of disasters as unspeakably terrible" (II, 198). Like Garczynski, Burlingame cannot resist inducing a shudder. W. H. Rideing, fresh from accompanying Hayden's survey party in the Colorado Rockies in the summer of 1873, says that although Americans are likely to have heard of Pike's Peak, Gray's Peak, and Long's Peak, "we are hazy as to their altitudes and characteristics, and could much more easily answer questions about the Alps, the Andes, or the Himalayas" (II, 482). Hayden's survey would change all that. Rideing emphasizes, as had Professor Josiah Whitney, that the great number of high peaks is the most impressive thing about the Rockies, and in this way they surpass the Alps. From Mount Lincoln, named for the president during the Civil War (when it was thought to be 18,000 feet high), one can see 130 peaks at least 13,000 feet high, and fifty over 14,000. Still, he says, "one misses the beauty of the pure Alpine mountains, with the glaciers streaming down their sides" (II, 485–86).

Rideing also misses the evidence of habitation present in the Alps and in mountain regions of the East. He struggles to express his confusing feelings about this "strange world," where "the heart of man is not felt" (II, 488, 492). He would find it easier "to go into ecstasies over the home-like view from Mount Washington" than over these "peaks that are more than twice as high" (II, 488).[38] This response is common among Easterners confronting the West for the first time.

At any rate, this region of high peaks with trackless snowfields, where the risks to climbers were evident, did not require any theatrics on the artist's part to convey a sense of sublimity. Theatrics, such as Bierstadt had used in some of his paintings, were, in fact, becoming suspect. Clarence King, in the voice of a fictional artist, had pointedly criticized Bierstadt, saying his mountains were "too high and too slim: they'd blow over in one of our fall winds."[39] On the other hand, King followed Ruskin in admiring Turner's depictions of mountains and wished for a painter like Turner to "arise and choose to paint our Sierras as they are."[40] By 1872, when some critics were calling Thomas Moran the American Turner, Bunce had much to gain by commissioning him to create images of the Rockies based on Jackson's photographs. Bunce could cut costs and circumvent charges of overblown representations through the use of photographs, while including works signed by the most admired artist of Western landscapes.

The treatment of the Colorado Rockies is somewhat fuller than that of the Sierras, but only the few mountains already famous in the early 1870s are depicted. There is no sweeping panorama matching the description of the view from Mount Lincoln, perhaps because Jackson made none or because such a view would not have been effective as a small-scale wood engraving. In addition to the recently celebrated Mountain of the Holy Cross, already discussed in chapter 5, most of the mountains mentioned in the text are included: Pike's Peak, Long's Peak (in both a wood engraving and the steel engraving after Worthington Whittredge's acclaimed painting *The Rocky Mountains*), Gray's Peak (named after the famous scientist Asa Gray, who had climbed it in 1872), and Snow-Mass, named by Hayden

6.21 Thomas Moran, "Chicago Lake," *Picturesque America*, II, 491. Wood engraving, 9⁵⁄₁₆" x 6⁵⁄₁₆".

and renowned for its large snowfield. Also included is Moran's rendering, after one or more Jackson photographs, of "Chicago Lake" (fig. 6.21), which lies, Rideing says, "at the foot of Mount Rosalie" (II, 494)—suggesting inevitable comparisons to Bierstadt's highly dramatic *Storm in the Rocky Mountains, Mount Rosalie* (1866).[41] The contrast could hardly be greater between Moran's tonally rich but straightforward depiction of the pristine lake crisply reflecting the domed mountains (II, 491) and Bierstadt's sharp peak almost lost in the swirling clouds. Awareness of this contrast may have led some readers to place greater credence in *Picturesque America*'s images as accurate representations of the Western mountains and less in Bierstadt's paintings. Certainly the book presented an impressive number of snowy peaks, very different from the forested mountains of the East, while stressing that uncounted others were yet to be climbed and depicted.

   Agricultural landscapes receive scant attention in *Picturesque America*, considering that a majority of the population still lived on farms in 1870 and that the nation's agricultural productivity greatly impressed visitors from abroad. When Anthony Trollope saw the grain pouring into Chicago and Buffalo, he said he "began to know what it was for a country to overflow with milk and honey, to burst with its own fruits, and be smothered in its own riches."[42] Yet only about thirty-five views, or about 3 per cent of the series total, include either farming operations, hay wagons, or livestock. In almost every case, the farmers and their activities are in the middle or background and appear very small, their importance diminished. This seems emblematic of their peripheral role in the increasingly industrial and urban nation, and of the extent to which the agrarian ideology of the early nineteenth century had waned.

Certainly for the team of city dwellers involved in this project, farm landscapes were primarily of nostalgic interest. When the writers or artists dealt with agrarian subjects, they utilized several conventional approaches emphasizing the country's fertility, the continuity of rural life, and the predominance of the self-sufficient family farm. In several instances, the artists placed cows or sheep in the foreground of a city view, suggesting undisturbed survival of the pastoral landscape adjacent to the city (II, 37, 106, 154, 239, 240, 570). Artists also represented farming primarily in the Northeast, where the scene could more readily include a river and mountains in the background. Yet, the farm population of the Northeast had been decreasing for years as the major grain producing areas had shifted west, first to Ohio, Indiana, and Illinois, and more recently to the fast-developing regions of Minnesota, Dakota Territory, Nebraska, and Kansas. Furthermore, with two exceptions the artists ignored agriculture in the South, which had been devastated in many regions during the war and raised difficult questions about labor supply under the new social order. The exceptions to this are scenes of family farms, one in the mountains of North Carolina (I, 140) and one in Virginia (I, 349). No farming is shown west of the Mississippi.

The depictions were also nostalgic in that they showed small groups, presumably families, working their own land with hand tools or simple plows and one or at most two teams of mules, oxen, or horses. In a time when large-scale operations involving huge tracts of land, many hired hands, and new tools and machinery were becoming more common, *Picturesque America* ignored such developments altogether. There is no picture remotely like those in the composite that appeared in *Harper's Weekly* September 23, 1871, showing farming operations on a sixty-five-square-mile

6.22 J. D. Woodward, *Cambridge from Charles River, Mass.*, Sept. 30, 1872 (detail). Pencil and white on beige paper, 7⅞" x 10½". Courtesy the Diocese of Virginia.

tract in Illinois.[43] Smillie described his reaction to seeing a mechanical reaper in California on the way to Yosemite, highlighting the difference between old and new methods:

Nothing could be more foreign to Eastern eyes than the huge machinery, barn-like in dimensions, drawn by a score of mules, "heading" a swathe of at least fifteen feet wide. Every thing was in proportion to the vast fields, of thousands of acres each, that had to be worked over. (I, 467)

But Smillie did not stop to draw this "foreign" operation; rather, he hurried on to Yosemite Valley.

The farm views also subtly reconfirm the longstanding celebration of the fertility of the country's soil by depicting two of the activities most emblematic of nature's bounty—haymaking and pumpkin gathering.[44] Alterations on the woodblocks to several of Woodward's drawings show that this emphasis was intentional. To his drawing of Cambridge, Massachusetts, from the

6.23 J. D. Woodward, "Charles River," *Picturesque America*, II, 246. Wood engraving, 4" x 9¼".

Charles River, originally including only two small haystacks on the flats, he added a towering haystack, several men with pitchforks, and two wagons (figs. 6.22, 6.23). These additions, along with the strong vertical of the sailboat's mast in the foreground, added interest to the largely horizontal composition. They also highlighted the continuing pastoral nature of the region and nature's abundance. Similarly, Woodward altered his image of a farm complex near Lenox, Massachusetts, by adding three men loading pumpkins into a cart (II, 308). Pumpkin gathering also appears in the foreground of a view of Albany (II, 470).

The pictorial message of scenes of harvesting and loading for market is that the farmers are still in control of marketing their produce. This was still true in many long-settled areas but was frequently not the case in the more recently developed farming regions dependent on the railroad, where middlemen controlled and profited from marketing the produce of others.

Several of *Picturesque America*'s rural scenes also show nostalgic attitudes in the artist's depiction of tending livestock or harvesting as pleasant, almost idyllic, recreation. Two views show children tending cows (I, 351, II, 570), and Waud's "Moss Gatherers" (I, 272) suggests a leisurely activity involving much rest. The artists also show very few women working in the fields, which many thought was more characteristically a necessity of Europe's peasant class than of American farm families.

Is there no other change
for thee, that lurks
Among the future ages?
Will not man
Seek out strange arts to wither
and deform
The pleasant landscape which
thou makest green?
Or shall the veins that feed
thy constant stream
Be choked in middle earth,
and flow no more
For ever, that the water-plants
along
Thy channel perish, and the
bird in vain
Alight to
drink?

6.24   Harry Fenn, [". . . strange arts to wither and deform"], in William Cullen Bryant, *The Story of the Fountain* (1872), 46. Wood engraving by J. Karst, 6" x 4⅛"; page size, 8⅜" x 6½".

In addition to great changes in the means of agricultural production, during this period there were unprecedented increases in manufacturing, mining, and lumbering. As Allan Nevins characterized the years 1865 to 1878, "More cotton spindles were set revolving, more iron furnaces were lighted, more steel was made, more coal and copper were mined, more lumber was sawed and hewed, more houses and shops constructed and more manufactories of different kinds established, than during any equal term in our earlier history."[45] Some were acutely aware that such activities had negative as well as positive results and questioned whether their proliferation could continue without destroying many beautiful and picturesque aspects of the landscape. The usually optimistic Appleton firm aired such concerns in its 1872 gift book, *The Story of the Fountain*, where Bryant asked at the end whether the "strange arts" of the future would "wither and deform / The pleasant landscape" the stream makes green. Accompanying these lines were Fenn's images of railroad construction and a nightmarish industrial landscape (fig. 6.24).

Yet *Picturesque America* communicates an interesting counterpoint regarding such developments: The dominant theme of the pictures is that the means of production have changed little, as in agriculture, and that mills and factories can be easily incorporated as parts of picturesque landscapes. Images of old mills and forges figure prominently in the book. When steam-powered factories and steel mills are included, on the other hand, they are small and distant. The few images dealing with mining or lumbering operations likewise show old-fashioned, small-scale operations or focus on the dramatic setting and the flurry of transportation activity, as at Mauch Chunk and along the Susquehanna.

In the text, however, the writers frequently express great pride both in the new technologies that facilitated increased production and in the role of the United States as supplier of numerous products to a world market. They also boast of the country's great wealth of mineral and forest resources. Several writers also clearly welcome the spread of industrial activities to the South and the West. The author of the section "On the Savannah" mentions with approval that "Augusta has been quietly solving the problem whether cotton fabrics can be manufactured profitably in cotton-growing sections, by establishing and successfully working a large factory, which now employs over five hundred operatives" (I, 131). In the West, along the Truckee River in California, Burlingame was pleased to hear "the buzzing saw-mills of an incipient civilization hum with homelike New-England sound on its banks" (II, 194).

Such attitudes were in accord with the still prevalent notion that introducing the "factory in the forest"—thus utilizing and making productive the power of nature's watercourses without altering the country's predominantly agrarian quality—was a sign of advancing civilization.[46] De Fontaine's musings about future industry along the French Broad in North Carolina epitomize such attitudes:

Doubtless the time is not far distant when the whistle of the locomotive, the hum of the woollen spindle and loom, the noisy life of the forge and trip-hammer, and the whir of the factory, will be heard blending with the melody of the rushing waters, and adding new strains to those which Nature has sung alone in these wild scenes since the creation. (I, 146)

Lumbering in the Eastern states was less welcome, however. The attitude toward large-scale timbering was the exception to the general enthusiasm for "progress" in the form of expanding manufacturing and resource extraction. It is not surprising that the writers object to the aesthetics of heavily timbered areas or that the artists generally avoid depicting them, considering the widespread love of trees and their role as important compositional elements in most images of picturesque and beautiful scenery. Negative attitudes toward lumbering had been aroused by extensive timbering in the East and by the contemporary reassessment of clear-cut lumbering as wasteful. There was also a growing recognition of the connection between the destruction of forests and problems of erosion and water supply.[47]

Several writers stress other negative visual impacts of industrial development. They resent the "unsightly encroachments" of "progress" that mar their beloved waterfalls in order to utilize their power (II, 287, 352). Richards is vexed because the view of the falls of the Housatonic at Falls Village, Connecticut, known as Canaan Falls, is "blemished" by "the ugly shanties and shops" of "factories, forges, and furnaces, useful indeed, but which we would fain banish into caverns, or at least into unlovely corners" (II, 295). Yet Woodward's view of the falls shows no sign of these "blemishes" (II, 292).[48]

In several other instances, the writers describe manufacturing cities with a mixture of revulsion and excitement: Although Garczynski says the factories of Harrisburg and Troy "vomit" black smoke (a recurring metaphor), he finds their chimneys "aspiring" and "inspiriting" (II, 208, 465). In describing Pittsburgh, long known as the "Smoky City," Woolson compares it to the "aspect of a volcano" and makes the inevitable allusion to Blake's "dark Satanic mills":

A cloud of smoke rests over it, and at night it is illuminated by the glow and flash of the iron-mills filling its valley and stretching up its hill-sides, . . . ever ceaselessly gleaming, smoking and roaring. Looking down on Pittsburg at night from the summit of its surrounding hills, the city . . . seems satanic. . . . But it is the smoke and the fires of Pittsburg that give it its character. . . . Anthony Trollope wrote, "It is the blackest place I ever saw, but its very blackness is picturesque." . . . What a grand, lurid picture Turner, Ruskin's art-god, would have made of Pittsburg at night! (II, 153–54)

Compared to this vivid description, the pictorial images of Pittsburgh are tame. Waud's original drawing from Reservoir Hill does show a city darkened by smoke, but in the wood engraving the sky and background hills are lighter and the smoke less pervasive (II, 148).[49] The attention to church towers and the addition of a cow, pigs, and several figures in the foreground also tend to link the scene with earlier picturesque views of cities and thus diminish its "lurid," "satanic" quality. Similarly, the distant views of Harrisburg and Troy contain very little smoke, despite what the text says, and are rendered picturesque by foreground details of trees (II, 206) and, in the case of Troy, by the inclusion of an old man and child and the device of an oval format set within a composite of attractive nearby scenes (II, 467). Although the writers were quick to describe "enterprising" and "bustling" manufacturing centers (II, 466), the artists depicted them from a distance, as picturesque and little different from other cities.

The writers also give attention to mineral extraction in a way the artists do not. The artists' avoidance of such scenes is not surprising considering how radically mining disturbs an area's terrain. A compelling case for national pride, however, could not ignore the nation's mineral wealth. In the article about Lake Superior, Woolson boasts that the "Iron Mountain" near Marquette yields "thousands of tons year after year" and "scarcely misses them from its massive sides" (I, 400). She claims that the copper mines at Keweenaw are the greatest in the world, now "supplying the whole country" and even aiding "the Old World" (I, 401–2). Similarly, de Fontaine speculates that in the not far distant future the Cumberland Gap region "must yield to the march of improvement, and pour forth the treasures of the mineralogical wealth now latent in its soil" (I, 237). Burlingame and Rideing mention mining operations in Colorado (II, 490) and Nevada (II, 192), but no images are included.

As with mining, writers could not overlook the relatively new and highly profitable industry of drilling and refining oil to produce kerosene (gasoline was still considered a useless by-product). Woolson's excitement about the as-yet-unfathomed potential of this "fiery fluid" coupled with awareness of its danger results in a passage elaborately layered with metaphors—kerosene is a monarch accompanied by Death, one of the Four Horsemen of the Apocalypse. From the Pennsylvania petroleum district, she says, to the refineries of Cleveland

comes that fiery fluid which, hidden through all these centuries, has crowned the nineteenth with its dangerous splendor. Here it is purified, and sent forth into the wide world to fulfil its mission. In its train is power as yet but half discovered; in its train is light as yet but half developed. But with it rides Death on a fiery steed, taking his victims hourly; . . . So far, our new slave of the lamp is a dark master; and the world waits for the mind which shall put the yoke upon this doubtful, dangerous servant, and make it do its work in safety, as steam and electricity do theirs. (I, 529)

Although Woolson says Cleveland's oil refineries, "which line the river-valley for miles," are its distinctive feature (I, 529), Woodward does not depict them.

Thus, while the text of *Picturesque America* gave considerable attention to the development of natural resources, industry, and railroads, the images reassured readers that the impact of such activities on the landscape was minimal—and sometimes positive. Adhering to the traditional subjects of picturesque views, the artists focused primarily on the abundance and variety of picturesque and sublime scenic features and on older, more familiar modes of industry, agriculture, and transportation—like mills, oxcarts, and sailboats. By utilizing familiar conventions when depicting factories and trains, they incorporated these elements into attractive "scenes," clearly recognizable as picturesque, conveying the message that the potentially disturbing visual aspects of progress could be hidden or dwarfed by nature's abundance. In views of the Northeast, artists followed the traditional approach of river journeys, concentrating on peaceful villages and pastoral scenes, and avoiding the numerous manufacturing centers. In the West they stressed sublime nature still wild and untouched, pointedly avoiding any evidence of recent enterprise.

By including descriptions and image after image of rocky coasts and snowclad mountains, the contributors countered some of the most prevalent negative impressions about the landscape of the United States. In addition, their attention to numerous unusual geological features made the case that extraordinary "natural monuments" could adequately compensate the lack of ancient architectural monuments. Finally, the text and pictures stressed that in its incomparable scenic variety—from the cascades, forested mountains, and island-dotted lakes of the Northeast, to the exotic swamps of Florida, to the glaciated peaks, giant trees, bizarre rock formations, and unfathomed canyons of the West—no other country could match the United States. Its "Book of Nature" offered those who would "read" it unprecedented opportunities to learn of the power and benevolence of divine creation.

A Civilization Advancing

Bunce and his co-contributors to *Picturesque America* also had a keen desire to demonstrate that the cities of the United States were centers of "civilization," whose inhabitants cared about more than money and acquisition. Both writers and artists enthusiastically embraced the mission to document such cultural advancement. They did so by showing that many cities possessed not only historic buildings, but also attractive parks and squares with monuments and fountains comparable to those in London or Paris, monumental public buildings, numerous educational, social, and cultural institutions, substantial homes and businesses of brick and stone, fashionable suburbs, and orderly, well-dressed residents who knew how to appreciate and use these amenities. These recent improvements often implicitly demonstrated the compatibility of democracy and "civilization," with civic-minded philanthropists taking initiatives to build public parks and monuments comparable to those built in Europe by royalty. The text and pictures join in celebrating both those historic aspects of cities considered picturesque, such as notable older buildings and busy harbors, and the latest amenities that signified advanced "civilization" and a citizenry of culture and taste.

These different but parallel emphases can be illustrated by two of Woodward's images of Detroit, a city Anthony Trollope had dismissed on

6.25 J. D. Woodward, *Glimpse of Detroit from Vances Mill, Windsor*, June 28, 1872. Pencil and white on tan paper, 10½" x 8⅜". Courtesy the Diocese of Virginia.

his 1861 visit as "half-finished" and "uninteresting"—"neither pleasant nor picturesque."[50] Woodward titled his drawing of an old windmill *Glimpse of Detroit from Vances Mill, Windsor,* and indeed, the city can be seen in the background (fig. 6.25). But the extremely picturesque old structure, apparently dating from the early period of French settlement, suggests the long history of the region and a link with the Old World (see the wood engraving, I, 545), complementing Woolson's claim that Detroit was already "a century old" when Cleveland and Buffalo were born (I, 547). The other image shows the city's center as viewed from the top of the new city hall. Woodward's drawing emphasizes that building's large urns and balustrade and the elegant Second Empire style building and church tower across the square (fig. 6.26). For a city that had grown from 3000 to more than 80,000 in the past forty years, *Picturesque America*'s wood engraving attested to considerable elegance (fig. 6.27). With the addition of a well-dressed man, with his dog, enjoying the view, and more pedestrians and vehicles in the engraving, the scene recalls European plazas—perhaps even Venice's Piazza San Marco as viewed from the basilica.

Given these two parallel missions, the neglect of the "unfinished," rude cities more typical of fast-growing regions or those heavily damaged during the war, like Chattanooga, is not surprising. Either the artists did not draw these places, or Bunce rejected the drawings. Waud's rendering of Duluth, Minnesota, a town just beginning to undergo rapid growth and termed "thriving" by Rideing (II, 538), was not used. Its "ungroomed" waterfront and boxlike wooden buildings were neither elegant nor picturesque.[51] More in keeping with the conventions was Fenn's dynamic image of city building created for *The Song of the Sower* (fig. 6.28). Yet such images of construction were deemed inappropriate for *Picturesque America*—perhaps because they depicted a transitory rather than a lasting condition.

In celebrating cities and towns of the United States, the artists and writers continue the tradition of picturesque viewbooks in several notable ways: they show great appreciation for trees, particularly old and stately ones; they prefer irregular sites and street plans; and they greatly admire older sections that are reminiscent of Europe.

Throughout *Picturesque America*, the presence of many trees renders cities and towns attractive. Woolson says that Cleveland, where "the houses are embowered in foliage," is "universally considered the most beautiful town on the Great Lakes" (I, 527). The steel engraving after

6.26 J. D. Woodward, *Detroit from top of City Hall*, June 29, 1872. Pencil and white on tan paper, 10½" x 8⅜". Courtesy the Diocese of Virginia.

6.27 J. D. Woodward, "Glance at Detroit from the City Hall," *Picturesque America*, I, 548. Wood engraving, 8⅞" x 6 3/16".

Sprinkle the furrow's even trace
   For those whose toiling hands uprear
The roof-trees of our swarming race,
    By grove and plain, by stream and
       mere;

6.28   Harry Fenn, ["The roof-trees of our swarming race"], in William Cullen Bryant, *The Song of the Sower* (1871), 26. Wood engraving by Harley, 6" x 3⁵⁄₁₆"; page size, 8⅝" x 6½".

Warren shows the city from Reservoir Walk, where fashionably dressed strollers look toward the lake across a dense stand of trees dotted with churches and elegant residences (I, opp. 529). In contrast, Bunce considers the village of East Eden (now Bar Harbor, Maine) inappropriately named because it is built upon a "treeless plain" and the cottages "erected by wealthy gentlemen of Boston" stand "without trees, garden, or other pleasant surroundings" (I, 3). The conviction that trees were crucial elements in beautifying cities and in creating attractive settings for homes had grown stronger since its popularization in the works of Andrew Jackson Downing beginning in the 1840s. The Appleton firm had promoted harmonizing houses with the landscape in books like *The Art of Beautifying Suburban Home Grounds of Small Extent* and in the pages of *Appletons' Journal.*[52] The widespread interest in planting trees in public spaces as well is indicated by the proliferation of Village Improvement Societies, of which there were two hundred in New England alone in the 1870s. Among their goals was "to improve and ornament the streets and public grounds of the village by planting and cultivating trees."[53]

Cities were also judged by the extent to which they displayed the picturesque hallmarks of variety and unevenness. Thus, Boston's Beacon Street, with its "buildings piled irregularly one above the other," rising toward the State House, seemed to G. M. Towle very like "that most picturesque of British cities," Edinburgh (II, 234). On the other hand, flat sites were dull, just as the rectangular grid street pattern, fostered by the Land Ordinance of 1785 and now spreading across the continent in the railroad towns, was seen as monotonous and stiff, particularly if the streets were also narrow, as in Philadelphia (II, 25). More appealing was the irregular pattern of Hartford (II, 70).

The enthusiasm for architectural antiquities in text and pictures clearly imparts the message that appreciation of "ruins" and historic buildings indicates that a person values art and understands the principles of picturesque touring. For those still developing this capacity, *Picturesque America* offered instruction by precept and example. The artist could teach appreciation of ruins, just as he or she could instruct in appreciation of nature. A prime example of this is Bunce's elaboration of how he "discovers the use of his eyes" with Fenn in Charleston. Although the "rude surfaces and antique color" of the city's old brick houses might at first displease "Northerners reared amid the supreme newness of our always reconstructing cities," with an artist's instruction the visitor learns

6.29 Harry Fenn, "Canal, Richmond," *Picturesque America*, I, 80. Wood engraving by John Filmer, 6⅜" x 4¾".

to appreciate the charms of Charleston's "time-tinted mansions" and fine bits of "dilapidation" (I, 199–200).

Other examples of such "fine bits of dilapidation" include several of Fenn's illustrations of St. Augustine (I, 186–87, 192–93), said to resemble "some of the old towns of Spain and Italy" more than any place else in the United States, and a scene beside the canal in Richmond that includes "ramshackle porches of the negro tenements" and the walls of a warehouse partially destroyed during the war, with Gothic windows that bring to mind a ruined abbey (fig. 6.29). Richmond native J. R. Thompson recognized a number of ironies connected with Fenn's "sketch,"

which, at first glance, looks as if it were designed to set before us a quaint, old, tumble-down nook or corner of some European city. Upon examination, however, one sees the African element of the population in such force . . . as to determine the locality in a Southern town of the United States. One cannot help recognizing in this sketch how much more effective in the hands of the artist is dilapidation than tidiness, and a ruin than a perfect structure. (I, 81)

Thompson then notes that Richmond still shows "in the marks of her great conflagration, much of that undesirable picturesqueness that belongs to ruins" (I, 81). Similarly, Ruskin had objected to what he called the "heartless picturesque," when the artist, concerned only with visual attributes, had no sympathy for the subject.[54] Having suffered through the "ravages" of the war, Thompson cannot limit his reactions to the visual or aesthetic alone when considering Richmond's ruins. It was obviously easier for the visiting artist from the North to find this scene of poverty and destruction exotically picturesque. The tenements closer to home in New York City are not treated in the book; this is, in fact, the only tenement shown.

Some Northern "bits of dilapidation" appear in Fenn's illustrations of East Hampton, Long Island. A view from the church belfry shows the village with its windmills, "reminding one forcibly of the quaint old mills in Holland which artists have always delighted to paint" (I, 255, fig. 6.30). Two scenes (I, 254, 255) show the home of John Howard Payne, composer of "Home, Sweet Home" (1823), which was experiencing a resurgence in popularity in this period when many were nostalgic for the home they had left.

In accord with the growing movement to preserve the nation's past, Bunce finds it "inexcusable" that the old belfry was destroyed shortly after

6.30 Harry Fenn, "East Hampton, From the Church Belfry," *Picturesque America*, I, 253. Wood engraving by Harley, 8⅞" x 6⅛".

Fenn made his sketch from it, and pleads for the preservation of Payne's home (I, 256). Elsewhere in the book, other writers urge the preservation of such historic sites as the forts at St. Augustine, Florida, and Ticonderoga, New York. This movement, which *Appletons' Journal* also supported by a series on historic houses almost simultaneous with "Picturesque America," had slowly been gaining momentum since the Mount Vernon Ladies' Association formed in 1853.

Attention in cities and towns, however, was not limited to conventional picturesque features. Both text and pictures gave equal, or sometimes greater, space to recent monuments, fountains, public buildings, and municipal parks and squares similar to those that so impressed travellers in Britain and Europe. Bunce and his contributors made a special effort to show that "civilization" was flourishing not only in the older cities of the Eastern seaboard, but also in the growing population centers of the Middle West, like Chicago, St. Louis, Cincinnati, Cleveland, Milwaukee, and Detroit.

Commemorative monuments and statues demonstrated that a citizenry valued its history and honored its heroes. Several sections featuring cities open with an illustration of a major monument, such as Richmond's equestrian statue of Washington by sculptor Thomas Crawford (I, 70); Providence's Soldiers and Sailors' Monument, erected in 1871 (I, 496, described 505–6); and Baltimore's famous Washington Monument, a landmark since its erection in 1812 (II, 97; described 103–4).[55] A number of other statues and obelisks celebrating the nation's heroes are illustrated, including the monument to the Revolutionary War general Nathanael Greene in Savannah (I, 122); the statue of Commodore Matthew C. Perry in Newport (I, 375); and the tomb of James Monroe in Richmond (I, 70).[56]

Similarly, the monumental fountains that often required major civic works programs to bring clean water into the city figure prominently in both text and pictures. Thompson notes that the fountain in Savannah's Forsyth Park, depicted in a fine wood engraving after Fenn (I, 121), is modeled on the one in Paris's Place de la Concorde (I, 119). A composite by Perkins shows nine fountains in Philadelphia, including the "largest and one of the most beautiful" in Franklin Square (II, 28). The writer, C. D. Gardette, praises the "humane and enlightened labors and taste of a few gentlemen" who formed a Fountain Society in 1869 to provide numerous street fountains offering "wholesome refreshment . . . to the parched throats of hundreds of thousands of their fellow-creatures" (II, 31). The "fellow-creatures" shown are primarily well-dressed women and children, although a few appear to be laborers.

This reference to organized private benevolence in Philadelphia is one example from many. The *Picturesque America* writers give considerable recognition to the proliferating public and private educational and charitable institutions, such as colleges, libraries, hospitals, and asylums for the deaf and insane. The need for these institutions was becoming ever more obvious as many left their families behind in the move from farms or villages to cities. As immigrants from various backgrounds swelled the population of cities, numerous charitable organizations outside the framework of churches formed to try to educate the new groups in the ways of middle-class respectability.[57] The text shows that organized private charities were a major force at this time, while governmental support of social services and education was growing gradually.[58]

The writers also praised cities that had built or were building imposing public structures, and the wide avenues that set them off—foreshadowing the City Beautiful movement of the 1890s and early twentieth century. The artists, in turn, depicted numerous such buildings and avenues. Towle noted, with evident relief, that Washington, D.C., thanks to sizable expenditures and a "newly-born pride in the government," presented "sights agreeable to the eye and mostly in good taste," especially the "magnificent white marble capitol," the Post Office Department, and the "yet-handsomer Patent Office" (II, 565). In contrast, T. M. Clark faulted Providence for having "no civic building of any description that deserves notice" (I, 500) but pointed out recent "measures" to erect a new state house that would "fairly represent the wealth and culture of the city and the State" (I, 500). He expressed great pride, however, in Providence's new State Hospital, built "entirely by private munificence."[59]

Among other buildings constructed with private funds, churches received considerable attention in both text and illustrations. The Gothic Revival style was particularly admired, and two churches in that style by Richard Upjohn were depicted: Trinity Church in New York (II, 551) and Grace Church in Providence (I, 500, 504). An adaptation of the more flamboyant High Victorian Gothic championed by Ruskin, with chromatic decoration, was seen in Mauch Chunk's "new, picturesque church" (I, 113). The artists were fond of depicting church towers and domes of civic buildings, which served the dual purpose of giving evidence of advanced "civilization" and providing the vertical accents needed for an interesting composition. Describing the proliferation of towers in Milwaukee, Bunce, with uncharacteristic ironic humor, suggested that some comparisons with Europe result from wishful thinking: "The city has so many domes, turrets, cupolas, spires, and towers, that you might imagine yourself in some Mediterranean port, especially if it happened that you had never been in a Mediterranean port" (II, 524).

Regarding building materials, there was a strong preference for brick and stone over more combustible wood. When Rideing visited Montreal, he was impressed by how much more substantially built it was than most American cities, with miles of limestone wharves and finely paved streets lined with stone buildings (II, 379). But many American cities were shown to have substantial buildings as well. The brick and stone buildings along Milwaukee's riverfront were impressive in Waud's illustration (II, 527). So, too, were the relatively uniform buildings of Chicago's business district, rebuilt after the fire of 1871 (II, 516).

The artists and writers of *Picturesque America* also devoted a great deal of attention to parks and open spaces—another arena in which Americans hoped to rival European cities. Steeped in the belief that encounters with nature would prove beneficial to all, and were especially needed by those living in crowded cities and unable to travel to the country often, *Picturesque America* endorsed making "rural beauty and sylvan seclusion" accessible to city dwellers. The contributors describe with admiration the earliest examples of large parks, the "rural cemeteries," like Boston's Mount Auburn (1831) and Brooklyn's Greenwood (1842), built on the outskirts of cities by private subscription as churchyards ran out of space. Not solely "cities of the dead," they served as picturesque parks to which many flocked for strolls and picnics, as well as to contemplate mortality and honor family members. They combined many of the features most sought-after by excursionists, as Towle's description of Mount Auburn reveals:

While Nature has been lavish with foliage and picturesque prospects, art has bestowed every various and appropriate adornment. There are lakes and ponds, elaborate tombs and monuments, nooks and grottos, and an abundance of flowers, quiet paths beside modest graves, and, on the summit of the highest hill, a large gray tower rising above the trees, whence a panorama of Boston and its suburbs, for miles around opens upon the view. (II, 252)

Woodward's illustrations accompanying this description show Mount Auburn's tower crowded with visitors enjoying the view, and a lake and fountain, with a family feeding swans (II, 250, 251). Other cemeteries mentioned or pictured include Magnolia Cemetery outside Charleston (I, 210), Mount Hope near Rochester (II, 363), Oakwood in Troy (II, 467), and Washington Park in Albany (II, 469). The enthusiasm and pride they engendered is seen in Bunce's description of Greenwood as "the handsomest cemetery, probably, in the world" (II, 564).

The recognition that ever-larger cities were to be a permanent fixture of the American scene soon fostered interest in preserving or restoring nearby open areas as public parks. The writers and artists of *Picturesque America* depict the parks of Savannah, Baltimore, Philadelphia, Hartford, Boston, Chicago, St. Louis, and Oakland, among others, stressing the variety of scenery, as well as the union of art and nature they represent. Some, such as New York's Central Park, had been molded by art from a refuse dump. Bunce says it "only needs a little more maturing of the trees to be one of the handsomest parks of the world" (II, 557). Boston's Public Garden, similarly "redeemed . . . from the waters of the Back Bay," stirs Towle's pride. Viewed from the steeple of the Arlington Street Church, it is

one of the most striking and noble scenes which any American city presents—a scene of brightness, beauty, luxury, adorned by the elegances of horticultural, architectural, and sculptural art . . . and gifted by Nature with fine contrasts of elevation, declivity, and outline. (II, 233)

Anticipating the Centennial Exposition in 1876 planned for Philadelphia's Fairmount Park, Gardette predicted that in "twenty years, Fairmount will be as famous in its way as the Bois de Boulogne of Paris, Hyde Park of London, the Pincian Hill of Rome, the Cascine of Florence, or the Prater of Vienna" (II, 42–43). His list showed that such parks were familiar to many Americans, as well as models to emulate. Yet in all the space devoted to parks in *Picturesque America*, the writers failed to give any sustained attention to a favorite theme of American park planners like Frederick Law Olmsted—how parks would help alleviate the major contemporary urban problems of poor public health and the increasing separation of rich and poor. This silence is entirely in keeping with the goal of presenting a reassuring picture of the country.

The text and pictures also show undiluted admiration for the private family parks of the new suburbs growing on the outskirts of cities, a trend that would lead to the typically American pattern of central business district surrounded by residential areas instead of the mixture of businesses

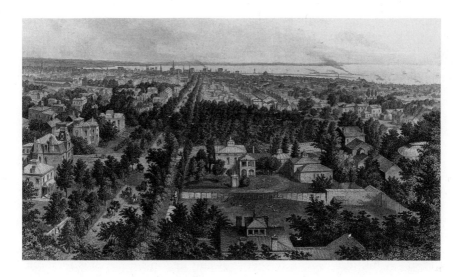

6.31 A. C. Warren, "City of Buffalo," *Picturesque America*, I, opposite 521. Steel engraving by W. Wellstood, 5⅜" x 9⅛".

and residences typical of older cities. The preference for picturesque scenery was an important impetus toward suburbs, but it was the railroad or streetcar that made such living arrangements practical. Many came to regard the picturesque suburb, with curving, tree-lined streets and spacious lots, as the most desirable living environment (unless, of course, they could afford even larger estates). Indeed, it would be interesting to know how many *Picturesque America* contributors lived in suburbs; certainly Fenn did. Even then much of the appeal was to withdraw from the "turmoil" of New York to "the serene quiet and sylvan charms" only an hour's ride away in New Jersey (II, 50). Similarly, Woolson says, without apparent irony, that Cincinnati's Clifton Hills contain "beautiful, castle-like mansions" where the people "retire" when work is over with "an air of calm contentment and indifference to the rest of the world" (II, 163).[60] A. C. Warren's bird's-eye view of Buffalo includes several such mansions in the foreground, while relegating the older, denser city to the background (fig. 6.31). This depiction is in keeping with Woolson's stress on the theaters, horse races, club houses, and balls that establish Buffalo's "social reputation" (I, 520).

Whereas before the Civil War there had still been considerable antipathy towards mansions as evidence of aristocratic, foreign taint, this was not true in the postwar period.[61] The writers make no attempt to mask their enthusiasm for the new villas and mansions—"palatial" or "castle-like"— and the wealth necessary to build them. They admire industriousness and consider wealth the reward of practicing thrift and succeeding in the competitive struggle. The old republican emphasis on restraint and self-denial has disappeared. Towle's description of Boston's Back Bay neatly reconciles the conflicting values of thrift and luxurious expenditures:

You reach the quarter of elegance and luxury and lavish taste which has sprung up entirely within twenty years . . . [I]t symbolizes Boston in its present and future prosperity; it tells the story of what fruit, in domestic luxury and architectural display, persistent thrift in commerce, and the busy competition in the active walks of life, bring forth in these latter days. (II, 238)

Such attitudes coincided with those of Henry Ward Beecher, who compared the successful businessman to the great elm tree in the social garden and encouraged the rich to spend money on noble private residences as well as on art galleries, public parks, and monuments. He legitimized such expenditures by maintaining that stately mansions and gardens benefited the entire community, providing examples of beauty that educated and elevated the poor.[62] His endorsement of conspicuous display of wealth represents a sea-change from his father, Lyman Beecher's, warning against the moral dangers of opulence—"debasing the mind and enervating the body."[63]

The pride in grand civic buildings, mansions, and suburban villas spills over into considerable interest in architectural styles. Clark finds Providence, with its wooden houses in the old-fashioned Greek Revival style, unattractive. Although opinions vary, a number of writers express enthusiasm for new buildings with mansard roofs, in the Second Empire style so popular in the 1860s and 1870s. Towle says that "Mansard is the tutelar architectural saint" of the entire Back Bay (II, 238, 244). W. F. Williams describes the same preferences at work as "city-folk" transform old Dutch farmhouses of Orange Mountain, New Jersey, with verandas, larger windows, and "even" mansard roofs (II, 50). Indeed, William Henry Appleton had recently converted his Greek Revival style country estate in Riverdale, New York, Wave Hill, to a Second Empire villa.[64]

This highly positive view of elegant suburban residences bespeaks the aspirations of many in this period. Just as *Picturesque America* provided an ideal model of travel, it offered a model of residential luxury to strive toward. The writers' frequent linking of such "fruits" with the virtues of thrift and enterprise also bespeaks the continuing force of the ideology that the United States was a fluid, open society in which merit would be rewarded and all who were industrious could become capitalists—that is, people with property and savings. Careful examination of the pictures reveals that the images of cities and suburbs are overwhelmingly peopled by those who have already attained this goal—based on the clues of their dress and manner. Like those engaged in picturesque touring, those depicted in cities are mainly fashionably dressed men and women with the leisure to stand at ease in the streets, to enjoy the parks, fountains, and monuments with their children, and to gather in small groups for conversation.

Picturesque America's cumulative picture of an orderly, elegantly dressed, highly homogeneous population in the cities of the Northeast and Middle West needs to be placed alongside factual data about the period and some very different interpretations in other contemporary sources. By the early 1870s, U.S. cities were highly heterogeneous in terms of ethnicity, religion, and wealth. Waves of Roman Catholic Irish immigrants had settled in New York, Boston, and the manufacturing centers of Connecticut and Massachusetts. In 1873 more immigrants entered the country than in any previous year—460,000, including Swedes, Slavs, Bohemians, Italians, and French Canadians, as well as large numbers of Britons, Germans, and Irish.[65] In 1869 in *The Great Metropolis: A Mirror of New York*, reporter Junius Henri Browne wrote that a walk in the city's streets was "like a voyage around the globe."[66] Many immigrants traveled no farther than the tenements of New York, which were receiving much attention in the press for their crowded, unhealthy conditions, and the growing number of street children. Another journalist, Edward Crapsey, maintained, in "The Nether Side of New York" (*The Galaxy*, 1872), that more than half of the city's population was "crammed into the deadly tenements." He also claimed he received an average of five requests for food each day at his own house, as did most of his friends.[67]

As poverty became more visible, so did displays of wealth. Browne was keenly aware of this. The first chapter of his book was "Rich and Poor" and included a picture of a mansard-roofed mansion next to a hovel. He was also aware that virtue and industriousness were not the only roads to wealth, and that many of the "new rich" had "profited by contracts and speculation during the War."[68] Although *Picturesque America* was silent about it, everyone knew that corruption had led to great fortunes in the post-Civil War years as well. Like Browne, *Appletons' Journal* gave some attention to the problems of poor and immigrant populations and possible solutions, notably in Charles Loring Brace's series "The Dangerous Classes of New York," advocating that children of the streets be relocated with farm families.

Aside from mentioning Castle Garden as "the great *entrepot* through which the vast bodies of immigrants from the Old World pass into the life of the New World" (II, 549) and the Chinese laborers in shoe factories in North Adams, Massachusetts (II, 314–15), *Picturesque America* gives no attention to recent immigrants. Images of people who are obviously poor are also scarce. Several illustrations show people from different economic circumstances, apparently enjoying the amenities of cities. For example, the steel engraving of "The Terrace, Central Park" (II, opp. 557) shows a black servant and a seated man who appears to be begging, while numerous groups of well-dressed people enjoy the fountain area. Judging from their clothes, one of the families relaxing by the lake at Mount Auburn cemetery is that of a laborer (II, 250).

Such images convey social harmony and order, yet many were concerned about increasing disorder during this period. Street demonstrations sometimes led to violence, such as the clash in New York between Irish Protestants and Catholics on July 12, 1871, when militiamen fired into the crowd, killing thirty-one people.[69] Shortly after this bloody incident, a "Table-Talk" column in *Appletons' Journal* commented on social unrest with notable detachment, as if those who produced and read the magazine looked down on such events from a lofty plain, with underlying confidence that inevitable assimilation would solve such problems. The writer (perhaps Bunce) said, "All these contrasted and contending features in our communities produce throughout the country a picturesque turbulence that recalls the commotion of Rome, Constantinople, or Alexandria."[70] Through the lens of the picturesque, the writer saw life in American cities, especially New Orleans, San Francisco, Chicago, and New York, where there were demonstrations of all kinds, as "full of social liberty, contrast, activity, collision, a life exuberant, loud and expansive." Nevertheless, such picturesque "turbulence" and "contrasts" were not featured in *Picturesque America*. Aside from Thorpe's reference to the "Babel of tongues" in New Orleans (I, 273), a view of Broadway congested with vehicles of all sorts (II, 553), and small images of parades in St. Louis (II, 324) and Philadelphia (II, 25), the message of the book is that city life is orderly and leisurely.

Few images actually relate to work, and women, in particular, appear as a group at leisure. They relax with their children and acquaintances in

6.32 A. R. Waud, "Bridges on the Mississippi, at Dubuque" (detail), *Picturesque America*, II, 329. Wood engraving by John Filmer, 6⅛" x 9⅛".

the parks and squares—wearing long dresses over bustles and shaded by elaborate hats and parasols. The exceptions are those who, by their dress or their race, can be identified as caretakers of well-dressed children and a few women carrying burdens and dressed for work (see fig. 6.16). Life inside the home, the sphere of work for most women, is not shown. What is shown, however, seems to support Ann Douglas's notion that during this period, "the lady's leisure, whether hypothetical or actual, was increasingly treated as the most interesting and significant thing about her."[71]

For men, the most frequently depicted arena of work in the city is near the docks or on boats. The well-dressed men also appear to have much leisure time in the city, although, again, the streets were not their sphere of work. A few images show laborers and affluent men in the same image. An interesting example is a view of Dubuque, which includes a black worker with a lunch pail walking up the road and a white man leaning against a sidewalk railing. They eye each other steadily. Waud drew both at the same scale, perhaps implying that both are necessary to the social order (fig. 6.32).[72]

In general, the images of work in *Picturesque America*, like those of agricultural labor in particular, represent activities that had changed little from earlier in the century—or from earlier centuries. Although no millers are actually depicted at work, Bunce's florid comments about the "poetic calm" of working in a brookside mill "under the sweet and inspiring conditions of musical water-falls, shadowy forests, soft airs ladened with the perfume of wild-flowers" (I, 222) show his romantic view of this traditional mode of labor. At least fifty people are shown fishing, in rural as well as city views—engaged in a timeless activity that appeared flexible and largely self-directed and that took advantage of nature's bounty. Many are shown engaged in work connected with the older types of transport—hauling, boating, operating ferries, and so on. Such images suggest independent laborers with a degree of control over the use of their time.

In fact, by 1870, in much of the Northeast most workers were not self-employed. In Pennsylvania 65 to 75 percent of the population worked for someone else; and in Massachusetts 75 to 85 percent did.[73] Many of these worked in large-scale factories where for ten or twelve hours a day they performed dull, repetitious tasks subject to the pace of whatever machine they operated.[74] The writers and artists of *Picturesque America*, however, like many of the educated elite who assumed that both poverty and manual labor would prove temporary conditions for the industrious, focused on the triumphs of invention and ignored the new kind of work they created. The most conspicuous machines, locomotives and steam engines, were, after all, associated with power and freedom rather than confinement.

Furthermore, as Daniel T. Rodgers has suggested, as recent immigrants, frequently from peasant backgrounds, filled more and more of the jobs in factories, "prejudice joined ignorance in shaping widespread indifference to industrial monotony."[75] Such attitudes can be seen in *Picturesque America* when Richards reduces the workers in "factories, forges, and furnaces" to something less that fully human by calling them "gnomes" (II, 295), and, less clearly, in Fenn's image of Poughkeepsie's foundries in which the tiny workers, in fact, resemble gnomes. Over and over again, the book's emphasis on incorporating factories and foundries into the picturesque landscape resulted in confining attention to visual aspects. This allowed indifference to what went on inside. This was the aspect of approaching one's environment through the picturesque lens that Ruskin and others objected to, including Thompson in his comments about the ruined factory in Richmond.

6.33 Harry Fenn, "A Ferry on the French Broad" (detail), *Picturesque America*, I, 145. Wood engraving by J. Karst, 6¼" x 8⅞".

This indifference toward the plight of immigrants and others working in factories extended also to the black population of the United States. Although the writers and artists give somewhat more attention to blacks than to immigrants, they sidestep the controversial issues of granting blacks political rights and economic opportunities. The writers tend to patronize, describing blacks as inherently childlike, inept, and therefore amusing.[76] Bunce says that observing "the various aspects of negro character" in Southern cities "is an endless source of amusement . . . the buxom and turbaned negro 'aunties,' the solemn but ragged negro 'uncles,' the gay and chattering negro young folk."[77] Furthermore, observing that the black ferrymen at the Ashley River do not use a rope to aid the passage, he comments that "our Southern Africans" are "proficient in the art of how not to do a thing" (I, 203–6).

The artists frequently show blacks as idle and with the exaggerated features of the racial stereotype that was appearing more and more often in the popular press. Occasionally blacks are depicted as working with dignity or skill, such as Fenn's image of the woman selling sweet potatoes near Charleston (see fig. 3.7) and Bunce's reference to the "consummate skill" of the New River boatmen (I, 344). More often, however, blacks are set apart as different, as ruled more by instincts, and therefore as picturesque. Fenn's image of "A Ferry on the French Broad" includes a rather grotesque figure of a black male sprawled on the ground apparently asleep, as well as two young boys with exaggerated features (fig. 6.33). The latter pair stands out because of their frontal stance and gaze directly toward the viewer, and by the rather puzzling fact that the same pair, in the same clothes, appears in Fenn's "Street in St. Augustine" (I, 187). Perhaps Fenn referred to a photograph in making both illustrations. If so, this suggests a lack of confidence on his part about representing blacks, and supports the idea that he and some of the other contributors saw blacks as very different from themselves.

Woolson's article on the Ohio River contains the most striking example of viewing blacks as happy children, an attitude that eliminated any need to think about difficult social issues. From the passing steamers, she says, "the jolly laugh of the negro echoes out almost constantly, for he laughs, as the birds sing, by instinct" (II, 149). Her description of the "antics" of the "negroes" during a night landing is even more picturesque:

An iron basket, filled with flaming pine-knots, is hung out on the end of a pole, and then, down over the plank stream the negro hands, jerking themselves along with song and joke, carrying heavy freight with a kind of uncouth, dancing step, and stopping to laugh with a freedom that would astonish the crew of a lake-propeller accustomed to do the same work in half the time under the sharp eye of a laconic mate. (II, 167)

Considering blacks as exotic and picturesque was common during this period, as can been seen in many periodical illustrations and such articles as Henry C. Wood's "A Southern Corn Shucking," which appeared in the *Appletons' Journal* that launched the "Picturesque America" series November 12, 1870. Wood describes a night scene, also lighted by pine torches, in which a negro with a powerful voice sings "nonsense song" atop the huge pile of corn to set the rhythm for the shuckers. The writer finds the feasting afterwards highly picturesque, "worthy the pencil of a master-artist . . . the dark background of pines and cabins, with the dusky revellers banqueting beneath the arching limbs of the lofty trees, their swarthy features lighted by the fitful glare of the numerous torches, while mirth and jest held undisputed sway" (517).

The messages about American Indians conveyed in the text and pictures sometimes parallel those about blacks. The writers call American Indians "children of Nature" and describe them as yet to evolve to "civilization"; the artists use figures of Indians to enhance the picturesque quality of a scene. The 1870 *Appletons' Journal* series "Glimpses of Indian Life" had conveyed similar attitudes, stressing the "humorous" side of a vanishing race.[78] More attention is given to American Indians than to blacks, however, and that attention is sometimes even more baldly derogatory. There are also striking differences between the references to Indians in the East and in the West and between the text and pictures. By 1872 many American Indians had been removed from the East, or died out. In the West, however, clashes with tribes of the Great Plains and Northwest increased as greater numbers of settlers than ever tried to establish themselves and as mining spread to more areas. Before 1869 the army undertook frequent forays against Indians, but when Grant assumed the presidency, he forbade such initiatives. His peace policy favored confining them to reservations and promoting their "civilization" or assimilation to the dominant culture. In light of this situation, it is not surprising that *Picturesque America*'s writers tend to emphasize the rich history of Eastern tribes but express irritation at and disdain for the tribes encountered in the West.[79] Both the text and pictures frequently suggest that the American Indians' day is over, that they have no future. In the images, however, the artists generally cast them in a positive light, as picturesque, whereas the text is often much more disparaging.

In the East, where the diminished tribes no longer posed a threat, the writers find much of interest in their histories. Woolson includes a rare specimen "of the original poetry of the Indian race before intercourse with the white man had corrupted its simplicity," a translation of an aged chief's praise and farewell to Mackinac Island (I, 291). She also describes with admiration the "cities of refuge" maintained by the "remarkable confederacy" called the "Neutral Nation" along the Sandusky River (I, 536). Several of the writers empathize with Indian anger at being tricked out of their lands, as in the "Walk of 1737" (I, 103). Ward contrasts the homeless condition of the tribes who had formerly met in an old Iroquois Council House with the time when they "could call all these wild passes, royal forests, and broad acres, their own" (II, 357).[80] Furthermore, Garczynski regrets that more is not known about the extinct tribes of the Mississippi Valley. Nevertheless, expressing an implicit theme with regard to American Indians, he finds it preferable that whites have displaced them:

Their place has been taken by the thrifty and energetic pale-faces, who have made the Mississippi's borders a long succession of smiling fields and cheerful habitations, and who have built up great cities, destined to be in the future what Nineveh and Babylon were to Asia. (II, 321)

The widespread assumption that the land rightfully belonged to those who knew how to use it by cultivating it and establishing permanent settlements was a powerful rationalization for disregarding the rights of American Indians in this period.

The "doomed Indian" genre appears both overtly and subtly in *Picturesque America*.[81] At the end of her article on Lake Superior, Woolson reminds the reader that Longfellow made the lake "the scene of the final disappearance of Hiawatha." Before quoting the lines describing his sail into "the fiery sunset," she makes a comparison that startles today's reader, but, considering the usually temperate tone of *Picturesque America*, must have represented one commonly discussed possible outcome to the "Indian Question." Woolson writes, "The lines are no inapt representation of the final disappearance of the Indian race from among men" (I, 411). Similarly, Runkle urges that native place names be retained to commemorate "a vanishing race" (I, 36). Moran's opening illustration for "The Plains and the Sierras" conveyed a more subtle message that the Indians' era was closing in the West. In it the setting sun silhouetted an American Indian on horseback, with raised spear, before Witches' Rocks in Weber Canon, Utah (II, 168). The case for this interpretation is strengthened by the fact that none of the figures in the illustrations that follow appear to be Indians—in fact, several of them carry rifles and look like soldiers.

The sections on the Rockies and the canyons of the Colorado focus almost exclusively on the splendors of the landscape without giving attention to any native peoples seen along the way.[82] The coverage of Yosemite Valley, northern California, and the Columbia River, however, gives considerable attention to American Indians in both text and pictures. The only description of actual interaction with Indians as well as the only close-up images appear in James Smillie's article "The Yosemite." He is both attracted to and repelled by the fifty Indians that "straggle, vagrant and worthless, through the region" (I, 483). His description and illustration of three young "squaws" who surprised him "by deliberately preparing for a bath, not a hundred feet" from him in the Merced River, must have shocked or at least titillated some by its departure from "civilized" customs. Although he termed it "a charming picture," his description of these "children of Nature," disporting themselves "with all the grace of mermaids," also suggests he viewed them as of a different order. He tried to oblige some friendly "squaws" who insisted that he try their *chemuck*, a gruel made from acorn flour. But his stomach rebelled. In the end he retained the attitudes he came with about "the inevitable decay of the race" (II, 483).

The articles on northern California and the Columbia River convey even more negative attitudes toward American Indians in the texts. But in a striking discrepancy, the graphic images are either neutral or positive, apparently governed by nostalgia for the time when the tribes were free ranging, before their way of life was changed by contact with settlers.

Gifford's diary and letters show that he came with preconceived notions about exotic "savages," and that he was not disappointed. His party encountered members of the Flathead tribe spearfishing at the Dalles on the Columbia and another tribe in camp near the McCloud River in northern California. He found the latter the "most savage fellows" he had seen, with naked, greased bodies and "stripes of black paint across their faces." Although armed with bows and arrows, they met the intruders with curiosity rather than hostility, and Gifford bought from them "a beautiful bow & quiver of arrows" for his studio.[83] On occasion Gifford took time to sketch individuals, dwellings, and canoes, and included distant figures and teepees in some of his compositions (see fig. 5.44). More such details were added to the wood engravings to enliven the foreground and middleground.

These images of small groups of peaceful American Indians contrast with the sharply derogatory comments in the text. Garczynski stresses that parts of northern California are still "infested with quarrelsome Indians, who are continually committing depredations on the settlers and upon travellers" (I, 426). He seems to be aware of the discrepancy between his comments and the accompanying illustrations, for he says that although from a distance their camps "are somewhat picturesque," "a nearer look destroys the charm" (I, 420). In the distant view of the camp in Smillie's "Mount Shasta," none of the squalor described in the text is apparent (I, opp. 424).

Similarly, Gifford's images of American Indians in the Columbia River area do not suggest the characteristics that Runkle finds so loathsome in the Trascopin tribe. The bare ground and bare trees of the camp he depicts imply a meager existence, but the woman and child are not repugnant (I, 50). Runkle's earlier experience at a Catholic mission among the Potawatamies had convinced her that they were incapable of anything but rote learning and would not be able to be assimilated (I, 49–50). Referring to Cooper's writings and to Nahum Ward,[84] whose discovery of a mummy in Mammoth Cave in 1816 had made the spot famous, she says of her Western encounters:

We nowhere saw the forest-god whom Cooper believed in, nor yet the statuesque and noble hunter whom Ward has found. It is not possible to imagine human creatures more unromantic, more indecent, more loathsome, more inhuman, than the visible Indian who appears along every line of travel from the Kansas border to the northwestern boundary. (I, 47–48)

In this age which admired industriousness as a prime virtue, she says the Indian "belongs to the universal genus *loafer*" (I, 48). She objects greatly to the Trascopins' wasteful spearing of more salmon than they need, and even suggests that "Darwin himself" would accord them many centuries to evolve to the level of "the poor fish they slaughter" (I, 49).[85] To Runkle, American Indians are "step-children" rather than children, "of Nature," and the sum of all the tribes does not equal in value the life of young Loring, the reporter killed by Apaches in 1871. She tempers her comments slightly by calling for a "proper Indian policy somewhere between the indiscriminate wiping out which the frontiersman insists on and the peppermint-candy wiles" of some (I, 49). Bunce could have edited out these extremely negative attitudes had he wanted to. Instead, he let them stand prominently in the third section of the book. Bunce and the Appleton firm probably shared some of these attitudes, as did many others promoting the spread of "civilization" to all parts of the continental nation. Indeed, inevitable progress implied that the "thrifty and energetic pale-faces" would transform the land into "smiling fields" and "great cities."

Picturesque America's strong message with regard to "civilization" in the United States was that advancement was steady and sure. Both text and pictures gave great attention to historic cities and towns and quaint old buildings that demonstrated "civilization" on these shores dated back several hundred years, as well as to the latest civic improvements that suggested cultural sophistication even in the burgeoning cities of the Midwest. By depicting an orderly, homogeneous, and well-dressed society and by omitting discussion in the text and suggestions in the images of such contemporary problems as increasing poverty, unhealthy tenements crowded with immigrants, unjust treatment of blacks and American Indians, poor working conditions in factories and mines, and corruption in business and government, the book reinforced the inclinations of many readers toward complacency and self-satisfaction.

Picturesque America seemed to promise that the diffusion of culture and education would eventually enable all who practiced thrift and industry to obtain such "prizes of life" as "a tasteful home," fashionable clothes, books, pictures, and the opportunity to travel to scenic attractions and cultural centers. Most people shown in the book had already attained these pleasures, as had those producing it. For those who had not, the book offered instruction in some of the values, attitudes, and activities of the cultured elite and thus could function as an etiquette book. It provided models of how polite society went about touring, using their leisure, contemplating scenery, choosing their homes and surroundings, and assigning appropriate roles by gender and race.

Balancing continuity and change, blending valued aspects of tradition with carefully selected emblems of technological advancement and urban sophistication, the words and pictures of *Picturesque America* offered reassurance to many Americans. Despite unprecedented and unsettling change on many fronts, they could still go in search of picturesque, beautiful, or sublime scenes and not go unrewarded; or take a different turn to enjoy cities on a par with Europe; or yet another to admire the nation's industrial development and potential. In the face of such evidence, only a curmudgeon would fail to join the chorus of praise for American scenery and progress.

CHAPTER 7

From Cultural Landmark
to Relic

Picturesque America's confident assertion that Americans could retain the old while embracing the new was evidently welcome, for the serialized book was hugely successful. By 1880 payments to agents had reached $2.4 million, indicating approximately 100,000 subscriptions had been sold at $24 a set.[1] The offering continued to be available for many years, and some sources claim as many as a million copies were eventually distributed.[2] After the parts were bound—either by the Appleton firm or a local binder chosen by the subscriber—the book typically took its place on the center table of the parlor[3] (see fig. 7.1 and appendix D.6).

During its original publication as a subscription book from 1872 to 1874, *Picturesque America* continued to have a direct impact on the content of the illustrated periodicals. *Appletons' Journal* itself occasionally reprinted some of the material, noting "This article and illustrations are selected from 'Picturesque America,' publishing in parts by D. Appleton and Company."[4] In the fall of 1873, *Harper's Weekly* launched a series of its own on the American West, with illustrations by Jules Tavernier, who had done one section for *Picturesque America*, and another Frenchman, Paul Frenzeny.[5] *Scribner's Monthly* continued to include attractive views of the American landscape, and in July 1873 initiated the comprehensive series "The Great South," by Edward King with illustrations by James Wells Champney.[6] *The Aldine's* series of American views continued prominently through the years *Picturesque America* was published and after, with Thomas Moran and J. D. Woodward as leading contributors.[7]

That *Picturesque America's* subjects and presentation appealed to many was no accident. The book was carefully crafted by Bunce, Fenn, and the firm's leadership to fulfill several cultural functions. These ranged from

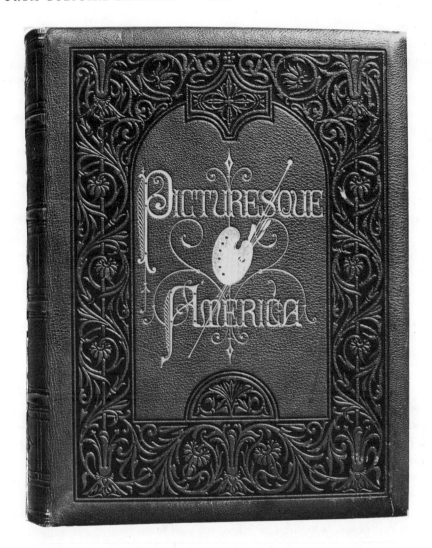

7.1 A volume of *Picturesque America* in D. Appleton's finest binding. Courtesy of William Abt.

instructing in picturesque touring and serving as a status symbol, to enhancing American art and publishing, to fostering a positive self-image of the United States, and thus nationalism and tourism, to allaying uneasiness about disturbing changes of all sorts. Before the onset of the world-altering events that began to shape the peculiar nature of our own century, *Picturesque America* became a cultural landmark beyond the imaginations of its designers.

In an age that valued encounters with nature and art as essential means of "improving" the populace, *Picturesque America* could serve its subscribers as both a symbol of cultural attainment and a vehicle for cultural aspirations. By displaying the book prominently, Americans could signal their enthusiasm for scenery and picturesque touring as well as their intention to enrich the family circle through books and landscape art. In addition, support of this renowned, large-scale art project provided families of moderate means a way to become patrons of art—like many of the wealthiest Americans during this period. For those striving to learn the mores of "polite society" it set forth didactic models: of leisurely touring that would yield spiritual benefits, of orderly behavior and fashionable dress appropriate for the public spaces of cities, and of the most admired dwelling type, elegant suburban mansions.

For a larger circle, including subscribers but extending beyond them, *Picturesque America* built pride in American art and American illustrated books and magazines. The high quality of its widely distributed images fostered appreciation of American landscape artists and illustrators and enhanced their reputations and opportunities. Woodward, for example, was in 1875 termed "the celebrated drawer on wood and illustrator of 'Picturesque America.'"[8] This appreciation led, in turn, to a proliferation of similar projects.

The success of *Picturesque America* also helped to overcome the American people's feelings of inferiority and build confidence regarding their sophistication in terms of art. An 1874 *New York Times* notice about Appleton's Christmas books nourished this pride, claiming that "almost every crowned head in Europe" had subscribed to *Picturesque America* and that Pope Pius IX was so pleased with his copy he sent the publishers a silver medal.[9] Many must have taken great satisfaction in such responses as that of the London *Graphic* to subscription sales in England, begun in 1873, under the imprint of Cassell, Petter, Galpin and Company. The *Graphic* called it a "magnificent work," of which the publishers, the editor,

Bryant, and the "principal artist, Mr. Fenn . . . may well be proud." The *Graphic* went on to say that it was

satisfactory to find that art is so highly appreciated in the United States. . . . We hope that the English publishers will look to their laurels. Surely there is a public sufficiently appreciative to make it a profitable enterprise to issue work in England of this high class, instead of the poor-looking photographs of used up engravings which do duty now with us.[10]

Thus in the opinion of some, American art publications had surpassed English ones. This was a great change from the situation at mid-century when Americans still depended on England for most of their illustrated books, and whole editions of printed sheets were imported for American publication.[11] It was also quite an advance from the 1860s, when their trade journal criticized American publishers for depending on electrotypes from abroad and making books out of "all sorts of odds and ends." With the English importing *Picturesque America*, that process was reversed.

Pride in the nation's bookmaking was also given a boost at the Centennial Exposition in 1876, where *Picturesque America* was prominently displayed in the publishers' exhibit in the Main Building. D. Appleton and Company cleverly placed a specially bound copy of *Picturesque America* alongside their first book, the three-inch-square *Crumbs from the Master's Table*, issued in 1831. This had the desired effect, as René Fouret commented in the "Report of the French Commission":

By the side of this plain volume, showing the first efforts of Messrs. Appleton and Company, there was displayed a superb copy, richly bound of Picturesque America, a typographical monument, erected by them to their country. . . . The arrangement of the text, and the style of printing, compare favorably with similar works published in France and England, in fact, this publication does the greatest honor and credit to its publishers, and may from a typographical and artistic point of view, be considered the best of all original publications from the American press.[12]

Picturesque America was again displayed at the 1878 World's Fair in Paris in the collective exhibit by American publishers.[13] Shortly afterward, A. Quantin of Paris issued an abridged and reorganized version translated into French by Benedict-Henry Revoil.[14] The complete book was issued in four volumes by the London publishers Cassell and Company beginning in 1881 and reissued in 1889 and 1894.[15] A German publication, *Amerika in Wort und Bild* (1883–85), by Friedrich von Hellwald, reused approximately half of *Picturesque America*'s wood engravings in an even larger format, 10¾" x 14¼".[16]

Furthermore, the next generation of artist-illustrators after Harry Fenn regarded *Picturesque America* as a publishing landmark because it created a highly favorable climate for illustrated books and magazines. American writer and artist F. Hopkinson Smith (1838–1915), speaking in the persona of "the Doctor" in *American Illustrators* (1892), said that Fenn was entitled to be called "the Nestor of his guild" not only for the high quality of his *Picturesque America* illustrations, but also because of the book's "enormous financial success." As "the first illustrated publication on so large a scale ever attempted," it demonstrated "the commercial value of pictures" and "paved the way" for later illustrated works. Soon, "there were not enough artists to go around." If Fenn's efforts had been "a dead failure," some "distinguished illustrators" of his day might have been "measuring tape at Macy's."[17] Joseph Pennell, one of those "distinguished illustrators" of the 1890s, agreed with Smith's assessment of Fenn's work for *Picturesque America*. He called the book "the high-water mark of American publishing enterprise" and counted Fenn, Woodward, and Moran "among the pioneers of American landscape illustration."[18]

Some, though by no means all, of the heavily illustrated publications stimulated by the success of *Picturesque America* came from the Appleton firm. Bunce and his employers followed up with two similar projects. The first, *Picturesque Europe*, came out in parts between 1875 and 1879. This was another sound business decision, for, despite the landscape chauvinism and "see America first" emphasis of *Picturesque America*, Americans obviously continued to be fascinated with Europe. The poet and travel writer Bayard Taylor (1825–78), whose translation of Goethe's *Faust* had been published 1870–71, edited the text. The omission of the writers' names made even clearer than with *Picturesque America* that this was primarily an art project. Once again, Harry Fenn served as principal artist, beginning work on it in late 1873 or early 1874, before *Picturesque America* was completed. A publisher's announcement inside the wrapper of part 43 of *Picturesque America* stated that a companion series on Europe had been in preparation for some time; another in part 45 added that January 1, 1875, was the projected date for beginning publication (see appendix D.5). Yet to cover all of Europe was more than one artist could accomplish in any reasonable amount of time; thus, in addition to Fenn, some twenty-five British artists drew for the wood engravings. The works of still others, including Birket Foster, were reproduced as steel engravings. Woodward also participated in this project, going to London for the Appletons in 1875.[19] The title page credits "European and American Artists" for the illustrations. Perhaps the order here reflects continuing deference to European art; on the other hand, in a book of images of Europe it seems appropriate to give first billing to European artists.

Picturesque Europe followed its predecessor quite closely in format and types of subjects, although traces of human history were much more conspicuous. The early announcement stressed that the numerous ancient monuments in Europe would offer "more varied subjects than in our own country, where the artist has little more than scenes of Nature to inspire his pencil"—quite a surprising statement considering the efforts made in *Picturesque America* to demonstrate the rich variety of the American scene. Yet perhaps the success of *Picturesque America* had buoyed confidence sufficiently to allow unabashed admiration of Europe. In his Preface, Taylor stressed that Europe's chief interest for Americans lay in the evidence of history—for this was "the past" of their "own stock." These words reveal both Taylor's typically limited concept of *American* as well as the contemporary interest in Anglo-Saxon and Teutonic origins.

Like its predecessor, this new Appleton venture met with success. It also inspired a competitive response from *The Aldine*, recalling that magazine's rivalry with *Appletons' Journal* in 1871–72: In its June 1875 number, *The Aldine* launched a series of views also entitled "Picturesque Europe." By touting subjects never before brought to the notice of Americans and "necessarily unattainable elsewhere," the magazine attempted to hold the interest and subscriptions of its audience.[20]

In 1877, when half of the parts of *Picturesque Europe* had been published, the Appleton firm began planning a third "picturesque" publication—about the Holy Land. This project had long been a dream of George S. Appleton, who died in 1878 before it appeared. In 1878 and 1879, the firm sent Harry Fenn and John Douglas Woodward on extensive tours to make drawings. *Picturesque Palestine, Sinai and Egypt* was issued in parts between 1881 and 1883. The editor was Col. Charles William Wilson (1840–1924), "formerly Engineer to the Palestine Exploration Society" of Britain, who had published *The Recovery of Jerusalem* in 1871. The other writers were Americans and Britons described as "the most eminent Palestine explorers, etc." In this case, their names appeared in the table

of contents. Although the ancient architecture and unusual land formations provided the artists with especially rich material and the book was
quite successful, the wood engravings are frequently less attractive than
those in *Picturesque America*. In some cases tonal areas are difficult to
"read," lines are less precise, and contrasts too harsh.[21]

Yet another Appleton project provided commissions for American
artists and highlighted their work. *The Art Journal*, launched in 1875 and
also edited by Bunce, was a large-format monthly modeled on and sharing
material from a long-established London publication by the same name
(published since 1839 by Virtue and Company). It took over from
Appletons' Journal the role of disseminating art to the home in the form of
wood engravings.[22] Continuing attention to American scenery, it featured
three series of views by John Douglas Woodward, of the Hudson River,
Colorado, and the scenery along the transcontinental railroad.[23]

Other publishers, impressed by the success of Appleton's "picturesque"
books, used them as models and in so doing provided yet more commissions for artists. From 1882 to 1884, Belden Brothers in Toronto issued
Picturesque Canada, a handsome subscription book edited by George
Monro Grant.[24] Almost identical to *Picturesque America* and *Picturesque
Europe* in size, page format, and type, it contained more than 550 wood
engraved illustrations.[25] The title page indicates the art was supervised by
the president of the Royal Canadian Academy, L. (Lucius) R. O'Brien,
who contributed many designs himself. But the work of an American
artist, Frederic B. Schell, dominated the publication to an even greater
extent than Fenn's did *Picturesque America*. Originally from Philadelphia,
Schell furnished more than half the views, either working alone or with
Thomas Hogan, with whom he had frequently collaborated for *Harper's
Weekly*.[26] Schell, Hogan, O'Brien, and two other Americans, W. T. Smedley
(1858–1920) and W. C. Fitler (1857–1915), provided most of the apparently on-the-spot drawings of specific Canadian localities, people, and
industries. Several *Picturesque America* artists, including Fenn, Moran,
Gifford, Waud, Gibson, and Woodward, also furnished at least one illustration for the book. Examination of their contributions, however, suggests
that, in some cases, instead of making sketching trips for the publication,
they based their drawings on photographs or drawings already in their
portfolios.[27] Certainly the publishers hoped to profit from the use of their
names and the link with the earlier successful work. *Picturesque Canada*
contains many excellent wood engravings, some decidedly impressionistic

in style, and numerous interesting examples of experimental formats in which elements in the composition leap out of the frame, giving depth and drama to the page (see, for example, I, 22, 137.).

A few years after completing work on *Picturesque Canada*, Schell carried the tradition to another part of the world, becoming art director and artist for *The Picturesque Atlas of Australasia*, published in 1886.[28] In 1888, John Muir's *Picturesque California*, published in San Francisco by J. Dewing, expanded the tradition in a different way by utilizing etchings, photogravures, process halftones, and even some colored inks, as well as wood engravings, to reproduce works by Moran, Fenn, and other artists.[29] In this same period countless "picturesque" viewbooks featuring specific cities or regions were produced all over the country.[30]

Other heavily illustrated publications not dealing with landscapes were influenced by the success of *Picturesque America*. Two outstanding projects of the late 1870s and 1880s that were similar in scale and quality were William Cullen Bryant and Sydney Howard Gay's *Popular History of the United States* (1876–81) and *The Century* magazine's series on "Battles and Leaders of the Civil War" (1884–87). Several *Picturesque America* artists and engravers were involved in these projects, as were many others.[31]

Such projects further increased the prestige of artist-illustrators, as is clear from their greater participation in clubs and exhibitions, particularly those of the American Watercolor Society. Sometimes publishers submitted drawings by their staff artists for exhibition, and they were displayed alongside the prints made from them.[32] Two societies specifically for illustrators organized in this period, the Salmagundi Club (1871) and the Society of Illustrators (1901). Fenn and Woodward joined both. Several *Picturesque America* artists exhibited works at the Centennial Exposition in Philadelphia in 1876, where the American landscape paintings were especially admired, most notably Moran's *Mountain of the Holy Cross*. Fenn's *Picturesque America* subjects—*Old Convent Gate, St. Augustine, Florida* and the *Old Fireplace* of John Howard Payne's "Home, Sweet Home,"—appeared with the American Watercolor Society's exhibition.[33] In a sense, the display of art at the Centennial marked the culmination of interest in landscape painting in the realistic-Romantic mode. Thereafter artists more and more would experiment with impressionistic styles and new techniques and subject matters. The preponderance of panoramic views and conventional picturesque images would give way to more intimate landscapes featuring atmospheric effects, influenced by the Barbizon school, and to figure paintings and urban scenes.[34] Illustrations soon followed the same course.

As the demand for inexpensive printed images grew, engravers and publishers experimented with reproduction methods as well. Their objective was twofold: to produce images truer to the artist's original work and to discover processes that were faster and cheaper. One new approach involved a further elaboration of wood engraving; the other resulted in bypassing the engraving process entirely. Beginning in the late 1870s, the virtuoso wood engravings of the "New School" led by Frederick Juengling, Timothy Cole, and Elbridge Kingsley emphasized tone, value, and texture, instead of line, as had Linton and Quartley. Their works would gain much favor with the public and with artists who thought the different emphasis led to more faithful reproductions of their oil or watercolor paintings.

In the 1880s, development of photoengraving, first with the Moss process, eventually made it possible to reproduce the lines of ink drawings exactly on a relief plate, without the intervention of an engraver. The magazines and books of this decade are filled with works by Howard Pyle, A. B. Frost, Joseph Pennell, and, indeed, Harry Fenn, J. D. Woodward, and W. L. Sheppard reproduced by this method and refinements of it. It took longer to figure out how to reproduce tonal works such as watercolors and oils, and for a time wood engravers still had a hand in interpreting these. Eventually, however, the halftone process would be improved enough to effectively and inexpensively reproduce many types of original media—chalk, pencil, wash—and even the transparent colors of watercolor.[35] The new techniques facilitated distinctive expressions of personal artistic visions, leading to the "golden age of American illustration" in the 1880s and 1890s.[36] The appeal that illustrated magazines held for artists at this time is clear from Joseph Pennell's comment that "an illustrator receives more publicity from a magazine which publishes illustrations than any other artist . . . an illustrated magazine is an art gallery for the world."[37]

By the decades around the turn of the century, the United States was the acknowledged leader in this arena of art. In 1894 the English art critic Henry Blackburn commented on the "fashion" to admire American magazine illustrations, which he thought had outstripped those of all other nations. He said, "it is common to meet people in England asking 'Have you seen the last number of *Harper's* or the *Century Magazine?*' "[38] Here at last was a realm of art in which Americans could justifiably take pride in their nation's superiority. The success of *Picturesque America* was an important step toward these later achievements.

In addition to fostering pride in American art and illustrated books and magazines, *Picturesque America* contributed greatly to Americans' self-image, a national identity arising from shared information and positive interpretations of the natural and cultural landscape. After the wrenching years of secession and Civil War, this re-creation of a collective identity was sorely needed. The earlier pride in the republican experiment and confidence in the superiority of the constitutional system had been shaken by the terrible war itself, as well as the political corruption of the Tweed Ring, the Grant administration, and the Credit Mobilier scandal exposed in 1872. Tweed's manipulation of poor voters in New York City aroused fears about the viability of democracy, as the excesses of the Paris Commune of 1871 aroused fears of revolution and radical reform. Clearly a foundation for national pride other than the government itself was needed. For many, the land—with its picturesque, beautiful, and sublime scenery and rich natural resources—defined the national identity more strongly than before.

Picturesque America was ideally suited to aid in displacing doubts about democratic process with pride anchored in place, in geography, and in history. The basic assumption that the landscape of the United States was of sufficient beauty and interest to be represented in detail by a troupe of artists, as the countries of Europe had been in earlier decades, undergirded the project, as did the corollary assumption that scenery worthy of the attention of artists certainly deserved the admiration of tourists. The volumes' comprehensiveness made the case for tourism as never before, offering a great advance over earlier surveys in the quantity and range of sites depicted. And the attention to previously unnoticed "charming nooks" in the "byways of travel" as well as to the stars of American scenery suggested the tourist in search of the picturesque could never exhaust the landscape's riches.

By presenting numerous images of conventionally picturesque scenery in the South, as well as of the exotic plants and animals of Florida, and by suggesting these regions as appropriate tourist destinations, *Picturesque America* helped reinstate the South in the national self-image. The book's timely depictions of the unusual and often spectacular scenery of the West were instrumental in integrating that region into the national consciousness, and vital in strengthening nationalism. The mountain ranges, waterfalls, and ancient forests of the West were comparable to and in some cases surpassed the famous attractions of Switzerland, long admired by American travellers. And no country in Europe had anything to compare with the vivid pastels and impressive rock formations of Yellowstone Canyon, or the unfathomable depth and countless stratifications of the canyons of the Colorado River. As Joshua Taylor observed,

These bold expressions of the West were not simply the landscape of the Hudson expanded; they represented a whole new phase in America's identification with nature. There was something about these gargantuan landscapes that could make even the city-bound inhabitant proud in incorporating the unmatched Western images into his visual depiction of America. Finally, America had the mountains that could be claimed to match her men.[39]

In the years following *Picturesque America*'s appearance the geography of the West became a national preoccupation, and Yellowstone Park and the Grand Canyon came to rank as the premier icons of the American landscape, as Niagara Falls had been earlier. This is clear from their prominence in periodicals and books like *America Illustrated*, produced in 1879, which opened with "The Valley of the Yellowstone" and a wood engraving of "The Lower Falls."[40] In 1882, when D. Appleton and Company assembled *Our Native Land*, reusing many wood engravings from *The Art Journal, Picturesque America*, and *Appletons' Journal*, the first area featured was "The Cañons of the Colorado."[41] Even before these two regions were developed for tourism, reports about them as well as about the more readily accessible rock formations and deep canyons along the Union and Central Pacific railroads had already altered perceptions of the United States. In the preface to *Our Native Land* (1882), George T. Ferris noted that whereas earlier travellers from abroad sneered "at what was rude and crass in our social forms," since the Civil War a "great influx of travel has crowded every nook and corner of our country with keen and competent observers." Among them "the feeble sneer has been lost in big notes of amazement and pleasure at the wonders scattered profusely by the hand of Nature, and the no lesser marvels wrought by the energy of man."

In 1882 just as in 1872, the enthusiastic promoter of American tourism was little troubled by the potential of "the energy of man" to disturb and alter the wonders of nature. Certainly not in the West, which seemed too vast to ever be completely known, much less settled and developed. By focusing on largely untouched natural scenery, the Western images of *Picturesque America* reinforced this attitude, and comments in the text supported it. Burlingame, for example, stressed how little the railroad had encroached upon the plains, which "close behind the scudding train like the scarce broader ocean behind the stoutest steamer of the moderns—a vast expanse as silent and unbroken and undisturbed as it lay centuries before ever rail or keel was dreamed of" (II, 169). Further, Burlingame exulted that the railroad had made accessible such wonders of nature as Echo and Weber canyons in Utah, unique in all the world. He predicted that they would come to be regarded as essential sights on the Western journey, just as the stretch of the Rhine from Mainz to Cologne was considered "the river." Not perspicacious enough to foresee the automobile, whose roadways would take over and expand the railroad's roadbeds and alter the canyons greatly, or the impetus to build dams for water storage and power, he believed the canyons were immune from destruction by cities and settlements (I, 178).

Easier to comprehend was the threat to wildlife from "the energy of man," for the obliteration of the buffalo for their skins as well as sport was already well advanced. In his article on "The Coast of California," Garczynski, always quick to find reasons for national pride, pointed out that the seals and sea lions on Seal Rock were protected from hunters, despite the value their skins would bring in "the New-York market." He said, "Little touches of sympathy with universal Nature, such as this, are truer subjects whereon to claim American superiority than all the inventions with which the Yankees have blessed the world" (I, 566).

In the East, where industry's demands for power generation had already led to widespread destruction of waterfalls and forests—two of the best-loved elements of the natural landscape—the task of promoting tourism and "progress" simultaneously was more complicated. To accomplish it, *Picturesque America* combined several strategies. The artists omitted coverage of natural resource extraction almost completely, while the writers spoke with pride of the potential riches yet to be developed, and the rewards they would bring. The writers recommended routes that avoided concentrations of factories, while both artists and writers gave attention to mills and forges of the previous era. In addition, the artists surrounded their few representations of more recent industry with conventionally picturesque natural elements.

By these approaches, *Picturesque America* endorsed the very elements that would eventually transform much of the American landscape. Some individuals did have misgivings about progress and the disappearance of the wilderness—in 1851 Emerson had said, "I cannot accept the railroad and telegraph in exchange for reason and charity" and warned that "things are in the saddle and ride mankind."[42] Yet such disenchantment was not widespread in the popular culture. *Picturesque America* further allayed such doubts with its reassuring message that little had changed, that the picturesque landscape and social order persisted, while labor-saving machinery increased productivity and enabled the United States to supply its own citizens and the world.

This message allowed, or subtly promoted, the practically unbounded enthusiasm for steam power that was embodied a few years later in the 1876 Centennial Exposition in Philadelphia, where the undisputed star of the show was the huge Corliss steam engine that powered some eight thousand other machines. Guidebooks directed visitors to make it a first stop, and the excitement it evoked was a prime example of the technological sublime. The fervor expressed suggests such encounters increasingly provided alternatives to the sublime in nature or art:

The first thing to do is to see the tremendous iron heart, whose energies are pulsating around us. . . . Poets see sublimity in the ocean, the mountains, the everlasting heavens; in the tragic elements of passion, madness, fate; *we* see sublimity in that great flywheel, those great walking-beams and cylinders, that crank-shaft, and those connecting rods and piston-rods,—in the magnificent totality of the great Corliss engine.[43]

In his review of the Exposition for the *Atlantic Monthly*, William Dean Howells said he saw in the Corliss engine, rather than in the displays of American painting, sculpture, or literature, the truest expression of "the national genius."[44]

By depicting factories as aesthetically appealing while ignoring their workers, *Picturesque America* corroborated the widespread confidence that growth of machine technology and industrial capitalism were evidence of the gradual evolution of civilization. Appletons' *Popular Science Monthly* revealed this ideology more clearly in reaction to an 1872 strike among New York's industrial craftspeople, including printers. Admitting some grievances, Youmans said that peaceful strikes were legitimate, but violence and coercion were never justified. Rather, the working classes must "accept the spirit of civilization, which is pacific, constructive, controlled by reason, and slowly ameliorating and progressive."[45]

In general, *Picturesque America*'s implicit message with regard to those groups outside the Anglo-Saxon Protestant cultural mainstream was that by learning to conform to the mores and values of "polite society"—as depicted in the book's pages—they could participate in the nation's public life and share in its rewards. By sidestepping the obstacles that would prevent many from doing this, and most often adopting a patronizing view of blacks as happy children and American Indians as doomed to be replaced by "energetic pale-faces," the book fostered complacency with regard to social and economic problems and self-satisfaction of those already belonging to the leading cultural group.

There is an element of self-glorification, or group glorification, in the omnipresent fashionable and orderly city dwellers, whether in Central Park or at Trenton Falls. Yet the primary motivation for including them was to counteract deep-seated feelings of inadequacy about the nation's cultural life. In its emphasis on urban amenities, such as parks, monumental buildings, and avenues, *Picturesque America* asserted that at last the United States had cities to compare with Paris and London, and seemingly without their problems. Furthermore, the book promoted admiration of the elegant new "villas" cropping up in the cities and suburbs as testimony of the good taste of the nation's most successful entrepreneurs, and thus endorsed the type of ostentatious display of wealth that would become ever more prevalent in what would soon be termed the Gilded Age. The fact that the other extreme—tenements and hovels—were omitted made it easier to celebrate the mansions of the fortunate and remain detached from the problems of the poor. Furthermore, the positive emphasis on city life also indicated how urban-oriented the nation was becoming, in a great change from the earlier agrarian emphasis.

For many Americans in the 1870s (and some into the 1880s) *Picturesque America* offered a reassuring picture of themselves and their land, retaining much of the familiar and revered past but at the same time growing and changing in exciting new ways and taking a leading role among the nations of the world. The book continued the long-valued tradition of touring in search of the picturesque, while presenting countless new regions to discover and appreciate. It demonstrated the continuing power of encounters with nature to evoke gratitude for divine creation and lift the spirit, while discussing recent theories about the earth's formation. It honored the traditional family farms and close-knit communities from which most Americans had come, while celebrating cities as centers of culture and opportunity. The volumes admired the picturesque mill or small factory in the forest, while they boasted of the nation's phenomenal industrial output. They represented wilderness unaltered by man, while promoting tourism and the expansion of the railroad, and boasted of the nation's abundant natural resources. *Picturesque America* continued to rely on Europe as the standard to emulate, while it claimed to have met or surpassed the standard in many ways. This multifaceted, often paradoxical, synthesis of continuity and change formed a national image that appealed to many from all across the nation. Fostering pride in the present and hope for the future, it helped establish the confident base from which the nation expanded and grew in the increasingly cosmopolitan and imperialistic era that followed. Yet it was a synthesis that could not last.

By the time D. Appleton and Company issued a revised version of *Picturesque America* in 1894, the world had changed sufficiently to make a number of revisions advisable.[46] In a less romantic, increasingly matter-of-fact period, the Appleton firm presented a pared down, vastly less-expensive version that was delivered to subscribers by the U.S. Postal Service. The thirty weekly parts costing ten cents each, for a total of $3.00, contained no table of contents identifying the writers and artists of each section. The revised text emphasized accurate information for travellers, and although still prominent, the traditional aesthetic categories have diminished in significance as a means of understanding the world. The growing reliance on empirical observation and scientific analysis made such a shift inevitable. Indeed, it had been foretold twenty years earlier by Clarence King when he contrasted scientific observation with letting "Nature impress you *in the dear old way* with all her mystery and glory, with those vague, indescribable emotions which tremble between wonder and sympathy."[47] Such old-fashioned responses are less prominent, while objective descriptions and quantitative measurements and comparisons are more so. Gone are most of the quotations from poetry and much of the highly charged prose, as are many of the derogatory references to American Indians and blacks. For example, although Garczynski's comment that an unbounded view is "saddening" remains in "The Susquehanna" article, the theatrics about the view stirring deep emotions and sending tears to the eyes have been deleted. The language

7.2 Charles Dana Gibson, "Picturesque America: Anywhere Along the Coast," in *Americans* (1900), unnumbered.

used in comparing American scenery with European and in descriptions of industrial sites is similarly tempered, less enthusiastic, indicating the synthesis of nature appreciation and optimism about technological progress demonstrated in the 1870s was more tentative in the popular culture two decades later. Although the publishers obviously felt the book was still appealing enough to warrant a revised edition, attitudes had changed sufficiently to cause deletion of numerous examples of emotional responses to the landscape and technological change.

In 1896 *Picturesque America* was still considered a cultural landmark by an Illinois educator who included it in his "Culture List" of "the one hundred best productions of literature, science, art and music, which ought to be considered in any scheme of education or of self-culture."[48] By the turn of the century, however, its significance as an artistic and cultural force had definitely been undermined. The ubiquitous, familiar concept of "Picturesque America" was now old-fashioned, appropriate for jest and satire. In 1900, Charles Dana Gibson used the phrase as an ironic title for one of his cartoons of American beauties (fig. 7.2). And in 1909, Harry

7.3 Harry Grant Dart, "Picturesque America," in *Men, Women, and Mirth* (1909), unnumbered.

Grant Dart used "Picturesque America" as the satirical title of an image of a city choked by crowds, traffic, advertising, and vendors (fig. 7.3).

The explanation of this dramatic change in *Picturesque America*'s fate lies in the increasingly conspicuous intensification of the social and economic problems that Bunce, Fenn, and the other contributors had been able to sidestep. By the turn of the century, these problems were clearly so pressing that a work restricting its attention to aesthetics, to visual aspects and surfaces, was clearly too limited to warrant serious consideration.

Americans were shaken by a series of economic depressions followed by disruptive strikes that resulted in many deaths, beginning with the nationwide railroad strike in 1877, followed by Chicago's Haymarket Square riot in 1886, and the Homestead, Pennsylvania, strike in 1892. It was becoming all too obvious that the complex industrial economy was prone to wild fluctuations and that many workers and small farmers were not benefiting from growth in productivity. It was also clear that fewer and fewer of those in power valued the common good above personal gain. Thus, to be confident of civilization's inevitable advance was more difficult. William Dean Howells seemed to find it impossible in 1888 when he wrote, "After fifty years of optimistic content with 'civilization' and its ability to come out all right in the end, I now abhor it, and feel that it is coming out all wrong in the end, unless it bases itself anew on a real equality."[49]

This coexistence of technological progress and social chaos was, as John Kasson has said, the "overriding paradox" of the late nineteenth century. Seeing little children at work in "factories where labor-saving machinery has reached its most wonderful development" and "large classes maintained by charity," Henry George felt "the promised land flies before us like a mirage."[50] Such discrepancies prompted George's *Progress and Poverty* (1879), as well as Jacob Riis's *How the Other Half Lives* (1890) and Henry Demarest Lloyd's *Wealth Against Commonwealth* (1894). Others dreamed of utopian schemes to correct the imbalances of wealth and labor. Edward Bellamy's 1888 novel, *Looking Backward,* was widely read and discussed, as was Howells's depiction of a humane technological order in *A Traveler from Altruria* (1894). In contrast, the populist politician Ignatius Donnelly, in *Caesar's Column* (1884), forecast nightmarish conditions in the United States of 1988, ruled by a tyrannous merchant prince and his council.

Other related aspects of the American scene were equally disturbing, including the speed of change, commercialism, and materialism satirized in Dart's cartoon. Henry James found the United States profoundly altered when he visited in 1902 after living abroad for twenty years. He felt disoriented in a land where economic considerations outweighed aesthetic values and traditions. He saw everywhere a "crudity of wealth" and a "perpetual repudiation of the past." The changed landscape included a novel and disturbing source of sublimity: Overhanging the well-loved landmark of Trinity Church in New York's Wall Street was a new skyscraper—a "vast money-making structure" that seemed to him "as high and wide as the mountain-wall that drops the Alpine avalanche."[51] He was also shaken by a visit to Ellis Island, where the numbers of immigrants the United States was "ingurgitating" impressed him as never before. Thereafter everywhere he went he was aware of their presence and their claim to share in the life of the nation.[52]

In sum, by the turn of the century many experienced their homeland as vastly altered from that of their youth. Reactions to this disorienting transformation varied. Some could still take comfort in nostalgia and interest in history, but of more remote times than *Picturesque America* depicted. Henry Adams, for example, retreated to the Middle Ages. Others glorified the "discovery of America," the early explorers, and the colonists, stressing the values of the Founding Fathers—and the continuing primacy of their descendants. Some involved themselves in active reforms, seeking solutions to the nation's problems through science, education, religion, labor unions, or political parties. Others retired into cynicism, or simply tended their own gardens—or estates.

Whatever the response, however, for most of these citizens of the new century, especially the urban dwellers, the phrase "picturesque America" could call up an image like the satiric cartoon as readily as a cascading waterfall. Although enthusiasm for scenery and touring was still strong, confidence that nature appreciation, picturesque touring, and books of landscape art were sufficient civilizing forces had waned. And *Picturesque America*, with its old-fashioned steel and wood engravings, could no longer function to inspire confidence and "cement" patriotism as it had in the 1870s. The parlor where it was still likely to be displayed near the family Bible was not the well-appointed one of up-to-date city dwellers, but rather a "musty chromo-hung and horsehaired" country parlor.[53] The "monument of native art" had become a relic.

APPENDIX A

Biographies of
Picturesque America's Artists

Note: Brief biographies of the artists who made on-the-spot drawings or paintings for *Picturesque America* follow. Not included are those artists whose only connection with the project was the inclusion of steel-engravings after one or more of their works, such as Kensett, Casilear, and Darley. Information on these artists is readily available in standard reference works.

In preparing the biographies that follow, standard sources such as the *Dictionary of American Biography* and *The National Cyclopedia of American Biography* have been used, as well as the *M. & M. Karolik Collection of American Water Colors & Drawings, 1800–1878*, Sinclair Hamilton, *Early American Book Illustrators and Wood Engravers, 1670–1870*, Mantle Fielding, *Dictionary of American Painters, Sculptors and Engravers*, the National Museum of American Art's *Index to American Art Exhibition Catalogues through 1876*, and the Inventory of American Paintings of the National Museum of American Art, Smithsonian Institution. The most helpful sources specific to particular artists are listed at the end of each biography.

HARRY FENN
Born Richmond, England, 1837 (?); died Montclair, New Jersey, 1911.
Work signed: H.F., H. Fenn
or

As a youth Fenn was apprenticed to the Dalziel Brothers wood engraving firm in London, where he was considered one of the cleverest pupils. About 1857, he sailed to Canada and the United States with fellow apprentice Charles Kingdon. He settled in New York and worked as a wood engraver for *Frank Leslie's Illustrated*

293

Newspaper, and probably for other publishers as well. He married Marian Thompson of Brooklyn around 1860. After studying art in Italy in the early 1860s, upon his return to New York he pursued drawing and painting rather than engraving. Among his earliest book illustrations were contributions to Frank B. Goodrich's *The Tribute Book* (Derby and Miller, 1865) and Whittier's *National Lyrics* (Ticknor and Fields, 1865). Fenn also did many illustrations for Ticknor and Fields's *Our Young Folks*, and received much praise for special illustrated editions of Whittier's *Snow-Bound* (1868) and *Ballads of New England* (1870). He was one of the early members of the American Society of Painters in Water Colors (later the American Watercolor Society), elected at the second meeting, January 2, 1867. He remained active in the Society and exhibited regularly in their shows.

He was a frequent contributor to *Appletons' Journal* from its inception in 1869. As the initial artist for the "Picturesque America" series in the *Journal*, he travelled widely on the East Coast, beginning in mid-1870, often with editor Oliver Bell Bunce. His work clearly dominates volume I of *Picturesque America*, for which he illustrated the following sections: "On the Coast of Maine," "St. John's and Ocklawaha Rivers, Florida," "Lookout Mountain and the Tennessee," "Richmond, Scenic and Historic," "Natural Bridge, Virginia," "Mauch Chunk," "On the Savannah," "The French Broad," "The White Mountains," "St. Augustine, Florida," "Charleston and Its Suburbs," "Weyer's Cave, Virginia," "Cumberland Gap," "Watkin's Glen," "Scenes in Eastern Long Island," "Our Great National Park," "Niagara," and "Trenton Falls." For Volume II, he illustrated many of the Northeast's most famous scenic areas—"Highlands and Palisades of the Hudson," "The Catskills," "Lake George and Lake Champlain," "Mount Mansfield," and "The Adirondack Region"—as well as "The Mohawk, Albany, and Troy" (with Woodward) and "New York and Brooklyn."

The success of *Picturesque America* established Fenn as a leading landscape illustrator and prompted D. Appleton and Company to produce similar surveys of Europe and Palestine. In 1873 Fenn went to Europe, settling his family near London, to begin work on *Picturesque Europe*. His illustrations would dominate this publication as well, although a number of British artists also contributed. Fenn covered parts of the British Isles, Spain, Italy and Sicily, Switzerland, and Germany. In 1878 and 1879, he travelled extensively with J. D. Woodward in the Holy Land and Egypt to sketch for *Picturesque Palestine, Sinai, and Egypt*.

After returning to New York in 1881, Fenn was a frequent contributor to such popular periodicals as *Harper's Weekly*, *Harper's Monthly*, *Century*, and *St. Nicholas*. In 1884, Roberts Brothers (Boston) issued a special "Harry Fenn Edition" of Gray's *Elegy in a Country Churchyard*. He was heavily involved in the *Century's* "Battles and Leaders of the Civil War" series (1884–87). As photoengraving replaced wood engraving, Fenn's pen drawings could be reproduced exactly as drawn, and his renderings of architecture were much appreciated. Joseph Pennell said Fenn "might almost be said to have invented the artistic illustration of architecture in America" (*Pen Drawing*, 302).

Fenn lived in Montclair, New Jersey, although he usually maintained a New York studio. He was a member of the Salmagundi Club and the Society of Illustrators. He received a gold medal at the World's Columbian Exposition in 1893. Numerous institutions own works by Fenn, including the Montclair Art Museum, the Metropolitan Museum of Art, the Library of Congress, and Cooper-Hewitt Museum.

References:

[Dalziel, George and Edward]. *The Brothers Dalziel: A Record of Work, 1840–1890.* London: B. T. Batsford Ltd., 1978. Reprint of the original 1901 edition, London: Methuen and Company.

Typescripts, newspaper clippings, etc. The Montclair (New Jersey) Historical Society.

(The author plans a study of Fenn's life and works.)

WILLIAM HAMILTON GIBSON
Born Newtown, Connecticut, 1850; died Washington, Connecticut, 1896.
Work signed: W. H. Gibson

Gibson was educated at the Gunnery in Washington, Conn., and at the Brooklyn Polytechnic Institute. After his father's death in 1868, he attempted to support himself as an artist. His early works appeared in *Frank Leslie's Boys' and Girls' Weekly* and *Frank Leslie's Chimney Corner*. He contributed botanical sketches to the *American Agriculturalist* and to Appletons' *American Cyclopaedia*. In 1872, editor O. B. Bunce commissioned him to make drawings of Rhode Island, and later of the Connecticut coast, for *Picturesque America*'s sections "Providence and Vicinity" (vol. I) and "The Connecticut Shore of the Sound" (vol. II). He also did some of the Brooklyn images.

From the late 1870s he became well known as author and illustrator of nature articles appearing in *Harper's Monthly*, *Scribner's Monthly*, and *Century* magazines. Some were reprinted as books, such as *Highways and Byways, or Saunterings in New England* (1883) and *Strolls by Starlight and Sunshine* (1891).

He exhibited works at the Boston Art Club and the American Watercolor Society, of which he became a member in 1885. He first exhibited with the Society in 1874 (Seventh Annual Exhibition), when his contribution was "Leaves from a Sketch Book." He designed greeting cards for Prang & Company. In the 1880s he maintained a studio in his Brooklyn home.

References:

Adams, John Coleman. *William Hamilton Gibson, Artist-Naturalist-Author* (New York: G. P. Putnam's Sons, 1901).

Jussim, Estelle. "William Hamilton Gibson (1850–1896): The Artist Using the Camera's Eye." In *Visual Communication and the Graphic Arts: Photographic Technologies in the Nineteenth Century* (New York and London: R. R. Bowker, 1983), ch. 6, 149–94.

R. SWAIN GIFFORD

Born Naushon Island, Massachusetts, 1840; died New York City, 1905.

Work signed: R. Swain Gifford, RSG

or:

The son of a sailor and fisherman, Gifford was raised near New Bedford, Massachusetts. He was encouraged to paint by two local marine artists, William Bradford and Albert van Beest, and by Mrs. Lydia Swain, the wife of his father's employer, who took a special interest in him from childhood. He achieved success early and moved to Boston in 1864. Two years later he moved to New York, where he taught for many years at Cooper Union. He was one of the eleven founding members of the American Watercolor Society and, like Fenn, was present at the second meeting, January 2, 1867. That same year he was elected an associate of the National Academy, becoming a full member in 1878.

Gifford was artist for three sections about the West Coast in volume I of *Picturesque America*: "Up and Down the Columbia," "Northern California," and "On the Coast of California." The wood engravings were based on sketches or paintings made during the summer of 1869, when Gifford went West on the newly-completed transcontinental railroad. From San Francisco, he travelled to Portland by steamer and up the Columbia (where he met and became friendly with Vice President Schuyler Colfax and his party). He returned to San Francisco overland by private carriage. His letters reveal he had done work for the Appleton firm in early 1869, and he may well have been asked to provide some West Coast illustrations for the new *Appletons' Journal*. However, because the *Journal*'s "Picturesque America" series was first conceived in mid-1870, it is not accurate to say that Gifford set out with a commission to do work for the series or the book.

Gifford returned from his three-months' journey with sketches in oils, watercolors, and pencil, as well as photographs, rare minerals, furs and Indian "curiosities" (*Daily Mercury*, New Bedford, Oct. 15, 1869). The Whaling Museum, Old Dartmouth Historical Society, New Bedford, Massachusetts, owns a number of these artworks, as well as Gifford's diary and numerous letters from the journey.

Reproductions of two sketches similar to illustrations in *Picturesque America* appeared in the catalog of a 1974 exhibition: *R. Swain Gifford: 1840–1905*, which has an informative essay by Elton W. Hall.

In early 1870 Gifford exhibited a number of oils and watercolors from his trip in New York, at the National Academy of Design and elsewhere (see *Index to American Art Exhibition Catalogues to 1876*). Later that year Gifford travelled extensively in Europe, Egypt, and Morocco with Louis C. Tiffany. After his marriage in 1873 to Frances Eliot, also an artist, he and his wife further explored North Africa. His sketches from these journeys provided the material for many paintings. In 1877 he was one of the organizers, with James D. Smillie, of the New York Etching Club, and thereafter made a number of etchings.

References:

Hall, Elton W. "R. Swain Gifford and the New York Etching Club." In *Prints and Printmakers of New York State, 1825–1940*. Edited by David Tatham. Syracuse, N.Y.: Syracuse University Press, 1986.

Letters and Diaries. Robert Swain Gifford Papers, Whaling Museum Library, Old Dartmouth Historical Society, New Bedford, Mass.

R. Swain Gifford, 1840–1905. New Bedford, Mass.: Old Dartmouth Historical Society, 1974.

CASIMIR CLAYTON GRISWOLD
Born Delaware, Ohio, 1834; died 1918.
Work signed:

Griswold studied wood engraving in Cincinnati, and came to New York in 1850. He first exhibited at the National Academy of Design in 1857, where he was elected an Associate Member in 1866 and a full member in 1867. (The NAD has a portrait of him by Oliver Ingraham Lay.) In the late 1860s, he was mentioned frequently in the New York and Boston newspapers as a promising young landscape artist. By 1869 he had established himself in the studio building at 51 West Tenth Street. He was part of the artistic circle associated with the American Pre-Raphaelites (*The New Path: Ruskin and the American Pre-Raphaelites*, 16, 66), although few of his works have been located. He lived in Rome from 1872–86.

Griswold specialized in seacoast scenes, especially of Newport. Several of his dramatic coastal views in the "Newport" section of *Picturesque America* may have been based on existing oil paintings. (Five wood engravings carry his monogram, while others in the section are signed "Hogan & Schell). His *Purgatory Point,* exhibited at the Union League Club in February 1869 (*The Evening Post* [New York], Feb. 12, 1869), may have been the basis for the *Picturesque America* wood engraving titled "Purgatory" (which had appeared January 22, 1870, in *Appletons' Journal*). He also was artist for the steel engraving of "East Rock, New Haven" (II, opposite 444). (The designation of the artist as C. G. Griswold in the plate and the List of Engravings on Steel is surely an error.)

Although primarily a painter in oils around the time of *Picturesque America*, Griswold also worked as an illustrator, providing designs for an 1869 edition of the popular *Katrina* by J. G. Holland and for Field, Osgood & Company's *Winter Poems* (1871). Along with Fenn, Perkins, Homer, Hennessey, and others, he contributed four landscape designs to Appletons' 1871 edition of Bryant's *The Song of the Sower*.

Reference:

Ferber, Linda S., and William Gerdts. *The New Path: Ruskin and the American Pre-Raphaelites*. New York: Brooklyn Museum, 1985.

WILLIAM M. HART

Born Paisley, Scotland, 1823; died Mt. Vernon, New York, 1894.

Work signed:

In 1831, Hart's family moved from Scotland to Albany, New York, where young William painted carriages for a carriage maker. Self-taught, he thereafter supported himself painting portraits, spending three years in Michigan. He studied and travelled briefly in Scotland, returning to America in 1852. By 1854 he had a studio in New York and was specializing in landscape painting. He became an associate of the National Academy in 1854 and a full member in 1858. In 1856 he became the first president of the Brooklyn Academy of Design. He was one of the organizers, in 1866, of the American Watercolor Society, where he would have had contact with Fenn and R. Swain Gifford. Hart became president of the society in 1870.

For *Picturesque America*, Hart provided the illustrations for the "Lake Superior" section in vol. I, including the steel engraving "Baptism Bay, Lake Superior." He had visited the region during the summer of 1870. He spent other summers at Lake George and near Keene Flats in the Adirondacks. His younger brother, James M. Hart, also a landscape painter, was artist for the steel engraving "Adirondack Woods" in volume II of *Picturesque America*. William Hart occasionally contributed illustrations to books, including sixteen designs for an "artist's edition" of *The Sketch-Book of Geoffrey Crayon* (1864). In the early 1870s he maintained a studio in the YMCA building at Twenty-third Street and Fourth Avenue, as did J. F. Kensett, David Johnson, R. Swain Gifford, and numerous other artists.

References:

Sullivan, Mark. *James M. and William Hart: American Landscape Painters.* Philadelphia: John F. Warren, 1983.

"William Hart," *Cosmopolitan Art Journal* 3 (September 1858): 183–84 (includes wood-engraved portrait).

THOMAS MORAN

Born Bolton, Lancashire, England, 1837; died Santa Barbara, California, 1926.

Work signed:

Moran's family emigrated to Philadelphia when he was seven. At fifteen he was apprenticed to the wood engravers Scattergood and Telfer, where he drew on the block. After three years there he joined his older brother Edward in a studio, where Edward instructed him in painting and etching. In 1856 he exhibited five watercolors at the Pennsylvania Academy of the Fine Arts. In 1862 he studied Turner and Claude in England and also married Mary Nimmo.

During the 1860s and 1870s, much of his income came from book and magazine illustrations. He was a principal illustrator for *Scribner's Monthly* from its inception in November 1870. Working on illustrations of the Yellowstone region for *Scribner's* whetted his desire to go there, which he did as a guest of Hayden's expedition the summer of 1871. Upon his return he established a studio in Newark, New Jersey, and began work on his large canvas, *The Grand Canyon of the Yellowstone* (1872). Congress purchased this painting in 1872 for $10,000, which solidly established Moran's reputation as a leading artist of Western landscapes.

Thereafter Bunce hired Moran to illustrate all three sections on the West in volume II of *Picturesque America*, as discussed in detail in chapter 5, in the section "Using Photographs to Depict the West." For "The Plains and the Sierras," Moran travelled with his artist wife, Mary Nimmo Moran, to San Francisco on the Union and Central Pacific railroads, beginning August 24, 1872 (see Wilkins, chapter 5, for details of Moran's travels). His illustrations were based primarily on photographs by A. J. Russell, aided by personal observation.

The next summer (July 1873) Moran again went West with commissions from the Appleton firm, to southern Utah Territory and the Grand Canyon (see Wilkins, 78–81). With the aid of photographs by John K. "Jack" Hillers, the photographer of the Powell expedition, Moran prepared illustrations for *Picturesque America*'s section "The Cañons of the Colorado." He also prepared illustrations for *Scribner's Monthly* and *The Aldine*, and his large oil, *The Chasm of the Colorado* (1873–74), was based on sketches made during the visit.

Finally, Bunce commissioned Moran to prepare illustrations of "The Rocky Mountains" for *Picturesque America,* using photographs by W. H. Jackson made in conjunction with the Hayden survey during the summer of 1873. Moran was so intrigued with the photographs of the Mountain of the Holy Cross that he arranged to go there himself the next summer. His painting *Mountain of the Holy Cross* (1875) attracted much admiration at the Centennial Exposition in Philadelphia in 1876.

In the years following, Moran made numerous trips to the West, revisiting Yellowstone, the Grand Canyon, and Colorado several times. He became seriously interested in etching in 1877, as did his wife. In 1884 they built a studio in East Hampton, Long Island, which also served as a summer home. In 1916, Moran moved to Santa Barbara, California.

Moran was a member of the National Academy of Design, the American Watercolor Society, the New York Etching Club, and the Royal Society of Painter-Etchers, London.

References:

Bassford, Amy O., and Fritiof Fryxell. *Home-Thoughts from Afar: Letters of Thomas Moran to Mary Nimmo Moran.* East Hampton, N.Y.: East Hampton Free Library, 1967.

Clark, Carol. *Thomas Moran: Watercolors of the American West.* Austin: University of Texas Press, 1980.

Fern, Thomas S. *The Drawings and Watercolors of Thomas Moran.* Notre Dame, Ind.: Art Gallery, University of Notre Dame, 1976.

Kinsey, Joni Louise. "Creating a Sense of Place: Thomas Moran and the Surveying of the American West." Ph.D. diss., Washington University, 1989.

_____. *Thomas Moran and the Surveying of the American West.* Washington, D.C.: Smithsonian Institution Press, 1992.

Morand, Anne, and Nancy Friese. *The Prints of Thomas Moran in the Thomas Gilcrease Institute of American History and Art.* Tulsa, Oklahoma: Thomas Gilcrease Museum Association, 1986.

Wilkins, Thurman. *Thomas Moran: Artist of the Mountains.* Norman, Okla.: University of Oklahoma Press, 1966.

GRANVILLE PERKINS
Born Baltimore, Maryland, 1830; died New York City, 1895.
Work signed:G.P.

As a boy, Perkins was instructed in art by William E. Smith, son of John Reuben Smith, of Philadelphia. At the age of fifteen he began working as an assistant to another of Smith's sons, J. R. Smith, scene-painter for Philadelphia's Chestnut

Street Theatre. He became so expert that at least once, in Richmond, the audience shouted for "Young Perkins" after the curtain rose (*The Aldine*, February 1872, 48).

He painted stage sets for the elaborate productions of the Ravel family, and in about 1850 he set out with them on a long trip through Cuba, Jamaica, Yucatán, and Central America, returning to Philadelphia in 1856 with many sketches and studies. For a time thereafter he studied with the marine painter James Hamilton. He exhibited at the Pennsylvania Academy of the Fine Arts in 1856. After marrying in 1857, he began to illustrate books and periodicals for publishers in New York, Boston, and Philadelphia. In 1859 and 1860 he worked for *Frank Leslie's Illustrated Newspaper*, contributing numerous marine and landscape views. By 1861, he was working for the rival *Harper's Weekly*. At the same time, he painted in oils, exhibiting frequently at the National Academy of Design after 1860.

During Cuba's struggle for independence from Spain beginning in 1868, Perkins took advantage of his familiarity with the island, contributing numerous Cuban views to periodicals, including several to *Leslie's* (February 1869 and February 1871) and *Appletons' Journal* (August 14, 1869). Throughout the early 1870s he was a frequent contributor to *Appletons' Journal*, *The Aldine*, and *Every Saturday*.

For *Picturesque America*, Perkins illustrated much Eastern river scenery, as well as Philadelphia and Baltimore, two cities he knew well. He illustrated the following: vol. I: "Delaware Water-Gap," "Neversink Highlands," "Scenes on the Brandywine," and "Harper's Ferry"; vol. II: "Philadelphia and Its Suburbs," "Baltimore and Environs," "The Juniata," and "The Susquehanna." He contributed designs for six steel engravings: "Delaware Water-Gap," "The Highlands of the Neversink," "Harper's Ferry by Moonlight," "Philadelphia, from Belmont," "Baltimore from Druid-Hill Park," and "The Susquehanna."

Perkins contributed paintings to the exhibitions of the American Watercolor Society beginning in 1875 and was elected a member in 1877. The February 1872 *Aldine* said that his paintings were much admired for "their warmth of color, and for the natural life-like beauty of their sky and water effects." Works by Perkins are in the collections of the Mystic Seaport Museum, Mystic, Connecticut, and the Peabody and Essex Museum, Salem, Massachusetts.

References:

Gambee, Budd Leslie, Jr. "*Frank Leslie's Illustrated Newspaper*, 1855–1860: Artistic and Technical Operations of a Pioneer Pictorial News Weekly in America," ch. 6: "Henry Louis Stephens and Granville Perkins." Ph.D. diss., University of Michigan, 1963.

"Granville Perkins," *The Aldine* 5 (February 1872): 48 (includes portrait).

Manthorne, Katherine Emma. *Tropical Renaissance: North American Artists Exploring Latin America, 1839–1879*. Washington, D.C.: Smithsonian Institution Press, 1989, esp. 188.

WILLIAM LUDWELL SHEPPARD
Born Richmond, Virginia, 1833; died there in 1912.
Work signed: W.L.S.

As a young man, Sheppard designed labels for tobacco manufacturers. After winning awards in 1855 and 1857 for paintings exhibited at the Mechanics Institute in Richmond, Sheppard went to New York to study art in 1858. He was studying in Paris when the Civil War broke out in 1861 and immediately returned home to join the Confederate Army. He became a Second Lieutenant in the Richmond Howitzers. His later assignment to the Topographical Department of the Army of Northern Virginia provided many opportunities to draw.

After the Civil War his career as an illustrator flourished; his initials appear frequently on wood engravings in *Harper's Weekly*, *Every Saturday*, *Appletons' Journal*, and, later, *St. Nicholas*. He specialized in drawing figures, rather than landscapes. His earliest work for *Appletons' Journal*, "Charcoal Sketches" (February 12, 1870), featured Southern blacks, as did the four-part "Southern Sketches" (summer of 1870). Although considered highly adept at depicting blacks (*Harper's Weekly*, 1872, 555), many of his engraved figures are characterized by the exaggerated features of the racial stereotype.

The regions Sheppard illustrated for *Picturesque America* were not far from Richmond: "Scenes in Virginia" and "Washington" in volume I, including the steel engravings "The Chickahominy" and "Washington, from Arlington Heights."

He illustrated numerous books of popular and juvenile fiction, as well as accounts of the war. Particularly striking are his illustrations for John Esten Cooke's *Justin Harley* (1874). From 1877–78 Sheppard studied art, first in London, then in Paris under the engraver Paul Soyer. In the 1880's he taught art at the Mechanics Institute in Richmond. He also designed several sculptures in Richmond, including the Howitzers Monument and the Soldiers and Sailors Monument.

The Valentine Museum, the Museum of the Confederacy, and the Commonwealth Club, all in Richmond, own a number of his paintings and drawings. The Valentine Museum held a retrospective exhibition of his works in 1969.

Reference:
William Ludwell Sheppard: A Retrospective Exhibition of His Works. Richmond, Va.:
    Valentine Museum, 1969.

James David Smillie
Born New York, 1833; died there in 1909.
Work signed:

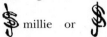 millie   or

Son of the prominent engraver James Smillie (1807–85), James David Smillie was trained as a steel engraver by his father as a child, as was his brother George Henry Smillie (1840–1921). A highly skilled practitioner of the art, he often collaborated with his father on bank note vignettes for the American Bank Note Company. After a trip abroad in 1862, however, he aspired to paint, and exhibited a landscape in oils at the National Academy of Design in 1864. He and his brother George often sketched in the Adirondacks in the summer and worked the rest of the year in their studio at Tenth Street and Broadway in New York. In 1866 he helped found the American Watercolor Society, and served as its president from 1871 to 1877.

Thus Smillie was already a prominent artist when he travelled to California by train in the summer of 1871. He had already provided material for *Appletons' Journal*, a view of "Placid Lake" included in a September 24, 1870, feature on "Adirondack Scenery" illustrated primarily by his brother. It is not surprising that he was asked to prepare illustrations of the Yosemite Valley for *Picturesque America*. He also wrote the accompanying text in early 1873, for which he was paid $80, as recorded in his diary. Smillie's drawings for the wood engravings were acquired by the Huntington Art Collections, San Marino, California, in 1992. His trip West also provided the opportunity to paint two subjects reproduced as steel engravings for the book—"Mount Shasta" and "The Golden Gate"—as well as exhibition pieces. At the Fifth Annual Exhibition of the American Watercolor Society in the following winter (1871–72), he exhibited three paintings of Yosemite landmarks: *The Half Dome, Yosemite, from Cloud's Rest, Face of the Half Dome from Tenaya Cañon, Yosemite*, and *Glacier Point, from Tenaya Cañon, Yosemite*. A painting dated 1872 of *Half Dome, Yosemite* was included in the 1979 exhibition *Beyond the Endless River: Western American Drawings and Watercolors of the Nineteenth Century* (Phoenix Art Museum, 1979) and reproduced in the catalog (172). In 1873, at the Sixth Annual Exhibition of the AWS, he exhibited *Scene in the Yosemite—Horse Racing*. This might be the watercolor in the M. & M. Karolik Collection at the Museum of Fine Arts, Boston, no. 662, *Rough Sport in the Yosemite*.

Smillie's contribution to the second volume of *Picturesque America* was to illustrate the only Canadian views included, based on a trip up the St. Lawrence to Montreal and up the Saguenay in July 1873. His father accompanied him, revisiting the scenes of his youth (see Mary Macaulay Allodi and Rosemarie L. Tovell, *An Engraver's Pilgrimage: James Smillie in Quebec, 1821–1830* [Toronto: Royal Ontario

Museum, 1989]; the authors inform me that Smillie included a portrait of his father in a top hat at the foot of Breakneck Stairs [*Picturesque America*, II, 379]. The section "The St. Lawrence and the Saguenay" appeared toward the middle of the second volume.

In the following years, Smillie experimented further with other graphic media. After being elected to the National Academy of Design in 1876, he helped organize the New York Etching Club in 1877, and became an ardent promoter of painter-etching as an art. Collections of his etchings, dry points, and aquatints are at the Museum of Fine Arts, Boston, and the New York Public Library.

References:
James D. Smillie: Drawings. New York: Jill Newhouse, American Drawings, 1981.
Schantz, Michael W. *James D. Smillie: American Printmaker, 1833–1909.* Philadelphia, Penn.: Woodmere Art Museum, 1991.
_____. "James David Smillie and the Evolution of American Printmaking." Ph.D. diss., University of California at Los Angeles, 1988.
Schneider, Rona. "The Career of James David Smillie (1833–1909) as rendered in His Diaries." *The American Art Journal* 16, no. 1 (1984): 5–33.
_____. "James David Smillie: The Etchings (1877–1909)." *Imprint: Journal of the American Historical Print Collectors Society* 6, no. 2 (Autumn 1981): 2–13.
Smillie, James D. Diaries. Archives of American Art, mfm. rolls 2849–51 (index to artists mentioned at Archives of American Art, Washington, D.C.).
Witthoft, Brucia. *The Fine-Arts Etchings of James David Smillie, 1833–1909: A Catalogue Raisonné.* Lewiston, N.Y.: Edward Mellen, 1992.

JULES TAVERNIER
Born Paris, France, 1844; died Honolulu, 1889.
Work signed: Jules Tavernier

The son of English citizens of French Huguenot ancestry, Tavernier entered the Paris atelier of Felix Barrias, member of the École des Beaux Arts, in 1861. He exhibited in the Paris Salon from 1865 to 1870. He fought in the Franco-Prussian War, but after the armistice went to London, where he joined the staff of *The Graphic.*

In 1872 he emigrated to New York with Allen Measom, who had engraved his works for *The Graphic.* He quickly became an illustrator for the New York *Graphic* and *Harper's Weekly.* His striking close-up view of Niagara from below was the front-page illustration for the November 1872 *Aldine.* This was probably based on a painting titled *Niagara* exhibited in the Sixth Annual Exhibition of the American Watercolor Society (1873) and owned by *The Aldine*'s publisher, James Sutton.

Tavernier probably made drawings in early 1873 for *Picturesque America*'s "Scenes in Northern New Jersey," which appeared early in the second volume, first distributed in mid-1873. Evidently he was still learning to create the illusion of depth in black and white, for most of the wood engravings, several of which were executed by Allen Measom, have a flat quality. His view of Passaic Falls (II, 57) is similar in viewpoint to the one of Niagara mentioned above.

Later in 1873 Tavernier and Paul Frenzeny, another artist-illustrator from France, were commissioned by *Harper's Weekly* to embark on a sketching tour from New York to San Francisco. The wood engravings based on their drawings began appearing on October 18, 1873, and continued sporadically through 1876. The announcement of their expedition stressed that they would "make long excursions on horseback into regions where railroads have not yet penetrated." Thus *Harper's* sought to compete effectively with *Picturesque America* and similar series. With primary attention to human activity distinctive to the West, such as cattle herding, this series was quite different from *Picturesque America*'s focus on scenery. Interestingly, the payment received by Tavernier and Frenzeny has been recorded: $75 for a full page, $150 for a double page (see Taft, *Artists and Illustrators of the Old West*, ch. 7). In 1874, at the Seventh Annual Exhibition of the American Watercolor Society, the Harper firm exhibited a wood block deriving from their journey, titled "Old Cotton Mill." (Their names were misspelled in the catalog: Paul T. Fenzeny and Jules Favernier).

After their sketching expedition, Tavernier remained in San Francisco, where he was involved in the San Francisco Art Association and the Bohemian Club. In 1875 he moved to Monterey, a spot popular with artists. Always seeking to get out of debt, Tavernier went to Hawaii in 1884, where, as one of the few professional artists, he made numerous paintings of volcanoes. He died in Honolulu in 1889.

References:

Ewing, Robert Nichols. "Jules Tavernier (1844–1889): Painter and Illustrator." Ph.D. diss., University of California, Los Angeles, 1975.

Taft, Robert. *Artists and Illustrators of the Old West: 1850–1900.* New York: Charles Scribner's Sons, 1953, ch. 7.

ASA COOLIDGE WARREN
Born New York, 1819; died Boston, 1904.

The son of a portrait painter, Warren learned steel engraving from George G. Smith and, later, Joseph Andrews. Then for a number of years, he engraved vignettes for the New England Bank Note Company and book illustrations for Ticknor and Fields.

The extremely close work of engraving threatened to damage his eyesight, causing him to turn to drawing on wood for a time. In 1863 he moved to New York, where he engraved for various publishers and the Continental Bank Note Company. He turned more and more to drawing and painting.

Warren had been a frequent contributor of city views to *Appletons' Journal*, and he prepared nine such views for *Picturesque America*, reproduced as steel engravings: vol. I: "City of Providence," "City of Buffalo," "City of Cleveland," "City of Detroit"; vol. II: "New York, from Brooklyn Heights," "City of Cincinnati," "City of Louisville," "The City of St. Louis," and "City of Milwaukee." It is not known whether he travelled to make on-the-spot renderings for these works.

He lost the sight of one eye in 1899 and gave up his profession altogether.

ALFRED R. WAUD
Born London, 1828; died Marietta, Georgia, 1891.
Work signed: A. R. Waud, or A.R.W.

Trained at the School of Design, Somerset House, and at the Royal Academy, London, Waud came to the United States with his older brother, William, in 1850. He worked as a staff artist for the *New York Illustrated News*. When the Civil War started, he was hired by *Harper's Weekly* as a "special artist," travelling with the Army of the Potomac. His on-the-spot drawings of battle scenes, reproduced as wood engravings, were considered remarkably accurate. Several depicted the cypress swamps of Louisiana (e.g., May 9, 1863, and Dec. 8, 1866), settings he later illustrated for *Picturesque America*. The Library of Congress has many Civil War sketches by both Alfred and William Waud.

After the war, in 1866, *Harper's Weekly* sent him to Kentucky, Tennessee, Louisiana, and elsewhere to record the conditions. He contributed to *Appletons' Journal* from its beginning, furnishing drawings for several fold-out cartoons, including "The Levee at New Orleans" (April 24, 1869), "A View on the Hudson" (November 20, 1869), and "A Southern Garden" (April 16, 1870). In 1871, on assignment for the new periodical *Every Saturday*, Waud travelled to New Orleans, Louisville, Mammoth Cave, and St. Louis, then to Chicago to cover the fire (October 9, 1871). Soon after *Every Saturday* discontinued illustrations at the beginning of 1872, Waud began assignments for *Picturesque America*.

Waud provided the illustrations for "The Lower Mississippi" in volume I of *Picturesque America* and for four sections in volume II: "The Upper Mississippi," "Chicago and Milwaukee," "A Glance at the Northwest," and "The Mammoth Cave." He was also artist of the steel engraving "City of New Orleans." Waud occasionally reused sketches from earlier travels in preparing *Picturesque America* views.

The largest group of his drawings of cities and scenery, including many for

Picturesque America, is owned by the Historic New Orleans Collection. The Missouri Historical Society also has a number of his drawings, as does the Chicago Historical Society (including some of the destruction caused by the Great Fire). Waud's journal from his 1872 journey to Minnesota, Wisconsin, Illinois, and the Dakota Territory for *Picturesque America* is also at the Historic New Orleans Collection.

In later years, Waud contributed many illustrations to both Bryant and Gay's *A Popular History of the United States* and *Battles and Leaders of the Civil War*. He died while on assignment in Marietta, Georgia.

References:

Alfred R. Waud: Special Artist on Assignment: Profiles of American Towns and Cities 1850–1880. New Orleans: Historic New Orleans Collection, Kemper and Leila Williams Foundation, 1979.

"The Creole Sketchbook of A. R. Waud." *American Heritage* 15, no. 1 (December 1963): 33–48.

"Down the Mississippi: From the North Woods to New Orleans with an Artist-Reporter of the Last Century." *American Heritage* 35 (June/July 1984): 86–95.

Ray, Frederic E. *Alfred R. Waud, Civil War Artist* (New York: Viking Press, 1974)

Taft, Robert. *Artists and Illustrators of the Old West: 1850–1900*. New York: Charles Scribner's Sons, 1953, 58–62.

JOHN DOUGLAS WOODWARD

Born Middlesex County, Virginia, 1846; died New Rochelle, New York, 1924.

Work signed: J.D.W. or

(late in Vol. II): $\mathcal{JW}$; or his later monogram:

Woodward's family moved from Virginia to Covington, Kentucky, in 1849. In 1861, Douglas Woodward began his art instruction with F. C. Welsh in Cincinnati. After the Civil War his family settled in Richmond, where he knew the sculptor Edward V. Valentine and artists William Ludwell Sheppard and John Adams Elder. In 1866 Woodward went to New York and studied art at Cooper Union. He first contributed to *Appletons' Journal* about 1870. He travelled extensively in the South in the spring and summer of 1871, making drawings for *Hearth and Home*.

In 1872 and 1873 Woodward was commissioned by the Appleton firm to work on *Picturesque America*. He was the second most prolific contributor to that work, illustrating more sections in volume II than Fenn. In volume I he illustrated "Mackinac" and "South Shore of Lake Erie"; and in volume II: "Valley of the Connecticut," "Boston," "Valley of the Housatonic," "Valley of the Genesee,"

"Eastern Shore," "Lake Memphremagog," "The Mohawk, Albany, and Troy" (with Fenn), "The Upper Delaware," and "Water-Falls at Cayuga Lake." Many of Woodward's original drawings for *Picturesque America* were given by his widow to Shrine Mont, a conference center of the Episcopal Diocese of Virginia.

In 1876 and 1877 Woodward travelled for *Picturesque Europe*, covering parts of Germany, Norway, Sweden, and Russia. He and Fenn travelled together in the Holy Land and Egypt in 1878 and 1879 for *Picturesque Palestine, Sinai, and Egypt*. Woodward contributed many illustrations to *The Aldine*, *The Art Journal*, and *Century* magazine in the 1870s and 1880s. Like Fenn, he participated in the "Battles and Leaders of the Civil War" series in the *Century*.

Woodward longed to paint in oils rather than for illustration. He spent much time at the artists' colony at Pont Aven, France, and especially enjoyed trying to capture the atmospheric effects of the Italian Lakes. In the 1880s and 1890s he was a regular exhibitor at the National Academy of Design. In 1891 he was Secretary of the Pennsylvania Academy of the Fine Arts. In 1894, an inheritance provided adequate income, and thereafter he devoted himself to painting. In 1905, he built a home and studio at New Rochelle, New York, overlooking Long Island Sound.

References

"An Artist Abroad in the Seventies: Letters by John Douglas Woodward." Unpublished typed transcription of manuscript letters. Virginia State Library, Richmond, Virginia.

"J. D. Woodward," in *American Art and American Art Collections*. Edited by Walter Montgomery. 1889; reprint, New York: Garland Publishing Co., 1978.

Rainey, Sue. "J. D. Woodward's Wood Engravings of Colorado and the Pacific Railways, 1876–1878," *Imprint: Journal of the American Historical Print Collectors' Society* 18, no. 2 (fall 1993): 2–12.

Two Versions of the Preface

Earlier Preface—Unsigned

The design of "Picturesque America" is to present a full description and elaborate pictorial delineation of all the different portions of our country. The wealth of material for the purpose is very great. Our country borders on two oceans and comprises within the vast space that lies between them a variety of scenery that no other people can boast of. There are a few mountains in other portions of the globe that attain a greater altitude, but the number and the distinct character of our mountain-ranges are remarkable; the White Mountains, the Catskills, the Alleghanies, the Rocky Mountains, and the Sierra Nevada, embrace some of the wildest and most beautiful mountain-scenes in the world, while the gigantic cañons of the far West are unapproachable in grandeur. Our rivers are among the largest and our lakes are the noblest of either continent; our water-falls are among the masterpieces of Nature's handiwork; our forests are of the primitive growth; our prairies and savannas possess a novelty and beauty that fill the beholder with surprise and admiration. No country in the world possesses a succession of such varied pictures, while probably no country has so many features and places entirely unfamiliar to its own people. It is quite safe to assert that a book of American scenery like "Picturesque America" will afford American readers more novel scenes than would a similar work on Europe. We are all acquainted with the Hudson, Niagara, and the Yosemite, either by direct observation or by paintings and photographs, but there are innumerable places which our artists and tourists have rarely visited, and hence many strange, picturesque, and charming scenes will for the first time become familiar to the general public through these pages. Our purpose has been to illustrate, with greater fulness and artistic excellence than has hitherto been attempted, all the spots endeared to us by association, and, at the same time, to bring into public appreciation the many glorious scenes that lie in the by-ways of travel.

The design of the work includes, not only the natural beauties of our country, but the various aspects that civilization has impressed upon it. It will give views of our cities and towns, exhibit the animated life that marks our rivers and lakes, and portray those features of our life and habits that have a picturesque element.

The illustrations, in almost every instance, are from drawings made on the spot, by artists sent by the publishers for the purpose. Photographs, however accurate, have not the spirit and personal quality which an accomplished painter or draughtsman succeeds in infusing into his picture. The engravings here presented would lose half their charm if simply obtained by the ordinary method of photography; and the publishers, with due modesty, claim for "Picturesque America," in addition to the truthfulness of the scenes, a spirit, animation, and beauty, which give to the work an art value higher than could be derived from mere topographical accuracy.

Preface Signed by William Cullen Bryant

It is the design of the publication entitled "PICTURESQUE AMERICA" to present full descriptions and elaborate pictorial delineations of the scenery characteristic of all the different parts of our country. The wealth of material for this purpose is almost boundless.

It will be admitted that our country abounds with scenery new to the artist's pencil, of a varied character, whether beautiful or grand, or formed of those sharper but no less striking combinations of outline which belong to neither of these classes. In the Old World every spot remarkable in these respects has been visited by the artist; studied and sketched again and again; observed in sunshine and in the shade of clouds, and regarded from every point of view that may give variety to the delineation. Both those who see in a landscape only what it shows to common eyes, and those whose imagination, like that of Turner, transfigures and glorifies whatever they look at, have made of these places, for the most part, all that could be made of them, until a desire is felt for the elements of natural beauty in new combinations, and for regions not yet rifled of all that they can yield to the pencil. Art sighs to carry her conquests into new realms. On our continent, and within the limits of our Republic, she finds them—primitive forests, in which the huge trunks of a past generation of trees lie mouldering in the shade of their aged descendants; mountains and valleys, gorges and rivers, and tracts of sea-coast, which the foot of the artist has never trod; and glens murmuring with water-falls which his ear has never heard. Thousands of charming nooks are waiting to yield their beauty to the pencil of the first comer. On the two great oceans which border our league of States, and in the vast space between them, we find a variety of scenery which no other single country can boast of. In other parts of the globe are a few mountains which attain a greater altitude than any within our limits, but the mere difference in height adds nothing to the impression made on the spectator. Among our White Mountains, our Catskills, our Alleghanies, our Rocky Mountains, and our Sierra Nevada, we have some of the wildest and most beautiful scenery in the world. On our majestic rivers—among the largest on either continent—and on our lakes—the largest and noblest in the world—the country often wears an aspect in which beauty is blended with majesty; and on our prairies and savannas the spectator, surprised at the vastness of their features, finds himself, notwithstanding the soft and gentle sweep of their outlines, overpowered with a sense of sublimity.

By means of the overland communications lately opened between the Atlantic coast and that of the Pacific, we have now easy access to scenery of a most remarkable character. For those who would see Nature in her grandest forms of snow-clad mountain, deep valley, rocky pinnacle, precipice, and chasm, there is no longer any occasion to cross the ocean. A rapid journey by railway over the plains that stretch westward from the Mississippi, brings the tourist into a region of the Rocky Mountains rivalling Switzerland in its scenery of rock piled on rock, up to the region of the clouds. But Switzerland has no such groves on its mountain-sides, nor has even Libanus [Lebanon], with its ancient cedars, as those which raise the astonishment of the visitor to that Western region—trees of such prodigious height and enormous dimensions that, to attain their present bulk, we might imagine them to have sprouted from the seed at the time of the Trojan War. Another feature of that region is so remarkable as to have enriched our language with a new word; and *cañon*, as the Spaniards write it, or *canyon*, as it is often spelled by our people, signifies one of those chasms between perpendicular walls of rock—chasms of fearful depth and of length like that of a river, reporting of some mighty convulsion of Nature in ages that have left no record save in these displacements of the crust of our globe. Nor should we overlook in this enumeration the scenery of the desert, as it is seen in all its dreariness, not without offering subjects for the pencil, in those tracts of our Western possessions where rains never fall nor springs gush to moisten the soil.

When we speak of the scenery in our country rivalling that of Switzerland, we do not mean to imply that it has not a distinct and peculiar aspect. In mountain-scenery Nature does not repeat herself any more than in the human countenance. The traveller among the Pyrenees sees at a glance that he is not among the Alps. There is something in the forms and tints by which he is surrounded, and even in the lights which fall upon them, that impresses him with the idea of an essential difference. So, when he journeys among the steeps, and gorges, and fountains of Lebanon and Anti-Lebanon, he well perceives that he is neither among the Alps nor the Pyrenees. The precipices wear outlines of their own, the soil has its peculiar vegetation, the clouds and the sky have their distinct physiognomy.

Here, then, is a field for the artist almost without limits. It is no wonder that, with such an abundance and diversity of subjects for the pencil of the landscape-painter, his art should flourish in our country, and that some of those by whom it is practised should have made themselves illustrious by their works. Amid this great variety, however, and in a territory of such great extent, parts of which are but newly explored and other parts yet unvisited by sketchers, it is certain that no country has within its borders so many beautiful spots altogether unfamiliar to its own people. It is quite safe to assert that a book of American scenery, like "Picturesque America," will lay before American readers more scenes entirely new to them than a similar book on Europe. Paintings, engravings, and photographs, have made us all, even those who have never seen them, well acquainted with the banks of the Hudson, with Niagara, and with the wonderful valley of the Yosemite; but there are innumerable places which lie out of the usual path of our artists and tourists; and many strange, picturesque, and charming scenes, sought out in these secluded spots, will, for the first time, become familiar to the general public through these pages. It is the purpose of the work to illustrate with greater fulness, and with superior excellence, so far as art is concerned, the places which attract curiosity by their interesting associations, and, at the same time, to challenge the admiration of the public for many of the glorious scenes which lie in the by-ways of travel.

Nor is the plan of the work confined to the natural beauty of our country. It includes, moreover, the various aspects impressed on it by civilization. It will give views of our cities and towns, characteristic scenes of human activity on our rivers and lakes, and will often associate, with the places delineated, whatever of American life and habits may possess the picturesque element.

The descriptions which form the letter-press of this work are necessarily from different pens, since they were to be obtained from those who had personally some knowledge of the places described. As for the illustrations, they were made in almost every instance by artists sent by the publisher for the purpose. Photographs, however accurate, lack the spirit and personal quality which the accomplished painter or draughtsman infuses into his work. The engravings here presented may with reason claim for "Picturesque America," in addition to the fidelity of the delineations, that they possess spirit, animation, and beauty, which give to the work of the artist a value higher than could be derived from mere topographical accuracy.

The letter-press has passed under my revision, but to the zeal and diligence of Mr. Oliver B. Bunce, who has made the getting up of this work a labor of love, the credit of obtaining the descriptions from different quarters is due. To his well-instructed taste also the public will owe what constitutes the principal value of the work, the selection of subjects, the employment of skilful artists, and the general arrangement of the contents.

William Cullen Bryant.

Placement of Steel Engravings in the Parts of *Picturesque America*

Part Number	Title of Steel Engraving	Date on Print
1	Title page vignette, vol. I	none
	On the Coast of Florida*	1871
2	Mount Desert, Coast of Maine	1871
3	Richmond from the James*	1871
4	Delaware Water Gap	1872
5	The Rocky Mountains	1871
6	Mirror Lake, Yosemite Valley	1872
7	The Mount Washington Road*	1872
8	The Highlands of the Neversink*	1872
9	The City of Detroit*	1872
10	Cumberland Gap*	1872
11	The Terrace, Central Park	1872
12	Washington from Arlington Heights	1872
13	City of Cleveland	1872
14	City of Louisville	1872
15	The Chickahominy*	1872
16	City of Providence	1872
17	West Point and the Highlands	1869
18	City of Cincinnati	1872
19	Niagara* (used as frontispiece, vol. I)	1873
20	Mouth of the Moodna on the Hudson	1870
21	Indian Rock (Narragansett)	1873
22	City of Milwaukee	1872
23	Native Californians Lassoing a Bear	1873
24	City of Buffalo	1873
25	Philadelphia from Belmont*	1873
26	The Catskills	1873

27	Lake George	1873 or 1874
28	City of Baltimore*	1873
29	City of Boston	1873
30	Lake Superior (Entrance to Baptism Bay)	1873
31	New Orleans	1873
32	The Susquehanna	1873
33	City of New York	1872
34	Emigrants Crossing the Plains	1869
35	Golden Gate (From Telegraph Hill)	1873
36	The Upper Yellowstone Falls	1873
37	The Housatonic*	1874
38	Mount Shasta	1873
39	The Adirondack Woods	1874
40	The Smoky Mountains	1873
41	On the Beverly Coast, Massachusetts	1874
42	East Rock, New Haven*	1873
43	Mount Hood, from the Columbia	1874
44	City of St. Louis	1872
45	Connecticut Valley from Mount Tom	1874
46	Quebec	1874
47	Harpers Ferry by Moonlight	1874
48	Title page vignette, vol. II	none

* Subject of steel engraving corresponds to subject covered in the part.

Notices on the Wrappers of the Parts of *Picturesque America*

Note: Because *Picturesque America* was issued in parts over a long period, considerable variation occurs in the content and placement of the announcements. Although I have not made an exhaustive study, I think the order and timing suggested here accurately represents the first appearance of the different notices.

D.1. Part 24 (tipped inside front wrapper).

N O T I C E.

THE publishers having been applied to in several instances to bind the first volume of " Picturesque America," the last article of which is reached in the present number (24), deem it necessary to notify subscribers that this volume is not yet complete, and that, if bound now, will be imperfect. Several steel engravings connected with articles in the first volume are yet to come, while some of the steels already issued must have their permanent place in the second volume. This fact has prevented us from preparing tables of contents, index, etc., all of which will be necessary for the completeness of the volume, and which will be given to the subscribers at the end of the issue.

For those who desire a secure and convenient receptacle for their numbers until they are ready for the binder, we have prepared a box, covered with muslin, and stamped in gilt, which will hold twenty-four parts. Price, $2.50. Those desiring it may notify the delivery agent, who will bring it for their inspection.

D. APPLETON & CO.

D.2. Part 35 (on verso of front wrapper).

TO SUBSCRIBERS.

As proof that the Publishers of " Picturesque America" have more than kept their promises in regard to the outlay upon this work, they beg to offer the following statements :

The full cost of the steelplates, woodcuts, and articles, was estimated in their first announcement at eighty thousand dollars ; subsequently, finding that this amount would not cover the investment, the figures in the prospectus were placed at one hundred thousand. It is now quite certain the cost of the engravings and the literary work will reach all of a hundred and thirty thousand dollars. This estimate has no reference to cost of paper and printing.

The cost of the illustrations and articles in the first volume averaged twenty-four hundred and forty-one dollars ($2,441) per number (total for the volume, $58,584), while the cost of these items in the ten numbers of volume second, so far published, averages thirty-two hundred and seventy-five dollars ($3,275) per number, or eight hundred and thirty-four dollars over the average cost of the earlier parts. This additional average cost arises from the greater number of illustrations now given in each number. These facts speak for themselves.

D. APPLETON & COMPANY.

D.3. Part 37 (on verso of front wrapper).

NOTICE.

WE have many inquiries in regard to the *binding* of the volumes of "PICTURESQUE AMERICA" when completed. We beg to inform our subscribers that we have designs in preparation of unusual elegance, and that in due time specimens of various styles will be exhibited by our *number deliverers,* who will then be authorized to receive the parts for binding. In all instances where orders are intrusted to our regular deliverers we will be responsible for style of execution and prompt return, but would caution subscribers against applications from irresponsible persons. It is important, in a work of this kind, that the binding should correspond with the contents.

For those who are too remote to transmit their numbers to us for binding, we shall have *cases* in cloth and morocco, stamped with the elaborate and appropriate designs we are having prepared, which any local binder can attach. Prices will be given hereafter.

D. APPLETON & CO.

With Part 37, the back wrapper begins to carry an announcement about the new revised edition of *Appletons' Illustrated American Cyclopaedia.* Four of the sixteen projected volumes were then ready, and the whole was to be sold by subscription only. Some parts contained sample pages of the *Cyclopaedia.*

D.4. Parts 39 through 46 (on front wrapper, running vertically along
left side); and parts 47 and 48, below "To the Binder."

☞ CAUTION TO SUBSCRIBERS.—Subscribers are particularly cautioned against giving up their Numbers to bind to irresponsible persons. A printed form of receipt, bearing the name of D. Appleton & Co., and properly signed, should IN ALL CASES be required. Offers of unusually cheap bindings should be regarded with extreme suspicion, as designing persons sometimes use such pretenses to cover fraudulent intentions.

D.5. Parts 43 through 46 (on verso of front wrapper).

PICTURESQUE EUROPE.

ILLUSTRATED ON STEEL AND WOOD.

A COMPANION VOLUME TO

PICTURESQUE AMERICA.

THE undersigned have had for some time in active preparation a work designed to correspond, in style and character, to PICTURESQUE AMERICA (a publication that has attained a popularity unequaled bv any publication of its kind in the history of American literature), which is to consist of views of the more notable and attractive places in Great Britain and the Continent. The illustrations for this work will be engraved solely from fresh and original sketches, made by artists who have visited, for this purpose, the places selected for illustration.

It is designed to give the most comprehensive and, at the same time, artistically perfect series of views of picturesque places in the Old World ever published. The success which has attended PICTU-RESQUE AMERICA, and which encouraged the publishers to increase the number of engravings in the later parts, and to extend the cost many thousands of dollars beyond the sum first intended, has warranted in the undertaking now announced an outlay of the most liberal character, and has determined the undersigned to spare no expense in making it in every way a splendid art-gallery of the picturesque and the beautiful in the storied lands abroad. In this work the innumerable old ruins, the splendid cathedrals, the ancient abbeys, the monuments of art scattered everywhere, will secure more varied subjects than in our own country, where the artist has little more than scenes of Nature to inspire his pencil.

D. APPLETON & CO., Publishers,

549 & 551 Broadway, New York.

Appended to the above with part 45:

The undersigned hope to be able to begin the publication of this great work by

JANUARY 1, 1875

Before which time further particulars will be given.

D. Appleton & Co., Publishers
549 & 551 Broadway, New York.

D.6. Parts 47 and 48 (on front wrapper running vertically on left and right sides).

☞ NOTICE TO SUBSCRIBERS.—We hereby respectfully notify our numerous subscribers to "PICTURESQUE AMERICA," that we have prepared elaborate and elegant styles and stamps for binding this valuable work, and are now prepared to receive their numbers, giving receipts for the same at prices herein stated. Our deliverers will take pleasure in showing specimens of our binding, which may also be seen at our office. Subscribers residing at a distance can have their copies bound and delivered to them at the same prices, and without additional expense, by forwarding their numbers to our address.

PRICES OF BINDING.

Full Turkey Morocco Antique, Gilt,	$10.00 per Volume.
French Morocco Antique,	8.00 "
Half Morocco, Extra Gilt,	6.00 "
Half Morocco, Best,	7.00 "

D. APPLETON & CO., Publishers, 549 & 551 Broadway, New York.

On verso of front wrapper.

TO THE BINDER.

In binding the volumes of this work, the binder will note that the steel plates are not usually, as stitched in the numbers, rightly placed. By consulting the Lists of Steel Illustrations in the last part, the order and place of each plate will be found indicated, the page given in the list being that which the plate is to face.

The title-page and preface for volume one will be found in part first; the title-page of volume second, the table of contents and list of steel illustrations for volume one, and table of contents and list of steel illustrations for volume two, will all be found accompanying part *forty-eight.*

Notes

Preface

1. Neil Harris, *The Artist in American Society: The Formative Years, 1790–1860* (1966; reprint, Chicago: University of Chicago Press, 1982), 196.

2. See Peter B. Hales, introduction to *Silver Cities: The Photography of American Urbanization, 1839–1915* (Philadelphia: Temple University Press, 1984), esp. 4–5, and "Transforming the View: 1871–1878," in *William Henry Jackson and the Transformation of the American Landscape* (Philadelphia: Temple University Press, 1988), 95–139.

Chapter 1

1. *Publishers' Weekly* 17 (May 1, 1880): 455. Grant Overton, *Portrait of a Publisher* (New York: D. Appleton, 1925), 10.

2. James M. Patterson, "Agriculture as a Force of Civilization," *Appletons' Journal*, Dec. 18, 1869, 567.

3. "Literature in America in 1871," *Publishers' and Stationers' Weekly Trade Circular* 1, Jan. 18, 1872: 4. Prior to January 1872, this trade journal was titled *The American Literary Gazette and Publishers' Circular*.

4. Gerard R. Wolfe, *The House of Appleton* (Metuchen, N.J.: Scarecrow Press, 1981), 171.

5. "A Plea for Culture," *Atlantic Monthly* 19 (January 1867): 33.

6. Thomas Carlyle, "Shooting Niagara: and After?" *Macmillan's Magazine* 16 (1867): 319–36 (reprinted in *New York Tribune*, Aug. 16, 1867); Walt Whitman, "Democracy," *Galaxy* 4 (December 1867): 923, cited in Thomas Bender, *New York Intellect* (New York: Knopf, 1987), 155.

7. March 1869, 354. Also appeared under the title "Oil Painting by Machinery," in James Parton, *The Triumphs of Enterprise, Ingenuity and Public Spirit* (Hartford: A. S. Hale, 1871; sold by subscription).

8. Parton, *Triumphs of Enterprise*, 77. An earlier version of this description of Chicago appeared in the *Atlantic Monthly* 19 (March 1867).

9. Parton, *Triumphs of Enterprise*, 75.

10. Parton, *Triumphs of Enterprise*, 615. Originally published in 1867 in the *Atlantic Monthly*.

11. Parton, *Triumphs of Enterprise*, 620.

12. Samuel Bowles, *The Switzerland of America: A Summer Vacation in the Parks and Mountains of Colorado* (Springfield, Mass.: Samuel Bowles, 1869), 16, 17.

13. Charles Dudley Warner, "What Is Your Culture to Me?" *Scribner's Monthly* 4 (1872): 475.

14. Ralph Waldo Emerson, "Wealth," in *The Conduct of Life* (1860), *Ralph Waldo Emerson. Essays and Lectures* (The Library of America, 1983), 995.

15. Frederic Hudson, *Journalism in the United States From 1690 to 1872* (New York: Harper & Brothers, 1873), 705.

16. Quoted in *The Aldine*, inside back wrapper, December 1871. Special Collections, Alderman Library, the University of Virginia.

17. Eugene Benson, "French and English Illustrated Magazines," *Atlantic Monthly* 25 (June 1870): 687.

18. The *Ledger*'s circulation was close to 400,000, according to James D. Hart, *The Popular Book: A History of America's Literary Taste* (1950; reprint, Westport, Conn.: Greenwood, 1976), 95. Michael Denning, in *Mechanic Accents: Dime Novels and Working-Class Culture in America* (New York: Verso, 1987), says the *Ledger* claimed a circulation of 377,000 by 1869 (fn. 1, p. 214 n).

19. See *Godey's Lady's Book*, April 1870. In 1872 such concerns led to the arrest of the editor of *Fireside Companion* for publishing obscene materials, on the initiative of the Society for the Suppression of Vice, organized by Anthony Comstock. Denning, *Mechanic Accents*, 50–51.

20. Wolfe, *House of Appleton*, 145, 152–54, 169, 183. The successive addresses in Manhattan were 443–445 Broadway, 90–92–94 Grand Street, and 549 and 551 Broadway.

21. Advertisement in the back matter of W. F. Rae, *Westward by Rail* (New York: D. Appleton, 1871). It also suggested that having such a reference on hand might "directly contribute to the business success of the party concerned."

22. Wolfe, *House of Appleton*, 76.

23. Advertisement in the *American Literary Gazette and Publishers' Circular*, July 1, 1869, includes these two books, plus *Evenings at Home* "in words of one syllable by Mary Godolphin."

24. Perennial favorites included Cornell's *Geographics* and *Physical Geography* and G. P. Quakenbos's *Arithmetics, English Grammar and Composition*, and *Elementary History of the United States*. During these years, the firm also offered the Masterly Series for learning French and German.

25. Quoting the well-known landscape gardener Egbert L. Viele, in an advertisement in the *New York Tribune*, Dec. 15, 1870.

26. Phineas Camp Headley's *Life and Military Career of Major-General Philip Henry Sheridan* (1865) and Gen. Adam Badeau's *Military History of Ulysses S. Grant* (1868), the first of three volumes.

27. Wolfe, *House of Appleton*, 46.

28. For example, on human origins: St. George Mivart's *On the Genesis of Species* (1871) and Edward Fontaine's *How the World Was Peopled* (1872); on astronomy and geology: Richard A. Proctor's *Other Worlds than Ours* (1871), J. Norman Lockyer's *Elements of Astronomy* (1870), and Lord (John Benn Walsh) Ormathwaites's *Astronomy and Geology Compared* (1872). More practical works of geology were *Resources of the Pacific Region* (1869) and *The Coal Regions of America—Underground Treasures, Where and How to Find Them* (1872).

29. For example, W. E. H. Lecky, *History of European Morals from Augustus to Charlemagne* (1869), Sir John Lubbock, *The Origin of Civilization and Primitive Conditions of Man* (1870), and S. Baring-Gould, *The Origin and Development of Religious Belief* (1870).

30. "American Notice of a New System of Philosophy by Herbert Spencer," in Herbert Spencer, *Illustrations of Universal Progress: A Series of Discussions* (New York: D. Appleton, 1865), ix. *A New System of Philosophy* was later retitled *Synthetic Philosophy.*

31. Herbert Spencer, "Progress: Its Law and Cause," in *Illustrations of Universal Progress*, 3, 58.

32. See Herbert Spencer, "Over-Legislation," in *Essays: Moral, Political and Aesthetic* (New York: D. Appleton, 1871).

33. Spencer, "Progress: Its Law and Cause," 60

34. "American Notice of a New System of Philosophy," vii.

35. Also, the Duke of Somerset's *Christian Theology and Modern Skepticism* (1872) and John William Draper's *History of the Conflict Between Religion and Science* (1874).

36. Joseph Le Conte, *Religion and Science* (New York: D. Appleton, 1873), 243.

37. Luise Mühlbach was the pseudonym of Klara Mundt, one of the "Gartenlaube" school. The firm brought out twenty of Mühlbach's books over the next two years and published translations of works by other German writers, including A. E. Brachvogel, Frederick Gerstäcker, and Heinrich Zschokke. Wolfe, *House of Appleton*, 128.

38. In addition to being written by the famous former British prime minister, the book dealt with such controversial subjects as the Irish separatist movement and Jesuit intrigue. See Vernon Bogdanor's introduction to Benjamin Disraeli, *Lothair* (London: Oxford University Press, 1975). Bret Harte parodied this novel in "Lothair—or the Adventures of a Young Gentleman in Search of a Religion," in *Every Saturday* (April 29, 1871).

39. Scott's Waverley novels were also offered in 1868 at twenty-five cents each, and Cooper's novels, illustrated by F. O. C. Darley, were offered at fifty cents in 1872. Women writers on Appleton's list included Britons Rhoda Broughton, Mrs. Oliphant, and Julia Kavanaugh and Americans Alice B. Haven and Christian Reid (the pen name of Frances C. Tiernan).

40. Some first appeared in *The Home Book of the Picturesque* (New York: George P. Putnam, 1852).

41. Advertisement in the *New York Times*, Dec. 23, 1869.

42. Electrotypes were made by galvanic action—direct current electricity in a precipitating cell containing dilute sulfuric acid and copper plates. A beeswax mold of the type or woodcut was covered with a thin coat of graphite and placed in the cell, which was then connected with a galvanic battery. The electric current would slowly deposit a thin shell of copper on the mold, which was later backed with type metal to make it extremely durable. See Michael Winship, "Printing with Plates in the Nineteenth-Century United States," *Printing History* 5, no. 2 (1983): 20–21. An earlier process, stereotyping, had adequately duplicated letterpress type but was less successful with wood engravings.

43. Probably as an incentive, the same number featured the innovation of reproducing numerous sample pages from illustrated books as advertisements.

44. Quoted in advertisement in the *New York Times*, Dec. 19, 1871. David Tatham comments on the "lack of consistency of style and interpretation" in *The Song of the Sower*'s illustrations, and the greater harmony of those in *The Story of the Fountain* (*Winslow and the Illustrated Book* [Syracuse, N.Y.: Syracuse University Press, 1992], 98–101).

45. See, for example, Benson, "French and English Illustrated Magazines," 681–87.

46. For example, an advertisement in the Dec. 15, 1869, *New York Times* announced that *Putnam's Magazine* for January 1870 would be "ready at 12 o'clock today"; similarly, on Dec. 22, 1869, an advertisement for *Harper's Monthly* said it would be ready at one o'clock.

47. John Fiske, *Edward Livingston Youmans: Interpreter of Science for the People* (New York: D. Appleton, 1894), 255.

48. From Youmans's letter to his mother, Sept. 15, 1868, in Fiske, *Edward Livingston Youmans*, 256.

49. *Round Table*, April 10, 1869.

50. *American Literary Gazette*, July 1, 1869.

51. Letter of April 27, 1869, in Fiske, *Edward Livingston Youmans*, 260.

52. The main literary attraction in the early numbers was Victor Hugo's *The Man Who Laughs; or, By the King's Command*, published simultaneously with the original *L'Homme qui rit*, presumably fruit of Youmans's scouting trip abroad.

53. Quoted in an advertisement in *The Aldine* (January 1870).

Chapter 2

1. *Appletons' Journal*, Oct. 29, 1870.

2. Dec. 18, 1869.

3. The text was by Thomas W. Knox. The numerous illustrations included double-page specials of Western scenery by Joseph Becker and smaller views based on photographs by A. J. Russell.

4. *New York Evening Post*, Nov. 23, 1870.

5. December 1869 and January 1870. Its claim to furnish yearly "twenty-five per cent more literature than the largest of the monthly magazines" reflects the period's infatuation with quantitative measurement, as had *Leslie's* touting "21 square feet of engravings." Plans for 1870 included a new serial novel by Dickens (the Mystery of Edwin Drood), short stories by Annie Thomas, "novelties in the way of pictorial visits to famous places and sketches of travel and adventure," and papers on science and social topics.

6. *Every Saturday*, n.s., Jan. 1, 1870, 2. Thomas Bailey Aldrich (1836–1907) was editor of *Every Saturday*. The junior member of Fields, Osgood & Co., James R. Osgood (1836–92), persuaded James T. Fields to change the magazine, according to Carl J. Weber, *The Rise and Fall of James Ripley Osgood: A Biography* (Waterville, Me.: Colby College Press, 1959), 113–14.

7. "The Handsomest Illustrated Newspaper," *Frank Leslie's Illustrated Newspaper*, 28 (Jan. 8, 1870), 274.

8. Numerous works by Houghton made a circuitous journey, as the artist sent drawings from his American travels back to London for a *Graphic* series called "Graphic America"; thereafter, they appeared in *Every Saturday*. See Julian Treuherz, *Hard Times: Social Realism in Victorian Art* (London: Lund Humphries, and Mt. Kisco, N.Y.: Moyer Bell, 1987), ch. 7, "The Graphic"; and Paul Hogarth, *Arthur Boyd Houghton* (London: G. Fraser, 1981) and *Arthur Boyd Houghton: Introduction and Check-list of the Artist's Work* (London: Victoria and Albert Museum, 1975). In the latter, Hogarth says that Houghton's satiric views of certain aspects of life in New York and Boston generated considerable adverse reaction among Americans (13). A publisher's note in the Oct. 29, 1870, *Every Saturday* revealed the source of the magazine's foreign illustrations, stressing its exclusive "honorable arrangement" with *The Graphic*. This wording could not fail to suggest a favorable comparison with periodicals that copied images without compensating the source.

9. By the fall of 1870, when the "Picturesque America" series began in *Appletons' Journal*, and thereafter, many American works appeared, including landscapes by A. R. Waud and

Homer Martin, and scenes of American life by W. J. Hennessy, Winslow Homer, F. O. C. Darley, C. G. Bush, W. L. Sheppard, and Sol Eytinge, Jr. With some exceptions, the quality of the wood engravings of these American works did not measure up to the electrotypes imported from *The Graphic*. Most of the text continued to be reprinted from European periodicals throughout 1870, and thus was different in appeal from *Appletons' Journal*.

10. Prominently featured were illustrations by the French artist Gustave Doré (1832–83), including several of his illustrations to the Bible and the *Divine Comedy*. *The Aldine* may have had an arrangement with the London publisher of these editions, Cassell, Petter & Galpin.

11. Other magazines also jumped on the illustration bandwagon. For example, in June and August 1870, *Lippincott's*, which had started without illustrations in 1868, but had gradually added several full-page wood engravings each month, suddenly "discovered" American scenery with "The Virginia Tourist" by Edward A. Pollard. The August feature, with seven small unsigned vignettes, was the most heavily illustrated piece *Lippincott's* had run.

12. Edward Eggleston, "Josiah Gilbert Holland," *Century Magazine* 23 (December 1881):165. Quoted in Robert J. Scholnick, "J. G. Holland and the 'Religion of Civilization' in Mid-Nineteenth Century America," *American Studies* 27 (Spring 1986): 58. For an account of the founding of *Scribner's Monthly*, which became *The Century* in 1881, see Arthur John, *The Best Years of the Century: Richard Watson Gilder, Scribner's Monthly, and the Century Magazine, 1870–1909* (Urbana: University of Illinois Press, 1981), ch. 2.

13. Important general works about this period include: Allan Nevins, *The Emergence of Modern America 1865–1878* (1927; reprint, Chicago: Quadrangle Books, 1971); Roy F. Nichols and Eugene H. Berwanger, *The Stakes of Power, 1845–1877* (1972; rev. ed., New York: Hill and Wang, 1982); and Alan Trachtenberg, *The Incorporation of America: Culture and Society in the Gilded Age* (New York: Hill and Wang, 1982). See also Henry Nash Smith, ed., *Popular Culture and Industrialism 1865–1890* (New York: New York University Press, 1967).

14. Nichols and Berwanger, *Stakes of Power*, 193. By 1872 there were approximately 70,000 miles of track.

15. This topic has been dealt with by, among others, Barbara Novak, *Nature and Culture, American Landscape and Painting, 1825–1875* (New York: Oxford University Press, 1980), and Joshua C. Taylor, "The Virtue of American Nature," in *America as Art* (Washington, D.C.: Published for the National Collection of Fine Arts by the Smithsonian Institution Press, 1976), 97–130.

16. William Wordsworth, "The Tables Turned" (1798), stanza 6.

17. Hugh Davids, "On Expression in Art. Painting," *Lippincott's Magazine* (July 1868), 57.

18. See the classic studies of this topic: Christopher Hussey, *The Picturesque: Studies in a Point of View* (1927; reprint, London: Cass, 1967); Elizabeth W. Manwaring, *Italian Landscape in Eighteenth-Century England* (New York: Oxford University Press, 1925); Walter John Hipple, Jr., *The Beautiful, the Sublime, and the Picturesque in Eighteenth-Century British Aesthetic Theory* (Carbondale: Southern Illinois University Press, 1957); and Paul Shepherd, *Man in the Landscape* (New York: Knopf, 1967). Also see Malcolm Andrews, *The Search for the Picturesque: Landscape Aesthetics and Tourism in Britain, 1760–1800* (Stanford: Stanford University Press, 1989).

19. The complete stanza runs: "Enough of science and of art; / Close up those barren leaves; / Come forth, and bring with you a heart / That watches and receives" ("The Tables Turned," stanza 8).

20. Christopher Mulvey, *Anglo-American Landscapes: A Study of Nineteenth-Century Anglo-American Travel Literature* (Cambridge: Cambridge University Press, 1983), 193.

21. Thomas Cole, "Essay on American Scenery," in *American Art, 1700–1960: Sources and Documents*, ed. John W. McCoubrey (Englewood Cliffs, N.J.: Prentice-Hall, Inc., 1965), 98, 99. See Kenneth Myers, *The Catskills: Painters, Writers, and Tourists in the Mountains 1820–1895* (Yonkers, N.Y.: The Hudson River Museum of Westchester, 1987), 38–40.

22. Warren Burton, *The Scenery-Shower, with Word-Paintings of the Beautiful, the Picturesque, and the Grand in Nature* (Boston: Ticknor, 1844), based on lecture delivered before the American Institute of Instruction in 1841.

23. Edmund Burke's influential essay, *Philosophical Enquiry into the Origin of Our Ideas of the Sublime and the Beautiful* (1756), delineated these constrasting responses and supplied a descriptive terminology that was in popular use until the end of the nineteenth century. See Elizabeth McKinsey, *Niagara Falls: Icon of the American Sublime* (New York: Cambridge University Press, 1985), esp. chs. 2 and 4, for the development of literary conventions in response to Niagara Falls.

24. See Price, *An Essay on the Picturesque* (1794), and Knight, *Analytical Inquiry into the Principles of Taste* (1805).

25. See Carl Paul Barbier, *William Gilpin: His Drawings, Teachings, and Theory of the Picturesque* (Oxford: At the Clarendon Press, 1963).

26. See Peter Bicknell, *Beauty, Horror and Immensity: Picturesque Landscape in Britain, 1750–1850* (Cambridge: Cambridge University Press and Fitzwilliam Museum, 1981). Whereas such eighteenth-century Associationist philosophers as David Hartley had conceived of the action of the mind in associating as "automatic," or physiologically based, this was no longer widely held by the 1860s and 1870s.

27. See Beth Lynne Lueck, "The Sublime and the Picturesque in American Landscape Description 1790–1850," Ph.D. diss., University of North Carolina, 1982; Edward J. Nygren, "From View to Vision," in Edward J. Nygren, with Bruce Robertson, *Views and Visions: American Landscapes before 1830* (Washington, D.C.: Corcoran Gallery of Art, 1986), 3–81; Mulvey, *Anglo-American Landscapes*; and McKinsey, *Niagara Falls: Icon of the American Sublime,* chs. 1–4.

28. Aquatint, an etching process with effects resembling watercolor painting, was becoming very popular and was well suited to depicting the moist British atmosphere (see Andrews, *The Search for the Picturesque,* 36). The aquatint process involves creating tonal areas by sprinkling resin dust on the copper plate prior to using acid. Among the outstanding aquatint series in Britain were Philip de Loutherbourg, *The Romantic and Picturesque Scenery of England and Wales* (London: Bowyer, 1805), and William Daniell and R. Ayton, *A Voyage Round Great Britain* (London: Longman, Hurst, Rees, Orme, and Brown, 1814–25).

29. English publishers commissioned artists including J. M. W. Turner, Thomas Allom, David Roberts, Samuel Prout, Clarkson Stanfield, and William Henry Bartlett to prepare drawings for steel engravings.

30. See McKinsey, *Niagara Falls: Icon of the American Sublime,* ch. 3, esp. 57–59.

31. Andrews states, "The English Gothic revival, a distinctly nationalistic phenomenon, performed a great service in promoting the aesthetic appeal of the ruins of native antiquities, and thereby consecrating them for inclusion in quasi-Claudean British landscape paintings" (*The Search for the Picturesque,* 36).

32. These series are reproduced in black-and-white in Gloria-Gilda Deák, *Picturing America 1497–1899* (Princeton: Princeton University Press, 1988), 2, 315, 320. On the engraver, John Hill, see Tobin Andrews Sparling, *American Scenery: The Art of John & John William Hill* (New York: New York Public Library, 1985), and Richard J. Koke, "John Hill, Master of Aquatint," *New-York Historical Society Quarterly* 43 (January 1959), 51–117. A major series of aquatints depicting primarily Western scenes, Prince Maximilian of Wied's *Travels in the Interior of North America*, with plates after paintings by the Swiss artist Karl Bodmer, was published in London, Paris, and Koblenz (1839–41), and was intended for European and British audiences.

33. Described in James T. Callow, *Kindred Spirits: Knickerbocker Writers and American Artists, 1807–1855* (Chapel Hill, N.C.: University of North Carolina Press, 1967), 164–67; and Frank Weitenkampf, "Early American Landscape Prints," *Art Quarterly* 8 (Winter 1945), 64–65.

34. See Edward Halsey Foster, "Picturesque America: A Study of the Popular Use of the Picturesque in Considerations of the American Landscape, 1835–1860," Ph.D. diss., Columbia University, 1970, 27–40. Foster calls Willis "the American Gilpin." On the travels of Bartlett and Willis, see Alexander M. Ross, *William Henry Bartlett: Artist, Author, Traveller* (Toronto: University of Toronto Press, 1973), 26; and Eugene C. Worman, Jr., "A Biblio-historical Reconstruction: Bartlett's Travels in the United States (1836–1837)," *AB Bookman's Weekly*, Oct. 30, 1989, 1643–51. For details of Virtue's business dealings, see Worman, "George Virtue's New York Connection, 1836–1879," *AB Bookman's Weekly*, March 30, 1987, 1350–63. See also Ross, *William Henry Bartlett*, 111, and Worman, "*American Scenery* and the Dating of Its Bartlett Prints," parts 1 and 2, *Imprint: Journal of the American Historical Print Collectors Society* 12, no. 2 (Autumn 1987): 2–11, and vol. 13, no. 1 (Spring 1988): 22–27.

35. *Meyer's Universum* included steel engraved views of many parts of the world, including the United States. It was published in parts as an annual by the Bibliographisches Institut in Hildburghausen, Germany, from 1833 to 1864, and in other countries at various times. An English-language edition was published in New York by Hermann Meyer in 1852 and 1853. See Angelika Marsch, *Meyer's Universum: Ein Beitrag zur Geschichte des Stahlstiches und des Verlagswesens im 19. Jahrhundert* (Lüneburg: Nordostdeutsches Kulturwerk, 1972).

36. For Western views, these works' engravings tended to be based on earlier paintings or prints. For example, several of Bodmer's views in *Travels into the Interior of North America* served, without any attribution, as the basis for later plates: see, for example, "The Stone Walls, Upper Missouri," in *The Scenery of the United States*, and "Elkhorn Pyramid, Upper Missouri," "Bison and Elk, Upper Missouri," and "The Ohio Cave-in Rock" in *Landscape Annual*.

37. Myers discusses this reciprocal relationship in *The Catskills*, 37–63.

38. For example: Franconia Notch (June 1852), "The Landscape of the South" (May 1853), Lake George (July 1853), Niagara (August 1853), the Susquehanna (October 1853), "The Virginian Canaan" (December 1853),the Catskills (July 1854) "Virginia Illustrated" (December 1854), the Juniata (March 1856), the Dismal Swamp (September 1856), the valley of the Connecticut (August 1856), "North Carolina Illustrated" (March 1857). The accompanying illustrations, many by T. Addison Richards or David Hunter Strother ("Porte Crayon") were often not very attractive.

39. "Fenn, Harry," *National Cyclopedia of American Biography* (New York: James T. White), 6:368. A similar account appears in [George and Edward Dalziel], *The Brothers Dalziel: A Record of Fifty Years' Work 1840–1890*, foreword by Graham Reynolds (1901; reprint, London:

B. T. Batsford, 1978) 344. In this version, at a dinner party, after the Englishman's remarks, Fenn said to the representatives of the Appleton firm, "Give me the chance and you shall see what a variety of beautiful material you have got in America." The response was, "Well, you shall have a try if you like. Do a few drawings and let us see."

40. Obituary, *New York Times*, July 7, 1878.

41. According to the *National Cyclopedia of American Biography* article on George S. Appleton: "To him the firm and the world of readers and art lovers were indebted for the magnificent series of superbly illustrated works known as 'Picturesque America,' 'Picturesque Europe,' and 'Picturesque Palestine,' each of which required an investment of about a quarter of a million dollars. The idea was that of George S. Appleton, and the charge of the artistic and literary department of these beautiful works was in the hands of the late Oliver B. Bunce, to whose fine literary intelligence, remarkable critical powers in matters of art, and thorough business knowledge and experience, it was due that the performance of the work reached so high a standard of excellence" (2:510).

42. See Harry Fenn, "The Bishop and the Boy," *St. Nicholas* 37 (June 1910): 705–6.

43. The Montclair (N.J.) Historical Society has typescripts of several accounts of Fenn's life, mainly obituaries. Unofficial records of his birthdate differ, but 1837 appears most likely.

44. American artists who started out learning either engraving or lithography include Asher B. Durand, John F. Kensett, John W. Casilear, James D. Smillie, Winslow Homer, and Thomas Moran. See Kathleen Adair Foster, "Makers of the American Watercolor Movement: 1860–1890," Ph.D. diss., Yale University, 1982, 46–47.

45. Budd Leslie Gambee, Jr., "*Frank Leslie's Illustrated Newspaper*, 1855–1860: Artistic and Technical Operations of a Pioneer Pictorial News Weekly in America," Ph.D. diss., University of Michigan, 1963, 365. Gambee says Fenn made engravings published in vols. 4, 5, and 6 of *Leslie's*, either working alone or with other engravers, including Speer.

46. *American Bookmaker* 9, no. 3 (September 1889): 1.

47. See two essays in *American Paradise: The World of the Hudson River School*, ed. John K. Howat (New York: Metropolitan Museum of Art, 1987): John K. Howat, "A Climate for Landscape Painters," esp. 66–67; and Doreen Bolger Burke and Catherine Hoover Voorsanger, "The Hudson River School in Eclipse," 71–90. See also Carol Troyen, "Innocents Abroad: American Painters at the 1867 Exposition Universelle, Paris," *American Art Journal* 16 (Autumn 1984): 2–29, recounting the poor reception of the American landscape paintings at the Paris Exposition. The only American honor for art was a silver medal awarded to Church for *Niagara*. The exposition influenced many American collectors to start buying European, especially French, artworks (19).

48. See also those accompanying Harriet Beecher Stowe's "Little Pussy Willow" (September and October 1866), 547, 626, and Maria S. Cummins's "The Girl and the Gleaner" (November 1866), 663.

49. Ralph Fabri, *History of the American Watercolor Society: The First Hundred Years* (New York: American Watercolor Society, 1969), 12–13. American Watercolor Society Papers, 1866–1955, Archives of American Art, mfm. roll N68-8. The society's name from 1866 until 1877 was The American Society of Painters in Water Colors. An earlier organization called The New York Water Color Society lasted from 1850 to 1855. See Foster, "Makers of the American Watercolor Movement."

50. See Kathleen A. Foster, "The Pre-Raphaelite Medium: Ruskin, Turner, and American Watercolor," in Linda S. Ferber and William H. Gerdts, co-curators, *The New Path: Ruskin and the American Pre-Raphaelites* (New York: Brooklyn Museum, 1985), 80–81.

51. Techniques used included superimposing washes, using opaque bodycolor or gouache in certain areas, and applying flecks of undiluted color with a dry brush. See Jane Bayard, *Works of Splendour and Imagination: The Exhibition Watercolor, 1770–1870* (New Haven: Yale Center for British Art, 1981), esp. 15–20; and Andrew Wilton and Anne Lyles, *The Great Age of British Watercolor, 1750–1880* (London: Royal Academy of Art, and Munich: Prestel-Verlag, 1993).

52. The 1866 Ticknor and Fields edition had only Fenn's title page illustration. See Sarah Burns, *Pastoral Inventions: Rural Life in Nineteenth-Century American Art and Culture* (Philadelphia: Temple University Press, 1989), 261–62.

53. Fenn had very deliberately gone about this re-creation of the past, as is shown in his account of his visit to Whittier's boyhood home (Harry Fenn, "The Story of Whittier's *Snow-Bound*," *St. Nicholas* 22, no. 6 [April 1893]: 427–30). The old homestead had changed so much that Whittier, then living some distance away, did not even want him to see it. Fenn insisted, however, claiming the publisher had ordered him to go there. It took all his powers of persuasion to induce the immigrant woman renting the house to let him in, but then he even got her permission to remove the cooking stove from the fireplace, revealing the old cranes, and to retrieve some furniture from the attic. When he showed Whittier his drawings, tears came to the sixty-year-old poet's eyes.

54. The article on Fenn in the *National Cyclopedia of American Biography* says that *Snow-Bound* (1868) and *Ballads of New England* (1870) were "the first illustrated gift-books produced in this country," and many later writers have repeated this errant claim. On early gift books, see Ralph Thompson, *American Literary Annuals and Gift Books, 1825–1865* (New York: H. W. Wilson, 1936).

55. David Tatham, *Winslow Homer and the Illustrated Book* (Syracuse, N.Y.: Syracuse University Press, 1992), 102.

56. *Atlantic Monthly* 24 (December 1869): 767. Fenn's wave of popularity continued into the next gift book season when his contributions to both Bryant's *Song of the Sower* (D. Appleton, 1871) and the anthology *Songs of Home* (Scribner, 1871) were singled out as "deserving the award of highest merit" (*The New York Evening Post*, Dec. 5, 1870, and "Books and Authors at Home," *Scribner's Monthly* [Jananuary 1871], 349). In "French and English Illustrated Magazines," Benson names Fenn as one of the artists who had done "the best work for American publications"; the others were Darley, Homer, Sheppard, Hows, Eytinge, Vedder, Cary, La Farge, Parsons, and Hennessy (683).

57. Their friendship is mentioned in a May 17, 1869, letter from Parsons's daughter-in-law, Alice Brigham Parsons, to her mother, quoted in *Charles Parsons and His Domain* (Montclair, N.J.: Montclair Art Museum, 1958), 16. Parsons had first worked as a lithographer for Endicott & Company, New York, where he advanced from an apprentice to director of the art department. His marine views drawn on stone for Currier and Ives also gained him much recognition.

58. Of the eight illustrations, Fenn provided four; another is signed by Darley and three are unsigned, but probably after Darley. Fields was so taken with Murray's lively stories that he rushed them out by April. See Warder H. Cadbury's introduction to William H. H.

Murray, *Adventures in the Wilderness*, ed. William K. Verner (1869; reprint, Syracuse, N.Y.: Syracuse University Press for the Adirondack Museum, 1970), 39.

59. Horace Bushnell, *Work and Play; or Literary Varieties* (New York: Charles Scribner, 1864), 16.

60. See David Strauss, "Toward a Consumer Culture: 'Adirondack Murray' and the Wilderness Vacation," *American Quarterly* 39, no. 2 (Summer 1987): 270–86.

61. See William G. McLoughlin, *The Meaning of Henry Ward Beecher* (New York: Alfred A. Knopf, 1970), 54–83.

62. Ford advertised, "The artistic fancy and graceful pencil of Mr. Fenn have produced some rare effects" (*New York Times*, Dec. 18, 1869). *Hearth and Home* of the same date published Fenn's drawing of Beecher looking out over his Peekskill farm, based on a photograph. Perhaps Harriet Beecher Stowe called her brother's attention to Fenn, presuming she was pleased with his illustrations for her *Religious Poems* and stories in *Our Young Folks*. As an editor of *Hearth and Home* earlier in 1869, she might have solicited his contributions.

63. By early 1872, the first and only volume of Beecher's *Life of Jesus, the Christ* had achieved "phenomenal sales," according to the *Publishers' and Stationers' Weekly Trade Circular*, which called it "a noble work, glowing with the essence of faith, while admitting to modern criticism that difficulties have crept into the letter of the Gospel text" (Feb. 1, 1872). Evidently Beecher was distracted by the much-publicized accusations of his adultery with one of his congregation, which eventually led to a trial in 1875. When J. B. Ford & Co. failed in 1875, they blamed Beecher's procrastination and the heavy expenses already incurred in the project. (See *Rocky Mountain News* [Denver], Aug. 12, 1875.) Nevertheless, Beecher's influential ministry and lecture career continued until his death in 1887. The majority of the public believed him unjustly accused. See Clifford E. Clark, Jr., *Henry Ward Beecher: Spokesman for a Middle-Class America* (Chicago: University of Chicago Press, 1978), esp. chs. 10 and 11.

64. The two illustrations were accompanied by a brief article by the popular humorist T. B. Thorpe, who would write the text for the first article in the "Picturesque America" series.

65. "Harry Fenn: An Appreciation: by a Friend," *Harper's Weekly*, May 13, 1911, 10.

Chapter 3

1. Frank Luther Mott gives the date as 1872 (*A History of American Magazines* [Cambridge, Mass.: Harvard University Press, 1938–57], 3:417). The article on Carter in the *Dictionary of American Biography* says he resigned in 1873 to take part in the revision of the *American Cyclopaedia*, suggesting that Bunce stepped up in 1873.

2. Bunce's coworker for several years was "Colonel" Charles H. Jones (1848–1913), a young Georgian who had come to New York in 1865 and edited Appleton's *Southern Tour* (1866), but Bunce clearly played the dominant role in directing the *Journal*. On Jones, see *The National Cyclopedia of American Biography*, 1:386; and Don C. Seitz, *Joseph Pulitzer: His Life and Letters* (New York: Simon & Schuster, 1924), 193ff. Jones had entered the Confederate army at the age of 15. The fact that James Wyman Barrett, city editor of the *World*, where Jones later worked, puts "colonel" in quotation marks indicates he had not earned the rank. See Barrett, *Joseph Pulitzer and his World* (New York: Vanguard Press, 1944), 153.

3. Bunce and Brother also published *Mrs. Ann S. Stephens' Monthly*, serializing her work. See Adrienne Siegel, *The Image of the American City in Popular Literature 1820–1870* (Port Washington, N.Y.: Kennikat Press; National University Publications, 1981), 72–73.

OTES TO PAGES 47–52

4. "Obituary: Oliver Bell Bunce," *Publishers' Weekly*, May 17, 1890, 649. This obituary also says he instigated the publication of Cooper's works illustrated with steel and wood engravings after F. O. C. Darley. This probably refers to those editions of Cooper's novels published by W. A. Townsend (New York) beginning in 1860 and continued in 1862 by the firm's successor, James C. Gregory. The Gregory firm also published steel engravings after Darley in *The Cooper Vignettes* (1862). Perhaps Bunce worked for the Townsend firm and stayed on after the change of ownership.

5. Edited by Frederick Saunders, priced at $15. See David Tatham, *Winslow Homer and the Illustrated Book* (Syracuse: Syracuse University Press, 1992), 89–90. Homer's contribution was his first drawing for a gift book.

6. Some Northern booksellers did not welcome the book at first. The illustrations were striking in their combination of spareness and drama, utilizing large areas of white space and contrasting areas of dark. Tatham, *Winslow Homer and the Illustrated Book*, 67–68.

7. The standard biographical accounts of Bunce say that he also worked briefly as a literary reader for Harper & Brothers before joining D. Appleton and Company in 1867.

8. William H. Rideing, *Many Celebrities and A Few Others* (Garden City, N.Y.: Doubleday, Page & Company, 1912), 79. The article on Bunce in *The Dictionary of American Biography* also mentions these gatherings: "His Sunday evening suppers were a happy institution among New York literary men."

9. Rideing, *Many Celebrities and A Few Others*, 77–79. Bunce's obituary in *Publishers' Weekly*, May 17, 1890, says his "irritability" grew "out of physical pain" (650). S. G. W. Benjamin, *The Life and Adventures of a Freelance* (Burlington, Vt.: Free Press Company, 1914), says Bunce was kind-hearted, but had a curt, "unfortunate manner."

10. *Publishers' and Stationers' Weekly Trade Circular*, Feb. 15, 1872, 142.

11. The series ran in eleven sporadic installments beginning Feb. 19, 1870. Brace described his Christian Aid Mission and its program to send children of the streets to live with and work for families in the West.

12. "About Our Trip to Colorado," *Appletons' Journal*, Oct. 18, 25, 1873.

13. "The Nearest Way Home," *Appletons' Journal*, Nov. 4, 1871, 516–19.

14. This series by Edward King, with illustrations based on drawings by James Wells Champney, ran from July 1873 to November 1874, and was issued in expanded form as a book in 1875 by the American Publishing Co. of Hartford. See Sue Rainey, "Images of the South in *Picturesque America* and *The Great South*," in *Graphic Arts & the South: Proceedings of the 1990 North American Print Conference*, ed. Judy L. Larson (Fayetteville: University of Arkansas Press, 1993), 185–215.

15. David C. Miller, *Dark Eden: The Swamp in Nineteenth-Century American Culture* (New York: Cambridge University Press, 1989), 59.

16. Dec. 12, 1869. See Elliott James Mackle, Jr., "The Eden of the South: Florida's Image in American Travel Literature and Painting, 1865–1900," Ph.D. diss., Emory University, 1977.

17. *Harper's Monthly* published "Six Weeks in Florida" by George Ward Nichols, with small, rather dull illustrations, and the Oct. 15, 1870, *Every Saturday* included brief text and several illustrations about Florida—including a full-page one by A. R. Waud. *Lippincott's Magazine* followed suit in December with "Florida: How to Go and Where to Stay," by J. P. Little, without illustrations.

18. A series of three articles, "In Search of Health and the Picturesque," appeared Aug. 25 and Sept. 1 and 8, 1860.

19. Thorpe probably had read these lines from Henry Wadsworth Longfellow's *Evangeline*: "Over their heads the towering and tenebrous boughs of the cypress / Met in a dusky arch, and trailing mosses in mid-air / Waved like banners that hang on the walls of ancient cathedrals" (ll. 29–31). For a detailed account of how such literary conventions took shape and solidified in relation to a specific site, see Elizabeth McKinsey, *Niagara Falls: Icon of the American Sublime* (New York: Cambridge University Press, 1985). "Quoting" from previous writers was common.

20. See Joni Louise Kinsey, *Thomas Moran and the Surveying of the American West* (Washington, D.C.: Smithsonian Institution Press, 1992), ch. 2, "Landscape as Metaphor."

21. The wood engraving (*Picturesque America*, I, 48) is similar to Fenn's watercolor entitled *Everglades* owned by the Metropolitan Museum of Art, reproduced in *American Watercolors from the Metropolitan Museum of Art* (New York: American Federation of Arts and Harry Abrams, 1991), cat. no. 78. It is not known whether this work was made on-the-spot or was a later work based on such a drawing.

22. Similarly, advertising for the monthly part in the *New York Evening Post*, Nov. 19, 1870, especially promoted the illustrations—"a superb steel engraving" designed by Darley, as well as Fenn's "fourteen superb designs" for "Picturesque America."

23. *Appletons' Journal*, Oct. 16, 1869, 1. See also *Charles Lanman: Landscapes and Nature Studies*, curated by Harry Frederick Orchard (Morristown, N.J.: Morris Museum of Arts and Sciences, 1983).

24. July 2, 1870, 22–23; July 30, 1870, 142.

25. The text in the Dec. 17, 1870, and Jan. 7, 1871, numbers was by H. E. Colton, author of *Mountain Scenery: The Scenery of the Mountains of Western North Carolina and Northwestern South Carolina* (1859). For the book, Bunce commissioned F. G. de Fontaine to write about this region.

26. Although the "Picturesque America" series was a prominent feature in the *Journal* during these months, the magazine did not neglect other timely subjects, such as the Franco-Prussian War. Gustave Doré's representations of "Peace" and "War" appeared as "extra sheets" in the December 3 issue.

27. Quoted in *Appletons' Journal*, April 22, 1871, 475.

28. Advertisement in the *New York Evening Post*, Oct. 29, 1870. The landscape illustrations announced in a *New York Times* advertisement, Nov. 19, 1870, evidently were Thomas Moran's views of "Fairmount," in Philadelphia, in the January 1871 number.

29. *The Aldine* touted its holiday number, with more than fifty illustrations, and announced a larger format for 1871 (*New York Times*, Dec. 3, 1870; *New York Evening Post*, Dec. 28, 1870); *Every Saturday*'s holiday number contained designs by such leading illustrators as F. O. C. Darley, Sol Eytinge, William Ludwell Sheppard, and Augustus Hoppin.

30. *New York Times*, Dec. 23, 28, 1870; *New York Evening Post*, Dec. 29, 1870. Those selected were "Noon on the Seashore" by J. F. Kensett, "Sunday Morning" by A. B. Durand, "Sunday Afternoon" by James Hart, "Emigrants Crossing the Plains" by F. O. C. Darley, "The River Road" by A. F. Bellows, "West Point and the Highlands" by Harry Fenn, "A Morning in the Tropics" by F. E. Church, "Lake George" by J. W. Casilear, "The Quiet Nook" by A. F. Bellows, and "Indian Rock" by [W. S.] Haseltine (*Appletons'* misspelled the name Hazeltine).

31. See Leo Marx, *The Machine in the Garden* (New York: Oxford University Press, 1964), esp. 190–209; also John F. Kasson, *Civilizing the Machine: Technology and Republican Values in America, 1776–1900* (New York: Grossman, 1976), esp. ch. 4, "The Aesthetics of Machinery."

32. In his 1828 sketchbook, The Detroit Institute of Arts, Archives of American Art, mfm. roll D-39, frame 227; as quoted by Kenneth Maddox, *In Search of the Picturesque: Nineteenth Century Images of Industry Along the Hudson River Valley* (Annandale-on-Hudson, N.Y.: Edith C. Blum Art Institute, Milton and Sally Avery Center for the Arts, Bard College Center, 1983), 23.

33. Fenn evidently made his pilgrimage to Natural Bridge on his first Southern tour in the fall of 1870.

34. "A Word to the Reader," *Every Saturday*, Jan. 7, 1871.

35. Ralph Keeler had gained considerable attention with his *Vagabond Adventures* (1870), recounting his rise from poor orphan to a "gentleman of culture," and made up largely of material that had already appeared in the *Atlantic Monthly* and *Old and New*. (See P. T. Barnum's letter quoted in an advertisement for the book in *Every Saturday*, Jan. 28, 1871, 87.) He died in a boating accident in 1873 in Cuba, where he was reporting for the *New York Tribune* (*Dictionary of American Biography*, 10:279–80). See also Ferris Greenslet, *The Life of Thomas Bailey Aldrich* (Boston: Houghton Mifflin, 1908), 100–101.

36. Probably photographs by C. L. Weed published by E. Anthony or E. and H. T. Anthony. See Weston J. Naef and James N. Wood, *Era of Exploration: The Rise of Landscape Photography in the American West, 1860–1885* (Buffalo, N.Y.: Albright-Knox Art Gallery, and New York: The Metropolitan Museum of Art, 1975), 33, 79–80.

37. The *Journal* credited W. W. Bailey for the sketch on which the illustration "Wright's Canyon" was based. Bailey was a young botanist who participated in Clarence King's Fortieth Parallel Survey in 1867. See William H. Goetzmann, *Exploration and Empire: The Explorer and the Scientist in the Winning of the American West* (1966; reprint, New York: Norton, 1978), 430–35.

38. William Cullen Bryant's *New York Evening Post* had given the series an endorsement on July 3, saying that a "delightful chapter on Charleston and its suburbs . . . admirably illustrated by Mr. Harry Fenn, forms a notable feature in the latest" *Appletons' Journal*.

39. It is not clear whether the unsigned article was by Bunce or W. T. Thompson, who wrote about Augusta for the later book.

40. During the remainder of 1871, sporadic additions to the series featured illustrations by artists other than Fenn, including views of Canandaigua Lake, New York, by Paul Dixon (November 11) and of a mill on the Brandywine River by Granville Perkins (November 25). Fenn did reappear November 18 with a full-page view of gnarled mulberry trees along the Savannah River at Augusta. Yet the *Journal*'s prospectus for 1872 indicated the series would continue (although the title was not used). The first item listed was: "American Localities and Scenery.—The series of Illustrated Papers depicting the Landscape and Places in America, which have been so popular a feature of the *Journal* heretofore, will be continued. . . . Harry Fenn, the most distinguished of our landscape-draughtsmen, will give his time exclusively to this series" (Dec. 23, 30, 1871).

41. In a May 2, 1872, letter to F. V. Hayden, Bunce described the coverage of the Yellowstone region in the *Journal* as "merely preliminary to the complete and perfect article in 'Picturesque America'" (National Archives, record group 57, mfm. 623, roll 2, frame 481). A number of views by Fenn and others appeared in the early months of 1872, but no more

reports of journeys by Bunce and Fenn appeared, despite the fact that the two visited the coast of Maine in July 1871 (*New York Evening Post,* July 15, 1871). Fenn's works appearing in early 1872 included "Schenectady, on the Mohawk" (Jan. 27), "Richmond, Historic and Scenic" (Feb. 3), "Cumberland Gap" (March 16), "The Fountain, Forsyth Park, Savannah" (April 13), and two views of Yellowstone Park based on photographs (May 11). In addition, George H. Smillie wrote and illustrated "From Denver to Gray's Peak" (March 9), and C. C. Griswold contributed a view of "The Spouting Cave, New-Port" (May 4).

42. *Publishers' Weekly* (May 17, 1890), 650.

43. Sept. 2, 1871, 414. On Oct. 28, *Leslie's* again chided those rivals importing or copying foreign engravings and claimed that because its own staff prepared all its pictures, "we are necessarily obliged to employ American art and industry to an extent far beyond any other publication—this fact alone should give us a superior claim upon the American public" (98).

44. Drawn by Matt.[hew Somerville] Morgan, an English artist brought to New York in 1870 by Frank Leslie to compete with Thomas Nast, and J. N. Hyde. (See Albert B. Paine, *Th. Nast: His Period and his Pictures* [New York: Macmillan, 1904], 227). *Leslie's* may well have chosen this emphasis as an alternative to natural scenery, as well as to compete with *Harper's Weekly.*

45. June 3, 1871. A few months later, *Harper's Weekly* reported a circulation of 275,000 for the issues covering the Chicago fire, but *Leslie's* said its circulation reached 327,000, and the following week was over 470,000.

46. By June 24, 1871, the following Homer designs had appeared: "The Robin's Note" (Aug. 20, 1870); "Chestnutting" (Oct. 29, 1870); "Trapping in the Adirondacks" (Dec. 17, 1870); "A Winter-Morning.—Shovelling Out" (Jan. 14, 1871); "Deer-Stalking in the Adirondacks in Winter" (Jan. 21, 1871); "Lumbering in Winter" (Jan. 28, 1871); "Cutting a Figure" (Feb. 4, 1871); "At Sea—Signalling a Passing Steamer" (April 1, 1871). *The New York Evening Post* also called attention to *Every Saturday*'s "admirable sketches" of New Orleans by Waud and of Virginia (especially of the "negro life") by W. L. Sheppard (July 3 and 20, 1871).

47. For example, from February to May 1871, *Harper's Monthly* ran "Along the Florida Reef," and in June 1871, it featured "An Excursion to Watkin's Glen," written and illustrated by "Porte Crayon" (David Hunter Strother). The illustrations for these articles were small and rather dull, but Charles Parsons's views of Montauk Point in the September number were more attractive.

48. *New York Evening Post,* July 24, 1871. *Scribner's* would become known in later years for the excellence of its printing after Theodore Low DeVinne took charge. It may have already been experimenting with methods that improved printing, however.

49. *Appletons' Journal,* Oct. 28, 1871. Other "commendations" from such prominent individuals as Vice-President Schuyler Colfax, Horace Greeley, and John Hay (whose *Pike County Ballads* [1871] and *Castilian Days* [1871] were currently popular) must also have given them pause.

50. *The Aldine*'s announced plans may well have been a factor in *Every Saturday*'s abrupt decision in January 1872 to abandon illustrations and revert to its less costly program of reprinting articles from foreign periodicals. Despite its claims of success quoted earlier, the magazine obviously had not gained the share of the market it hoped for and needed. Carl J. Weber, *The Rise and Fall of James Ripley Osgood: A Biography* (Waterville, Me.: Colby College Press, 1959), portrays Osgood as a brilliant and energetic publisher whose major failing was

lack of business sense. Osgood apparently once confessed to E. C. Stedman that he had lost $125,000 in the attempt to make *Every Saturday* the leading illustrated weekly (148). Frederic Hudson, *Journalism in the United States from 1690 to 1872* (New York: Harper & Brothers, 1873), 708, alludes to some "arrangement" with the Harpers at the time *Every Saturday* "abandoned pictures."

51. A young artist who had worked for the *Journal* and would soon work for *Picturesque America*, William Hamilton Gibson, indicated in a letter early in 1872 that his fellow New York illustrators considered *The Aldine* "the finest American illustrated journal"; they all congratulated him, saying "it is not a small thing to get a drawing accepted in the 'Aldine.'" John Coleman Adams, *William Hamilton Gibson, Artist-Naturalist-Author* (New York: G. P. Putnam's Sons, 1901), 168.

52. See James D. Hart, *The Popular Book: A History of America's Literary Taste* (Westport, Conn.: Greenwood, 1976), 150–52.

Chapter 4

1. The June 27, 1872, *Publishers' and Stationers' Weekly Trade Circular* contains a notice that D. Appleton and Company "are to publish" *Picturesque America* (602). I have not been able to locate advertisements for the beginning of the series. It is likely some appeared on the advertising pages that accompanied *Appletons' Journal* but were typically discarded before the magazines were bound into volumes.

2. By 1875, the firm had eleven agencies: 22 Hawley St., Boston; 922 Chestnut St., Philadelphia; 22 Post Office Avenue, Baltimore; 53 Ninth St., Pittsburgh; 100 State St., Albany; 42 State St., Rochester; 103 State St., Chicago; 30 W. 4th St., Cincinnati; 305 Locust St., St. Louis; 20 St. Charles St., New Orleans; 230 Sutter St., San Francisco (listed in an advertisement for *The Art Journal* in the back matter of *The Hudson River, by Pen and Pencil* [D. Appleton, 1875]).

3. Subscription lists of famous subscribers are reproduced in Grant Overton, *Portrait of a Publisher* (New York: D. Appleton, 1925), 59, 60.

4. The only sample book I have located, at the Library Company of Philadelphia, is not the earliest version, for it contains material from late in volume I. Rather elaborate, it is bound in brown morocco, with the title and a palette and brushes stamped in gold. It contains the engraved title page, followed by thirteen steel plates (an assortment from those issued with parts 1–20, as shown in appendix B). The title page and preface follow, and then pages 217–48, 337–44; 433–80 from vol. I—a fair cross section of less familiar as well as famous places in different parts of the country. There follows forty-two pages of ruled sheets for "Subscribers' Names," of which ten pages are filled in. Notations on these lists indicate that new subscribers often received "all the parts out" upon signing up for the work, presumably upon payment of the appropriate lump sum.

5. The preponderance of male subscribers could also be explained by the way this particular canvassing agent chose to work, for the Appleton office was on Chestnut Street and it was probably most convenient to solicit at nearby businesses and factories, where numerous potential customers could be found.

6. For example, Appleton's *The Poet and the Painter* (1869), with ninety-nine steel engravings, many reused, cost $20, and G. P. Putnam & Sons' *Gallery of Landscape Painters: American Scenery* (1870), with twenty-four large steel engravings, cost $50.

7. Knight, who was known for producing popular, relatively inexpensive books, also issued an 1853 edition with the expanded subtitle: *A Pictorial, Historical, and Literary Sketchbook of the British Islands, with Descriptions of Their More Remarkable Features and Localities.* William S. Orr & Co. also published *The Land We Live In* in 1853, with the same subtitle. The prolific illustrator William Harvey, a favorite pupil of the wood engraver Thomas Bewick, made most of the drawings for the book. *Picturesque America* is far superior to the earlier English work in the quality of the illustrations, typography, printing, and paper.

8. *Harper's Monthly Magazine* 45 (July 1872): 161–68.

9. Appleton-Century MSS, Lilly Library, Indiana University, Bloomington, Ind. Bryant mentions agreeing to the terms in a June 21 letter from D. Appleton and Company (unlocated).

10. Quoted in Parke Godwin, *A Biography of William Cullen Bryant*, 2 vols. (New York: D. Appleton, 1883), 2:347. Bryant's pay might have been similar to that Bayard Taylor received from Appleton and Company for editing *Picturesque Europe* (1875–79). A Sept. 2, 1875, agreement reveals he was paid $50 for "editing, preparing for the press and proofreading" each part of twenty-four pages (Appleton-Century MSS, Lilly Library, Indiana Universtiy, Bloomington, Ind.). If Bryant's pay was comparable, he would have earned $2,400 for editing the forty-eight parts (or somewhat less if he did not edit the earliest parts).

11. The region had attracted artists and writers earlier—Frederic Church in 1855. See John Wilmerding, "The Allure of Mount Desert," in *American Views: Essays on American Art* (Princeton: Princeton University Press, 1991), 3–15.

12. George William Curtis, *Lotus-Eating* (New York: Harper & Brothers, 1852), 139; James Fenimore Cooper, "American and European Scenery Compared," *The Home Book of the Picturesque* (New York: G. P. Putnam, 1852), 54.

13. The poem accompanied the wood engraving "Niagara Seen With Different Eyes," after Arthur Lumley, a humorous double-page spread depicting how various types, such as artists and poets, approached the falls.

14. John F. Sears, *Sacred Places: American Tourist Attractions in the Nineteenth Century* (New York: Oxford University Press, 1989), 184, 186.

15. Robert Swain Gifford Papers, MS. 12, S-g 1, Sr B, vol. 1, 1869, "Diary of Trip," Whaling Museum Library, Old Dartmouth Historical Society, New Bedford, Mass.

16. I am indebted to Roger B. Stein for the phrase "epistemological map."

17. In comments in his diaries on Sunday sermons, *Picturesque America* artist James D. Smillie approved such nonspecific theism. For example, he liked "the straightforward anti-doctrinal views" expressed by Dr. (Thomas S.) Hastings, of West Presbyterian Church, in an "earnest anti-hyper-Calvinist sermon." Diaries of James D. Smillie, Archives of American Art, mfm. roll 2849, March 6, 1870.

18. Similarly, in his article on Natural Bridge, Cooke writes that although "thoughtless persons have characterized" the most "remarkable curiosities in North America," Niagara Falls and Natural Bridge, as "freaks of Nature," on the contrary "in Nature—great, beneficent, and doing all things in order—there are no freaks. She shows her power in the grand cataract, spanned with its rainbow, and in the dizzy arch of the Natural Bridge, as in the daisy and the violet she shows her grace and beauty" (I, 82–83).

19. James Turner, *Without God, Without Creed: The Origins of Unbelief in America* (Baltimore: Johns Hopkins University Press, 1985), 173. Turner argues that in their attempt to make belief compatible with science American theologians and ministers identified God so closely

with the material world that they paved the way for agnosticism in the face of advancing scientific knowledge.

20. Letters of Gifford to Mrs. Lydia Swain, Jan.3, 1869, and July 30, 1869 (Robert Swain Gifford Papers, MS. 12, S-g 1, Sr A, S-s 2, folders 7, 10).

21. Anthony Trollope, *North America* (New York: Knopf, 1951), 98–99.

22. "About Our Trip to Colorado. II," *Appletons' Journal*, Oct. 25, 1873, 522. Later in *Picturesque America*, James D. Smillie quotes the geologist and writer Clarence King about Yosemite's Inspiration Point: "I always go swiftly by this famous point of view now, feeling somehow that I don't belong to that army of literary travellers who have here planted themselves and burst into rhetoric. Here all who make California books . . . dismount and inflate" (I, 477). From *Mountaineering in the Sierra Nevada* (Boston: James R. Osgood, 1872), 149.

23. There are numerous precedents for such metaphorical descriptions (and, indeed, they persist today). For example, in the account of his picturesque tour of the prairies in 1832, Washington Irving likens the experience of being in a lofty grove of trees in autumn to "the effect of sunshine among the stained windows and clustering columns of a Gothic cathedral" (*A Tour on the Prairies*, ed. John Francis McDermott [Norman: University of Oklahoma Press, 1956], 41). See Joni Louise Kinsey, *Thomas Moran and the Surveying of the American West* (Washington, D.C.: Smithsonian Institution Press, 1992), ch. 2.

24. Among those not reused were Paul Dixon's Hudson views (Feb. 25, April 5, June 10 and July 8, 1871); A. C. Warren's illustrations of "New-Hampshire Scenery" (March 11, 1871); A. R. Waud's Nevada and Snake River views (May 27, June 3, 1871); and some of George H. Smillie's images of Colorado scenery (March 9, 1872).

25. Three other small views in the Charleston article were not included, perhaps because of their size. An illustration of "The Old Bridge" in Schenectady appearing in *Appletons' Journal*, Jan. 27, 1872, was also dropped for no apparent reason.

26. See "On Clear Creek, above Georgetown," *Appletons' Journal*, March 9, 1872, and the unsigned "Gray's Peak," *Picturesque America*, II, 487.

27. *The Aldine* (August 1870) and the *New York Evening Post*, Oct. 11, 1870.

28. Announced in the *New York Evening Post*, May 16, 1871. See the Diaries of James D. Smillie, Archives of American Art, August 1871.

29. He visited Newport in the summer of 1867 and exhibited *Purgatory Point* at the Union League Club in February 1869 (*New York Evening Post*, June 13, 1867; Feb. 12, 1869).

30. This specialization is referred to in E. V. Lucas, *Edward Austin Abbey: Royal Academician: The Record of His Life and Work* (New York: Charles Scribner's Sons, 1921), 1:22, 45. Joseph Pennell chafed under the specialization imposed by A. W. Drake, art editor of *Scribner's* (later *The Century*). He wrote, "I was always to draw buildings" (Pennell, *The Adventures of An Illustrator* [Boston: Little, Brown, 1925], 65).

31. See *Godey's Lady's Book* (July 1871).

32. See especially, March 4, 1871, 201, and March 25, 1871, 277.

33. Waud's numerous illustrations appeared in *Every Saturday* beginning with the April 29, 1871, number. His drawings at the Historic New Orleans Collection also demonstrate how frequently and how well he sketched people. See "The Creole Sketchbook of A. R. Waud," *American Heritage* 15 (December 1963): 33–48.

34. "Art Gossip," *Frank Leslie's Illustrated Newspaper*, Feb. 27, 1869; *The Aldine* 5 (February 1872): 48.

35. Two clear instances of reuse are: "Moss Gathering Near Baton Rouge," *Every Saturday*, Aug. 5, 1871, 141, and "The Moss-Gatherers," *Picturesque America*, I, 272; and views of Mammoth Cave: "The Dead Sea," *Every Saturday*, May 13, 1871, 444, and the central scene in the composite "Scenes in Mammoth Cave," *Picturesque America*, II, 543.

36. The West Virginia images were "drawn by W. L. Sheppard, from sketches by David H. Strother," the writer of the piece. It is unclear whether Sheppard actually travelled for the assignment, although Strother refers to an unnamed artist accompanying him (I, 382). The close correspondence between illustrations in Strother's article on "The Mountains" of West Virginia in *Harper's Monthly* (June 1872 and November 1873) and the *Picturesque America* section suggests the same sketches were used for both.

37. Although two of George Smillie's Colorado views were reworked from the *Journal*, he is given no credit in *Picturesque America*, aside from his monogram on the wood engravings. I have not counted him among the *Picturesque America* artists. Nor have I counted the artists of at least two of the illustrations in the section on Newport—Frederic B. Schell and Thomas Hogan, who would later play a prominent role in *Picturesque Canada* (1882). "Schell & Hogan" appears in the wood engravings, but Griswold is given credit as illustrator of the section.

38. R. Swain Gifford also exhibited paintings of areas he illustrated for *Picturesque America*—Northern California and the Columbia River (see appendix A).

39. Those writers and artists who definitely travelled together were: Bunce with Fenn for "On the Coast of Maine," "Lookout Mountain and the Tennessee," "Mauch Chunk," "Charleston and its Suburbs"; Thorpe with Fenn for "The St. John's and Ocklawaha Rivers"; Henry A. Brown with Fenn for "The Catskills"; Rossiter Johnson with Fenn for "Mount Mansfield"; W. S. Ward with Woodward for "Valley of the Genesee"; J. E. Colburn with Moran for "The Cañons of the Colorado."

The text suggests that the following also travelled together: Bunce with Fenn for "Watkin's Glen"; G. W. Bagby with W. L. Sheppard for "Scenes in Virginia"; Garczynski with Fenn for "Niagara" and "Trenton Falls"; Burlingame with Fenn for "Highlands and Palisades of the Hudson"; Rideing with Woodward for "Lake Memphremagog" and "Water-Falls at Cayuga Lakes"; Rideing with Waud for "A Glance at the Northwest" and "The Mammoth Cave."

The following definitely did not travel together: Runkle and Gifford for "Up and Down the Columbia"; Clark and Gibson for "Providence and Vicinity"; Rideing and Moran for "The Rocky Mountains"; Burlingame and Moran for "The Plains and the Sierras"; Garczynski and Gifford for "Northern California"; Smillie and Rideing for "St. Lawrence and the Saguenay" (Smillie's diaries record travel with his father, not Rideing [Diaries of James D. Smillie, Archives of American Art, mfm. roll 2850, June 30–July 12, 1873]).

40. The letters, which are similar in content and style to her *Picturesque America* article, appeared sporadically in the fall and winter of 1869–70. Those covering Oregon appeared: Dec. 11, 18, 1869; Jan. 15, Feb. 5, 1870. They were signed "L. G. C." Apparently Mrs. Runkle remarried after the trip, as suggested in Gifford's letter of March 13, 1870, to Mrs. Lydia Swain: He mentioned breakfasting at Mrs. Runkle's, "formerly Mrs. Calhoun, who wrote those letters for the Tribune" (Robert Swain Gifford Papers, MS. 12, box 3, Whaling Museum, Old Dartmouth Historical Society, New Bedford, Mass.).

41. *Picturesque America*'s table of contents credits T. M. Clarke, spelled with a final e, but considering that Clark was closely associated with both Rhode Island and the Appleton firm, it seems likely he is the author. I can find no T. M. *Clarke* in the standard biographical sources.

42. See Cecil D. Eby, Jr., *"Porte Crayon": The Life of David Hunter Strother* (Chapel Hill: University of North Carolina Press, 1960); and Jessie F. Poesch, "David Hunter Strother: Mountain People, Mountain Images," in *Graphic Arts & the South: Proceedings of the 1990 North American Print Conference*, ed. Judy L. Larson (Fayetteville: University of Arkansas Press, 1993), 63–99.

43. In his 1872 "Note Book" Cooke recorded in the spring, "I have written this winter some sketches for 'Appleton's Journal': the Va. part of the 'Handbook of Travel,'" and he mentions corresponding with Carter and Bunce (John Esten Cooke Papers, Barrett Manuscript Collection, Alderman Library, University of Virginia). Cooke had already laid the foundation in his works for romanticizing colonial Virginia and antebellum plantation life, a growing trend in the following decades. See Thomas L. Connelly and Barbara L. Bellows, *God and General Longstreet: The Lost Cause and the Southern Mind* (Baton Rouge: Louisiana State University Press, 1982), ch. 2.

44. *Trow's New York City Directory* for 1873–74 lists a Rudolph E. Garczynski, reporter, at 41 Park Row.

45. See *Biographical Cyclopedia of American Women* (1925; reprint, Detroit: Gale Research Company, 1974) 2:113–15.

46. For Brock, see *The National Cyclopedia of American Biography*, 10:381. Her memoirs, retitled *Richmond During the War: Four Years of Personal Observation / by a Richmond Lady*, were republished in 1983 by Time-Life Books in the Collectors Library of the Civil War.

47. The table of contents of *Picturesque America*, vol. I, attributes the article "On the Savannah" to W. V. Thompson, but it seems likely that the prominent local editor W. T. Thompson would have been the author, and the middle initial merely a mistake or typographical error.

48. Appleton-Century MSS, Lilly Library, Indiana University, Bloomington, Ind. William Henry Rideing later recounted that in this period *Appletons' Journal* was one of a handful of New York periodicals that "paid a living wage." The others were [*Harper's*], *Scribner's*, *Hearth and Home*, and the *Galaxy* (William H. Rideing, *Many Celebrities and a Few Others* [Garden City, N.Y.: Doubleday, Page & Company, 1912], 77).

49. Smillie's diary entries for December 1873–March 1874 are sprinkled with references to his reworking the Yosemite article to suit Bunce. On Jan. 4, he wrote that Bunce had so "improved" it, "I do not acknowledge it as mine." Diaries of James D. Smillie, Archives of American Art, mfm. roll 2850.

50. Henry Armitt Brown (1844–79) was a young Philadelphia lawyer who had studied law at Columbia. He was active in politics and a distinguished orator.

51. "The Subscription Book Trade," *Publishers' and Stationers' Weekly Trade Circular*, July 25, 1872, 93–94.

Chapter 5

1. Christopher Mulvey, "*Ecriture* and Landscape: British Writing on Post-Revolutionary America," in Mick Gidley and Robert Lawson-Peebles, eds., *Views of American Landscape* (Cambridge: Cambridge University Press, 1989), 104.

2. Strother goes on to say he tired of waiting and rode on to Petersburg, where the artist joined him that evening, "elated with his sketch." This suggests Sheppard accompanied him on at least part of his travels in West Virginia. (See note 36, p. 339).

3. Diaries of James D. Smillie, Aug. 19, 1871, Archives of American Art, mfm. roll 2849.

4. John Coleman Adams, *William Hamilton Gibson, Artist-Naturalist-Author* (New York: G. P. Putnam's Sons, 1901), 40.

5. As did many watercolorists at the time. See Kathleen A. Foster, "The Pre-Raphaelite Medium: Ruskin, Turner, and American Watercolor," in Linda S. Ferber and William H. Gerdts, co-curators, *The New Path: Ruskin and the American Pre-Raphaelites* (New York: Brooklyn Museum, 1985), 89. See Waud's works at the Historic New Orleans Collection.

6. John Ruskin, *Modern Painters*, 1, *Library Edition of the Works of John Ruskin*, ed. E. T. Cook and A. Wedderbrun (London: George Allen, 1903–12), vol. 3, part 2, section 6, ch. 3, 623–24; and *The Elements of Drawing* (1857; reprint, New York: Dover Publications, 1971), 49; para. 42.

7. Ruskin's work in that show, the watercolor *Study of a Block of Gneiss* (c. 1854–55), was a vivid example of a close-up, detailed depiction of a single rock. For the influence of this exhibition and Ruskin on American artists, see Linda S. Ferber and William H. Gerdts, *The New Path: Ruskin and the American Pre-Raphaelites* (New York: Brooklyn Museum, 1985), esp. 14–19, 25–29, 42–46, 109–31. See also Roger B. Stein, *John Ruskin and Aesthetic Thought in America, 1840–1900* (Cambridge, Mass.: Harvard University Press, 1967), and *John Ruskin and the Victorian Eye*, organized by the Phoenix Art Museum (New York: Harry N. Abrams, 1993).

8. Ruskin frequently recommended the work of his former teacher. See, for example, *Modern Painters*, 1, *Works of John Ruskin*, vol. 3, part 2, section 4, ch. 1, 597-98 n. 2. Edward Austin Abbey wrote that in New York in the early 1870s an illustrator's reference library contained Harding's *Lessons on Trees*, among other works (E. V. Lucas, *Edward Austin Abbey, Royal Academician: The Record of His Life and Work* [New York: Charles Scribner's Sons, 1921], 29).

9. The drawing is in the collection of the Missouri Historical Society (1962.331.5). Waud's precision came to little in this case, for the wood engraving was very small and undistinguished, part of a composite of nine St. Louis views (II, 322).

10. For example, the art section of the *Atlantic Monthly* for August 1872 says that the "ordinary spectator" is tempted to see nothing in Thomas Moran's *Grand Canyon of the Yellowstone* but "a geological and geographical statement, another of those painted photographs of which we already have too many, and which have done so much to give our landscape art a name for childishness and journey-work" (246). The writer goes on to say this first impression is corrected upon a closer look, however.

11. See Joni Louise Kinsey, "Creating a Sense of Place: Thomas Moran and the Surveying of the American West" Ph.D. diss., Washington University, St. Louis, 1989, 14–15.

12. See, for example, I, 562, and II, 154.

13. In his first article in the series "The Taking of Pittsburgh" (*Every Saturday*, March 4, 1871), Ralph Keeler wrote that Fenn and the conductor of their train went "into joint ecstasies over the landscapes of Turner."

14. See Andrew Wilton, *Turner and the Sublime* (London: British Museum, 1980); W. G. Rawlinson, *The Engraved Work of J. M. W. Turner* (London: Macmillan, 1908); and Anne Lyles and Diane Perkins, *Colour into Line: Turner and the Art of Engraving* (London: Tate Gallery, 1989).

15. Henry T. Tuckerman, *The Book of the Artists* (New York: Putnam, 1867), 513.

16. John Ruskin, *Modern Painters*, 1, *Works of John Ruskin*, vol. 3, part 2, section 3, ch. 1, 343.

17. Waud's original drawing is owned by the Historic New Orleans Collection (1977.137.14.39).

18. See Eric de Maré, *The Victorian Woodblock Illustrators* (London: Gordon Fraser, 1980). Pages 49–50 concern electrotyping.

19. [George and Edward Dalziel], *The Brothers Dalziel: A Record of Fifty Years' Work 1840–1890*, (1901; reprint, London: B. T. Batsford, 1978), 193. The writer of "Art and Artists," *Daily Evening Transcript* (Boston, March 22, 1887), called Fenn "a pupil of Birket Foster."

20. Quoted from a letter to Charles Dudley Warner in Lucas, *Edward Austin Abbey*, 29. The library also typically included "Shakespeare, with John Gilbert's illustrations, Cassell's or Wood's Natural History" and "J. D. Harding's *Lessons on Trees*" (1850).

21. An 1878 edition of Bryant's poems was illustrated by Foster and Fenn, as well as Alfred Fredericks and others. *Wood-Side and Sea-Side* contained wood engravings after Dalziel, Hows, Duncan, Durand, and Weir, in addition to Foster.

22. The publication date is 1863. In this case the illustrations, engraved by the Dalziel firm, were primary, with the poems written to accompany them by Tom Taylor (whose play *Our American Cousin* was being performed at Ford's Theater when Lincoln was assassinated). See Taylor's preface and Jan Reynolds, *Birket Foster* (London: B. T. Batsford, 1984), 84.

23. This was true as early as 1835 according to Ann Bermingham, *Landscape and Ideology: The English Rustic Tradition, 1740–1860* (Berkeley: University of California Press, 1986), 73.

24. Fenn's image also recalls Bierstadt's *Haying, Conway Meadows* (1864), reproduced in Nancy K. Anderson and Linda S. Ferber, *Albert Bierstadt: Art & Enterprize* (New York: Brooklyn Museum, 1990), 191.

25. In *The Influence of Photography on American Landscape Painting, 1839–1880* (New York: Garland, 1977), Elizabeth Lindquist-Cock maintains that painters such as Bierstadt were striving to rival the three-dimensionality of the stereoscope (esp. ch. 3).

26. For examples of the advice given photographers about how to manipulate scenes to add charm and picturesque effect, see Richard N. Masteller, "Western Views in Eastern Parlors: The Contribution of the Stereograph Photographer to the Conquest of the West," *Prospects* 6 (1981): 60–62.

27. This is suggested by Robert L. McGrath in "The Real and the Ideal: Popular Images of the White Mountains," in *The White Mountains: Place and Perceptions*, exhibition catalog, published for the University Art Galleries, University of New Hampshire (Durham, N.H.: University Press of New England, 1980), 69. McGrath says of Fenn's views of the White Mountains: "It was especially the latter's [Timothy O'Sullivan and William Henry Jackson's] dramatic photographs of the Rockies and Yosemite, which first appeared in the East in the early 1870's, that provided the model for steep precipices, narrow paths, and soaring mountains in Fenn's engravings." Whereas some photographs may have served as models for Fenn, the timing would not have been right for Jackson's first photographs of the Rockies, made the summer of 1873, to influence Fenn's White Mountain views in *Picturesque America*, which appeared in parts 7 and 8.

McGrath is also critical of Fenn's "pictorial theatrics" in his "Descent from Mount Washington" (I, 158); he much prefers the "sober dignity and classic constraint" of Winslow Homer's portrayal of the same subject (*Harper's Weekly*, July 10, 1869). See McGrath, 69–70.

28. See *American Paradise: The World of the Hudson River School*, ed. John K. Howat (New York: Metropolitan Museum of Art, 1987), 203–4; Kenneth Myers, *The Catskills: Painters,*

Writers, and Tourists in the Mountains 1820–1895 (Yonkers, N.Y.: Hudson River Museum of Westchester, 1987), 36–55; plates 76, 77.

29. For a reproduction of William Guy Wall's "Palisades," aquatinted by John Hill, see Frank Weitenkampf, "Early American Landscape Prints," 57; or Gloria-Gilda Deák, *Picturing America 1497–1899* (Princeton: Princeton University Press, 1988), 2:321.

30. In a brief article in *The Art Journal* accompanying two of Fenn's Italian views—one of which depicted the famous Rialto Bridge from below, showing only a small part of it in a dramatic curve—the writer claimed: "Mr. Fenn has a very happy faculty of seizing upon unconventional points of view in a scene, and always succeeds in giving great freshness to the most familiar places. Often as the 'Rialto' has been painted and engraved, every one must admit that Mr. Fenn has succeeded in making as fresh and striking a picture as if the place were new to the world of Art. . . . His drawings are always truthful and vital; they have none of the dreary monotony of photographic views, which, while reproducing so clearly the forms and lines of a picture, lose its spirit, its expression, the true characteristics of sentiment and color" (January 1877, 19).

31. In contrast, the text by W. H. Rideing trivializes the encounter with Trinity Rock by focusing on the passengers' attempts to hit it with pebbles, at the suggestion of the crew (II, 394). Smillie's diaries for Aug. 21–23, 1873, reveal he struggled with this design in his studio after his return. On the third day of work on it, he wrote, "I don't believe that I will be able to make anything of the page block 'Under Trinity Rock'" (Archives of American Art, mfm. roll 2850.)

32. Ruskin, *Modern Painters*, 1, *Works of John Ruskin*, vol. 3, part 2, section 3, ch. 1, 344.

33. See John Wilmerding, *American Light: The Luminist Movement, 1850–1875* (Washington, D. C.: National Gallery of Art, 1980), esp. Earl A. Powell, "Luminism and the American Sublime," 69–94; and Barbara Novak, *Nature and Culture: American Landscape and Painting, 1825–1875* (New York: Norton, 1959), ch. 2.

34. The significance of the church steeple was reinforced when it was exhibited at the National Academy of Design in 1850: The listing for the painting was accompanied by these lines from William Cullen Bryant's poem "A Scene on the Banks of the Hudson": "O'er the clear still water swells / the music of the Sabbath bells." *American Paradise*, 111. For a color reproduction, see *The American Painting Collection of the Montclair Art Museum*, (Montclair, N.J.: 1977) 80; or *American Paradise*, 111.

35. Smillie had depicted an arrangement of trees and rocks similar to the tall trees and boat in this view in his oil painting *Woodland Scene* (1869), now at Vassar College Art Gallery, reproduced in Ella M. Foshay and Sally Mills, *All Seasons and Every Light: Nineteenth-Century American Landscapes from the Collection of Elias Lyman Magoon* (Poughkeepsie: Vassar College Art Gallery, 1983), 86.

36. As a precedent for this treatment, perhaps Woodward looked to Thomas Moran's "West Point and Cold Spring, from Garrison's Landing," that opened the *Scribner's Monthly* for July 1872, in which a pier also breaks the bottom of a circle. Woodward's pier is longer and projects more dramatically out from the picture plane.

37. Waud's design (Missouri Historical Society, 1962.331.43) was not used in the book, although one element of it, a waterfront scene, appeared in altered form in a composite (II, 322).

38. Diaries of James D. Smillie, Dec. 12, 1873, Archives of American Art, mfm. roll 2850.

39. The man lost in Yellowstone, Truman Everts, became an instant celebrity when his story, "Thirty-Seven Days of Peril," appeared in *Scribner's Monthly* (November 1871). Loring's death was announced in the "Table-Talk" column of the Dec. 9, 1871, *Appletons' Journal*, 666.

40. Joni Louise Kinsey, *Thomas Moran the Surveying of the American West* (Washington, D.C.: Smithsonian Institution Press, 1992), details the involvement of railroad interests, publishers, photographers, and artists, specifically Moran, as well as geologist-explorers, in promoting Yellowstone, the Grand Canyon, and the Colorado Rockies as tourist attractions—leading to the development of the regions. See also her dissertation, "Creating a Sense of Place."

41. Private Charles Moore, part of the military escort, and Walter Trumbull, a journalist. Kinsey, "Creating a Sense of Place," 125–26.

42. On page 522, Bunce thanks the Hon. Columbus Delano, Secretary of the Interior, for photographs. On March 20, 1872, Bunce had written Hayden: "The Yellowstone photographs came duly to hand and Mr. Fenn has already made several drawings which are now in the hands of the engravers. The photographs of the other locations which you agreed to lend us have not been received. I write especially now to ask if you will not undertake to prepare the article on the Yellowstone Valley. . . . Please try to find time to prepare this paper for us before you leave for the West" (National Archives, record group 57, mfm. 623, roll 2, frames 481–82). I am indebted to Kinsey, who quoted extensively from Bunce's correspondence with Hayden in her dissertation. Bunce's handwriting is difficult to decipher; in several instances my reading differs from Kinsey's.

43. Hayden must have seen an advance copy of the May 11 *Journal*. Bunce wrote Hayden, May 2, 1872:

> Your letter of yesterday greatly distresses me. I knew your name ought to be connected with those Yellowstone views, but I hadn't a single fact to go by, and I was in hope, ere the next illustrations came along, to be in receipt of your mss. and be enabled to make amends and do you justice. However these Journal publications are merely preliminary to the complete and perfect article in 'Picturesque America'—and for this I have depended on you. Now, my dear sir, if the press has neglected you and done you injustice heretofore, why not make the Journal the medium of setting you and your connection with the Park fully before the public. We will print what you may send us . . . and hereafter . . . give you full credit and make the public recognize its indebtedness to you in this matter. . . . If you absolutely can't prepare the article for 'Picturesque America,' please give us all the notes and memoranda you can." (National Archives, record group 57, mfm. 623, roll 2, frame 547–48)

44. May 14, 1872, Bunce wrote Acting Secretary of the Interior R. V. Corven: "In regard to the Yellowstone engravings we certainly should much prefer them to reach the public for scrutiny [solely] through our journal and 'Picturesque America,' but as we are under obligations to the Department for the photographs we feel it is our duty to comply with your request for electrotypes. If we can have full credit in the reports for the electros we should be willing to furnish them at the cost of electrotyping, if otherwise, would the department be willing to share any portion of the expense of the engraving?" (National Archives, record group 57, mfm. 623, roll 2, frames 405–6). Two wood engravings from *Picturesque America*, "The Lower Falls" and "Cañon of the Yellowstone," appeared in Hayden's official report of the 1872 expedition, *Sixth Annual Report of the United States Geological Survey of the Territories . . . for the Year 1872* (Washington, D.C.: Government Printing Office, 1873), plates 15 and 34.

45. Based on the watercolor *Upper Falls, Yellowstone,* 10in. x 8in., at the Gilcrease Museum (1236–1451). Reproduced in Thurman Wilkins, *Thomas Moran: Artist of the Mountains* (Norman: University of Oklahoma Press, 1966), after 128.

46. Moran mentioned working on these illustrations in a letter to Hayden as early as March 11, 1872 (National Archives, record group 57, mfm. 623, roll 2, frames 468–70), so their appearance was probably anticipated.

47. This discussion of the shortcomings of film in this period is based on Estelle Jussim, *Visual Communication and the Graphic Arts: Photographic Technologies in the Nineteenth Century* (New York: R. R. Bowker, 1983), 180.

48. Other comparisons can be made between reproductions of Jackson photographs in Peter B. Hales, *William Henry Jackson and the Transformation of the American Landscape* (Philadelphia: Temple University Press, 1988), and Fenn's *Picturesque America* views: "Valley of the Yellowstone," Hales, 102, with "The Yellowstone," I, 292; and "Tower Falls," Hales, 103, with "Tower Falls," I, 305.

49. The section entitled "A Glance at the Northwest," illustrated by Alfred R. Waud, deals mainly with Wisconsin scenery, giving cursory attention to the Red River dividing Minnesota from the Dakota Territory. This region had long been designated "the Northwest," and, more recently, "the Old Northwest."

50. The following images in "The Plains and the Sierras" section appear to be based on Russell photographs from *Sun Pictures of Rocky Mountain Scenery*: "Church Butte, Utah," "Monument Rock, Echo Cañon," "Devil's Slide, Weber Cañon," "Dial Rock, Red Buttes, Laramie Plains," "Cliffs of Green River" (similar to Russell's "Castle Rock, Green River Valley"), "Donner Lake, Nevada" (similar to Russell's "Summit of the Sierra Nevada"). I am indebted to Joni L. Kinsey, who suggested this source for Moran's illustrations in "Creating a Sense of Place."

51. W. H. Jackson also photographed this formation. See W. H. Jackson, *Picture Maker of the Old West* (New York: Scribner's Sons, 1947), 99; or see "1869 Summit Co" [Utah], W. H. Jackson photograph #30, U.S. Geological Survey Photographic Library (Denver).

52. Bunce to Hayden Jan. 3, 1873: "Mr. Moran is now making drawings of scenes along the Union and the Pacific roads. Shall then want scenes in Colorado, Nevada, etc; I am extremely grateful to you for your offer to give him the use of your photographs; and also for your consent to prepare the text" (National Archives, record group 57, mfm. 623, roll 3, frame 81).

53. Kinsey, "Creating a Sense of Place," 292–93. Kinsey presents evidence that until June 1873 Moran had hoped to visit the Grand Canyon with Hayden's survey, but then realized Hayden probably wouldn't get there (297–98). Moran wrote his wife he had commissions for "70 drawings for Powell, 40 for Appleton, 4 for Aldine, 20 for Scribners . . . besides the water colors and oil pictures" (Amy Bassford and Fritiof Fryxell, eds., *Home Thoughts from Afar: Letters from Thomas Moran to Mary Nimmo Moran* [East Hampton, N.Y.: East Hampton Free Library, 1967], 41–42). About the journey, see Don D. Fowler, *The Western Photographs of John K. Hillers: "Myself in the Water"* (Washington, D.C.: Smithsonian Institution Press, 1989),47–50; and Wilkins, *Thomas Moran,* ch. 5. Powell knew the area thoroughly from his ongoing explorations for the U.S. government and, as Special Commissioner of Indian Affairs, was well acquainted with the southern Utah tribes (Fowler, 47).

54. See "The Colorado Cañon: A Trip to the Verge of the Chasm," *New York Times,* Sept. 4, 1873; and Kinsey, "Creating a Sense of Place," 299, 302.

55. Most of his sketches were studies for the large oil painting he was planning, judging from the extant ones. See Kinsey, *Thomas Moran*, 117–24.

56. Kinsey, *Thomas Moran*, 122, reproduces Hillers's photograph of "Marble Pinnacle, Kanab Canyon" and Moran's *Picturesque America* image. Moran's black-and-white wash drawing, *In the Grand Canyon*, 1873 (#4292, Jefferson National Expansion Memorial) is similar to "Walls of the Grand Cañon" (II, 509), but it is so indistinct and lacking in detail it seems likely Moran also used a photograph to aid his memory in representing the intricate rock faces.

In 1875 Hayden asked Bunce for electrotypes of Moran's "Cañons of the Colorado" illustrations, assuming they had been made from photographs supplied by the Department of the Interior. Bunce pointed out the error to him (Bunce to Hayden, Oct. 29, 1875, National Archives, record group 57, mfm. 623, roll 5, frames 1050–52). Bunce's Nov. 5, 1873, letter informed Hayden of a $35.00 charge for some electrotypes, but it is unclear whether they were of Yellowstone, the Rocky Mountains, or, less likely, the Grand Canyon (mfm. 623, roll 5, frame 1054).

57. Except for routes west from Denver to various mining centers, as can be seen in Samuel Bowles's account of his trip in the summer of 1868, *The Switzerland of America: A Summer Vacation in the Parks and Mountains of Colorado* (Springfield, Mass.: Samuel Bowles, 1869). Isabella L. Bird, *A Lady's Life in the Rocky Mountains* (Norman: University of Oklahoma Press, 1960), recounts her difficulties reaching Estes Park and climbing Long's Peak in 1873. On the development of the Colorado Springs region as a tourist attraction by railroad promoters, with the support of English investors, see Kinsey, *Thomas Moran*, 153–60.

58. Bunce wrote: "I was in Denver about two weeks ago and there met Mr. Stevenson [Hayden's chief assistant] . . . who informed me that Mr. Jackson, photographer of your expedition, had taken photographs of all interesting points in the Rocky Mountains in Colorado. If this is so do you suppose we could obtain the use of a few of them—say fifteen or sixteen—for our 'Picturesque America,' the same way as with the Yellowstone scenes" (National Archives, record group 57, mfm. 623, roll 3, frame 485). "Answered by W. H. Jackson, Sept. 29" is written across Bunce's Sept. 23 letter.

59. Bunce's difficulties obtaining photographs and an article from Hayden are revealed in his letters of Dec. 11, 13 and 16, 1873 (National Archives, record group 57, mfm. 623, roll 3, frames 641, 646) and March 25 and 28 1874 (roll 5, frames 1044, 1047).

60. See Elizabeth Lindquist-Cock, *The Influence of Photography on American Landscape Painting*, 148–50, and Kinsey, *Thomas Moran*, ch. 8 and 161–62.

61. Kinsey, *Thomas Moran*, suggests the 1875 painting presents the mountain as "the object of a quest, an inspiration for a pilgrimage" (141). See also Linda C. Hults, "Pilgrim's Progress in the West: Moran's *The Mountain of the Holy Cross*," *American Art* 5 (Winter/Spring 1991): 69–85.

62. For example, the background of Moran's "Long's Peak, from Estes Park" (II, 483) relates closely to a Jackson photograph with the same title (#476, U.S. Geological Survey), but the foreground is either imaginary or derived from another photo (perhaps #998, U.S. Geological Survey); Moran's highly poetic "Frozen Lake, Foot of James Peak" (II, 486) takes considerable liberties with the likely model, Jackson's "Frozen Lake near James Peak" (#1308, U.S. Geological Survey); "Chicago Lake" (II, 491) is similar to Jackson's photo #1316 (U.S. Geological Survey), but from a different angle; and "Teocalli Mountain" (II, 497) could be derived from a combination of #1304, #402, and #1379 (U.S. Geological Survey).

Further study might determine more exact correspondences. Other possible ones are: parts of II, 493, with #894 and #1293; II, 496, and #384; II, 499, and #1039; II, 500, and #1042.

63. In his introductory "Letter to the Secretary," Hayden thanked D. Appleton and Company for permitting the Interior Department the use of electrotypes of illustrations from "their magnificent publication 'Picturesque America.'" *[Eighth] Annual Report of the United States Geological and Geographical Survey of the Territories, embracing Colorado and Parts of Adjacent Territories; being a report of Progress of the Exploration for the Year 1874* (Washington, D.C.: Government Printing Office, 1876), 16. The nine illustrations used were (*Picturesque America* title in parentheses): "Monument Park, Colorado," pl. 3 ("Eroded Sandstones, Monument Park"); "Gateway to the 'Garden of the Gods,' Colorado," pl. 8 ("Pike's Peak from the Garden of the Gods"); "Cathedral Rock, 'Garden of the Gods,' Colorado," pl. 9, ("Tower Rock, Garden of the Gods"); "Long's Peak and Estes Park, Colorado," pl. 11 ("Long's Peak from Estes Park"); "Boulder Cañon," pl. 12 ("Bowlder Cañon"); "Chicago Lake, Colorado," pl. 13 ("Chicago Lake"); "Mountain of the Holy Cross, Colorado," pl. 15 ("Mountain of the Holy Cross"); "View in the Snowmass Group," fig. 6 ("Snowmass Mountain"); "Cascade on Rock Creek, Colorado," fig. 8 ("Elk-Lake Cascade"). Some of these were later reused, as Kinsey has pointed out, "Creating a Sense of Place," 445: for example, "Bowlder Cañon" was reproduced in a *Union Pacific Sketchbook: A Brief Description of Prominent Places of Interest Along the Line of the Union Pacific* (Omaha: Passenger Department, Union Pacific Railroad, 1887): 85. "Long's Peak from Estes Park" appeared in George Crofutt's 1881 edition of *Grip-Sack Guide of Colorado* (Omaha: Overland, 1881).

64. Compare "Mirror Lake, Yosemite Valley" (I, opposite 465) with Muybridge's photograph, *Mirror Lake, Valley of the Yosemite* (1872), reproduced in Weston J. Naef and James N. Wood, *Era of Exploration: The Rise of Landscape Photography in the American West, 1860–1885* (Buffalo, N.Y.: Albright-Knox Art Gallery, and New York: The Metropolitan Museum of Art, 1975), plate 70. The steel engraving was originally distributed with part 6 of *Picturesque America*, well before Smillie's section on Yosemite was ready.

It is possible that some of the other *Picturesque America* artists besides Fenn and Moran also made use of photographs. Smillie mentioned "selecting photos" in Quebec (diaries of James D. Smillie, July 7, 1873, Archives of American Art, mfm. roll 2850). A slightly different use is indicated by the note, "See photo," at the bottom of a Waud sketch of Chestnut Street in St. Louis: Whoever drew the scene on the wood would have to depend on a photo for the details of the main building, which Waud failed to draw (Missouri Historical Society, 1962.331.40; *Picturesque America*, II, 322).

65. See Keith F. Davis, *George N. Barnard: Photographer of Sherman's Campaign* (Kansas City, Mo.: Hallmark Cards, Inc., 1990). Davis includes a facsimile of Barnard's *Photographic Views of Sherman's Campaign*, an album of sixty-one photographs published in 1866 at $100 per copy. The three photographs that seem to be the basis of Fenn's drawings are: pl. 47, "Savanah [*sic*] River, near Savanah, Ga." (cf. Fenn's image opening the section, I, 117); pl. 51, "Fountain" (cf. Fenn's "Fountain in Forsyth Park," I, 121); and pl. 48, "Buen-ventura [*sic*] Savanah, Ga," (cf. Fenn's "Bonaventure Cemetery," I, 124). Fenn may also have used the photographs of O. Pierre Havens, a Savannah photographer, whose image of "Madison Sq." could have been the basis for Fenn's "Bull Street" (I, 123). I am indebted to John D. Duncan, of Savannah, for pointing out the similarities between Fenn's works and the photographs of Barnard and Havens.

66. Adams, *William Hamilton Gibson*, 40–41.

67. On July 12, 1872, Fenn and Bunce "freely criticised" Smillie's Yosemite drawings at D. Appleton and Company (diaries of James D. Smillie, Archives of American Art, mfm. roll 2850). Smillie's diaries indicate he typically prepared a more finished drawing from his sketches and then traced it for transfer onto the block. Thereafter he "outlined" it. See, for example, Dec. 23, 24, and 27, 1872.

68. Adams, *William Hamilton Gibson*, 42–43. In addition, even for the later publications patterned on *Picturesque America*, *Picturesque Europe* (1875–79) and *Picturesque Palestine, Sinai and Egypt* (1881–83), the major artists, Harry Fenn and J. D. Woodward, were still drawing on woodblocks. John Douglas Woodward to his mother, Sept. 30 and Dec. 9, 1877 (John Douglas Woodward, *An Artist Abroad in the Seventies*, typescript of letters, Virginia State Library and Archives, Richmond, Virginia).

69. R. Swain Gifford noted the strain on his eyes in preparing blocks to illustrate a small format gift edition of *The Building of the Ship* (Fields, Osgood, 1870): "It is pretty hard work for the Eyes to do such fine work on the wood and I hope if I do any more for them that they will give me larger ones. I have never done anything so carefully before. It requires more care than etching on copper but not quite so much artistic ability—that is—in the most mechanical parts. Such as putting in shades &c of course the composition requires just as much ability" (letter to Mrs. Lydia Swain, Feb, 28, 1969, Robert Swain Gifford Papers, MS. 12, S-g 1, Sr A, S-s 2, folder 7, Whaling Museum Library, Old Dartmouth Historical Society, New Bedford, Massachusetts).

70. William J. Linton, *The History of Wood-Engraving in America* (Boston: Estes and Lauriat, 1882), 37. Facsimile ed. with introduction by Nancy Carlson Schrock, *American Wood Engraving: A Victorian History* (Watkins Glen, N.Y.: for the Athenaeum Library of the American Life Foundation and Study Institute, 1976).

71. July 20, 1872, diaries of James D. Smillie, Archives of American Art, mfm. roll 2850. After working several days on the "Big Trees" block (I, 466), Smillie wrote July 5, 1872: "I am not sufficiently familiar with drawing on wood to have the amount of confidence necessary to beget despatch."

72. A. V. S. Anthony, "An Art That Is Passing Away," in A. V. S. Anthony, Timothy Cole, and Elbridge Kingsley, *Wood-Engraving: Three Essays* (New York: Grolier Club, 1916), 20. The experience of Lucius O'Brien as art director for *Picturesque Canada*, which was modeled after *Picturesque America* and published in Toronto beginning in 1880, also demonstrated that drawing for wood engraving was a highly specialized skill. O'Brien planned to have the drawings done by fellow members of the Royal Canadian Academy, of which he was president. He was the only Academy member to catch on to drawing on wood, however, and the bulk of the drawings were eventually done by Americans familiar with the medium. See Dennis Reid, *"Our Own Country Canada": Being an Account of the National Aspirations of the Principal Landscape Artists in Montreal and Toronto 1860–1890* (Ottawa: National Gallery of Canada, 1979), 330–32.

73. Cash accounts at end of diaries for the years 1872, 1873, diaries of James D. Smillie, Archives of American Art, mfm. roll 2850.

74. Smillie's cash accounts for 1873 show an Aug. 5 payment of $250 for his "Saguenay trip," and a sheet inserted at the end of the 1872 diary lists his fifteen-day itinerary and travel expenses for the trip. Diaries of James D. Smillie, Archives of American Art, mfm. roll 2850.

Adams, *William Hamilton Gibson*, 42–43. Gibson also expected to receive about $400 for rendering fifteen sketches on the wood, an average of $27.35 per finished block.

75. "American Journalism" by the editor of *The Leisure Hour*, quoted in "Miscellany," *Appletons' Journal*, June 3, 1871, 661. A few years earlier, Julius Wilcox, in "Journalism as a Profession," *The Galaxy* 4 (November 1867), wrote that $30 a week was reckoned a fair salary, but that often the journalist needed to supplement that to make ends meet.

76. The Boston *Daily Evening Transcript* later stated Fenn earned $10,000 a year for his work on *Picturesque America* ("Art and Artists," March 22, 1887). For larger designs for *Harper's Weekly*, the team of Jules Tavernier and Paul Frenzeny were said to have been paid $75 for a full page, $150 for a double page drawn on the block, between 1873 and 1876 (Robert Taft, *Artists and Illustrators of the Old West* [New York: Charles Scribner's Sons, 1953], 97). In 1881, Thomas Moran received between $35 and $60 for illustrations of varying size for *Picturesque Canada*. See Moran's drawing receipt books at the East Hampton Free Library, cited in Allan Pringle, "Thomas Moran: *Picturesque Canada* and the Quest for a Canadian National Landscape Theme," *Imprint; Journal of the American Historical Print Collectors Society*, 14, no. 1 (Spring 1989): 13, 18.

77. See, for example, Jussim, *Visual Communication and the Graphic Arts*, 159–60.

78. Elbridge Kingsley, "Life and Work of Elbridge Kingsley, Painter-Engraver" (Papers of Elbridge Kingsley, Forbes Library, Northampton, Mass.; Archives of American Art, mfm. roll 48, TS), 39. On ruling machines, see Anthony Dyson, *Pictures to Print: The Nineteenth-Century Engraving Trade* (London: Farrand Press, 1984), 126–30.

79. Firms specialized in supplying woodblocks to publishers and engravers. Although Kingsley ("Life and Work," 46) said they could supply wood in any size and quality, it seems doubtful that blocks as large as 9in. x 6in. could be had.

80. Benson J. Lossing gave these numbers in his *Memorial of Alexander Anderson, M.D., The First Engraver on Wood in America* (New York: Printed for the subscribers of the New York Historical Society, 1872). Reported in "Dr. Alexander Anderson," *Frank Leslie's Illustrated Newspaper*, Nov. 12, 1870, 133. By the late 1880s, as photomechanical reproduction was gradually replacing wood engraving, the field would become overcrowded. Hiram Campbell Merrill said New York in the 1890s "was a regular Bull Pen. Every engraver came to New York and it was a fight for life" (quoted in Richard O. Hathaway, "Hiram Campbell Merrill, Wood Engraver [1866–1958]," *Vermont History News* 40, no.4 [July–August 1989]: 70).

81. In 1870, Frank Leslie's firm employed 68 wood engravers, and Harper & Brothers employed 35, according to *Frank Leslie's Illustrated Newspaper*, Nov. 12, 1870, 133. Some wood engravers worked in other publishing centers like Boston and Philadelphia.

82. Kingsley, "Life and Work," 35, recalled that when he worked for the J. W. Orr engraving firm, it was located first at 75 Nassau Street, then moved to 96 Nassau Street, "at the corner of Fulton Street, opposite the offices of the New York Herald. The Times and Tribune were only a few steps north of us." Also nearby were "Frank Leslies Weekly, corner of Elm & Pearl Streets and Harper's Weekly, corner of Cliff and Pearl Streets."

83. Kingsley, "Life and Work," 35–37.

84. Kingsley, "Life and Work," 40.

85. Linton, *The History of Wood-Engraving in America*, 37.

86. Kingsley, "Life and Work," 36, 45.

87. A member of the National Academy who concentrated on oil and watercolor painting, Hart was probably much less adept at the special techniques needed for wood engraving than many of the other contributors.

88. Although I have found no record of how *Picturesque America* was printed, the procedures suggested seem the most likely. High-speed rotary presses were being used for newspapers, but for fine illustrated books and magazines the stop-cylinder press was replacing the Adams press. See Theodore Low De Vinne, *Printing in the Nineteenth Century* (New York: Lead Mould Electrotype Foundry, 1924) and "The Growth of Wood-Cut Printing.II" *Scribner's Monthly* (May 1880), 34–35. De Vinne explains the advantages of the stop-cylinder press and the use of dry, calendered paper and overlays.

89. Cash accounts at end of diaries for 1872, 1873, Diaries of James D. Smillie, Archives of American Art, mfm. roll 2850.

90. Plates after Darley appeared in *Appletons' Journal*, Aug. 17, 1869, and March 5, 1870; one after Casilear, Oct. 23, 1869; one after Kensett, April 17, 1869; one after Haseltine, June 19, 1869; and one after Bellows, May 8, 1869. The steel engraving after Haseltine seems to be based on an 1863 oil painting of the same scene (reproduced in *Antiques Magazine*, August 1992), now in a private collection. Frequently the date was changed on the plate.

91. Casilear's "Lake George" is larger in *Picturesque America*: the height increased from 4 13/16in. to 5 5/16in. Added below the image were a copyright line and the artist's name, followed by "N.A." The title of Bellows's view was changed from "The River Road" to "The Housatonic," and the height increased from 4 15/16in. to 5 7/8in. The artist's signature was removed and a new copyright line added. One reason for the changes was probably to make these images comparable in size to the others in *Picturesque America*. Another reason might have been to produce more balanced, picturesque compositions. This is clearly the outcome with the Casilear view, in which a boat, rocks, and shrubs were added to the foreground.

92. See the section on Whittredge in *American Paradise*, esp. 186–88, about several similar versions of the same scene and differing opinions about which one the engraver, Robert Hinshelwood, used.

93. Robert Hinshelwood (1812–after 1874) was the steel engraver contributing the largest number of plates to *Picturesque America*: twelve in vol. I, and eleven in vol. II. Hinshelwood was born in Edinburgh, where he learned engraving. After settling in America in about 1835, Hinshelwood worked as a landscape engraver for Harper & Brothers and *The Ladies' Repository*. Hinshelwood frequently engraved major works by well-known artists, such as Cole's *Voyage of Life* series. He was an artist in his own right and sometimes engraved his own compositions, such as the folio size "Natural Bridge, Virginia," which appeared in the *Gallery of Landscape Painters: American Scenery* (New York: G. P. Putnam, 1872).

Samuel Valentine Hunt (1803–92) made the plates for six steel engravings in vol. I and five in vol. II. Hunt was born in England and came to America in 1834. Early in his career he did plates for *The Home Book of the Picturesque* (1852).

Other well-known engravers with five or six plates in *Picturesque America* were William Wellstood (1819–1900) and E. P. Brandard (1819–98). Wellstood was born in Edinburgh, but learned engraving after moving to the United States with his family in 1830. Like Hinshelwood and Hunt, he did much work for the Western Methodist Book Concern of Cincinnati, which regularly published landscape plates in *The Ladies' Repository*.

A native of Birmingham, England, Edward Paxman Brandard was brother and pupil of Robert Brandard, who engraved many plates after Bartlett and Turner. It is not clear whether Edward spent some years in America or whether plates executed by him were shipped from England.

94. The ruling machine for metal engraving was invented in 1790 by an English engraver, Wilson Lowry. For a description and illustrations, see Dyson, *Pictures to Print*, 127–30.

95. Jussim, *Visual Communication*, 32.

96. Jussim, *Visual Communication*, 33.

97. Prints from the *Picturesque America* steel engravings vary in quality; one comes across prints that have a "thin" look, with less density of ink in the darks and more prominent lines in lighter areas. This could result either from worn plates or poor printing technique.

98. Although it has been claimed that the steel-plate engravings of *Picturesque America* were printed on this press (Stephen D. Tucker, "History of R. Hoe & Company 1834–1885," in *American Antiquarian Society, Proceedings*, ed. Rollo G. Silver, 1972, 82, 439; and Frank E. Comparato, *Chronicles of Genius and Folly: R. Hoe & Company and the Printing Press as a Service to Democracy* [Culver City, Calif.: Labyrinthos, 1979], 690), this could not have been true of the printings before 1876. The Jan. 5, 1878, *Publishers' Weekly* commented about steel engravings:

> Those of the trade who have had occasion to deal with this branch of the art of illustration have been much interested for the past two years in the 'Neale steam-press' for printing from steel plates, which has hitherto been a slow and expensive hand process. In fact, driving it out of use for the large editions of illustrated books of the day, and as a consequence, the art of engraving on steel has itself been declining. It is already difficult to find good steel engravers. The success of the Neale Press, which does its own inking, wiping, polishing, and feeding, and turns off ten impressions a minute, is likely to put a new face upon this branch of work. It has been in use for several months in printing the steel plates for Appleton's Art Journal. . . ."(22)

Comparato states in his article on D. Appleton and Company in *Publishers for Mass Entertainment in Nineteenth Century America*, ed. Madeleine B. Stern (Boston: G. K. Hall, 1980), 19, that *Picturesque America*'s steel engravings were printed on the steam-powered press developed by Neale. But since Comparato, in *Chronicles of Genius and Folly*, dates that press from 1876 (as does the quote from *Publishers' Weekly*) it could not have been used before then. Perhaps it was used for later impressions. The "successful" printing of engravings from D. Appleton and Company's *Art Journal*, *Picturesque America*, and *Picturesque Europe* mentioned in an invitation to see the press in operation in November 1878 quoted by Comparato (*Chronicles*, 691) probably referred to printing trials using the existing plates.

99. "An October Idyl," *Harper's Monthly Magazine* 41 (November 1870): 907.

100. *Publishers' Weekly* 17 (May 1, 1880): 455. Grant Overton, *Portrait of a Publisher* (New York: D. Appleton, 1925), 10. See appendix D.2.

Chapter 6

1. These pages were first assembled in their proper order when the volumes were bound, but Bunce must have considered the choices early on.

2. See Alan Trachtenberg, *Brooklyn Bridge: Fact and Symbol* (1965; reprint, Chicago: University of Chicago Press, 1979), 75–76.

3. A popular subject, the Capitol building, without its later dome, had also been used for the opening illustration in the first issue of the German edition of *Meyer's Universum* (1833) and the engraved title page of N. P. Willis's *American Scenery* (1837–39). See John W. Reps, *Washington on View: The Nation's Capital Since 1790* (Chapel Hill: University of North Carolina Press, 1991).

4. William H. Goetzmann theorizes that artists found Texas, in all its variety, daunting, and that it was difficult for them to decide which features were representative. See "Images of Texas," in *Texas Images and Visions*, catalogue by Becky Duval Reese (Austin: Archer M. Huntington Art Gallery, University of Texas at Austin, 1983), 21.

5. Other designations he suggested for the period were education, scientific investigation, political inquiry, and "cheap literature." "Editor's Table," *Appletons' Journal*, July 19, 1873, 89.

6. See Roy F. Nichols and Eugene H. Berwanger, *The Stakes of Power, 1845–1877*, rev. ed. (New York: Hill and Wang, 1982), 222–26.

7. Completed in 1869 after an abortive earlier attempt, they accomplished keeping the railroad open despite blizzards similar to the one that trapped the ill-fated Donner party in 1846–47, rendering the spot notorious. See Nancy K. Anderson, "'The Kiss of Enterprise,' The Western Landscape as Symbol and Resource," in *The West as America: Reinterpreting Images of the Frontier, 1820–1920*, ed. William H. Truettner (Washington, D.C.: National Museum of American Art, 1991), 259–68. Although Moran probably based his image on a photograph that lacked the snowshed, choice was still a factor, for he had seen the actual spot. The same is true of his image of the cliffs of the Green River, in Wyoming Territory, which omitted the famous railroad bridge that replaced one of the most dangerous fords on the Oregon Trail. See Anderson, "'The Kiss of Enterprise,'" 243–47.

8. It was also a characteristic of many paintings of the West in this period, as several recent exhibitions have stressed. See Truettner, ed., *The West as America*, and William Cronon, "Telling Tales on Canvas: Landscapes of Frontier Change," in Jules David Prown, et al., *Discovered Lands, Invented Pasts: Transforming Visions of the American West* (New Haven: Yale University Press, 1992), 80–81.

9. Isabella L. Bird, *A Lady's Life in the Rocky Mountains* (Norman: University of Oklahoma Press, 1960), 33.

10. Alfred R. Waud manuscript, 1872: "From Duluth to Bismarck," Mss 106/12, 31. Historic New Orleans Collection.

11. "Essay on American Scenery," in *American Art, 1700–1960: Sources and Documents*, ed. John W. McCoubrey (Englewood Cliffs, N.J.: Prentice-Hall, Inc., 1965), 105. This passage is also quoted in David Tatham, "The Artists of Trenton Falls," in *The Art of Trenton Falls, 1825–1900*, exhibition organized by Paul D. Schweizer (Utica, N.Y.: Museum of Art, Munson-Williams-Proctor Institute, 1989), 17. See also Barbara Maria Stafford, *Voyage into Substance: Art, Science, Nature, and the Illustrated Travel Account, 1760–1840* (Cambridge, Mass.: The Massachusetts Institute of Technology Press, 1984), 242–49.

12. Christopher Mulvey, *Anglo-American Landscapes: A Study of Nineteenth-Century Anglo-American Travel Literature* (Cambridge: Cambridge University Press, 1983), 187–208; see also Elizabeth R. McKinsey, *Niagara Falls: Icon of the American Sublime* (New York: Cambridge University Press, 1985); Jeremy Elwell Adamson, ed. *Niagara: Two Centuries of Changing Attitudes, 1697–1901* (Washington, D.C.: Corcoran Gallery of Art, 1985); and Christopher W. Lane, *Impressions of Niagara: The Charles Rand Penney Collection* (Philadelphia: Philadelphia Print Shop, 1993).

13. See McKinsey, *Niagara Falls: Icon of the American Sublime*, ch. 5, "'To be rendered useful'—The Selling of Niagara Falls."

14. John Ruskin, *Modern Painters*, 1, in *Library Edition of the Works of John Ruskin*, ed. E. T. Cook and A. Wedderbrun (London: George Allen, 1903–12), vol. 3, part 2, section 5, ch. 3, 556.

15. Gilpin had written, "Happy the pencil that can seize the spirit, agitation, and brilliancy of a broken cascade" ("Analysis of Romantic Scenery," *Tour to the Lakes*, quoted in Hussey, *The Picturesque*, 117).

16. Compare, for example, Thomas Cole's *Falls at Catskill* (ca. 1828–29) (reproduced in Kenneth Myers, *The Catskills: Painters, Writers, and Tourists in the Mountains 1820–1895* [Yonkers, N.Y.: The Hudson River Museum of Westchester, 1987], pl. 73), and Thomas Doughty's "Catskill Falls" engraved for *The Northern Traveller*, 1828 (reproduced in Edward J. Nygren with Bruce Robertson, *View and Visions: American Landscapes before 1830* [Washington, D.C.: Corcoran Gallery of Art, 1986], 62), where the rocks of the foreground provide a resting place for the viewer.

17. Reproduced in Myers, *The Catskills*, 77.

18. Travellers found the view from Mount Holyoke especially appealing because of the evidences of intense cultivation and long history. *Arcadian Vales / Views of the Connecticut River Valley* (Springfield, Mass.: George Walter Vincent Smith Art Museum, 1981), 14.

19. Charles Dickens, *American Notes and Pictures from Italy* (London: Oxford University Press, 1957), 171–72, 187; quoted in Mulvey, *Anglo-American Landscapes*, 227–28. See also ch. 12 of Mulvey, "The Mississippi: The Nightmare Landscape."

20. [Thomas Hamilton], *Men and Manners in America*, 3 vols. (Edinburgh: Blackwood, 1833), 2:192–94. Quoted in Mulvey, *Anglo-American Landscapes*, 215.

21. Compare the drawing reproduced in *American Heritage* (December 1963), 35.

22. An example of this convention from earlier in the century comes from the description of St. Michael's Mount in *Picturesque Views on the Southern Coast of England, from drawings made principally by J. M. W. Turner* (2 vols; London: John and Arthur Arch, Cornhill, 1826), vol. 2, unpaged): "It is calculated to attract the attention of the naturalist, to awaken the inquisitive spirit of the historian, to inspire the imagination of the poet, and to court the imitative powers of the painter."

23. See Barbara Novak, *Nature and Culture: American Landscape and Painting, 1825–1875* (New York: Norton, 1959), ch. 4, esp. 52.

24. See for example, I, 59, 92, 258–261, 296; II, 127, 278, 307, 500.

25. Similarly, Rossiter Johnson wrote of Vermont's Green Mountains: "If Professor Rogers's theory of mountain-formation be correct—that elevated ranges have been produced by a sort of tidal wave of the earth's once plastic crust—then the Green Mountains must be the softened undulation that followed the greater billow which crested and broke in Mount Washington and Mount Lafayette" (II, 278–79).

26. See Virginia L. Wagner, "Geological Time in Nineteenth-Century Landscape Painting," *Winterthur Portfolio*, 24, 2/3 (Summer/Autumn 1989): 153–63.

27. See Carol Gordon Wood, "'Only Second in Fame to Niagara'—Trenton Falls and the American Grand Tour," in *The Art of Trenton Falls*, 43–44.

28. See Virginia L. Wagner, "John Ruskin and Artistical Geology in America," *Winterthur Portfolio*, 23, 2/3 (Summer/Autumn, 1988): 152.

29. See John F. Sears's chapter on "Mammoth Cave: Theater of the Cosmic" in *Sacred Places: American Tourist Attractions in this Nineteenth Century* (New York: Oxford University Press, 1989), 31–48.

30. *Modern Painters*, 1, *Library Edition of the Works of John Ruskin*, ed. E. T. Cook and A. Wedderbrun (London: George Allen, 1903–12), vol. 3, part 2, sec. 4, ch. 1, 427; and 4, vol. 6, part 5, ch. 20, 418. Part 5 of *Modern Painters*, first published in 1856 as vol. 4, is entitled "Of Mountain Beauty."

31. Wagner, "John Ruskin and Artistical Geology in America," 167.

32. For example, Cole painted Mount Aetna in Sicily and Church painted Cotopaxi in Ecuador. Eastern mountains that appeared to derive from volcanic action, like Mount Chocorua in the White Mountains and Mount Katahdin in Maine, were also favored as subjects. Reports from Oregon Territory of the impressive snow-covered volcanic peaks of the Cascade Range generated public enthusiasm and drew artists to the Northwest, including Bierstadt, who exhibited his large painting of Mount Hood in 1865. See Nancy K. Anderson, "'Wondrously Full of Invention': The Western Landscapes of Albert Bierstadt," in Nancy K. Anderson and Linda S. Ferber, *Albert Bierstadt: Art & Enterprise* (New York: Brooklyn Museum, 1990), 85.

33. Especially Bret Harte's stories and Joaquin Miller's "Songs of the Sierras," called the literary "sensation" of 1871 by the *Publishers' and Stationers' Weekly Trade Circular*, Jan. 18, 1872, 5.

34. *Publishers' and Stationers' Weekly Trade Circular*, Feb. 15, 1872, 141.

35. "Shasta," *Atlantic Monthly* (December 1871), 720. In his diaries, Smillie recorded reading both Whymper's *Scrambles amongst the Alps* (Dec. 30, 1872) and King's *Mountaineering in the Sierra Nevada* (Jan. 1, 1873) at the same time he was struggling to write his article on the Yosemite Valley (diaries of James D. Smillie, Archives of American Art, mfm. roll 2850).

36. Quoted in Novak, *Nature and Culture*, 68, from Alexander von Humboldt, *Cosmos*, trans. E. C. Otte, 2 vols. (New York: Harper & Brothers, 1850), 2:93.

37. Discovered by his exploring party in the fall of 1870.

38. Rideing goes into "healthy raptures" over the more "tender, almost pastoral scenery" of Twin Lakes, which "transports" him to the Scottish Highlands (II, 498). Amid the high peaks, however, his "admiration and wonder are mingled with a degree of awe that restrains expression"(II, 488). He likens the feeling to grief, to standing "on the brink of a grave." If this is similar to the "stern, strong accord" with the "lifeless region" above timberline that King describes, King seems to relish the experience more than Rideing. The response of the young Rideing seems more shaped than that of the other writers by awareness of recent theories that the earth had evolved through arbitrary occurrences rather than divine plan.

39. King, *Mountaineering in the Sierra Nevada* (Boston: J. R. Osgood, 1872) 207–210.

40. Linda S. Ferber, "Albert Bierstadt: The History of a Reputation," in Anderson and Ferber, *Albert Bierstadt*, 48–49.

41. See Anderson, "'Wondrously Full of Invention,'" 88–90.

42. Anthony Trollope, *North America* (New York: Knopf, 1951), 158.

43. "Farming in the Great West—The 'Burr Oak' Farm, Illinois, Comprising Sixty-Five Square Miles," drawn by Theodore Davis. Reproduced in Sarah Burns, *Pastoral Inventions: Rural Life in Nineteenth-Century American Art and Culture* (Philadelphia: Temple University Press, 1989), 70. Burns, 71, reproduces a later view of steam threshing machines in Dakota Territory, from *Frank Leslie's Illustrated Newspaper*, Oct. 19, 1878.

44. See Burns, *Pastoral Inventions*, ch. 2, "The Poetry of Labor."

45. Allan Nevins, *The Emergence of Modern America 1865–1878* (1927; reprint, Chicago: Quadrangle Books, 1971), 32.

46. See Thomas Bender, *Toward an Urban Vision: Ideas and Institutions in Nineteenth-Century America* (Louisville: University of Kentucky Press, 1975), ch. 2; and John F. Kasson, *Civilizing the Machine: Technology and Republican Values in America, 1776–1900* (New York: Grossman, 1976), 62.

47. George Perkins Marsh's *Man and Nature*, first published in 1864, was an important impetus toward preserving and properly managing forests. See John Brinckerhoff Jackson, *American Space* (New York: Norton, 1972), 87–99. A second edition of Marsh's book, retitled *The Earth as Modified by Human Action*, was published in 1874.

48. Garczynski describes how about a mile above the manufacturing village of Cohoes, "the Lowell of New York," the Mohawk is "hemmed in by a dam, and a great portion of its waters drawn off" to supply power for "the great Harmony Cotton-Mills" and "some twenty-five woollen-mills, besides paper factories and other industries" (II, 465). The same page, however, shows a highly romantic view of "Cohoes Falls" by Woodward with no hint of factories or dams.

49. Waud's drawing is reproduced in *Alfred R. Waud: Special Artist on Assignment* (New Orleans: Historic New Orleans Collection, 1979), 4.

50. Trollope, *North America*, 122.

51. This drawing is in the Historic New Orleans Collection, no. 1977.137.31.4.

52. See, for example, "Table-Talk," *Appletons' Journal*, October 14, 1871, 442.

53. As quoted in Jackson, *American Space*, 103. The enthusiasm for tree-planting also led to the establishment of Arbor Day, which started in Nebraska in 1874 and became a national observance, and an effort to celebrate the Centennial by planting "Centennial" trees and groves (37).

54. *Modern Painters*, 4, in *Works of John Ruskin*, vol. 5, part 5, ch. 1, 19.

55. Exemplifying the dual emphasis on old and new, the views of monuments in Richmond and Providence are placed next to pictures of historic buildings in each city.

56. Other examples include a monument commemorating the massacre in Wyoming Valley in 1778 (II, 227); one to Uncas in Norwich (II, 449); and the Bunker Hill Monument in Boston (II, 237). The four rather incongruous monuments in Boston's Public Garden embody the period's simultaneous enthusiam for scientific advances, art, and history: the Ether Monument, commemorating the discovery of anaesthetics, "Venus rising from the Sea," and statues of George Washington and Massachusetts politician and orator Edward Everett (II, 234, 237). Also described, but not pictured, are a new statue of Lincoln in Philadelphia (II, 36) and a column in Augusta to Georgia's signers of the Declaration of Independence (II, 129).

57. See Paul Boyer, *Urban Masses and Moral Order in America, 1820–1920* (Cambridge, Mass.: Harvard University Press, 1978), esp. 122.

58. Savannah is cited for a plethora of private benevolent organizations that support homes for the poor and orphaned and hospitals, as well as cultural organizations that support libraries and historical societies. At the same time, the "best and most influential citizens . . . sustained by the liberal provision of the municipal government," have inaugurated a public-school system "which is justly pronounced equal to that of any city in the Union" (I, 125).

59. The architect, A. C. Morse, had selected a popular Gothic Revival style considered especially picturesque. Clark says of the Italian Gothic building, "no more perfect specimen of this style may be found even in the old cities of Northern Italy" (I, 504). Gibson includes a view of the hospital and its grounds (I, 501).

60. Other suburbs praised in *Picturesque America* include Brookline and Roxbury, near Boston, which "have been well compared to those of Paris" (II, 242–44), Llewellyn Park on Orange Mountain, New Jersey (II, 50), the outlying residential streets of Chicago (II, 524), and Summerville, near Augusta, Georgia (I, 131).

61. Jan Cohn, *The Palace or the Poorhouse: The American House as a Cultural Symbol* (East Lansing: Michigan State University Press, 1979), 122.

62. William G. McLoughlin, *The Meaning of Henry Ward Beecher* (New York: Knopf, 1970), 146, 128, 110–13.

63. Quoted in Kasson, *Civilizing the Machine*, 36, from Lyman Beecher, "The Gospel the Only Security for Eminent and Abiding National Prosperity," *National Preacher* 3 (March 1829), 147.

64. Gerard R. Wolfe, *The House of Appleton* (Metuchen, N.J.: Scarecrow Press, 1981) 130.

65. Nevins, *The Emergence of Modern America*, 48–9; John Higham, *Strangers in the Land: Patterns of American Nativism, 1860–1925* (New Brunswick, N.J.: Rutgers University Press, 1955), 15.

66. Junius Henri Browne, *The Great Metropolis: A Mirror of New York* (Hartford: American Publishing Company, 1869), 339.

67. *The Galaxy* 13 (March, April 1872): 314, 321. In 1869, the "Home and Foreign Gossip" column of *Harper's Weekly* had described the magnitude of the problem similarly: "One half of the entire population of New York city are said to dwell in tenement-houses, and the most wretched under-ground cellars are homes for many thousands—if such desolate holes can be miscalled homes. Enormous rents are extorted from the poor for unventilated, inconvenient, dark damp rooms" (13 [June 26, 1869]: 414. Quoted in Sally Lorenson Gross, *Toward an Urban View: The Nineteenth Century American City in Prints* [New Haven: Yale University Art Gallery, 1989], 28.)

68. Browne, *The Great Metropolis*, 35.

69. Boyer, *Urban Masses and Moral Order in America, 1820–1920*, 125.

70. *Appletons' Journal*, Aug. 5, 1871, 162.

71. Ann Douglas, *The Feminization of American Culture* (New York: Knopf, 1977), 55.

72. The figures are essentially the same in Waud's original drawing in the Historic New Orleans Collection, acc.no. 1977.137.13.6. Several other images show garden laborers in the vicinity of more well-dressed people at leisure: I, opposite 497, II, opposite 569; II, 551; II, 251.

73. Daniel T. Rodgers, *The Work Ethic in Industrial America 1850–1920* (Chicago: University of Chicago Press, 1978), 35.

74. Winslow Homer had created an image of a young woman involved in such labor for *The Song of the Sower* (29), but the overall design is so appealing that it fails to convey the monotony of the work.

75. Rodgers, *The Work Ethic in Industrial America*, 67–69.

76. Albert Boime discusses how in the "paternalism that dominated the thought of the privileged classes," the "happy worker" succeeded the cheerful slave, in *The Art of Exclusion: Representing Blacks in the Nineteenth Century* (Washington, D.C.: Smithsonian Institution Press, 1990), 114. See also 88–114.

77. Also amusing is the "motherly solicitude" of the "little negro lass of about twelve years" who is "maid and master of all work" at the hotel on Lookout Mountain and who loves to polish boots (I, 56, 58).

78. Four installments, beginning Aug. 13, 1870, were written by T. B. Thorpe and illustrated by W. M. Cary, who had travelled to the "Plains."

79. Brian Dippie has described the disparate attitudes toward Indians in the East and West as "pity" and "censure." See "The Moving Finger Writes: Western Art and the Dynamics of Change," in Jules David Prown, et al., *Discovered Lands, Invented Pasts*, 94.

80. Describing the 1872 rededication of this Council House, when the grandsons of former chiefs passed the pipe of peace given to Red-Jacket by George Washington, Ward revealed his expectation that this was "no doubt the last Indian council that will ever be held in the valley of the Genesee" (II, 359).

81. See Julie Schimmel, "Inventing 'the Indian,'" in *The West as America*, esp. 168–78.

82. Moran and Colburn encountered many on their journey, as shown by Moran's letters (see Thomas Moran, *Home-Thoughts from Afar: Letters of Thomas Moran to Mary Nimmo Moran*, ed. Amy O. Bassford and Fritiof Fryxell [East Hampton, N.Y.: East Hampton Free Library, 1967]) and Colburn's article, "The Colorado Cañon: A Trip to the Verge of the Chasm," *New York Times*, Sept. 4, 1873.

83. Encountering a group engaged in a burial ritual a little farther on, Gifford questioned one who knew some English about what was happening (Robert Swain Gifford Papers: diary [MS 12, S-g 1, Sr 13, vol. 1, 1869] and letter of Sept. 26, 1869, to Mrs. Lydia Swain [MS 12, S-g 1, Sr A, S-s 2, folder 10], Whaling Museum Library, Old Dartmouth Historical Society, New Bedford, Mass.).

84. Sears, *Sacred Places*, 32.

85. The vigor with which the fishermen wield their spears in Gifford's "Salmon Falls" suggests something of what she sees as "wantonness of cruelty" (I, 48), but Gifford makes no such observation in his diary, and the fisherman could have been added to the image on the block by another hand.

Chapter 7

1. *Publishers' Weekly* 17 (May 1, 1880): 454.

2. Grant Overton claimed "nearly a million" copies of *Picturesque America* eventually sold (*Portrait of a Publisher*, [New York: D. Appleton, 1925], 10). J. C. Derby, in *Fifty Years Among Authors, Books and Publishers* (New York: G. W. Carleton, 1884), wrote that *Picturesque America, Picturesque Europe*, and *Picturesque Palestine* all "continue to sell largely and by subscription only." *Picturesque America* was issued in a variety of ways, including a six-"division" set, with all parts dated 1872. A five-part set is noted in the annotated bibliography in Anne Morand and Nancy Friese, *The Prints of Thomas Moran in the Thomas Gilcrease Institute of American History and Art, Tulsa, Oklahoma* (Tulsa: Thomas Gilcrease Museum Association, 1986), 237.

3. According to Fenn's obituary in *Harper's Weekly* (May 13, 1911, 10), it was found "on the center-table of every orthodox parlor."

4. For example, "The Coast of California" (Oct. 11, 1873); "Mount Mansfield" (Feb. 21, 1874); and some of the illustrations for the "Summer Resorts" series in August and September 1874.

5. The *Weekly* stressed that their artists would go beyond the usual route on "long excursions on horseback into regions where railroads have not yet penetrated" (Nov. 8, 1873, 994). Beginning Oct. 18, 1873, the series continued sporadically through 1876. Some of the handsome, double-page wood engravings excelled in depicting frontier life and American Indian customs. See Robert Taft, *Artists and Illustrators of the Old West* (New York: Charles Scribner's Sons, 1953), ch. 7.

6. Champney's drawings were frequently reworked on the block by Thomas Moran or W. L. Sheppard. The series continued through 1874 and was published as a book in 1875 (Hartford: American Publishiing Co.). Other notable landscape illustrations were those by Thomas Moran for "Traveling by Telegraph: Northward to Niagara" in May and June 1872, and "West Point" in July 1872.

7. Moran's views included Lake Superior (January 1873), the Yellowstone Region (April 1873), Utah (January and September 1874; April 1875), Lake George (April 1874), the Missisquoi and Vermont (May 1874), and Idaho (June 1876). Woodward's included Virginia (February and July 1873; March 1874), Florida (May 1874), the Palisades and Hudson (August 1874; February 1876), the Delaware Water Gap (January 1875); and Newport (November 1875). Despite such high quality illustrations, *The Aldine* ceased publication in 1879. Perhaps by then it was clear that less expensive photoengraving was destined to replace wood engraving.

8. "Art and Artists," *Daily Evening Transcript* (Boston), Oct. 1, 1875.

9. Dec. 9, 1874, 8, col 3. I am indebted to Alan Ramsier for this reference.

10. Quoted in Bunce's "Table-Talk" column, *Appletons' Journal*, May 24, 1873.

11. See *Appletons' Journal*, Jan. 17, 1874, 92.

12. "Printing and Publishing" ("Extracts from the Report of the French Commission"), U.S. Centennial Commission, *International Exhibition, 1876, Reports and Awards*, ed. Francis A. Walker (Philadelphia: J. B. Lippincott, 1879), vol. 10, group 27, Educational Systems, Methods and Libraries, 245. The copy displayed was "one of the foremost competitors for the award of fine binding . . . in brown levant, inlaid in red and blue calf, lined with brown watered silk, and most richly tooled." The binder was William Matthews, head of Appleton's manufacturing plant. Also displayed was the silver medal the pope sent D. Appleton and Company in recognition of the gift of a copy of *Picturesque America* (*Publishers' Weekly* 233 [July 1876]: 16).

Although many still considered France the leader in illustrated art books, *Picturesque America* was at least a close contender (see *Reports and Awards*, vol. 10, group 28). American paper and binding received much praise, and the United States was considered the leader in textbook manufacturing. See vol. 2, group 13, pp. 3, 5.

13. *Publishers' Weekly*, 324 (March 30, 1878): 350.

14. *L'Amerique du Nord pittoresque: Ouvrage rédigé par une réunion d'écrivains américains. Traduit, revu et augmenté par Benedict-Henry Revoil.* (Paris: A. Quantin, 1880). This version omits the steel engravings, as well as Bryant's name as editor and his preface and the writers and artists' names. The publishers had the use of large numbers of the wood engravings, almost certainly in the form of electrotypes. The contents were rearranged according to geographical location, beginning with New York, then covering the Northeast, the mid-Atlantic, the South, and the West, ending with California and the Columbia River area.

15. The English editions understandably dropped "The Land We Live In" from the subtitle. Volumes I and II (1881 and 1882) were published by Cassell, Petter, Galpin & Co.,

London. The imprint of Volumes 3 and 4 was "London: Cassell & Co.," as it was for the later reissues.

16. Friedrich von Hellwald, *Amerika in Wort und Bild: Eine Schilderung der Vereinigten Staaten*, 2 vols. (Leipzig: Heinrich Schmidt and Carl Günther, 1883–85). Hellwald's organization was completely different from *Picturesque America*'s, moving from the Northeast and Middle-Atlantic states to the South, Gulf States, Southwest, Midwest, and Far West. The coverage of geographic regions was also more comprehensive. Illustrations in addition to those from *Picturesque America* included some from *The Great South*, numerous images of North American animals (after H. Leutemann), hotels, trains, Chinese immigrants, the Mormons in Salt Lake City, and sensational images of American Indians attacking, even scalping, travellers. No steel engravings were included. Some full-page wood engravings (mostly from *Picturesque America*) were treated as special plates (*Tafeln*), printed on heavier paper with no printing on the back.

17. F. Hopkinson Smith, *American Illustrators* (New York: Charles Scribner's, 1892), 62. Smith praised Fenn's drawings for their "delicacy, truth and refinement," but said they could also "be criticized for being precise."

18. Joseph Pennell, *Modern Illustration* (London and New York: G. Bell & Sons, 1895), 31, 127. Pennell also quoted Smith's words about Fenn being "the Nestor of his guild" (127).

19. Among the other artists contributing most heavily to *Picturesque Europe* were W. H. J. Boot, P. Skelton, R. P. Leitch, and T. L. Rowbotham. British engravers were employed, including, most conspicuously, E. Whymper. Many of the wood engravings are unsigned. The lists of steel engravings did not include the engravers, as *Picturesque America* had, perhaps indicating some loss of status.

20. In 1875 and early 1876 *The Aldine* featured Germany, whereas *Picturesque Europe* gave attention during 1875 to the British Isles. *The Aldine* later followed Appleton's example of producing a book from a magazine series: *Europe Illustrated* was published in 1888 by the Aldine Book Publishing Co., Boston.

21. The occasional use of screens of dots to create light tonal areas indicates the engravers were experimenting with new techniques.

22. In July 1876, the firm changed *Appletons' Journal* into a smaller format monthly magazine of "General Literature," dropping the emphasis on illustrations. The number of illustrations steadily diminished to virtually none by the time the *Journal* was discontinued in 1881. The *Art Journal* was better suited to compete with *The Aldine*, being large format and printed with great care on heavier paper. Its wood engravings were comparable in quality to *The Aldine*. Its subscription price was nine dollars a year, compared to five dollars for *The Aldine* in 1875 (justified in part by a greater number of pages), whereas *Appletons' Journal* by the late 1870s was reduced to three dollars a year. The new magazine was published through 1887.

23. In 1875, with Fenn abroad working on *Picturesque Europe*, Bunce turned to Woodward for the new *Art Journal*. His views of the Hudson River valley were regular features throughout 1875, as were his views of Colorado in May–July 1876, and of "The Scenery of the Pacific Railway" in 1877. These series later yielded two books for the Appleton firm: *The Hudson River, By Pen and Pencil* in 1875 and *The Scenery of the Pacific Railways and Colorado* in 1878, with text by William Henry Rideing. See Sue Rainey, "J. D. Woodward's Wood Engravings of Colorado and the Pacific Railways, 1876–1878," *Imprint: Journal of the American Historical Print Collectors Society*, 18, no. 2 (Fall 1993): 2–12.

24. The Beldens, who had moved to Toronto from Chicago in 1876, published county atlases by subscription. See George L. Parker, *Canadian Notes and Queries*, 25 (July 1980): 7–8.

25. In place of steel engravings, it included a number of fine wood engravings, featured by being printed on heavier, whiter paper, with no printing on the back.

26. Schell studied at the Pennsylvania Academy of the Fine Arts and joined *Leslie's* in 1863 as special artist. Later he was art director for Harper & Brothers. He died in Chicago in 1905. (Stephen W. Sears, ed., *The American Heritage Century Collection of Civil War Art*, [New York: American Heritage, 1974], 309.)

27. For example, Fenn's eight contributions included: five flower studies; one view of rapids near Niagara Falls that could well be based on a sketch from his trip to that area for *Picturesque America*; "A Laurentian Bluff"; and a "Forest Stream, and Timber Slide" (opp. 699) supposedly on the Lower St. Lawrence of the Saguenay, but clearly based on sketches made near Eastport, Maine, now in the collection of the Royal Ontario Musem, Toronto (acc. #980.145). Fenn drew a birch bark canoe on one side of the sheet and a waterfall, rocks, and trees on the other. For the wood engraving, he combined the two and added a timber slide. (I am grateful to Mary Allodi for calling these sketches to my attention.) The one or two views each contributed by Waud, Gibson, Gifford, and Woodward could have been based on previous drawings or photographs. On Moran's contribution, see Allan Pringle, "Thomas Moran: *Picturesque Canada* and the Quest for a Canadian National Landscape Theme," *Imprint: Journal of the American Historical Print Collectors Society* 14, no. 1 (Spring 1989): 12–21. Pringle maintains that interest in hydraulics was the dominant theme of the publication.

28. The title page reads: "Andrew Garran, ed. Illustrated under the supervision of Frederic B. Schell, assisted by leading colonial and American artists. With over eight hundred engravings on wood. Sydney, Melbourne, London, & Springfield, Mass.: Picturesque Atlas Publishing Company, Limited, 1886–88. 3 vols."

29. Dewing simultaneously issued a ten-volume edition, a condensed two-volume edition, and a one-volume trade edition. See Estelle Jussim, *Visual Communication and the Graphic Arts: Photographic Technologies in the Nineteenth Century* (New York: R. R. Bowker, 1974), 285–86.

30. For example, *Picturesque Washington* (1889), *Picturesque Richmond* (1891), *Picturesque Chicago and Guide to the World's Fair* (1892), *Picturesque Detroit and Environs*, (1893), *Picturesque Berkshire* (1893), *Picturesque Pittsburgh and Allegheny* (1898), and *Picturesque Colorado* (1900). As the halftone process was refined, these books came to rely increasingly on photography for their images.

31. The first volume of Bryant and Gay's *Popular History of the United States* was published by Scribner, Armstrong, and Company in time to be displayed at the 1876 Centennial Exhibition in Philadelphia. The subsequent three volumes appeared in 1878, 1879, and 1881, under the imprint Charles Scribners' Sons. (After Bryant's death in 1878, Gay carried on alone.) Contributing *Picturesque America* artists were Moran, Woodward, Sheppard, Waud, Perkins, Gibson, Smillie, and Warren. Among the artists from the next generation were E. A. Abbey, C. S. Reinhart, and Howard Pyle.

After its appearance over three years in *The Century* met with great popularity and commercial success, *Battles and Leaders of the Civil War* was published in 1888 by the Century Company in an expanded version in four volumes. Fenn, Woodward, Sheppard, and A. R. Waud were, once again, prolific contributors. Many of their original drawings are reproduced in Sears, ed., *The American Heritage Century Collection of Civil War Art*.

32. See Kathleen Adair Foster, "Makers of the American Watercolor Movement: 1860–1890," Ph.D. diss., Yale University, 1982, esp. 270–71.

33. *Old Fireplace* is in the collection of the Montclair Art Museum and reproduced in black and white in *The American Painting Collection of the Montclair Art Museum* (Montclair, N.J.: Montclair Art Museum, 1977), cat. no. 395, p. 234. The subject is the same as "Interior of Payne's 'Home, Sweet Home,'" *Picturesque America*, I, 255. Gifford showed mainly Egyptian subjects.

34. See *1876: American Art of the Centennial* (Washington, D.C.: National Collection of Fine Arts, 1976), essay by Susan Hobbs, esp. 12–15.

35. See Jussim, *Visual Communication and the Graphic Arts*, for a detailed account of the gradual development of satisfactory halftone processes.

36. Some of the most prominent illustrators of the period, in addition to Pyle, Frost, and Pennell, were Edward Austin Abbey, Charles S. Reinhart, W. A. Rogers, W. T. Smedley, E. W. Kemble, Alice Barber Stephens, George Wharton Edwards, and Frederic Remington. Within a few years Maxfield Parrish, Charles Dana Gibson, Howard Chandler Christy, N. C. Wyeth, and many more would join their ranks. With the exception of those few who specialized in landscapes and architectural views (Pennell, Fenn, Ernest Clifford Peixotto, and Jules Guerin), these illustrators focused on representing people—of every type and circumstance.

37. Joseph Pennell, *The Adventures of an Illustrator* (Boston: Little, Brown, 1925), 101.

38. Henry Blackburn, *The Art of Illustration*, 3rd ed. (1894; reprint, Edinburgh: John Grant, 1904), 185.

39. Joshua C. Taylor, "The Virtue of American Nature," in *America as Art* (Washington, D.C.: Published for the National Collection of Fine Arts by the Smithsonian Institution Press, 1976), 126.

40. *America Illustrated* was edited by J. David Williams and published by The New York Printing and Publishing House.

41. Frequently the blocks or electrotypes were cropped to fit the smaller 10⅜" x 7¼" format, altering compositions and often eliminating the signatures of the artist and engraver.

42. *The Complete Works of Ralph Waldo Emerson*, ed. Edward Waldo Emerson (Boston: Houghton, Mifflin, 1903–4), 9:78; 11:183–86.

43. Quoted in Kasson, *Civilizing the Machine: Technology and Republican Values in America, 1776–1900* (New York: Grossman, 1976), 164; from Richard Henry Stoddard, ed., *A Century After: Picturesque Glimpses of Philadelphia and Pennsylvania* (Philadelphia, 1876), 348.

44. William Dean Howells, "A Sennight of the Centennial," *Atlantic Monthly* 38 (July 1876): 96; discussed in Kasson, *Civilizing the Machine*, 165.

45. E. L. Youmans, "The Recent Strikes," *Popular Science Monthly* 1 (September 1872): 624.

46. The assembled parts contained 720 pages, almost one-third fewer than the original edition, and could be bound in either one or two volumes. The editor was Marcus Benjamin, a chemist who wrote for numerous Appleton publications and edited guides to winter and summer resorts. He noted that the changes were necessitated by the "great advances" in "railroad building" in the two decades since the first edition, which had made many localities described easily accessible. As a result, they had become popular resorts with fine hotels, rather than the "frequently incommodious inns of the past." Although the note claims "no other alterations of importance have been made," the much shorter version required condensing many sections and omitting several entirely, including the French Broad,

Charleston, and the Neversink Highlands. Some of the engravings were likewise omitted, and the steel engravings show evidence of retouched, worn plates, with less fine detail than in the earlier prints. Careful comparison reveals that many of the immediate details of the journeys have been deleted, presumably because they were no longer accurate, resulting in a less interesting text.

47. Italics added. Clarence King, *Mountaineering in the Sierra Nevada* (Boston: J. R. Osgood, 1872), 126.

48. Hiram M. Stanley [Lake Forest, Illinois] "A Culture List," *Education* (November 1896), 172–74.

49. Quoted in Kasson, *Civilizing the Machine*, 224, from Howells's letter to Henry James, Oct. 10, 1888, in *Life in Letters of William Dean Howells*, ed. Mildred Howells (Garden City, N.Y.: Double Day, Doran, 1928), 1:417.

50. Quoted in Kasson, *Civilizing the Machine*, 187, from Henry George, *Progress and Poverty . . .* (1873; reprint, Garden City, N.Y.: Garden City, 1912), 8.

51. Henry James, *The American Scene*, ed. Leon Edel (Bloomington: Indiana University Press, 1968), xi–xii, 83,

52. James, *The American Scene*, 84–86.

53. William H. Rideing, *Many Celebrities and a Few Others* (Garden City, N.Y.: Doubleday, Page, 1912), 77.

Select Bibliography

Adams, John Coleman. *William Hamilton Gibson, Artist-Naturalist-Author*. New York: G. P. Putnam's Sons, 1901.

Adamson, Jeremy Elwell, ed. *Niagara: Two Centuries of Changing Attitudes, 1697–1901*. Washington, D.C.: Corcoran Gallery of Art, 1985.

Alfred R. Waud: Special Artist on Assignment. New Orleans: Historic New Orleans Collection, 1979.

American Watercolor Society Papers, Archives of American Art, Smithsonian Institution, Washington, D.C. Mfm. rolls N68-8.

Anderson, Nancy K. "'The Kiss of Enterprise': The Western Landscape as Symbol and Resource." In *The West as America: Reinterpreting Images of the Frontier, 1820–1920*. Edited by William H. Truettner. Washington, D.C.: National Museum of American Art, 1991.

Anderson, Nancy K., and Linda S. Ferber. *Albert Bierstadt: Art & Enterprise*. New York: Brooklyn Museum, 1990.

Andrews, Malcolm. *The Search for the Picturesque: Landscape Aesthetics and Tourism in Britain, 1760–1800*. Stanford, Calif.: Stanford University Press, 1989.

Anthony, A. V. S. "An Art That is Passing Away." In A. V. S. Anthony, Timothy Cole, and Elbridge Kingsley, *Wood-Engraving: Three Essays*. New York: Grolier Club, 1916.

Barbier, Carl Paul. *William Gilpin: His Drawings, Teachings, and Theory of the Picturesque*. Oxford: Oxford University Press, Clarendon Press, 1963.

Barth, Gunther. *City People: The Rise of Modern City Culture in Nineteenth-Century America*. New York: Oxford University Press, 1980.

Bayard, Jane. *Works of Splendour and Imagination: The Exhibition Watercolor, 1770–1870*. New Haven: Yale Center for British Art, 1991.

Bender, Thomas. *New York Intellect*. New York: Alfred A. Knopf, 1987.

———. *Toward an Urban Vision: Ideas and Institutions in Nineteenth-Century America*. Louisville: University of Kentucky Press, 1975.

Benjamin, S. G. W. *The Life and Adventures of a Freelance*. Burlington, Vt.: Free Press Company, 1914.

Benjamin, Walter. "The Work of Art in the Age of Mechanical Reproduction." In *Illuminations.* Edited by Hannah Arendt; translated by Harry Zohn. New York: Harcourt, Brace & World, 1955.

Benson, Eugene. "French and English Illustrated Magazines." *Atlantic Monthly* 25 (June 1870): 681–87.

Bermingham, Ann. *Landscape and Ideology: The English Rustic Tradition, 1740–1860.* Berkeley: University of California Press, 1986.

Bicknell, Peter. *Beauty, Horror and Immensity: Picturesque Landscape in Britain, 1750–1850.* Cambridge: Cambridge University Press and Fitzwilliam Museum, 1981.

Boime, Albert. *The Art of Exclusion: Representing Blacks in the Nineteenth Century.* Washington, D.C.: Smithsonian Institution Press, 1990.

Boyer, Paul. *Urban Masses and Moral Order in America, 1820–1920.* Cambridge, Mass.: Harvard University Press, 1978.

Bowles, Samuel. *The Switzerland of America: A Summer Vacation in the Parks and Mountains of Colorado.* Springfield, Mass.: Samuel Bowles & Co., 1869.

Briggs, Peter M. "Timothy Dwight 'Composes' a Landscape for New England," *American Quarterly,* 40, no. 3 (September 1988): 359–77.

Browne, Junius Henri. *The Great Metropolis: A Mirror of New York.* Hartford: American Publishing Co., 1869.

Bryant, William Cullen. *The Story of the Fountain.* New York: D. Appleton & Co., 1872 (copyright 1871).

_____. *The Song of the Sower.* New York: D. Appleton & Co., 1871 (copyright 1870).

Burke, Doreen Bolger, and Catherine Hoover Voorsanger. "The Hudson River School in Eclipse." In *American Paradise: The World of the Hudson River School.* New York: Metropolitan Museum of Art, 1987.

Burns, Sarah. *Pastoral Inventions: Rural Life in Nineteenth-Century American Art and Culture.* Philadelphia: Temple University Press, 1989.

Burton, Warren. *The Scenery-Shower, with Word-Paintings of the Beautiful, the Picturesque and the Grand in Nature.* Boston: Ticknor & Co., 1844.

Bushnell, Horace. *Work and Play; or Literary Varieties.* New York: Charles Scribner, 1864.

Cadbury, Warder H. Introduction. In William H. H. Murray, *Adventures in the Wilderness.* Edited by William K. Verner. 1869; reprint, Syracuse, N.Y.: Syracuse University Press for The Adirondack Museum, 1970.

Callow, James T. *Kindred Spirits: Knickerbocker Writers and American Artists, 1807–1855.* Chapel Hill, N.C.: University of North Carolina Press, 1967.

Charles Parsons and His Domain. Introduction by Kathryn E. Gamble. Montclair, N.J.: Montclair Art Museum, 1958.

Cohn, Jan. *The Palace or the Poorhouse: The American House as a Cultural Symbol.* East Lansing: Michigan State University Press, 1979.

Cole, Thomas. "Essay on American Scenery." In *American Art, 1700–1960: Sources and Documents.* Edited by John W. McCoubrey. Englewood Cliffs, N.J.: Prentice-Hall, 1965.

Cronon, William. "Telling Tales on Canvas: Landscapes of Frontier Change." In Jules David Prown, et al. *Discovered Lands, Invented Pasts: Transforming Visions of the American West.* New Haven: Yale University Press, 1992.

Curtis, Eugene N. "American Opinion of the French Nineteenth Century Revolutions." *American Historical Review* 29 (January 1929): 249–70.

Curtis, George William. *Lotus-Eating.* New York: Harper & Brothers, 1852.

[Dalziel, George, and Edward Dalziel]. *The Brothers Dalziel: A Record of Fifty Years' Work 1840–1890.* Foreword by Graham Reynolds. London: B. T. Batsford Ltd., 1978. Reprint of the original 1901 edition, London: Methuen.

Danly, Susan, and Leo Marx, eds. *The Railroad in American Art: Representations of Technological Change.* Cambridge, Mass.: Massachusetts Institute of Technology Press, 1988.

Deák, Gloria Gilda. *Picturing America 1497–1899.* Princeton: Princeton University Press, 1988.

de Maré, Eric. *The Victorian Woodblock Illustrators.* London: Gordon Fraser, 1980.

Denning, Michael. *Mechanic Accents: Dime Novels and Working-Class Culture in America.* London & New York: Verso, 1987.

De Santis, Hugh. "The Democratization of Travel: The Travel Agent in American History." *Journal of American Culture* 1 (Spring 1978): 1–17.

De Vinne, Theodore Low. "The Growth of Wood-Cut Printing." Part I: *Scribner's Monthly* 19 (April 1880): 860–74; Part II: *Scribner's Monthly* 20 (May 1880): 34–45.

_____. *Printing in the Nineteenth Century.* New York: Lead Mould Electrotype Foundry, 1924.

Dippie, Brian. "The Moving Finger Writes: Western Art and the Dynamics of Change." In Jules David Prown, et al., *Discovered Lands, Invented Pasts: Transforming Visions of the American West.* New Haven: Yale University Press, 1992.

Douglas, Ann. *The Feminization of American Culture.* New York: Alfred A. Knopf, 1977.

Dunwell, Steve. *The Run of the Mill: A Pictorial Narrative of the Expansion, Dominion, Decline and Enduring Impact of the New England Textile Industry.* Boston: David R. Godine, 1978.

Dyson, Anthony. *Pictures to Print: The Nineteenth-Century Engraving Trade.* London: Farrand Press, 1984.

Eby, Cecil D., Jr. *"Porte Crayon": The Life of David Hunter Strother.* Chapel Hill, N.C.: University of North Carolina Press, 1960.

Fabri, Ralph. *History of the American Watercolor Society: The First Hundred Years.* New York: American Watercolor Society, 1969.

Ferber, Linda S., and William H. Gerdts, curators. *The New Path: Ruskin and the American Pre-Raphaelites.* New York: Brooklyn Museum, distributed by Schocken Books, 1985.

Fiske, John. *Edward Livingston Youmans: Interpreter of Science for the People.* New York: D. Appleton & Co., 1894.

Foshay, Ella M., and Sally Mills. *All Seasons and Every Light: Nineteenth Century American Landscapes from the Collection of Elias Lyman Magoon.* Poughkeepsie, N.Y.: Vassar College Art Gallery, 1983.

Foster, Edward Halsey. *The Civilized Wilderness: Backgrounds to American Romantic Literature, 1817–1860.* New York: Free Press, 1975.

_____. "Picturesque America: A Study of the Popular Use of the Picturesque in Considerations of the American Landscape, 1835–1860." Ph.D. diss., Columbia University, 1970.

Foster, Kathleen A. "Makers of the American Watercolor Movement: 1860–1890." Ph.D. diss., Yale University, 1982.

_____. "The Pre-Raphaelite Medium: Ruskin, Turner, and American Watercolor." In *The New Path: Ruskin and the American Pre-Raphaelites.* Linda S. Ferber and William H. Gerdts, curators. New York: Brooklyn Museum, distributed by Schocken Books, 1985.

Fowler, Don D. *The Western Photographs of John K. Hillers: "Myself in the Water."* Washington, D.C.: Smithsonian Institution Press, 1989.

Frederickson, George. *The Inner Civil War.* New York: Harper & Row, 1965.

Gambee, Budd Leslie, Jr. "*Frank Leslie's Illustrated Newspaper,* 1855–1860: Artistic and Technical Operations of a Pioneer Pictorial News Weekly in America." Ph.D. diss., University of Michigan, 1963.

Gifford, Robert Swain. Papers. Whaling Museum Library, Old Dartmouth Historical Society, New Bedford, Massachusetts.

Goetzmann, William H. *Exploration and Empire: The Explorer and the Scientist in the Winning of the American West.* 1966; reprint, New York: W. W. Norton, Norton Library, 1978.

_____. "Images of Texas." In *Texas Images and Visions,* catalogue by Becky Duval Reese. Austin: Archer M. Huntington Art Gallery, University of Texas at Austin, 1983.

Gross, Sally Lorenson. *Toward an Urban View: The Nineteenth Century American City in Prints.* New Haven: Yale University Art Gallery, 1989.

Hales, Peter B. *Silver Cities: The Photography of American Urbanization, 1839–1915.* Philadelphia: Temple University Press, 1984.

_____. *William Henry Jackson and the Transformation of the American Landscape.* Philadelphia: Temple University Press, 1988.

Harris, Neil. *The Artist in American Society: The Formative Years, 1790–1860.* 1966; reprint, Chicago: University of Chicago Press, 1982.

Hart, James D. *The Popular Book: A History of America's Literary Taste.* 1950; reprint, Westport, Conn.: Greenwood Publishers, 1976.

Higham, John. "From Boundlessness to Consolidation: The Transformation of American Culture, 1848–1860." Ann Arbor: William L. Clements Library, 1969.

———. "Hanging Together: Divergent Unities in American History." *The Journal of American History* 61, no. 1 (June 1974): 5–28.

———. *Strangers in the Land: Patterns of American Nativism, 1860–1925.* New Brunswick, N.J.: Rutgers University Press, 1955.

Hipple, Walter John, Jr. *The Beautiful, the Sublime, and the Picturesque in Eighteenth-Century British Aesthetic Theory.* Carbondale: Southern Illinois University Press, 1957.

Hofstadter, Richard. *Social Darwinism in American Thought.* Rev. ed. New York: George Braziller, 1959; originally published 1944.

Hogarth, Paul. *Arthur Boyd Houghton.* London: Gordon Fraser, 1981.

The Home Book of the Picturesque. New York: George P. Putnam, 1852.

Hoppin, Martha J., et al. *Arcadian Vales / Views of the Connecticut River Valley.* Springfield, Mass.: George Walter Vincent Smith Art Museum, 1981.

Howat, John K. "A Climate for Landscape Painters." In *American Paradise: The World of the Hudson River School.* New York: Metropolitan Museum of Art, distributed by Harry N. Abrams, 1987.

———. *American Paradise: The World of the Hudson River School.* New York: Metropolitan Museum of Art, 1987.

Howe, Daniel Walker, ed. *Victorian America.* Philadelphia: University of Pennsylvania Press, 1976.

Hudson, Frederic. *Journalism in the United States from 1690 to 1872.* New York: Harper & Brothers, 1873.

Hults, Linda C. "Pilgrim's Progress in the West: Moran's *The Mountain of the Holy Cross.*" *American Art* 5, nos. 1 and 2 (Winter/Spring 1991): 69–85.

Hunnisett, Basil. *Steel-Engraved Book Illustration in England.* Boston: David R. Godine, 1980.

Hussey, Christopher. *The Picturesque: Studies in a Point of View.* 1927; reprint, London: Cass, 1967.

Huth, Hans. *Nature and the Americans: Three Centuries of Changing Attitudes.* Berkeley: University of California, 1957.

Hyde, Ann Farrar. *An American Vision: Far Western Landscape and National Culture, 1820–1920.* New York: New York University Press, 1990.

Jackson, John Brinckerhoff. *American Space: The Centennial Years, 1865–1876.* New York: W. W. Norton, 1972.

John, Arthur. *The Best Years of the Century: Richard Watson Gilder, Scribner's Monthly, and the Century Magazine, 1870–1909.* Urbana: University of Illinois Press, 1981.

John Ruskin and the Victorian Eye. Phoenix Art Museum. New York: Harry N. Abrams, 1993.

Jones, Howard Mumford. *The Age of Energy: Varieties of American Experience 1865–1915.* New York: Viking Press, 1970.

Jussim, Estelle. *Visual Communication and the Graphic Arts: Photographic Technologies in the Nineteenth Century.* New York: R. R. Bowker, 1983.

Kasson, John F. *Civilizing the Machine: Technology and Republican Values in America, 1776–1900.* New York: Grossman, 1976.

Kelly, Franklin. *Frederic Edwin Church and the National Landscape.* Washington, D.C.: Smithsonian Institution Press, 1988.

Keyes, Donald D. *The White Mountains: Place and Perceptions.* Durham, N.H.: University Art Galleries, University of New Hampshire, 1980.

King, Clarence. *Mountaineering in the Sierra Nevada.* Boston: J. R. Osgood, 1872.

Kingsley, Elbridge, "Life and Work of Elbridge Kingsley, Painter-Engraver." Papers of Elbridge Kingsley, Forbes Library, Northampton, Mass. Archives of American Art, Smithsonian Institution, Washington, D.C. Mfm. roll 48.

Kinsey, Joni Louise. "Creating a Sense of Place: Thomas Moran and the Surveying of the American West." Ph.D. diss., Washington University, 1989.

_____. *Thomas Moran and the Surveying of the American West.* Washington, D.C.: Smithsonian Institution Press, 1992.

Korzenik, Diana. *Drawn to Art.* Hanover, N.H.: University Press of New England, 1985.

Laurie, Bruce. *Artisans into Workers: Labor in Nineteenth-Century America.* New York: Hill & Wang, 1989.

Le Conte, Joseph. *Religion and Science.* New York: D. Appleton & Co., 1873.

Lindquist-Cock, Elizabeth. *The Influence of Photography on American Landscape Painting, 1839–1880.* New York: Garland Publishing Co., 1977.

Linton, William J. *The History of Wood-Engraving in America.* Boston: Estes and Lauriat, 1882. In *American Wood Engraving: A Victorian History.* Facsimile Edition. Watkins Glen, N.Y.: Athenaeum Library of the American Life Foundation and Study Institute, 1976.

Lucas, E. V. *Edward Austin Abbey, Royal Academician: The Record of His Life and Work.* New York: Charles Scribner's Sons, 1921.

Lueck, Beth Lynne. "The Sublime and the Picturesque in American Landscape Description 1790–1850." Ph.D. diss., University of North Carolina, 1982.

Lyles, Anne, and Diane Perkins. *Colour into Line: Turner and the Art of Engraving.* London: The Tate Gallery, 1989.

McGrath, Robert L. "The Real and the Ideal: Popular Images of the White Mountains." In Donald D. Keyes, *The White Mountains: Place and Perceptions.* Durham, N.H.: University Art Galleries, University of New Hampshire, 1980.

Machor, James L. *Pastoral Cities, Urban Ideals and the Symbolic Landscape of America.* Madison: University of Wisconsin Press, 1987.

McKelvey, Blake. *The Urbanization of America, 1860–1915.* New Brunswick, N.J.: Rutgers University Press, 1963.

McKinsey, Elizabeth R. *Niagara Falls: Icon of the American Sublime.* New York: Cambridge University Press, 1985.

McLoughlin, William G. *The Meaning of Henry Ward Beecher.* New York: Alfred A. Knopf, 1970.

Maddox, Kenneth W. *In Search of the Picturesque: Nineteenth-Century Images of Industry Along the Hudson River Valley.* Annandale-on-Hudson, N.Y.: Edith C. Blum Art Institute, Milton and Sally Avery Center for the Arts, Bard College Center, 1983.

_____. "The Railroad in the Eastern Landscape: 1850–1900." In Susan Danly Walther, *The Railroad in the American Landscape: 1850–1900.* Wellesley, Mass.: Wellesley College Museum, 1981.

Manwaring, Elizabeth W. *Italian Landscape in Eighteenth Century England.* New York: Oxford University Press, 1925.

Marx, Leo. *The Machine in the Garden.* New York: Oxford University Press, 1964.

Masteller, Richard N. "Western Views in Eastern Parlors: The Contribution of the Stereograph Photographer to the Conquest of the West." *Prospects* 6 (1981): 55–71.

Miller, Perry. *Nature's Nation.* Cambridge, Mass.: Harvard University Press, Belknap Press, 1967.

Mitchell, Lee Clark. *Witnesses to a Vanishing America: The Nineteenth-Century Response.* Princeton: Princeton University Press, 1981.

Moran, Thomas. *Home-Thoughts from Afar: Letters of Thomas Moran to Mary Nimmo Moran.* Edited by Amy O. Bassford and Fritiof Fryxell. East Hampton, N.Y.: East Hampton Free Library, 1967.

Mulvey, Christopher. *Anglo-American Landscapes: A Study of Nineteenth-Century Anglo-American Travel Literature.* Cambridge: Cambridge University Press, 1983.

_____. "*Ecriture* and Landscape: British Writing on Post-Revolutionary America." In *Views of American Landscape.* Edited by Mick Gidley and Robert Lawson-Peebles. Cambridge: Cambridge University Press, 1989.

Myers, Kenneth. *The Catskills: Painters, Writers, and Tourists in the Mountains 1820–1895.* Yonkers, N.Y.: Hudson River Museum of Westchester, 1987.

Naef, Weston J., and James N. Wood. *Era of Exploration: The Rise of Landscape Photography in the American West, 1860–1885.* Buffalo: Albright-Knox Art Gallery, and New York: Metropolitan Museum of Art, 1975.

Nash, Roderick. *Wilderness and the American Mind.* 3d. ed. New Haven: Yale University Press, 1982.

Nevins, Allan. *The Emergence of Modern America 1865–1878.* 1927; reprint, Chicago: Quadrangle, 1971.

Nichols, Roy F., and Eugene H. Berwanger. *The Stakes of Power 1845–1877.* Rev. ed. New York: Hill and Wang, 1982.

Nicolson, Marjorie Hope. *Mountain Gloom and Mountain Glory.* New York: W. W. Norton, 1959.

Novak, Barbara. *Nature and Culture: American Landscape and Painting, 1825–1875.* New York: Oxford University Press, 1980.

Nygren, Edward J., with Bruce Robertson. *Views and Visions: American Landscape before 1830.* Washington, D.C.: Corcoran Gallery of Art, 1986.

Orchard, Harry Frederick, curator. *Charles Lanman: Landscapes and Nature Studies.* Morristown, N.J.: Morris Museum of Arts and Sciences, 1983.

Overton, Grant. *Portrait of a Publisher.* New York: D. Appleton & Co., 1925.

Parton, James. *The Triumphs of Enterprise, Ingenuity and Public Spirit.* Hartford, Conn.: A. S. Hale and Co., 1871.

Pearson, Andrea G. *"Frank Leslie's Illustrated Newspaper and Harper's Weekly:* Innovation and Imitation in Nineteenth-Century American Pictorial Reporting." *Journal of Popular Culture* 23, no.4 (Spring 1990): 81–111.

Pennell, Joseph. *The Adventures of An Illustrator.* Boston: Little, Brown and Co., 1925.

_____. *Modern Illustration.* London and New York: G. Bell & Sons, 1895.

_____. *Pen Drawing and Pen Draughtsmen.* New York: Macmillan, 1889.

Persons, Stow. *The Decline of American Gentility.* New York: Columbia University Press, 1973.

Powell, Earl A. "Luminism and the American Sublime." In John Wilmerding, *American Light: The Luminist Movement, 1850–1875.* Washington, D.C.: National Gallery of Art, 1980.

Prown, Jules David, et al. *Discovered Lands, Invented Pasts: Transforming Visions of the American West.* New Haven: Yale University Press, 1992.

Rainey, Sue. "Images of the South in *Picturesque America* and *The Great South.*" In *Graphic Arts & the South.* Edited by Judy L. Larson, with Cynthia Payne. Fayetteville: University of Arkansas Press, 1993.

Ramsier, Allen L. *"Picturesque America*: Packaging America for Popular Consumption." M.A. thesis, College of William and Mary, 1985.

Reps, John W. *Washington on View: The Nation's Capital Since 1790.* Chapel Hill, N.C.: University of North Carolina Press, 1991.

Reynolds, Jan. *Birket Foster.* London: B. T. Batsford, 1984.

Rideing, William H. *Many Celebrities and A Few Others.* Garden City, N.Y.: Doubleday, Page & Co., 1912.

Rodgers, Daniel T. *The Work Ethic in Industrial America 1850–1920.* Chicago: University of Chicago Press, 1978.

Ross, Alexander M. *William Henry Bartlett: Artist, Author, Traveller.* Toronto: University of Toronto Press, 1973.

Schimmel, Julie. "Inventing 'the Indian.'" In *The West as America: Reinterpreting Images of the Frontier, 1820–1920.* Edited by William H. Truettner. Washington, D.C.: National Museum of American Art, 1991.

Scholnick, Robert J. "J. G. Holland and the 'Religion of Civilization' in Mid-Nineteenth Century America." *American Studies* 27 (Spring 1986): 55–79.

Schuyler, David. *The New Urban Landscape: The Redefinition of City Form in Nineteenth-Century America.* Baltimore: Johns Hopkins University Press, 1986.

Sears, John F. *Sacred Places: American Tourist Attractions in the Nineteenth Century.* New York: Oxford University Press, 1989.

Shelton, William Henry. *The History of the Salmagundi Club as It Appeared in the New York Herald Tribune Magazine on Sunday December Eighteenth Nineteen Twenty Seven.* Privately printed, 1927.

Shepherd, Paul. *Man in the Landscape.* New York: Alfred A. Knopf, 1967.

Siegel, Adrienne. *The Image of the American City in Popular Literature 1820–1870.* Port Washington, N.Y.: Kennikat Press; National University Publications, 1981.

Smillie, James D. Diaries. Archives of American Art, Smithsonian Institution, Washington, D.C. Mfm. rolls 2849–2851.

Smith, Henry Nash. *Virgin Land: The American West as Symbol and Myth.* New York: Vintage Books, 1950.

Sparling, Tobin Andrews. *American Scenery: The Art of John & John William Hill.* New York: New York Public Library, 1985.

Stafford, Barbara Maria. *Voyage into Substance: Art, Science, Nature and the Illustrated Travel Account, 1760–1840.* Cambridge, Mass.: Massachusetts Institute of Technology Press, 1984.

Stein, Roger B. *John Ruskin and Aesthetic Thought in America, 1840–1900.* Cambridge, Mass.: Harvard University Press, 1967.

_____. *Susquehanna: Images of the Settled Landscape.* Exhibition catalogue. Binghamton, N.Y.: Roberson Center for the Arts and Sciences, 1981.

Strauss, David. "Toward a Consumer Culture: 'Adirondack Murray' and the Wilderness Vacation." *American Quarterly* 39, no.2 (Summer 1987), 270–86.

Taft, Robert. *Artists and Illustrators of the Old West.* New York: Charles Scribner's Sons, 1953.

Tatham, David. "The Artists of Trenton Falls." In *The Art of Trenton Falls, 1825–1900.* Exhibition organized by Paul D. Schweizer. Utica, N.Y.: Museum of Art, Munson-Williams-Proctor Institute, 1989.

_____. *Winslow Homer and the Illustrated Book.* Syracuse, N.Y.: Syracuse University Press, 1992.

Thernstrom, Stephen. *Poverty and Progress: Social Mobility in a Nineteenth-Century City.* Cambridge, Mass.: Harvard University Press, 1964.

Trachtenberg, Alan. *Brooklyn Bridge: Fact and Symbol.* 1965; reprint, Chicago: University of Chicago Press, Phoenix Editions, 1979.

_____. *The Incorporation of America: Culture and Society in the Gilded Age.* New York: Hill and Wang, 1982.

Treuherz, Julian. *"The Graphic."* In *Hard Times: Social Realism in Victorian Art.* Edited by Julian Treuherz. London: Lund Humphries, and Mt. Kisco, N.Y.: Moyer Bell, 1987.

Trollope, Anthony. *North America.* Edited by Donald Smalley and Bradford Allen Booth. New York: Knopf, 1951.

Troyen, Carol. "Innocents Abroad: American Painters at the 1867 Exposition Universelle, Paris." *American Art Journal* 16 (Autumn 1984): 2–29.

Truettner, William H., ed. *The West as America: Reinterpreting Images of the Frontier, 1820–1920.* Washington, D.C.: National Museum of American Art, 1991.

Tuckerman, Henry T. *America and Her Commentators.* New York: Charles Scribner, 1864.

_____. *The Book of the Artists.* New York: Putnam, 1867.

Turner, James. *Without God, Without Creed: The Origins of Unbelief in America.* Baltimore: Johns Hopkins University Press, 1985.

Wagner, Virginia L. "Geological Time in Nineteenth–Century Landscape Painting." *Winterthur Portfolio* 24, no. 2/3 (Summer/Autumn 1989): 153–63.

_____. "John Ruskin and Artistical Geology in America." *Winterthur Portfolio* 23, no. 2/3 (Summer/Autumn 1988): 151–67.

Weber, Carl J. *The Rise and Fall of James Ripley Osgood: A Biography.* Waterville, Me.: Colby College Press, 1959.

Weitenkampf, Frank. "Early American Landscape Prints." *Art Quarterly* 8 (Winter 1945): 40–67.

Wiebe, Robert H. *The Search for Order, 1877–1920.* New York: Hill and Wang, 1967.

Wilkins, Thurman. *Thomas Moran: Artist of the Mountains.* Norman: University of Oklahoma Press, 1966.

Wilmerding, John. "The Allure of Mount Desert." In *American Views: Essays on American Art.* Princeton: Princeton University Press, 1991.

_____. *American Light: The Luminist Movement, 1850–1875.* Washington, D.C.: National Gallery of Art, 1980.

Wilton, Andrew. *Turner and the Sublime.* London: British Museum, 1980.

Winship, Michael. "Printing with Plates in the Nineteenth Century United States." *Printing History* 5, no. 2 (1983): 15–26.

Wolfe, Gerard R. *The House of Appleton.* Metuchen, N.J.: Scarecrow Press, 1981.

Wood, Carol Gordon. "'Only Second in Fame to Niagara'—Trenton Falls and the American Grand Tour." In *The Art of Trenton Falls, 1825–1900.* Exhibition organized by Paul D. Schweizer. Utica, N.Y.: Museum of Art, Munson-Williams-Proctor Institute, 1989.

Worman, Eugene C., Jr. "A Biblio-historical Reconstruction: Bartlett's Travels in the United States (1836–1837)." *AB Bookman's Weekly* (Oct., 30, 1989): 1643–51.

_____. "*American Scenery* and the Dating of Its Bartlett Prints." *Imprint: Journal of the American Historical Print Collectors Society* 12, no.2 (Autumn 1987): 2–12; and 13, no. 1 (Spring 1988): 22–27.

_____. "George Virtue's New York Connection, 1836–79." *AB Bookman's Weekly* (March 30, 1987): 1350–63.

Index

Abbey, Edward Austin, 48, 140, 341n. 8, 360n. 31, 361n. 36
Adams press, 350n.88
Adams, Henry, 292
"Addums, Mozis." *See* Bagby, George W.
Adirondacks, 39; and *Adventures in the Wilderness* (Murray), 39; and *PA*, 202, 204
aesthetic categories, 27 (*see also* beautiful; picturesque; sublime)
Agassiz, Louis, 35, 229
agricultural landscapes in *PA*, 238–41
The Aldine (formerly *The Aldine Press*), 20–21, 58, 107, 359n. 20; and W. C. Bryant, 71–72; competition with *Appleton's Journal*, 71–72, 80, 279; prospectus for 1872, 71; and quality of wood engravings, 71–72, 182, 336n. 51; and Thomas Moran, 165, 169, 274, 299, 358n. 7; and Jules Tavernier, 107, 304; and J. D. Woodward, 106, 274, 308, 358n. 7
Aldrich, Thomas Bailey, 61, 325n. 6
American Agriculturalist, 295
American Indians, 159, 202, 204, 269–73; Western vs. Eastern, 269, 357n. 79; treatment of in text and illustrations, 269–73; and Swain Gifford, 271–72; and Thomas Moran, 270; and James Smillie, 270–71
American Literary Gazette and Publishers' Circular, 13, 47 (see also *Publishers' and Stationers' Weekly Trade Circular*)
American Pre-Raphaelites, 120, 297
American Scenery (Willis), 30, 148
American Watercolor Society, 35, 37, 39, 104–5, 107, 281, 329n. 49 (*see also* appendix A)
Anthony, A. V. S., 34–35, 177, 348n. 72
antiquities and ruins: 28, 30; natural features as substitutes for, 53, 84–85, 93, 119, 227, 229; in *PA*, 253, 255, 257

Appleton, D., and Company: establishment, 8; expansion, 8; and mission to educate and civilize, 4, 8–9, 15–18, 48–49, 87; as publisher of "PA" and *PA*, 1, 19–32, 50–51, 70–73; and history, 9; and literature, 11–12; and religion, 11–12; and revision of *PA* (1894), 288–89; and science, 9–10; and travel 9; and visual art, 12; other publications of 1865–80: *Alice's Adventures in Wonderland* (Carroll), 11; *Appletons' Journal* (see main entry); *The Art Journal*, 280, 284, 351n. 98, 359n. 22; *The Art of Beautifying Suburban Home Grounds . . .*, 9, 253; *Descent of Man* (Darwin), 10; *Education* (Spencer), 10; *First Principles* (Spencer), 10; *The Goethe Gallery*, 12; *How Shall We Paint Our Houses?*, 9; *Joseph II and His Court* (Mühlbach), 11; *Life of Stonewall Jackson*, 9; *Lothair* (Disraeli), 11, 324n. 38; *New American Cyclopaedia*; 6, 8–9, 46, revision of, 94, 109; *Our Native Land*, 284; *Picturesque Europe*, 110, 149, 278–79, 294, 308, 329n. 41, 337n. 10, 348n. 68, 351n. 98, 357n. 2, 359n. 19–20, 23; *Picturesque Palestine, Sinai and Egypt*, 279, 294, 308, 329n. 41, 348n. 68; *The Poet and the Painter*, 12, 336n. 6; *Popular Science Monthly*, 16, 286; *Primary Truths of Religion*, 11, 108; *Railroad and Steamboat Companion*, 9; *Religion and Science*, 11; *Robinson Crusoe*, 9; *The Schiller Gallery*, 12; *Song of the Sower* (Bryant), 14, 249, 324n. 44, 330n. 56, 356n. 74; *Southern Tour*, 9, 331n. 2; *Story of the Fountain* (Bryant), 14, 243, 324n. 44; *The Swiss Family Robinson*, 9; *Webster's Spelling Book*, 9; *Western Tour*, 9; *What to Read and How to Read*, 9; *Wood-Side and Sea-Side*, 13, 140, 342n. 21
Appleton, Daniel, 8

CREATING PICTURESQUE AMERICA

was composed in 10 on 13 Baskerville
with display type also in Baskerville
by D&T/Bailey Typesetting, Inc.;
printed on 60-pound, acid-free, Thor White Recycled paper,
with 80-pound colored endsheets and dust jackets printed in 3 colors,
Smyth-sewn and bound over 88-point binder's boards
in Roxite B-grade cloth,
by Thompson-Shore, Inc.
Both book and jacket design are the work of Gary Gore.
Published by Vanderbilt University Press,
Nashville, Tennessee 37235.